The British Empire through buildings

Manchester University Press

The British Empire through buildings

Structure, function and meaning

John M. MacKenzie

Manchester University Press

Copyright © John M. MacKenzie 2020

The right of John M. MacKenzie to be identified as the author of this work has been asserted by him in accordance with the Copyright, Designs and Patents Act 1988.

Published by Manchester University Press
Oxford Road, Manchester M13 9PL
www.manchesteruniversitypress.co.uk

British Library Cataloguing-in-Publication Data
A catalogue record for this book is available from the British Library

ISBN   978 1 5261 4596 3   hardback
ISBN   978 1 5261 7201 3   paperback

First published 2020
Paperback published 2023

The publisher has no responsibility for the persistence or accuracy of URLs for any external or third-party internet websites referred to in this book, and does not guarantee that any content on such websites is, or will remain, accurate or appropriate.

Typeset
by Toppan Best-set Premedia Limited

CONTENTS

Acknowledgements vi
List of illustrations vii

Introduction 1

1 Construction and destruction 23
2 Militarisation, mobility and the residencies of power 51
3 Cities, towns, civic buildings and hill stations 83
4 Institutions of the bourgeois public sphere and new technologies 124
5 Domestic residences and city improvement 164
6 The buildings of ritual: religion and freemasonry 195
7 Colonial cities: Valletta, Rangoon and new capitals 227

Conclusion 259
Select bibliography 273
Index 287

ACKNOWLEDGEMENTS

Throughout all my explorations of aspects of the history of the British Empire, I have had many stimulating companions. These have included colleagues such as Stephen Constantine and Jeffrey Richards, as well as collaborators Berny Sèbe, Giuseppe Finaldi, Bernhard Gissibl, Vincent Kuitenbrouwer, Matthew Stanard, Hermann Hiery, Sarah Longair and John McAleer, all of whom have opened intellectual doors. Research travels have produced a web of contacts and influences among scholars, including in South Africa, Vivian Bickford-Smith, Nigel Worden, Elizabeth van Heyningen, John Lambert and Jane Carruthers; in New Zealand Tom Brooking, John Cookson and Angela McCarthy; in Australia Libby Robin, Stephen Foster, Andrekos Varnava and the late Eric Richards; in the United States Stephanie Barczewski, William Roger Louis, Bryan Glass, Minnie Sinha, Dane Kennedy and Antoinette Burton; in Singapore, Michael Walsh; in Japan Masahiro Hirata, Shigeru Akita, Shoko Mizuno and Atsuko Mizobe; and in the UK Tom Devine, Marjory Harper, Giacomo Macola, James Belich, John Darwin, David Worthington and Andrew Mackillop.

So far as this book is concerned, particular thanks are due to David McNab and Rolf Johnson for various helpful suggestions, as well as to my long-standing editor at Manchester University Press, Emma Brennan. I am grateful for valuable comments by two anonymous readers and also Alan Lester.

Since my retirement to Scotland, I have developed fruitful relationships with colleagues in the Universities of Aberdeen, Stirling, St Andrews, Edinburgh and the Highlands and Islands. Nigel Dalziel has invariably accompanied me on all my travels and has shared the research. He has also been a tower of strength in editing projects, notably the Wiley-Blackwell *Encyclopedia of Empire*. He has always been a striking combination of helper, inspiration and guide.

ILLUSTRATIONS

The illustrations in this book, necessarily restricted in number by space and cost, are made up of a combination of personal photographs, historic postcards and two by permission of the Wellcome Foundation. An effort has been made to concentrate on the less familiar, and they are intended to be only representative of the large number of buildings mentioned in the text. Many of the others can be found illustrated on the web or in many of the books cited, so that the interested reader may be able to follow them up.

Note: In the captions of these illustrations, only the original colonial place names have been used. Modern equivalents can be found in the text or in the index.

1	Lovedale Mission Hospital, Eastern Cape, South Africa	2
2	Dhoby's House, Calcutta	12
3	Dunedin Railway Station	15
4	Toronto Union Railway Station	18
5	Gateway to the Lucknow Residency with the ruins of the city beyond, destroyed during the 1857 Indian Uprising	37
6	The Chattar Manzil, Lucknow, palace of the rulers of Awadh, destroyed during the 1857 Indian Uprising	38
7	Destruction of the Accommodation House, Tawarewa eruption, North Island, New Zealand, 1917	42
8	Brimstone Hill Fort, St Kitts	54
9	Jamrud Fort at the entrance of the Khyber Pass, Pakistan	55
10	Part of the huge tented encampment, Coronation Durbar, Delhi, 1911	62
11	Government House, Lagos	67

Illustrations

12	Ballroom of the Government House of Bengal, Calcutta	70
13	Government House, Madras	72
14	Plantation House, St Helena	73
15	Government House, Melbourne	75
16	Town Hall, Bombay	91
17	Town Hall, Singapore	93
18	Town Hall, Penang	94
19	Parliament building, Ottawa	99
20	Parliament House, Cape Town	101
21	High Court, Calcutta	102
22	High Court, Karachi	103
23	Candacraig, Maymyo, Burma	116
24	Albert Hall Museum, Jaipur	132
25	Colombo Museum, Ceylon	133
26	Tollygunge Club, Calcutta	140
27	Royal Bombay Yacht Club	141
28	Crawford Market, Bombay	143
29	Telegraph Office, Calcutta	149
30	Bank of Montreal, Montreal	153
31	Empress Hotel, Victoria, British Columbia	155
32	Midland Hotel, Castlemaine, Victoria, Australia	156
33	A 'native home', Trinidad	168
34	Shops and homes in Fort Street, Basseterre, St Kitts	169
35	St Nicholas Abbey, plantation house, Barbados	170
36	Fairview, plantation house, St Kitts	171
37	Craigdarroch, Victoria, British Columbia	174
38	Classic colonial bungalow in Lyttelton, South Island, New Zealand	177
39	Groote Schuur, Cape Town	181
40	St Paul's Cathedral, Calcutta	200
41	Anglican cathedral, Rangoon	202
42	St James's (Skinner's) Church, Delhi	204
43	Memorial Church, Cawnpore	206
44	Christ Church Cathedral, Zanzibar	206
45	St Andrew's Church, Calcutta	208
46	Presbyterian Church, Grahamstown, Eastern Cape, South Africa	211
47	Lovedale Mission, Eastern Cape, South Africa	213

Illustrations

48	Masonic Hall, Canning Place, Singapore	218
49	Manchester Unity of Oddfellows, Freetown, Sierra Leone	219
50	Victoria Gate and bastions, Valletta, Malta	228
51	Fort St Elmo, Valletta, Malta	229
52	Rebuilt railway station, Rangoon	233
53	Pegu Club, Rangoon	235
54	High Court, Rangoon	236
55	Strand Hotel, Rangoon	237
56	Anglican Cathedral, New Delhi	247
57	Thatched European bungalow, Lusaka, Northern Rhodesia	251
58	Government House, Maymyo, Burma	267
59	Victoria Falls Hotel, Southern Rhodesia	267
60	Bonsecours Market, Montreal	268

INTRODUCTION

Empires are underpinned by conceits. Of these, none is more potent than the belief in the cultural and intellectual superiority of the dominant people.[1] This conviction is at one and the same time explanatory, justificatory and instrumental. It follows that the imperial power invariably seeks to spread the characteristics of its cultural and intellectual pre-eminence across the extent of its empire, incorporating other peoples into this supposedly obvious superiority and its enabling benefits. This ambitious diffusion is achieved through the activities of a variety of imperial agencies and through a range of media, all of which both illustrate and utilise the technologies that facilitate the successful expansion of power. It follows that one of the objectives of empire is often to overlay the cultures of subordinate peoples with new, and for their time, supposedly 'modernising' elements. Occasionally, empires may even be judged (or judge themselves) according to their relative success in this enterprise. Moreover, it is sometimes the case that the central power has to begin the process by incorporating the peoples of its home area (sometimes seen as barbarians on the fringes) into what is perceived to be a potential common culture before expansion outwards can be achieved. Yet dominated cultures have a tendency to be resilient. They (or at least some of their populations) may accept the characteristics of the dominant people that suit them while seeking to protect cultural characteristics that are central to their identity.[2] The weakness of empires is often illustrated by such resilience and imperial decline is invariably accompanied by the reassertion of other cultures, both in the metropolis and in the colonies, even if such resurgence is characterised by significant aspects of cultural hybridity.

One of the most important expressions of such alleged cultural superiority lies in the built environment. Yet, in the many conventional histories of the British

1 Lovedale Mission Hospital, Eastern Cape, South Africa

Empire, buildings and the built environment have received relatively little attention. On the other hand, historians of architecture and planning have devoted much research and many publications to this important field, particularly in recent years. This book represents an attempt to bring these two streams together. It is a book which is deeply embedded in my past research and publications on aspects of visual and other forms of the propaganda of imperialism, on the cultural manifestations of the military, and on the manner in which Orientalism can be related to various of the western arts.[3] Such concerns were continued in work on the natural environment and on the role of hunting in both imperial relationships and aspects of interior aesthetics, on the social history of railway stations and museums as specific building types, and on the environmental and scientific aspects of Christian missions.[4] Interests later moved on to the significance of the different ethnic fragments of the United Kingdom and on the need to analyse the British Empire in terms of the 'four nations'.[5] This has a definite connection with the built environment since the various British ethnicities were known for different skills sets, a variety of architectural traditions and a range of activities in the field. The themes represented in most of these publications will be found to be woven through the chapters that follow.

Many of these scholarly interests were based on an upbringing in the city of Glasgow, a built environment which fascinated me from an early age. It

Introduction

was a city of self-consciously grand public buildings, where class residential zoning and the great range of its housing stock were particularly apparent, with extreme contrasts between striking bourgeois residences and proletarian tenements, largely influenced by its status as a significant port and industrial centre. It was also a city with major immigrant communities. It formerly prided itself on its imperial status, even adopting the much disputed 'Second City of the Empire' title. However fanciful that may have been, still in many respects it seemed to be a prototype for the imperial city. As we shall see in Chapter 5, it had also become a prototype for notions of 'city improvement' that went round the empire. Slum-clearance demolition and the creation of peri-urban council-housing schemes was very much on the 'improvement' agenda in the post-Second World War period. But the desire to create better housing and sanitation led to the abandonment of the old communities of the inner city, with their shops, libraries, swimming baths, theatres, cinemas, 'steamies' (laundries) and public houses that had been such a feature of an integrated social and cultural life. The result was areas of standardised council housing with new forms of deprivation. A focus on housing rather than community could be highly damaging. Such problems were eminently apparent in the Glasgow of the 1950s and 1960s, and there were parallels overseas.[6] In the 1950s, I also had experience of living in Northern Rhodesia (Zambia), where my father was a clerk of works in the Public Works Department (PWD), which was one of the key agencies of the colonies of the British Empire.

SOCIAL CLASSES, RACE, AND BUILT AND NATURAL ENVIRONMENTS

Experience of Glasgow and of Northern Rhodesia, together with all subsequent studies, created the conviction that empire was a highly complex and messy affair which endowed as well as endangered other societies (and reciprocally its own). It had the power to inspire as well as to injure, to be constructive as well as destructive. For all its inequalities and its undoubted violence, it was almost always a zone of cultural exchange in which the oppressed triumphantly maintained a degree of agency, speaking, negotiating, rejecting, adopting, adapting and reciprocating, however unequal the 'terms of cultural trade'. This indicates the manner in which the full range of peoples, as individuals and collectivities, are necessarily centre-stage in all cultural studies. In the profound modification of the imperial heartland, it is apparent that all talk of an 'absent-minded' ignoring of or ignorance of empire is misplaced.[7] In short, the cultural history of empire in its diverse and complex patterns has the capacity to illuminate all other aspects of imperial studies.[8] The built environment, no less than the natural environment, is vital in such analyses. After all, natural environmental phenomena mingle with the built in cities and towns, through squares and areas of parkland, as well as through the invasion of many different animals. City dwellers may attempt to control such mingling, but they are not always successful.[9] The built environment overlays, interacts with and is sometimes overwhelmed by the natural environment and cannot be separated from wider contexts. These include questions of geographical locations and attendant climates, with complex networks of conditioning factors affecting settlements whether coastal, on interior plains, in mountains, tropical, sub-tropical or temperate zones.

As we shall see, the perceived relationship between the built environment and health was an obsession of planners in both metropolis and empire and this conjunction unveils the paradoxes of empire, as well as the central relationship between development and under-development. Imperial cities and towns were, as far as possible, always divided into sectors according to race, into enclaves that were designed for the 'protection' of the dominant imperial people (or in British cities, in different ways, the dominant class), protection that might include various forms of security, whether from attack, from social 'contamination', or from the alleged dangers of disease, including the close proximity of the supposed insanitary settlements of indigenous (and working-class) people and the threatening health risks associated with them. On the other hand, there has always been a conflict between security and comfort in the empire. The comfort of the dominant imperial people often ensured that they should have staffs of servants to minister to them. In Asia, the Caribbean and Africa, such supporting staffs of servants were necessarily extensive in numbers and required to be on hand (if at times supposedly out of sight) to supply the supports the dominant people required. These dominant people have themselves to be disaggregated into different social groups, including a high-status administrative and military elite, a wealthy (but not necessarily high-status) entrepreneurial group, a large number of people of the more middling sort, and sometimes a poor white element seeking to distance itself from the indigenous population, not to mention groups of mixed-race people inhabiting specific economic niches, but often struggling to be accepted by either white or indigenous communities. Such a complex social mix varied in character in the various settings in Asia, Africa and tropical islands and, of course, was transformed over time.

Introduction

In the nineteenth century, the most important and virtually revolutionary change in the structure of social classes was the rapid emergence in Europe and elsewhere of a bourgeoisie with significant components of newly defined and organised professional, commercial and administrative classes. The cultural dominance of this bourgeoisie was powerfully reflected in the built environment, producing many buildings characteristic of the age. This key social class rapidly produced a nascent indigenous element which developed at different speeds and chronological contexts in the various imperial territories: in the nineteenth century in India and elsewhere in Asia, in the twentieth in New Zealand and Africa, and at a later date in Canada and Australia. This bourgeoisie became even more important in the territories of white settlement, where the complex white social hierarchy exhibited the full range of classes to be found in Europe (generally with the exception of the aristocracy, though aristocrats could be found among the administrative elite and even occasionally as landowning settlers). In many places, however, given the overblown residences and retinue of servants of some upwardly mobile individuals, there were those who aspired to be imperial aristocrats of wealth and privilege, if not of lineage. As Benedict Anderson observed, the colonial setting permitted 'sizeable numbers of bourgeois and petty bourgeois to play aristocrat off centre court, i.e. anywhere in the empire except at home'.[10] In white settler territories (with the exception of southern Africa) the indigenous people were rapidly overwhelmed in numbers (by war, disease or displacement) and were invariably, but not exclusively, located out of sight. In supposedly distant locations the processes of attempting to integrate them, if necessary by force, into white cultural norms could proceed apace, through education, missionary activity, and sometimes the removal of children.

OBJECTIVES OF THE BOOK

It is, however, necessary to register some disclaimers. This book is not a work of architectural history as architectural historians would understand it. It does not examine in detail the aesthetics of buildings, the background to their commissioning, aspects of their construction or the international movements with which they may be identified. Nor does it focus on the elaborate discussions by and about their architects, their predilections and the influences upon them. It is not concerned with architecture as art history, set into the history of ideas, as promoted by nineteenth-century commentators and others.[11] Another area which it merely touches upon is the contemporary debates by architects, engineers and commentators on 'purity' and 'hybridity' in architecture, notably in India, a field that has been ably introduced by Peter Scriver.[12] There are inevitably some glancing references to such material, but it is not the primary concern. This is also true of the highly technical and very important study of town planning.[13] Once again, town plans and zoning are necessarily mentioned, but are not primary interests. There has been a very extensive theoretical literature about the nature of colonial cities, their typologies ('primary', 'dependent', and so on), and the interaction of their economic and sociological constituents.[14] This work, by sociologists, geographers and others, is of great importance, but it would require several synoptic works to bring all these analyses together. Yet again, the intention here is different. In addition, the book clearly cannot presume to be in any sense a political history of empire. Some understanding of parallel political developments has been taken as read, although there will be some signposts on the way. Moreover, the approach of postcolonial historians, architectural historians and commentators, which tends to be jargon-laden and often convoluted in its theoretical positions, is avoided. Still, such writings contain significant insights, some of which have influenced aspects of this work.

The prime objective here is to examine the imperial built environment and analyse the importance of its function and meaning to the history of the British Empire. It is intended to be a readable introduction for the student and general reader, designed to confirm that the transformation of the environment into its built formations can be interpreted as a central aspect of imperial cultural relationships. It should illuminate the military matters, conquest, administration, politics and the economic, extractive and exploitative aspects of empire that have hitherto been the main focus of such histories. But it is concerned not just with the transfer of European forms and practices from metropole to periphery, as would have been the prime focus in the past, but their adaptation in new environments, and their manner of expressing settler and imperialist aspirations in relation not only to the cultures of indigenous people, but also to the advertising of the European presence (and its frequent desire to distance itself from metropolitan models), with all its political and economic ramifications. To a certain extent it is concerned to break down the centre–periphery paradigm. This could be reflected in the reciprocal effects of the constructional and architectural influences between Britain and both formal and informal empires. Modes of creating built environments in new urban spaces involved not just dispersal from centre to periphery, but were also represented in intercolonial webs, networks and consequently influences among colonies. This will serve to indicate the extent to which histories of architecture, the built environment and town planning have a capacity to illuminate imperial history in general in ways not always apparent in earlier studies.

The chapters that follow are therefore concerned with the messages conveyed by built structures and related manifestations of the white presence. In redressing the tendency of imperial histories to ignore aspects of the natural and built environments, it also seeks to be geographically synoptic. While there have been many works, both scholarly and popular, that have attempted to deal with the history of the entire British Empire, few have taken up global environmental issues.[15] Histories of imperial natural and built environments have tended to be highly specialist, with few attempting to deal in a comparative manner with the entire empire.[16] This effort to cover the wider British Empire may require some justification. It is perhaps inevitable that most attention has been paid to British buildings in India since there was such a notable pre-colonial, if highly heterogeneous, building tradition there. It was with regard to India that there was the greatest debate and the oscillation between imported European styles and the creation of striking and highly diverse hybridities. But there remain many comparative issues that relate to the full range of imperial territories.

The full diversity of the British Empire is reflected in the fact that it seems to have been made up of several empires. Indeed many histories have been focused on these various categories. There are six possible imperial divisions. The first might be seen as imperialism, political and cultural, within the British and Hibernian Isles, in which Ireland can be identified as the most significant element. Second, there was the empire of settlement, in other words, the colonies to which there were considerable movements of migrants from Britain (notably Ireland) and later from elsewhere in Europe and also from Asia, the latter stimulating considerable resistance. This was the empire which, after its origins in North America and the Caribbean in the seventeenth and eighteenth centuries, received a considerable check with the revolution in the thirteen colonies of the eastern seaboard of America between 1776 and 1783. After that trauma, the British were at pains to ensure that it did not happen again, at least until modern times. The white settlement territories of Canada, Australia, New Zealand and (in a somewhat different category) South Africa (the only one where the indigenous population remained in the majority and eventually took power) were led through a progression of constitutional changes that ensured their progress towards twentieth-century Dominion status within the Empire.

The third category consists of islands in the Caribbean and the Indian Ocean, acquired and settled between the seventeenth and nineteenth centuries. The most economically significant of these were concerned with plantation agriculture and therefore with slave labour supplied by the African slave trade until its abolition in 1807 and of the institution of slavery in 1833. In many of these the supply of African slaves was followed by the 'new system of slavery' – the migration of Indian indentured labourers to the islands (and later also East and southern Africa) where slavery had constituted the prime source of labour. This brought India and Indians into a key demographic connection with other parts of the empire, but India always enjoyed a separate status, partly because of its origins under the East India Company (EIC), which ruled large swathes of the Subcontinent until 1858, partly because of the scale and magnificence of the enterprise, and above all because of the notable indigenous states which it embraced. In India the British ruled peoples who had created their own historic and highly notable cultures, with built environments that matched or exceeded in grandeur and magnificence those of Europe.

The fifth category became known as the 'dependent empire', consisting of colonies in Africa, South-East Asia and Pacific islands, most of them acquired during the nineteenth century and generally moving through stages from 'protectorate' to crown colony. Pacific islands were to form a connection in terms of trade and labour with the Australian colonies (the 'Commonwealth' of Australia after 1901) and New Zealand, not least after German territories in the Pacific became League of Nations mandates for the two dominions after 1919. These mandated territories, in the British case in Africa and the Middle East, constituted another sub-category of relatively short duration in the twentieth century. The sixth category consists of smaller strategic posts which were generally acquired to protect the key trade routes of the British Empire or provide bases from which larger continental entities could be held within the system. Examples of these include Gibraltar, Malta, St Helena, Singapore and Hong Kong. Finally, there were outposts that have become known as 'informal empire' where there was no direct imperial control, but from which economic (and political) influence could be exerted in regions significant for the British world trading system. These would include the treaty ports and international settlements in China and Japan, as well as, in a rather different manner, the expatriate populations in South America, particularly Argentina. Another important category of largely informal empire was in the Middle East, where the British and others asserted their presence through the construction of buildings within a predominantly (but not exclusively) Islamic context, where they made their cultural presence felt despite the absence of formal imperial structures (except in Egypt between 1914 and 1922 and mandated territories from 1919).

It may well be asked: why should all these disparate colonial and imperial categories be lumped together? One answer is that, although the British never exercised a fully centralised control over these territories (which were handled and administered by at least three different ministries and secretaries of state in Whitehall), still their ruling and cultural predilections ensured that there were comparable responses to the development of their built environments. For a start, the British required similar buildings to pursue their aims. These included military fortresses and barracks, government houses, law courts, administrative buildings, company headquarters, police stations, prisons, harbour works and warehouses, educational and religious establishments, hotels and hostels, as well as such spatial arrangements as squares and parks. The buildings created to satisfy the tastes and cultural needs of the burgeoning bourgeoisie were created in almost all colonies. Such parallel developments justify a fully comparative approach. In addition, there were residential requirements for expatriates and workers, as well as buildings for leisure in clubs, sporting establishments, halls, theatres and later, cinemas. They represented a global dispersal of European forms.

Although there is no evidence that the British ever consciously set about creating a uniquely characteristic British style for imperial urban development, still distinctive British forms developed, often identifiably different from those of other European empires such as the Spanish, Portuguese, French or (briefly) German. Moreover, the British responded to the climatic conditions which necessarily came to modify the colonial built environment. It was in this area that natural and built environments interacted. The Canadian climate alternated between hot summers and winters that were much colder than those experienced in the temperate metropolis. Generally, however, the British had to respond to tropical and subtropical climates and the great majority of colonial built environments reflected to some degree the requirement to render the occupation of colonial buildings more comfortable in such conditions, not least for an imperial people whose natural environment was very different. Such climatic arrangements, sometimes initially hesitant or ill-judged, led to very considerable discussion and debates about appropriate forms to mitigate temperature extremes, to establish what became known as 'thermal comfort'. It took some time for such climatic responses to be fully worked out.[17]

The British Empire through buildings

THE LITERATURE

There were a number of commentators on the built environment of empire in the nineteenth century, of which the most quoted is perhaps Sir James Fergusson, whose name will reappear in the next chapter. In modern times, there are two distinct streams in the writing about imperial buildings. Given the visual appeal of buildings, there are many popular publications, but in recent times, more focused scholarly works have been published, reflecting the extent to which the practice of architectural history has expanded in many universities across the globe. Scholarly articles have also become a rich source, many in specialist journals. There are notable books relating to the architecture and buildings of the various dominions, while the built environment of Asia has become a major source of study. In the mainstream imperial architectural canon, India has always inspired most publications. Key (and generally specialised) works that have held the field include those by Sten Nilsson, Robert Grant Irving and Thomas Metcalf.[18] The latter has a strikingly broad range, while being particularly focused on Indo-Saracenic architecture (see below) and the building of New Delhi. Many more recent books have concentrated on specific styles in individual cities. Yet many serious scholarly works have seldom inserted studies of built environments into wider cultural and social contexts. They tend to be focused on the genesis, construction and aesthetic qualities of the buildings.

More popular books have tended to be celebratory (sometimes mildly denigratory) and have often lacked adequate historical contextualisation.[19] Morris's *Stones of Empire* (like her other books) is written in an engaging and sometimes arresting (if romantic) style, but its judgements are frequently eccentric. Philip Davies's *Splendours of the Raj* attempts some critical evaluation, but the general thrust is well represented in its title.[20] One rare attempt to cover the entire empire was a work edited (with his photographs) by Robert Fermor-Hesketh with a somewhat mixed bag of contributors including Jan Morris, Charles Allen, Gillian Tindall, Colin Amery and Gavin Stamp.[21] Some of the contributions tend to be dismissive of colonial architecture, treating it as inferior to the metropolitan version. This represents a kind of self-imposed 'cultural cringe', as well as being one that is noticeably Anglocentric in its tone.[22] To demonstrate the manner in which imperial buildings have often been an alluring subject, Clive Aslet, the editor of *Country Life*, published a lavishly illustrated book of empire buildings, written in equally lavish prose.[23] Also largely descriptive and celebratory, it is mainly about Britain, apart from a final chapter, though it usefully includes the architecture

Introduction

of entertainment. An imperial and military historian who turned his attention to architecture is Ashley Jackson, who examined eleven individual buildings in various territories of the British Empire, as well as Wembley Stadium in London.[24] These examples are generally presented in a descriptive way, although the material is sometimes illuminating. The notes found in the chapters that follow will demonstrate the wealth of other books that have appeared about specific cities or countries.

More significant publications about the buildings of empire include the one serious attempt to create a global overview. This is the volume edited by G.A. Bremner in the Oxford History of the British Empire companion series, a work containing twelve contributions by notable architectural historians covering most areas of the British Empire. This represents the bringing of a new professionalism to bear upon issues of material culture, imperial space and globalisation.[25] Bremner had already published extensively on the relationship of empire to buildings in Britain (for example the Imperial Institute and Westminster Abbey), and also on missionary architecture in Central Africa.[26] This culminated in his magnificent volume *Imperial Gothic*.[27] It set a new standard of contextualising buildings into their cultural, intellectual and religious settings, although some architectural historians have judged it somewhat conservative since it failed to take account of postcolonial theoretical positions. Of the large number of more specialist architectural histories, two that deserve mention are that notable classic of the globalisation of a style, Anthony D. King's *The Bungalow* of 1984 and Louis P. Nelson's more recent and significant architectural history of Jamaica.[28] Nelson importantly directs attention away from the buildings of 'high architectural art' and those illustrating power and authority in favour of residential structures that reflect the sugar economy of Jamaica together with the built legacies of plantations, slavery and the glaring discrepancies in social and economic status between blacks and whites. The highly influential King has published a sequence of works that connect his sociological concerns with urbanism and the development of cities in the imperial and postcolonial worlds.[29] A number of new postcolonial works are relevant to the study of the built environment of empire, dealing with individual cities and sometimes specific building types. Among a rapidly growing literature, a few examples would include Swati Chattopadhyay's *Representing Calcutta*, the volume edited by Chattopadhyay and Jeremy White on City Halls, a valuable collection of essays edited by Peter Scriver and Vikramaditya Prakash with the title *Colonial Modernities*, as well as work on tropical architecture by Jiat-Hwee Chang (note

2 Dhoby's House, Calcutta

17).³⁰ In a rather different category a new study of a specific institution has cleverly set the examination of an East African museum both literally and figuratively into its revealing architectural envelope.³¹ Another valuable work on Africa has been Myers's examination of the growth, urban layout and built environment of four cities (Nairobi, Lusaka, Zanzibar and Lilongwe) in colonial and postcolonial times.³² With the exception perhaps of the works of Nelson and Chattopadhyay, few of the books on imperial architecture deal with destruction as well as construction, a significant theme of the next chapter.

There is, however, a tendency for scholars in the field to speak to fellow practitioners and, through no fault of their own, frequently fail to inject their insights into wider historical contexts. This is probably true of other specialist fields such as art, theatre and sports history, as well as musicology and studies that operate, in a sense, in a different language. As already indicated, the objective of the present work is to bring architectural and spatial histories into the mainstream of imperial cultural history and perhaps into a wider readership of works about empire. Its manifesto is that the overall history of empire cannot be fully understood without taking into account these material cultural forms that interact in so many ways with the political, economic, social and environmental manifestations of the imperial phenomenon. Above all, such an integrative approach not only illuminates key racial relationships and the characteristic (and often reciprocal) interaction of cultural dominance and subordination of imperial peoples, but also indicates the manner in which postcolonial inheritors have invaded, converted and adapted the architecture of imperial predecessors. Efforts at the reinterpretation and reuse of imperial buildings will be examined in the concluding chapter.

It will become apparent in this book that the widest interpretation of the words 'built environment' has been used. Here it is taken to mean all structures, from the most flimsy and impermanent to the grandest of buildings. Indeed, few words have been subjected to more definitional discussion than 'architecture'. There is the high-flown approach, illustrated in the famous remark of Ruskin in *The Stones of Venice* that 'architecture is the work of nations', or in the notion that only the grandest buildings in identifiable styles considered to be aesthetically pleasing can be considered as architecture. Even the more restrained definition that architecture is structure embellished by art can sometimes seem elitist. The problem with the strictly aesthetic approach to buildings, though evident in each generation, is that it introduces such subjectivity that building forms often move from being valued to being vilified, sometimes remarkably quickly. But vilification can often lead to revaluation. Perhaps the classic British case is the rise, fall and rise again of London's St Pancras station (which was nearly demolished during its period of vilification), and similar examples can be found across the globe. Some buildings that are demolished when at the nadir of their reputations can later be profoundly missed and regretted. Aslet puts the Imperial Institute in South Kensington into this category.[33] Other artistic products can be put in the basement store or left on the shelves until rediscovered and revived. The built environment is not like that.

But an alternative approach to the elitist one is to say that structures, and possibly their putative architecture, are the work of anyone seeking shelter and attempting to make it both comfortable and appealing. Thus, all kinds of humble dwellings can still constitute aspects of the architecture of the built environment. Anyone with connections to Africa or to the practice of archaeology will recognise that all structures from classical times are ultimately based upon the hut, primarily the rectangular type (though round huts have also been influential), that leads to this all-embracing definition. The visitor to African villages soon sees the manner in which huts are amenable to distinctions of status and of gender, as well as realising that many who build huts try to give them some embellishment, the plus factor turning them into homes. Many huts are temporary residences, which influences their form and materials. Indeed, temporary structures can be significant for a period. In this book, even tents are included in the definition. They have structural forms, sometimes exceptionally grand ones, which have social, cultural, political and military meaning. Mongolian yurts constitute a form of the structural environment, not least to their occupants, and the popularity of yurts in the West, as well as of such leisure shelters as glamping pods (of various different designs), indicates the potential breadth of definition. Architecture is not simply the preserve of great civilisations. It produces forms in all cultures, and modern architects can be influenced by such ethnically diverse products. Moreover, in the twentieth century, many architects from non-European cultures, notably initially Chinese and Indian, have been trained in western methods and have been particularly sensitive towards hybridising possibilities, as well as to the ways in which modernism can be adapted to specific climates, locations and cultures. Less conventionally, an analysis of the ethnic origins of architects needs also to be extended to the contrasting ethnicities of the United Kingdom. It is apparent that there are different historic architectural traditions, as well as uniquely relevant forms and materials, in the 'four nations' of Britain and architects, for example from Scotland, often introduced ideas from the long-standing building traditions in which they had grown up, as well as from their modern architectural training. There is evidence that such distinctions are beginning to be studied by architectural historians.[34] It is certainly the case that the numbers of Scots architects working in the British Empire was out of proportion to the home populations, and is a phenomenon which needs to be understood. It may partly be explained by the prominence of Scots in the engineering and surveying professions, both in military and civilian contexts or of systems of training which helped in the overproduction of architects for domestic employment. Of course there were Irish, Welsh and English engineers and architects, but this work unveils the significance of Scots in these fields in the hope that others will identify distinctive skills of the other ethnicities of the 'four nations'. Such studies are important because it is clear that in some cases training practices and specific cultural influences were brought to bear on building types.

Once again, the intended 'audience' for the buildings of empire was different according to the type of territory. In India, the small European population was certainly seen as a significant 'consumer' of imperial buildings, but it was apparent that Indians were always going to be in a massive majority in cities and towns, as well as in the country as a whole. This was also true of the majority of African colonies. In territories of settlement such as Kenya, Southern Rhodesia

Introduction

3 Dunedin Railway Station

and South Africa, the audience was generally intended to be whites, although Africans were seen even in those countries as being a population to be influenced by missions, churches, schools and some public buildings. In Canada, Australia and New Zealand, the emphasis was again somewhat different. In Canada and Australia, the indigenous people were seen in the nineteenth century as being doomed. They were already being greatly reduced in numbers by European-imported diseases, and it was expected that they would be wiped out, culturally if not physically. The audience for the built environment was therefore seen as being almost entirely a white one. To a certain extent this was also true of New Zealand, although there the resurgence of the Maori people and their culture came somewhat earlier and Maori began to play a role in national life well ahead of the cultural reassertion of First Nations and Aboriginal peoples in more recent decades.

Given these differentials in the cultural and physical survival of the indigenous peoples of empire, it is necessary to analyse the racial dimensions of the experiences, events and performances – political, administrative and cultural – that took place within these material expressions of the built environment. In most colonies, indigenous peoples were seen by whites as being capable of being influenced by the very forms of architecture, but also by the contents of buildings (perhaps schools, libraries and museums are the best examples, each intended to convey world ideas and cultures to a local audience). In some cases in India, for example buildings such as museums in princely states, Indians were expected to be virtually the sole audience.[35] The chapters that follow set out to expose the multivalent aspects of imperial structures by concentrating on the delineation of a series of building types which illustrate on the one hand the phases and development of imperial rule and on the other the expansion of its functions and ambitions. As well as the aesthetic globalisation already mentioned, these building types symbolised the dispersal of military and administrative practices, economic activities, social and cultural habits and technological change, as well as the practice and dissemination of the Christian religion. The methodology throughout is thematic, with the chronological approach running through each chapter. Given the dynamic between imperial and postcolonial nomenclature, the names used will be those current during the imperial period, although on the first mention each place name will be accompanied by the modern version.

Following this introduction, Chapter 1 considers the extent of destruction as well as construction in the development of the built environment of empire, given the capacity of empires to overlay the cultural expressions in the built environments of their predecessors. Chapters 2 and 3 examine the search for military security and the necessity of mobility in the pursuit of power as the background for the creation of cities, towns and their public buildings. Such public structures were also essential in the creation of a wholly new type of town, hill stations, designed for the recuperation of health of whites, for rest and relaxation, as well as for cooler environments in which administration could be conducted. While closely associated with India, these emerged in many other colonies in South-East Asia, Africa and Australia, where climate seemed to demand them. Chapter 4 unveils the extensive built representations of institutions created to satisfy the tastes of the bourgeoisie during its global emergence from the early nineteenth centuries and its dramatic growth in the final decades of that century.[36] The key point about these institutional buildings was that they were part of the proselytisation and surveillance of other classes by the bourgeois. Domestic residences are also vital in the material environment, so Chapter 5 examines such residential structures in different forms throughout the colonies. The growth of towns and cities became so dramatic through inward migration that socially deprived areas became a common phenomenon leading to efforts at city improvement from the late nineteenth century. While revealing the working-out of economic, political, military and social forms of dominance, the built environment also saw the global expansion of European religious and ritualised forms, a spiritual material dispersal examined in Chapter 6. Chapter 7 analyses case studies of old and new capitals, the latter in the context of their extraordinarily late efflorescence in the twentieth century, offering insights into late imperial ideologies. Given the considerable breadth of the thematic treatment of the built environment in the chapters that follow, it is inevitable that the sources are predominantly (though not exclusively) secondary. Some primary source material was found at some of the locations themselves, while websites of buildings surveyed here often contain important information. The websites used were always those that might be called 'primary', that is, produced by the institutions themselves, often providing useful histories as well as information about the vicissitudes buildings have experienced leading to current survival and use.

In many ways, the book is essentially an individual statement, utilising examples from a range of building types in cities and towns of various colonies. The impossibility of being fully comprehensive necessitated the omission of colonial America as well as Ireland as a colony of England. There are some references to Mediterranean colonies as well as to informal empire in the Middle East and elsewhere, including the influence of British communities in Egypt and the Levant.[37] So far as styles are concerned, the book deals with those that fall within the imperial period, including for example twentieth-century Art Deco. But aspects of modernism and brutalism are omitted as being essentially developments of the post-imperial world.

One of the objectives of the book is to expose areas that have been little noticed – or have received no attention at all – in the literature to date. Being concerned with the humble and even impermanent as well as more notable buildings, it deals less with aesthetic judgements and more with social, economic and cultural contexts. Throughout, there will always be a number of key interactions in mind – between imperial and indigenous societies, colonists and metropolitan figures, administrators (or politicians) and leaders of economic forces or the companies representing them, and architects ('amateur' and professional) and their clients. Other significant issues addressed are the British grappling with environments and climates different from their own. As we have seen, the British were not a homogeneous people and that necessitates analysis of differentials in cultures, training, skills sets, forms of Christianity and building styles. With all this in mind, the imperial built environment will be set into dynamic and ever-changing cultural contexts. Given the extensive and impressive material remains of the British Empire, we can equally find there many clues to its

The British Empire through buildings

4 Toronto Union Railway Station

character, though the vast number of written records has had the effect of obscuring the significance of such material and cultural evidence. But while the built environment of modern imperial towns and cities strikingly reflected the hegemonic economic and social structures of imperial rule, it was never in a state of stasis, providing a dynamic of function and meaning as the nature of empire changed and finally gave way to a postcolonial world.

NOTES

1 For a comparative examination of many of these imperial myths, see John M. MacKenzie, 'Empires in World History: Characteristics, Concepts, and Consequences', introduction to the Wiley-Blackwell *Encyclopedia of Empire* (Malden, MA and Oxford, 2016), pp. lxxxiii–cx, particularly cv–cvii.
2 A valuable study of these processes is Brian L. Moore and Michele A. Johnson, *Neither Led Nor Driven: Contesting British Cultural Imperialism in Jamaica, 1865–1920* (Kingston, Jamaica, 2004).
3 John M. MacKenzie, *Propaganda and Empire* (Manchester, 1984); MacKenzie (ed.), *Imperialism and Popular Culture* (Manchester, 1986) and *Popular Imperialism and the Military, 1850–1950* (Manchester, 1992). MacKenzie (ed.), *European Empires and the People* (Manchester, 2011) is a comparative study in relation to other European empires. For Orientalism, MacKenzie, *Orientalism: History, Theory and the Arts* (Manchester, 1995).

Introduction

4 John M. MacKenzie, *The Empire of Nature: Hunting, Conservation and British Imperialism* (Manchester, 1988) was one of the first books to give hunting scholarly notice, but there have been many since, including important work by Jane Carruthers, Bernhard Gissibl, Angela Thompsell and Vijaya Ramadas Mandala. Environmental interests were developed further when I was co-ordinating editor of the journal *Environment and History* from 2000 to 2005. Also MacKenzie (ed.), *Imperialism and the Natural World* (Manchester, 1990); Jeffrey Richards and MacKenzie, *The Railway Station: A Social History* (Oxford, 1986). I contributed all the non-European chapters to this book. MacKenzie, *Museums and Empire: Natural History, Human Cultures and Colonial Identities* (Manchester, 2009); MacKenzie, 'Missionaries, Science and the Environment in Nineteenth-Century Africa' in Andrew Porter (ed.), *The Imperial Horizons of British Protestant Missions, 1880–1914* (Grand Rapids, MI and Cambridge, 2003), pp. 106–130; MacKenzie, 'Presbyterianism and Scottish Identity in Global Context', *Britain and the World*, 10, 1 (March 2017), pp. 88–112. Both of the latter articles deal with aspects of missionary and religious influence on the built environment.
5 John M. MacKenzie with Nigel R. Dalziel, *The Scots in South Africa* (Manchester, 2007); MacKenzie, 'Irish, Scottish, Welsh and English Worlds? The Four-Nations Approach to the History of the British Empire', *History Compass*, 6, 5 (2009), pp. 1244–1263; MacKenzie, 'Irish, Scottish, Welsh and English Worlds? The Historiography of the Four-Nations Approach to the History of the British Empire' in Catherine Hall and Keith McClelland (eds), *Race, Nation and Empire: Making Histories, 1750 to the Present* (Manchester, 2010), pp. 133–153. MacKenzie and T.M. Devine (eds), *Scotland and the British Empire* (Oxford, 2011).
6 Some of these issues were addressed in John M. MacKenzie, '"The Second City of the Empire": Glasgow – Imperial Municipality' in Felix Driver and David Gilbert (eds), *Imperial Cities* (Manchester, 1999), pp. 215–237. Such urban issues are considered in Chapter 5 below.
7 Bernard Porter, *The Absent-Minded Imperialists: Empire, Society and Culture in Britain* (Oxford, 2004).
8 Cultural studies of empire are now appearing: Barry Crosbie and Mark Hampton (eds), *The Cultural Construction of the British World* (Manchester, 2016), which deals with a number of disparate, but intriguing aspects of cultural connections. For settler societies, see Angela Woollacott, *Settler Society in the Australian Colonies: Self-Government and Imperial Culture* (Oxford, 2015) and Simon Sleight, *Young People and the Shaping of Public Space in Melbourne, 1870–1914* (Farnham, 2013).
9 In recent times it has become apparent in nature studies that urban environments have become places of opportunity for wild animals that often surprisingly, if dangerously, invade them.
10 Benedict Anderson, *Imagined Communities* (London, 1983), p. 150.
11 Mark Crinson, *Empire Building: Orientalism and Victorian Architecture* (London, 1996) is an example of an ideas-driven book as, in a rather different way, is G.A. Bremner, *Imperial Gothic Religious Architecture and High Anglican Culture in the British Empire, c. 1840–1870* (New Haven, CT and London, 2013).

12 Peter Scriver, 'Stones and Texts: The Architectural Historiography of Colonial India and its Colonial-Modern Contexts' in Scriver and Vikramaditya Prakash (eds), *Colonial Modernities: Building, Dwelling and Architecture in British India and Ceylon* (London, 2007), pp. 27–50.
13 For a valuable introduction, see Robert Home and Anthony D. King, ' Urbanism and Master Planning: Configuring the Colonial City' in G.A. Bremner (ed.), *Architecture and Urbanism in the British Empire* (Oxford, 2016), pp. 51–85.
14 Anthony D. King, *Urbanism, Colonialism and the World-Economy: Cultural and Spatial Foundations of the World Urban System* (London, 1990, republished 2015) provides an authoritative introduction to this work, as well as offering routes into the wider literature on cities, including planning.
15 Putting to one side more focused works, there is an enormous literature dealing in a global manner with the British Empire. Among the scholarly may be cited (as a select list): Bernard Porter, *The Lion's Share* (London, 1975); T.O. Lloyd, *The British Empire 1558–1983* (Oxford, 1984); John Darwin, *The Empire Project, the Rise and Fall of the British World-System, 1830–1970* (Cambridge, 2009) and *Unfinished Empire: The Global Expansion of Britain* (London, 2012); Denis Judd, *Empire: The British Imperial Experience from 1765 to the Present* (London, 1996); Bill Nasson, *Britannia's Empire: Making a British World* (Stroud, 2004); Ronald Hyam, *Understanding the British Empire* (Cambridge, 2010); Jeremy Black, *The British Seaborne Empire* (New Haven, CT, 2004). Among the popular (which often take up politically committed or polemical positions) are Lawrence James, *The Rise and Fall of the British Empire* (London, 1994); Piers Brendon, *The Decline and Fall of the British Empire 1781–1997* (London, 2007); Kwasi Kwarteng, *Ghosts of Empire: Britain's Legacies in the Modern World* (London, 2011); Richard Gott, *Britain's Empire: Resistance, Repression and Revolt* (London, 2011); Jeremy Paxman, *Empire: What Ruling the World Did to the British* (London, 2011); Niall Ferguson, *Empire: How Britain Made the Modern World* (London, 2003). Among more general postcolonial works may be cited Antoinette Burton, *The Trouble with Empire* (Oxford, 2015). In addition to these (and the distinction between scholarly and popular may sometimes be blurred), there is the five-volume *Oxford History of the British Empire* (Oxford, 1998–1999) under the general editorship of William Roger Louis, together with the 'companion series' on more specialist subjects.
16 The nearest to such a comprehensive approach are the Oxford History of the British Empire companion volumes, William Beinart and Lotte Hughes, *Environment and Empire* (Oxford, 2007) for the natural environment and Bremner (ed.), *Architecture and Urbanism* for the built environment.
17 Jiat-Hwee Chang, *A Genealogy of Tropical Architecture; Colonial Networks, Nature and Techno-Science* (Abingdon, 2016).
18 Sten Nilsson, *European Architecture in India, 1750–1850* (London, 1968); Robert Grant Irving, *Indian Summer: Lutyens, Baker and Imperial Delhi* (New Haven, CT, 1981) and Thomas R. Metcalf, *An Imperial Vision: Indian Architecture and Britain's Raj* (London, 1989).

Introduction

19 Jan Morris, *Stones of Empire: The Buildings of the Raj* (photographs and captions by Simon Winchester) (Oxford, 1983).
20 Philip Davies, *Splendours of the Raj: British Architecture and the Raj 1660–1947* (London, 1985).
21 Robert Fermor-Hesketh (ed.), *Architecture of the British Empire* (London, 1986).
22 The Church of Scotland is described as 'Nonconformist', which is nonsense in imperial terms since the Church of Scotland is an established church on a par with the Church of England. 'Cultural cringe' has its origins in the Australian critique of what was alleged to be the country's internationalised inferiority complex.
23 Clive Aslet, *The Age of Empire: Britain's Imperial Architecture from 1880–1930* (London, 2015). Aslet wrote (p. 6) that the imperial age from 1880–1930 was a time of 'great artistic sensitivity which coexisted with bombast, and earnest idealism walked the same pavements as opulence'.
24 Ashley Jackson, *Buildings of Empire* (Oxford, 2013).
25 Bremner (ed.), *Architecture and Urbanism*. It is intriguing that this book, in common with that by Philip Davies, has F.W. Stevens's great masterpiece, Victoria Terminus, Bombay (now Chhatrapati Shivaji Terminus, Mumbai), as the cover illustration.
26 Among various other articles on imperial architecture and British building, as well as mission architecture in southern Africa, see G.A. Bremner, '"Some Imperial Institute": Architecture, Symbolism, and the Ideal of Empire in Late Victorian Britain, 1887–93', *Journal of the Society of Architectural Historians*, 62, 1 (2003), pp. 50–73; '"Imperial Monumental Halls and Tower": Westminster Abbey and the Commemoration of Empire, 1854–1904', *Architectural History*, 47 (2004), pp. 251–282; 'The Architecture of the Universities' Mission to Central Africa: Developing a Vernacular Tradition in the Anglican Mission Field', *Journal of the Society of Architectural Historians*, 68, 4 (2009), pp. 514–539.
27 Bremner, *Imperial Gothic*.
28 Anthony D. King, *The Bungalow: The Production of a Global Culture* (London, 1984); Louis P. Nelson, *Architecture and Empire in Jamaica* (New Haven, CT, 2016).
29 Anthony D. King, *Colonial Urban Development* (London, 1976, republished 2007); *Aspects of Global Cultures: Architecture, Urbanism, Identity* (London, 2004); *Writing the Global City: Globalisation, Postcolonialism and the Urban* (London, 2016); *Urbanism, Colonialism and the World Economy* (Abingdon, 1990).
30 Swati Chattopadhyay, *Representing Calcutta: Modernity, Nationalism and the Colonial Uncanny* (London, 2005); Swati Chattopadhyay and Jeremy White (eds), *City Halls and Civic Materialism: Towards a Global History of Urban Public Space* (London, 2014); Scriver and Prakash (eds), *Colonial Modernities*. The latter contains a number of very valuable essays.
31 Sarah Longair, *Cracks in the Dome: Fractured Histories of Empire in the Zanzibar Museum, 1897–1964* (London, 2015).
32 Garth Andrew Myers, *Verandahs of Power: Colonialism and Space in Urban Africa* (Syracuse, NY, 2003).

33 Aslet, *Age of Empire*, pp. 7 and 33–34. Bremner, 'Some Imperial Institute' saw the architecture of the Institute as symbolic of imperial ideas in the late nineteenth century, not least the search for imperial unity. For an early history of the Institute, see John M. MacKenzie, *Propaganda and Empire*, chapter 5.

34 In 2017 there was a conference in Edinburgh examining the particular significance of Scottish architects in a global context. It is an obvious fact that architects from Scotland were particularly influential in eighteenth-century Britain and influenced buildings as far away as Russia. The presence of Scottish architects in India, South-East Asia, New Zealand and elsewhere will be noted in the chapters that follow.

35 This is true, for example, of the Albert Hall Museum in Jaipur (where the original name seems to have survived), designed by Swinton Jacob, and the museum in Trivandrum built by Fellowes Chisholm, each built in supposedly local styles. For the latter, see Paul Walker, 'Institutional Audiences and Architectural Style: The Napier Museum' in Scriver and Prakash (eds), *Colonial Modernities*, pp. 127–147.

36 Chattopadhyay and White (eds), *City Halls and Civic Materialism* makes an important contribution here, and we need more for other key building types.

37 For the British and Levantine community in Egypt, see James Whidden, *Egypt: British Colony, Imperial Capital* (Manchester, 2017); also James Whidden, 'The Levantine British: Defying Race Categories in Colonial Alexandria', *Britain and the World*, 12, 1 (March 2019), pp. 51–66.

1

Construction and destruction

It is an obvious truism that the creation of built environments involves destruction as well as construction, although the latter tends to be more noticed than the former. Not only is the natural environment overlaid by the built, but previously existing buildings, often part of rural economy and society, are also destroyed, together with the culture and lifestyles which they represented. In the empire, this is all the more strikingly true in terms of the subordinate societies which are colonised and dominated. The built environment thus becomes the key material presence of the racial hegemony of imperial rule. This chapter will consider in turn the physical materialisation of buildings, followed by the destruction wrought in the course of warfare and the construction of new (or replacement) cities and towns. It will also consider the means by which both construction and destruction were effected.

CONSTRUCTION AND MEANINGS

Imperial buildings lie at a complex intersection of ideas and economic imperatives, administrative requirements and technical innovations, cultural yearnings and religious needs, all expressed through a strongly visual and material existence. They are not mute, for they are designed to speak to their users as well as to those who merely observe them. All sorts of messages are inscribed upon them, whether of power and pomp, profit and piety or even poverty and practicality. They are thus documents that should be analysed like other documentary sources, even although they obviously differ in having a strongly spatial three-dimensional presence, in contributing to a land-, town- or city-scape. Unlike the other visual, musical or literary arts, structures and the forms in which they are presented are not a matter of consumer choice. Buildings cannot be avoided by those who live or work in them or their shadow. Whereas texts have to be sought out and are often directed at specific readerships, essentially through the particular medium of a language, architecture has multiple audiences. Edward Said pointed out that Orientalist texts were supposedly all directed at the portrayal of the East to western readerships, but the message of the built environment is clearly much more multidirectional.[1] The audiences for buildings included architectural practitioners and commentators, their viewers and their users, roughly a combination of the professional and the lay. Although at least initially (but increasingly less so later) the professionals would be largely from the imperial culture, viewers and users (as described in the Introduction) would combine imperial, colonial and indigenous categories. Moreover, viewers might well become users and racial and ethnic categories might become increasingly blurred. Thus buildings and the multiple ideas behind them were targeted at a variety of audiences who reacted to them in different ways, not least over the passage of time. The imperial built environment, though intended as a material display of sovereignty, did not present a monolithic set of ideas. Even if hegemonic power relationships were implicated in their construction, buildings could never represent a permanent and unchanging authority. Despite the hopes of their creators, they never maintained a set of homogeneous intentions.[2] Moreover, buildings and their design occupy a field in which cross-cultural influences have often been particularly potent. Metropolis and so-called periphery (as well as peripheral networks) have undoubtedly been involved in a dialogue in the development of imperial styles.[3]

In seeking to overlay the material culture of the people they dominate with replacements which they consider to be more 'civilised', more 'modern' or more fit for the cultural norms which they seek to inculcate, all empires have pursued the ambition of what today would be called 'globalisation', if initially within the boundaries of their known world. This became more of a reality once the expansion of the modern European empires took place, while the British had more opportunities than most to create an apparently genuine cultural globalisation. Yet, although economic globalisation has been much discussed, the accompanying cultural processes have, until recently, seldom entered the mainstream of professional imperial history.[4] There seem to be two explanations for this silence. The first is that the history of the British Empire has so often been written in isolation, remote from comparative approaches to other empires.[5] When we consider ancient or medieval empires such as the Roman or Norman, their cultural dimensions are invariably to the fore, given their striking material remains. It is now perfectly normal, for example, to consider aspects of the social history of the Romans from their gravestones and funerary monuments.[6] Roman sculptures, representing military and other events, as well as sites of memory, reveal a great deal about the scale and nature of empire as well as aspects of identity and concepts of 'othering'. Town planning, military structures, harbours and the building of walls and roads are also the stock-in-trade of all studies of the Roman Empire. Moreover, hybrid (for example Romano-British) cultures appeared and, with the retreat of the empire, indigenous peoples often came to reuse the buildings.[7]

Similarly, no one would think twice about considering the Normans in terms of architecture, their castle and cathedral building, military and religious innovations, layout of towns, effects upon the landscape, or compilation of data. All of these are vital to an understanding of British history. By extension, to achieve a fully rounded estimation of modern empires we need to analyse the buildings, towns and cities of empire, as well as the many cultural events that took place within them. For example, the cultures of ceremony and display, a characteristic of all empires, require to be understood, together with the ways in which buildings contributed to the many performative aspects of empires. Cities and towns are the obvious locations for cultural dispersal, but these may obscure similar effects, or the lack of them, in rural areas where most of the indigenous population were settled and often continued their traditional practices.

It is apparent that the British Empire not only spread peoples and a whole range of behavioural forms across the globe, it also dispersed building types and town planning; interior decoration and furniture; exclusive social clubs; the dressing of the human body; statuary, gardens (including the domestic variety) and parks; sports and all their associated clubs, grounds and related structures; the Christian religion with its churches, missions, educational and medical establishments; the press and publishing; institutions such as libraries, museums, art galleries, botanic and zoological gardens, intellectual associations, colleges and universities; the practice of western theatre, cinema, music and dance; and visual arts such as painting.[8] While few of these were unique to Britain, still they often took distinctively British forms. Some (like their architecture) were embedded in past 'cultures' in a conscious act of emulation of older imperialisms. Most material and cultural forms also went through rapid processes of adaptation in their new geographical and ethnic contexts. Thus, their dissemination demonstrates the manner in which cultures interpenetrate, interact and re-form and reconstruct in different geographical locations, climates and environments.

Moreover, the globalisation of material aspects of British culture leads us into informal imperial enclaves modified by interactions with adjacent societies.[9] Hybridisation and adaptation are vital themes of the dispersal of the British built environment, influenced by the dynamics of a debate between conservative cultural exclusiveness and quests for innovation and appropriate responsiveness to new conditions. Indigenous societies were very much involved in this search for accommodation.[10]

Urban and rural built environments reflect lives lived in agriculture and husbandry, the extractive processes of plantations, the manipulation of trade and commerce and the creation of mining centres and many other economic developments. Buildings also reflect the operations of the imperial military and the maintenance of order, the practices of authority, administration, legal affairs, religion, education, transportation systems, posts and telecommunications, medicine and health. In powerfully reflecting technological change as well as the hierarchy of social classes, race and status, they offer significant evidence of the social as well as economic and political history of empire. Buildings can encapsulate the other arts in their decoration, sculpture, mosaics, painted images and ceramics, all contributing to the projection of ideas and ideologies. Forms created to project the roles and activities they are designed to encapsulate and promote are also usually designed to produce emotional effects upon those who see or use them, though they may fail or stimulate resistance. Such effects can include a sense of power and authority, the majesty of the law, the mysteries of ideas to be transmitted through education and piety in intrusive forms of spirituality. Thus buildings are the most invasive and intrusive of the material deposits of empires.

For all these reasons, empires have been more or less obsessed with buildings and display, together with the great complex of concepts and types of command projected by them. Since empires are in the business of rule over both settlers and 'others', generally in exotic circumstances, their buildings are designed to exude power and the practice of its forms of authority in ways that supplement language. The practicality of early building types often assumes greater ideological overtones as control is consolidated. To return to the Romans and the Normans as specimen earlier empires, it is obvious that both used buildings to exert their command over the environment and its inhabitants, using the projection of the magnificence of their urban presence to imply cultural distancing from (and by implication superiority over) other peoples. Such structures had both practical and psychological effects. Throughout their imperial lands, fortresses and walls for the Romans, and great castles and fortifications for the Normans expressed the militarisation of their colonial territories.[11] Other buildings conveyed, in the Roman case, civilised agricultural settlement and the luxury of villas as well as venues for large-scale entertainments or appeals to the gods, while the Normans took Christian architecture in major new directions. As we shall see, the British drew on all of these in their empire as well as adding many more. But we should also note that the buildings of empire spanned a great range of structures, from those that reflected power and grandeur, like government houses or law courts, to the sometimes more humble examples associated with plantations, farms and migratory labour. Imperial government could be conducted in magnificent structures in capitals down to simple buildings in the provinces or even tents and spaces under trees. Moreover, we can note a distinction between the colonies of settlement and of rule. In the former, particularly as settlers secured more devolved powers, the intention was to demonstrate the adherence to the allegedly civilised values of the European origins of the white population. Increasingly, buildings in such territories vied with each other and with the metropole to showcase institutions that would simultaneously reflect the grandeur of the imperial project and the capacity of the settlers to emulate or even surpass the examples of the so-called 'mother country'. Eventually, this became part of the assertion of new national identities. In the empire of rule, imperialists displayed hegemonic purposes by spreading European types and styles on to a worldwide stage with diverse forms of aesthetic globalisation well ahead of the architectural homogenisation and apparently unstoppable spread of modernism in the twentieth century.

Thus, many of the buildings of empire spread European military forms and architectural styles, from the Renaissance fortress to highly historicist and allusive building types and architectural styles, neoclassical, Gothic, Italianate and modern Baroque. As well as the dispersed 'battle of the styles' that took place in the nineteenth century, they also took with them radical new aesthetic values as represented, for example, in Art Nouveau or more particularly Art Deco. Globalisation was indeed an aesthetically charged movement as well as a demographic, ideological and economic one. However, as suggested in the Introduction, the British never produced a standard imperial style and may not have been interested in doing so.[12] While it may be possible to see urban environments in the former British Empire as distinctively British, still fashion seems to have been more important in architecture than a consistent adherence to an ideology.

Nevertheless, in many places it took some time for imperial buildings to reflect the ambitions of colonisers. The real assertion of cultural difference came only after the initial pragmatic approach. The new built environment often adopted aspects of indigenous building, starting out by being insubstantial and flimsy, utilising natural materials like wood, bamboo and thatch. But later the imperial built environment exercised solidity, seeking a permanence which they imagined would both reflect the character of their rule and distance them from indigenous construction. Imperial buildings, reflecting their European origins, were often designed specifically to create enclosed spaces, symbolising privacy or privilege, with restricted entry supposedly inducing awe or reverence for ritualised public use. These might include law courts, administrative centres, banks, company headquarters or private clubs, though for many indigenous and lower-class people they might simply be places of work. A progressive social and racial opening-out might take place with public halls, Christian churches, and places of performance like theatres and, later, cinemas. Sports grounds were generally open, but even they had meeting rooms and clubhouses which included internal areas of restricted access. In most cases, buildings are designed not only to command the space of their footprints, but also to control their internal elements and immediate surroundings. Residences of various sorts, from the grandest to the relatively humble, would seek to create private space, at least in the case of whites, both in the buildings and in gardens, perhaps only to be invaded by servants. Many buildings were thus emblematic of deep social or racial divides. With the development of new technologies, however, buildings became specifically designed to open out to another world, through the portals of a railway station or the dockside warehouses or passenger accommodation of a port, later the terminals of airports. Most particularly, railway stations were open to all to satisfy the economic imperatives of ticket sales, but they too would have exclusive spaces to demarcate class and race.

Precolonial architecture encountered in the empire was often very different. In many places, as in North America, Africa and Australasia, it was invariably constructed from natural materials like wood and thatch which emphasised the essential relationship between structure and nature. Sometimes, such indigenous structures were consciously impermanent, ideal for moving on where certain ecologies demanded it, temporary arrangements spanning periods from seasons to several years (see Chapter 5 for more on this). Buildings of this sort were always grouped together into villages or kin groupings in which accessibility and a certain amount of openness were crucial to the sociability (and perhaps trading relationships) of the culture. Even in larger settlements, such openness was invariably more important than structural enclosure. While there were often defensive precautions against fellow humans or animals, in the form of stockades or the clever use of natural features, still each settlement related to others within the same or neighbouring cultures and societies. Where more solid building materials were used, such as masonry in India, the architecture was invariably climatically sensitive. While forts, palaces and large settlements would be surrounded by protective walls, as in Europe, villages still often maintained the structural and social openness to be found elsewhere. Nevertheless, despite deep social cleavages, the societies of the Subcontinent had produced a monumental architecture in which balconies, corridors and stairways were more likely to be open than enclosed, in which structural walls were generally pierced to permit the circulation of air, often from squares, courtyards and (for the elite) extensive surrounding gardens and water features. On the other hand, Islamic societies practised architectural enclosure in relation to the desire for the protection of women, with enclosed balconies from which women could observe either the outer or inner worlds or the structurally hidden harem or zenana space. With this notable exception, as well as the premium on defence in some places, indigenous architecture reflected an openness which was precluded both by climate and by social conventions in northern Europe. This was also reflected in the reverential architecture of religions, in shrines and spirit centres everywhere, in the mosques of Islam and the temples of Hinduism, Buddhism or Sikhism, all of them much more open than the strictly enclosed spaces of churches, missions and cathedrals, except again in relation to female space in mosques. However, builders of empire soon began to appreciate the climatic advantages, if not the social or religious ones, of the open characteristics of indigenous architecture.

In some cases, moreover, forms that were perceived to be exotic and indigenous to colonial territories were spread elsewhere in the world. This was most notably true of the bungalow derived from India or, less commonly, orientalised styles which were adopted, in various hybrid ways, in Asia and even spread to parts of Africa, Europe and elsewhere.[13] In grander buildings, there were two periods of striking architectural hybridity in India, the first in the late eighteenth century, the second in the later nineteenth and twentieth. It seems as though modern empires pass through three cultural phases (at least in respect of more highly developed, in material terms, subordinate cultures): a willingness to blend socially with indigenous culture in the early years (in architecture, mainly in residential terms), then a period of more intense cultural distancing and sense of superiority in the high point of imperialism in the early to mid-nineteenth century, followed by a modified return to a newly conceived and 'invented' hybridity (though never fully and convincingly adopted) as they declined. Thus, as empire began to weaken towards its fall, the British (and other Europeans) seemed to be more prepared to adopt culturally compromised styles, though with the weight still very much on the European side. This was particularly the case in British India with the development of the Indo-Saracenic style, though there was perhaps a retreat in the twentieth century symbolised by the reappearance of the neo-Georgian and the Baroque, with only a mild concession (for example) to Indian contexts in the new capital at New Delhi. It may be speculated that the retreat to older forms was designed to create a sense of reassurance as imperial decline became more apparent. These various phases will be examined in the chapters that follow.

Of course all of this building was conditional upon finance. The British Empire was notoriously parsimonious, such that the central treasury was seldom prepared to finance imperial developments – except in the case of the Royal Navy, required to assert global power, or with regard to specific military campaigns (though some of these were also paid for from colonial budgets). In the early territories of settlement, treasuries were invariably impecunious and budgets relied on the credit system to survive. Elsewhere, central government adopted an arm's-length approach, operating through chartered companies such as the East India and Hudson's Bay companies between the seventeenth and nineteenth centuries, or the four imperial chartered companies founded in the late nineteenth. It is, however, a myth to suggest that such devolution of powers made the operation any less imperial.[14] The charters were issued by the Crown and regulated by governments, while the populations of both the metropolis and of the resulting colonies saw little distinction between the operations of the company and the central authority that lay behind it. When they did identify such a distinction, as the missionary lobby did in the later nineteenth century, it was invariably to demand that imperial government become more directly involved. In any case chartered companies were a short-term device in modern times. Of the four founded in the 1880s as agencies for the extension of British power in Africa and Asia, two collapsed within a few years owing to financial weakness, while the other two gave way to central authority in the early 1920s and the 1940s, largely as a result of wars. Empire may have had essentially economic origins in the sense of being about a search for wealth through trade, but that did not make the material presence of empire any less imperial.

Nevertheless, colonies were generally expected to pay for themselves, either through the taxation of indigenous peoples (as in the case of India and many African colonies) or through fiscal policies relating to the products of hunting (as in North America in the earlier period), plantation and other agricultural production, forestry, raw materials and all the related commerce in export and import sectors. Many colonies enjoyed 'windfall' developments such as the discovery of major mining opportunities involving either precious or base minerals, like gold and diamonds or tin, copper and aluminium. Imperial buildings thus came to reflect not just the projection of power, but also the degree of tax-gathering potential or private wealth associated with economic development in specific territories. The magnificence of many imperial buildings in India was the product of the combination of tax levies upon a vast population and the scale of commerce of the Subcontinent. It was also a conscious reflection of the fact that India was the site of predecessor empires (notably the Mughal) whose public statements of power and grandeur had to be matched or exceeded in order to provide credibility to their British successors – or so they thought. It was perhaps inevitable that the buildings of African territories north of southern Africa were generally less impressive since they offered neither the tax-gathering potential nor the commercial scale or growth of India. Yet they still contrived to carry similar imperial messages. In settler territories, it was generally either highly successful agricultural or pastoral production and, even more so, the 'windfall' developments that stimulated urban growth and great building projects. The classic cases include the Australian colony of Victoria after the gold strikes of the 1850s or the territories in southern Africa after the discovery of diamonds in the late 1860s and gold in the 1880s. It was these economic developments which produced booms not only in the building of cities and towns, but also in the provision of infrastructures and great ports, as well as the development of new technologies. The growth of bourgeois classes was greatly stimulated, prompting the spread of all the emblematic institutions as well as cultural and educational opportunities that had developed in Britain itself as part of the 'bourgeois public sphere'. As we saw in the Introduction, not the least of the globalised effects of empire was the 'bourgeoisification' of the world, the great growth of the middle classes, and many buildings symbolised this major development in modern social ordering. They also reflected the power of the new companies that arose as a result of the booms, together with the technologies encapsulated in steamship companies and railways creating transport systems that rendered the territories of empire more accessible.

ENGINEERING, THE PROFESSIONALISATION OF THE ARCHITECTURAL PROFESSION, THE PUBLIC WORKS DEPARTMENTS, WORKERS AND RACE

The intersection of social classes and race is a key element in the construction of buildings. The creation of the imperial built environment ran through a sequence of phases starting with ad hoc, often informal arrangements through to the appearance of various aspects of professionalisation. The emergence of the architectural profession and its transfer to imperial contexts was very much a late development. In Europe, the concept of the architect only became widely used in the course of the sixteenth century, in Renaissance Italy through Andrea Palladio, and in England through John Shute, who staked his claim to the title in the 1560s. In Britain the most prominent names are figures such as Christopher Wren, Nicholas Hawksmoor, John Vanbrugh and the Scottish Adam family (father William and three sons, the most talented and prolific being Robert). Yet such men were seldom specifically trained in architecture. Wren, for example, was an anatomist, astronomer, mathematician and physicist. The Adam family were the most notable architects of the eighteenth century, pursuing interior decoration and design as much as architecture.[15] They educated themselves partly through the Grand Tour and through the works of the great masters, the ancient Vetruvius and the Renaissance Palladio. However, it was not until the nineteenth century that architects set out to identify themselves as a separate profession, thus no longer a craft or trade.[16] The establishment of professional status always required the foundation of a regulating body capable of controlling registration and therefore setting the standards of training and entry to the profession.[17] The Royal Institute of British Architects was founded in 1834 (the Irish equivalent in 1839), but legislation confirming the powers of registration was not passed until the twentieth century.[18] Nevertheless, the laying out of towns and the planning of buildings and structures in general tended to be arranged in a relatively informal and ad hoc fashion throughout the British Empire. In this, the military was very important, through its need for surveyors and engineers, the latter trained at the Royal Military Academy at Woolwich (founded in 1741) and at the East India Company's Addiscombe (1809). Later the Royal Engineer Establishment was founded at Chatham in 1812, followed by Cooper's Hill (the Royal Indian Engineering College), which operated between

1872 and 1906.[19] The provision of engineers became such a major professional requirement of the colonial regime in India, particularly in the major northern canal schemes like the Ganges Canal, that the British found it necessary to train Indians to assist in subordinate positions to European engineers. Such training started in Roorkee in the mid-1840s, later becoming the Thomason College of Civil Engineering, with grand neoclassical buildings.[20] European civilians were also involved in surveying and building. In remote plantations, often the planters themselves were their own surveyors and builders. In New South Wales, we know that convicts with some experience were employed on colonial buildings. Architectural pattern books became available in the eighteenth century and these were used by so-called amateurs, particularly engineers in India.[21] The full professionalisation of architecture in colonial territories only came later, with architectural institutes founded in South Africa in 1899 (another one in 1927, amalgamated in 1996), New Zealand in 1905, Canada in 1907, Australia in 1930, India in 1917, Egypt in the same year and Malaya in 1920.[22] All this professionalisation was to be important in the founding of architectural practices throughout the empire, leading into the postcolonial structure and regulation of the profession, but this was irrelevant to the development of the imperial built environment. Apart from the many other trades and professions involved, the really prestigious structures were often designed by the networks of British architects who worked both in Britain and in imperial territories. In Egypt, and sometimes elsewhere, other nationalities, particularly Italian, were active.[23]

However, the most influential bodies in India and the dependent colonies were the Public Works Departments (PWDs). The Central PWD of India was founded in 1854–55 under the Governor-General Lord Dalhousie and soon had a striking headquarters in Calcutta. Initially, the Indian PWD was dominated by military engineers who had performed most of the constructional activity in India since the eighteenth century. However, the building boom of the post-1857 Revolt period ensured that large numbers of civilian engineers (civil and mechanical) came to constitute the majority in the PWD, leading to rivalries and stresses between the different networks in what became a major bureaucracy.[24] PWDs were created in all the African colonies, once these had been established with formal administrations under the Colonial Office in the later nineteenth century. The PWD offices became one of the characteristic agencies of such colonies, established not just in the capitals, but also in the more significant provincial towns. Very often it was surveyors, inspectors and clerks of works in the PWDs who supplied plans for the 'bread and butter' colonial structures and supervised the choice and work of the contractors.²⁵ They developed a reputation for conservatism, and professionalised architects working on more prestigious projects often suspected the PWD of attempting to put the brakes on their stylistic and constructional innovations. As the constitutional progression of responsible and representative government (the latter involving the election of members of legislatures) proceeded in the settler territories, departments of public works necessarily became part of the apparatus of devolved government. In addition, private companies employed their own engineers and architects, a phenomenon particularly apparent with railway companies requiring not just the surveying of lines, but also the construction of headquarters buildings, railway stations and sometimes hotels. A few other large companies also directly employed their own surveyors and builders.

There were other agents and networks involved in the creation of the built environment of empire. Offices involved in land sales and allocations were important from the earliest days, indicative of the fundamental hegemonic and acquisitive functions of imperial expansion. The construction of buildings and other works required contractors, brickmakers, quarry masters, artisans and of course a multitude of labourers, illustrating the capacity of empires to marshal large labour forces and consequently transform environments. The racial mix of such a workforce was indeed highly complex and its make-up shifted according to colonial type. In Canada, Australia and New Zealand, almost all would have been drawn from white settlers, though sometimes from indentured labourers or, in eastern Canada, sometimes black loyalists who had migrated from the United States.²⁶ In South Africa and other African colonies, the most menial tasks were performed by blacks, though the craftsmen would usually have been white. In East and southern Africa, indentured Indian labour was used on large projects, such as the building of railway lines. Skilled black workers were trained and employed in those colonies where whites fulfilled only governmental, commercial, educational and missionary roles.²⁷ In India, most craftsmen would have been indigenous, supervised by whites, later by Indians. Both in India and the dependent colonies the large labour force was highly heterogeneous and at the lower end, was paid minimal wages, helping to keep the costs of imperial construction as low as possible. Often building workforces were sufficiently diverse that they spoke a variety of languages and exhibited different skills. This could lead to difficulties, tensions and delays in building schemes. Moreover, women were drawn into this workforce in the most menial, physically demanding and lowly paid tasks, mainly as load carriers of baskets of spoil or of raw materials.[28] Prisoners were also used as unpaid (and in effect forced) labourers in many parts of the British Empire.[29] However made up, the extensive base of the pyramid of workers was composed of the very people least likely to be able to make use of the buildings and amenities they were helping to construct. Thus, while buildings are invariably attributed to their designers and architects, great or humble, they achieve their material presence through the work of a host of unnamed workers who were the real builders of the architecture of empire. And they seldom, if ever, participated fully in the alleged benefits of the imperial condition. Such comparative labour issues help to justify the ambitious prospectus of taking an empire-wide approach, illuminating processes often examined in geographical isolation. In addition to all of this, many of the workers, in their struggle to survive, must have been aware of the elements of destruction in which they were, perhaps, the unwilling participants.

DESTRUCTION

As already observed, it would be grievously wrong to see the British Empire as being only about construction.[30] In desiring to overlay the built environment of predecessors, empires inevitably destroy in order to rebuild, a process that continues until modern times, and it is certainly the case that the British Empire was often set upon destruction.[31] To a certain extent, this reflects both imperial self-confidence and the quasi-religious commitment to what dominant cultures perceive as 'progress'. It could also reflect the violent confrontation of rival European empires, as in the destruction of Pondicherry (Puducherry) in India or of Quebec City in the Seven Years' War.[32] Throughout the empire, indigenous structures were destroyed in the name of what the British conceived as being 'progress' or the creation of a peaceful imperial order through 'pacification'. Other aspects of destruction include the disappearance of communities, of the spiritual significance of particular places, of indigenous craft skills and their outcomes, and much else. Such forms of destruction left many people bereft, but the focus here is on structures in the built environment.

The most striking examples of destruction happened in India, particularly at the time of the Revolt or 'Mutiny' of 1857, when entire areas of the great cities of Delhi and Lucknow were destroyed, including many remarkable buildings. It is true that the Mughals had themselves destroyed buildings as they created their empire, including in some cases Hindu temples (particularly in the reign of Aurangzeb). Indeed, Mughal Delhi had been built on the ruins of several predecessor cities. Moreover, the 1857 protagonists of the Revolt also set about destruction. As well as killing Christians, the rebels in the Agra area attacked and destroyed Christian churches. The Catholic Vicar Apostolic of Agra reported that in his area alone a cathedral, twenty-five churches and five seminaries had been damaged or destroyed, no doubt as condign revenge for attacks by the British regiments on mosques and temples, often turning them into temporary arsenals and barracks.[33] In the late 1850s, the British confidently set about remaking Delhi and Lucknow, creating new thoroughfares and urban routes as well as building the structures that reflected their own power. Nevertheless, some contemporaries were appalled by the scale of such destruction, as in the case of the Victorian architectural historian James Fergusson, who was particularly angered by the self-conscious demolition of much of the great Mughal palace in Delhi and its replacement by ugly barrack blocks (which still survive). Fergusson wrote of this destruction (it has been estimated that some four-fifths of the palace was swept away) that

> According to the native plan I possess, which I see no reason for distrusting, it contained three garden courts and some thirteen or fourteen other courts, arranged some for state, some for convenience, but what they were like we have no means of knowing. Not one vestige of them now remains. ... The whole of the harem courts of the palace were swept off the face of the earth to make way for a hideous British barrack, without those who carried out this fearful piece of vandalism, thinking it worthwhile to make a plan of what they were destroying or preserving any record of the most splendid palace in the world.[34]

William Dalrymple offers some detail of the destruction and redesign of Delhi.[35] Such destruction was to have repercussions in the twentieth century. When the British set about the creation of a new Indian upper-class district at Daryaganj, they used land that had been cleared of Mughal mansions after 1857.[36] The other notorious example of destruction and reordering in an Indian city is Lucknow, where the surprisingly eclectic architecture of the high point of the cultural and aesthetic activities of the court of the kingdom of Awadh was also severely damaged after the Mutiny, such that the British were able to set about the redesign of the city.[37] The celebrated correspondent of *The Times,* William Howard Russell, described Lucknow as the most 'striking and beautiful' city he had seen, more so than Rome, Athens or Constantinople. He wrote with horror

Construction and destruction

of its destruction and of the orgy of plunder indulged in by the imperial soldiers. When he returned to Lucknow on the visit of the Prince of Wales in 1876, he reported on the manner in which the city had been destroyed to make way for market gardens, 'parks, vistas, rides and drives' in place of the old 'streets, bazaars, palaces'. For him the rebuilding of Lucknow rendered it like 'oceans beneath which thousands of wrecks lie buried'.[38] In the case of both Delhi and Lucknow, the principal sources for the pre-British cities come from paintings and early photographs, particularly when a combination of British and Indian photographers became active in the later 1850s and 1860s. The devastation of Lucknow can be seen in a panorama of photographs taken by the photographer Felice Beato in 1858.[39] Efforts at the reconstruction of Lucknow continued into the twentieth century, when the town planner Patrick Geddes sought to introduce

5 Gateway to the Lucknow Residency with the ruins of the city beyond, destroyed during the 1857 Indian Uprising. Photograph by Felix Beato, *c.* 1858. Wellcome Collection. CC BY 4.0

6 The Chattar Manzil, Lucknow, palace of the rulers of Awadh, destroyed during the 1857 Indian Uprising. Photograph by Felix Beato, *c.* 1858. Wellcome Collection. CC BY 4.0

Arts and Crafts principles into street frontages.[40] Elsewhere, the destruction of villages and of indigenous urban habitations was commonplace in the search for security in opening up the field of fire for forts. The maidans in Calcutta and Bombay are the product of such clearance policies, as is the case with much open urban land elsewhere.

Another of the great cities of northern India, Lahore, also had mixed fortunes with the turnover of empires in the area. It had been an important residence for the Mughals after Babur had sacked the city in 1526. In the eighteenth century, with the decline of the Mughals, the city became prey to rival states, attacked by the Afghan ruler in 1765 and then the subject of a fierce contest between the Marathas and the Sikhs. It became an important city under the Sikh ruler Ranjit Singh, but by then its Mughal gardens and buildings were in decay. The British took it at the end of the Second Sikh War in 1849 and it became the capital of their Punjab province. The British squatted in and converted some of its buildings and destroyed others if they were considered to be inconvenient from the point of view of defence and the fort's field of fire. They soon decided that the old city was not appropriate for their residential and administrative requirements and inevitably built a cantonment and civil station outside the old town.[41] This established what has been described as the duality of the walled town and modernity, through the British attempt to create a new model town, which was in its turn 'colonised' by an Indian bourgeoisie as well as British imperial sojourners.[42] Outside these main centres, the British often set about reducing the fortresses of Indian rulers to ensure that they were not fortified against them again. Later, villages were cleared by the imperial forces from the Ridge above Delhi during the 1857 Revolt and again, more comprehensively, for the durbars held there in 1903 and 1911 and once more for the building of New Delhi. The British also considered that the tight alleys and lanes, together with the close patterns of buildings and their dense populations, were injurious to health and should be cleared, particularly when proximity to areas of British population seemed to endanger the representatives of the imperial power.[43] Though they were almost certainly not particularly effective, building regulations were introduced in order to ban specific aspects of Indian buildings considered to be dangerous.[44] An obsession with the notion that Indian settlement and culinary and other practices were redolent of dirt and disease became prominent in British thinking, particularly as the nineteenth century wore on.[45]

Architectural destruction was not, however, unique to India or to great cities like Delhi, Lucknow and Lahore. Elsewhere, wherever the British conquered, indigenous towns, palaces and forts were destroyed. The destruction of the Chinese imperial summer palace in 1860 by Lord Elgin is a notorious case in so-called 'informal empire'. After the second Anglo-Burmese War in the 1850s, the British destroyed the indigenous town on the banks of the Yangon River and set about building the new capital of Rangoon. In the third Anglo-Burmese War, the British demolished parts of Mandalay, although the destruction during the Second World War after the Japanese invasion was even more comprehensive. In Africa, the great Abyssinian fortress of Maqdala was totally razed to the ground after the British invasion in 1867–68. Part of the city of Kumasi and the then royal palace were destroyed by the British during the third Anglo-Asante War in 1874. In 1897, the city of Benin was seriously damaged in the British campaign. Attacks upon such cities also involved looting on a large scale, a conventional method in the British and other empires of incentivising the troops (and particularly their officers). This was the case with Benin art, much of which was relocated to Britain.[46] British regimental and other museums, as well as many private collections, particularly in great country houses, are full of such loot, never fully catalogued, but now the subject of a project to identify such material, create an inventory and interpret it appropriately.[47] In many parts of the world, villages were destroyed as acts of war or of revenge and punishment. This was true on the North-West Frontier of India, where Winston Churchill described the destruction of between twelve and fourteen villages and no fewer than thirty towers and forts blown up as reprisals for the failure to return rifles allegedly taken from British soldiers.[48] Many examples can also be found throughout Africa, notably in East Africa, in the British South Africa Company's seizure of Central Africa, and on the eastern frontier of the Cape.[49] And this is far from being a comprehensive list.

In many places in Africa, notably in the southern and central colonies, Africans were cleared off land to make it available to white settlers, a physical expulsion often effected by the invading settlers themselves and then sanctioned by land apportionment through the imposition of alien laws. This inevitably involved the destruction of countless African villages (and the construction of new ones elsewhere on so-called 'reserves', where, unlike their predecessors, they were intended to be permanent).[50] Sometimes, new settlements were also created for the use of the labour force desired by whites. During the Anglo-Boer War of 1899–1902, there was inevitably a great deal of destruction, not least through the notorious British torching of Afrikaans homesteads during the later guerrilla part of the campaign. In New Zealand, a large number of Maori fortified villages or *pas* were demolished during the Maori wars between the 1840s and early 1870s, when many of the great wooden carvings of the Maori people were either destroyed or removed to museums.[51] In Australia, white settlers regarded the Aboriginal hunting and gathering economy as wholly incompatible with their own desire to run domesticated stock. Conflicts led to massacres and clearance of peoples, destroying their, albeit temporary, settlements. This was, however, done with no respect at all for the Aborigines' spiritual relationship with nature and the mythic power of lands associated with their ancestors. The great carving traditions of the north-west coast of North America, a vital part of the architecture of the area, were raided extensively for museum displays.[52] At an early stage, First Nation Beothuk settlements in Newfoundland were destroyed by the new European immigrant fishing community. The new technologies were also highly destructive: countless settlements of both Métis and First Nations peoples were destroyed (despite sometimes having treaties with the whites) by the building of the transcontinental railway line (and by the arrival of European farming along its length) in Ontario, Manitoba, Saskatchewan and Alberta.[53] The railway of course produced explosive growth of the immigrant built environment across the same region. The building of such lines inevitably produced destruction everywhere, particularly in a densely populated country with historic cities and towns like India. Another effective mode of destruction was offered by the gunboat. On the British Columbian coast, Royal Navy gunboats were used to destroy Kwakiutl villages and canoes on the pretext of pursuing those who were regarded as murderers.[54] Such destructive gunboat actions occurred on coasts throughout the empire, notably in West Africa, South-East Asia and China.[55] In more recent times, the hostile use of air power resulted in destructive bombing deployed against villages in Somaliland, Iraq and elsewhere,[56] as well as in campaigns against Arab insurgents in Palestine in the late 1930s[57] and in Kenya or Malaya in the 1950s.[58] Such examples of the use of various modern technologies against settlements could be multiplied many times across the empire. In the Second World War, bombing also destroyed significant buildings in the colony of, for example, Malta.

There are of course many natural agents of destruction, which are indiscriminate in destroying imperial as well as indigenous elements of the built environment. These include earthquakes, volcanic eruptions, hurricanes, cyclones, typhoons, tidal waves and dereliction caused by abandonment and the encroachment of the natural world – always particularly potent in tropical regions. Among natural destroyers, termites have always been particularly effective demolition workers. To these we can add the accidents of fire, such as the great fire of St John's, New Brunswick in June 1877 when 200 acres and over 1,500 structures were destroyed, including eight churches and a number of banks and hotels. In 1917, the enormous explosion in Halifax, when a munitions ship in the harbour blew up after a collision, also had a devastating effect on many structures, including the Halifax Exhibition Hall. The Bombay Victoria Dock explosion of April 1944, when another munitions vessel blew up, devastated at least two square miles of the city. All these have served to damage and destroy imperial architecture, often leading to areas of reconstruction. In modern times, the demolition of colonial-era buildings has proceeded apace, many lost because of the imperative of development, because land becomes so valuable that smaller structures, however historically or aesthetically appealing, are doomed to disappear in order to make way for larger ones. Hong Kong is a former colony which has to a

The British Empire through buildings

7 Destruction of the Accommodation House, Tawarewa eruption, North Island, New Zealand, 1917

large extent renewed itself, with many buildings of the colonial era disappearing.[59] The scale of such demolition is readily illustrated by Sydney, New South Wales, where nostalgia for past residential architecture has led to publications to commemorate their existence.[60]

However, the overtly political destruction of buildings has never been solely a European imperial activity. Religious buildings have often provoked tensions, as they have continued to do in some parts of India in conflicts between Muslims and Hindus. This was particularly true in Egypt where the fortunes of the Anglican Church closely followed the ups and downs of the political relationship between Britain and Egypt. There were European (as opposed to indigenous, much older Coptic) Christian churches in Egypt for much of the nineteenth century. In 1876 one of these was upgraded to the status of cathedral. Considered inadequate in size, it was extended at various points in the 1890s, but after the declaration of the British protectorate in Egypt a new cathedral was considered necessary. It was consecrated in 1938. The 1956 Suez crisis was a disaster for the Anglican Church. All expatriate clergy were expelled and only a few indigenous clergy were left to run a number of churches.[61] In the post-British period, a number of the celebrated buildings of Cairo associated with Europeans were destroyed.

In the conditions of that time, there is a fine line between accident and arson. There seems to be little doubt that the famous Shepheard's Hotel, one of the most celebrated hotels in the world during its heyday, was deliberately burnt down during the anti-British riots and the accompanying massive fire in Cairo in 1952. The Khedivial opera house, opened in 1869 as part of the celebrations for the opening of the Suez Canal, was burnt down in 1971, although the circumstances of that fire are difficult to establish. Shepheard's and the opera house were subsequently rebuilt in more modern styles – in the case of the opera house an essentially Middle Eastern building was substituted for the original, which was French Second Empire in inspiration. Another aspect of what may be seen as inadvertent destruction is the damage caused to potential archaeological sites in the remains of past structures by the foundations of buildings, mainly in the Middle East.[62] This destruction has continued in the operations of modern warfare, such as the Iraq War of 2003 and the conflicts involving the Taliban in Afghanistan and Isis or Daesh groups across the Middle East.

In the Sudan in North-East Africa, a number of mission stations and churches were founded, notably by the Roman Catholics from the 1840s onwards. The Islamic regime of the Mahdi in the 1880s ordered the destruction of all of these, and the reappearance of Christianity and the erection of a new wave of Christian buildings only began after the British conquest in 1898 and the reconstruction of Khartoum. The Roman Catholic Cathedral of St Matthew was completed in 1908 on the banks of the Blue Nile. It still stands. However, the Anglican equivalent, All Saints Cathedral, was found to be unacceptably close to the presidential palace in a Muslim country. It was also alleged, almost certainly inaccurately, that there was a tunnel between the cathedral and the palace, convenient for the British but a security problem for their nationalist successors. The cathedral, which had come to be the principal church of the Episcopal Church of the Sudan, was confiscated in 1971. Its tower (towers are often controversial, both because of their symbolic significance and as a result of the manner in which they vie for prominence with the minarets of mosques) was demolished and the building itself was turned into a museum. The Sudanese government provided a plot for a new cathedral and money for the reconstruction, although the Episcopal Church insisted that the amount was inadequate.[63]

This alternation of construction and destruction is one of the themes of this book, a theme which helps to distance it from previous publications in the field.

However, as we shall see, in modern times a new factor has set about inhibiting the processes of destruction. This is the current obsession with heritage. If imperial buildings tended to reflect the restricted, power-based characteristics of empire building itself, we should recognise that the messages conveyed by such intrusive structures have a tendency to change over time.[64] They can pass through a sequence of aesthetic fashions, sometimes becoming for many commentators evidence of a debased taste of the past, only to be later revalued. Alternatively, they can be admired as demonstrating the superior values of an earlier generation. Eventually, they can become locations of a social and even political nostalgia. When empires pass away, they can be viewed as striking remains of a previous culture, however violent or brutal it may have been. The original meaning of buildings, as a projection of the ideology inherent in their creation, can be completely transformed as they come to be occupied, used and perhaps even valued in postcolonial ways. It is true that some of the buildings are allowed to fall into disuse, to become derelict or be demolished, but others are rediscovered and even converted into representing the outward display of independent, post-imperial states and their rulers. In some places, a new wave of concern for 'heritage' can convert such buildings into structures in which later generations can take pride, not least if they can come to symbolise the civilised behaviour of new nationalist generations, perhaps a particularly potent effect when it is recognised that such 'heritage' can significantly attract and influence tourism.[65] Sometimes, this conversion into heritage involves the convenient overlooking of sometimes baleful histories of such buildings, as for example in the case of slavery in the Caribbean. Heritage involves the reconstruction, in effect, of a new and symbolic historical façade. Nevertheless, such revaluation can take place at different levels, from those who walk in the streets and (possibly) like what they see, even viewing the built environment as contributing to the identity of their location, to those who like the places where they work, to the professional architects who wish to admire, analyse and preserve representative buildings. Perhaps most significantly, such new heritage façades can seem important for tourist offices trying to encourage more tourism in the respective city and territory. An interesting case, as will become apparent in Chapter 7, is that of Burma/Myanmar and in particular its former capital and now significant tourist destination of Yangon (colonial Rangoon). In some places, inherited buildings, such as those converted from government houses to state houses, can become almost symbolic of nationalist identity. There is thus some evidence that aspects of imperial architecture have come to be revalued for a post-imperial age. There will be further discussion of this effect in the concluding chapter.

NOTES

1 Edward Said, 'East Isn't East – The Impending End of the Age of Orientalism', *Times Literary Supplement*, 3 February 1995, p. 4. www.the-tls.co.uk/articles/private/east-isnt-east/ (accessed 16 January 2019).
2 Mark Crinson, *Empire Building: Orientalism and Victorian Architecture* (London, 1996), p. 6 and passim.
3 For discussions of the influence of the East on the West, see Patrick Conner, *Oriental Architecture in the West* (London, 1979); Raymond Head, *The Indian Style* (London, 1986); John Sweetman, *The Oriental Obsession: Islamic Inspiration in British and American Art and Architecture* (Cambridge, 1988); John M. MacKenzie, *Orientalism: History, Theory and the Arts* (Manchester, 1995), chapter 4. Deborah Howard has charted the interpenetration of East and West in *Venice and the East: The Impact of the Islamic World on Venetian Architecture 1100–1500* (New Haven, CT, 2000).
4 For aspects of globalisation, see Gary B. Magee and Andrew S. Thompson, *Empire and Globalisation* (Cambridge, 2010); A.G. Hopkins (ed.), *Globalisation in World History* (London, 2002).
5 John Darwin's *After Tamerlane* (London, 2007) has been a notable exception. Where empires have been examined in comparative ways, as in Jane Burbank and Frederick Cooper, *Empires in World History* (Princeton, NJ, 2010), Timothy H. Parsons, *The Rule of Empires* (Oxford, 2010) or Dominic Lieven, *Empire* (London, 2003), the approach has invariably been political. Sometimes a comparative approach has been introduced in order to 'exceptionalise' the British Empire. See my critique of this in John M. MacKenzie, 'The British Empire: Ramshackle or Rampaging? A Historiographical Reflection', *Journal of Imperial and Commonwealth History*, 43, 1 (March 2015), pp. 99–124.
6 Mary Beard pioneered such studies and unveiled significant aspects of Roman social life as a result. See www.eagle-network.eu/story/putting-ancient-inscriptions-in-the-limelight (accessed 25 October 2017). British graveyards and monuments in metropolis and empire also present intriguing opportunities for research.
7 On Hadrian's Wall, indigenous (round) structures often coexist with Roman (rectangular) ones. At Bothwellhaugh Roman bathhouse in central Scotland, a 'leisure centre' for the Antonine Wall, a hearth indicating later native occupation was found in the middle of the frigidarium. Lawrence Keppie and John M. MacKenzie, 'Bothwellhaugh Roman bathhouse', *Current Archaeology*, 52 (1976), pp. 154–156.
8 Some of these phenomena will be considered in another volume.
9 A valuable account which offers considerable insights into the Chinese treaty port of Shanghai is Robert Bickers, *Empire Made Me: An Englishman Adrift in Shanghai* (London, 2003). See also Bickers (ed.), *Settlers and Expatriates* (Oxford, 2010). A fascinating

account of the British community in a South American city is Michelle Prain (ed.), *The British Legacy in Valparaiso* (Santiago, 2011).

10 See, for example, Courtnay Micots, 'Status and Mimicry, African Colonial Period Architecture in Coastal Ghana', *Journal of the Society of Architectural Historians*, 74, 1 (March 2015), pp. 41–62, doi: 10.1525/jsah.2015.74.1.41. Micots examines hybrid, colonial-period architecture in Anomabo between the 1870s and 1820s, arguing that mimicry of colonial styles constituted not just a search for status and modernity, but also a means of resistance to colonial rulers.

11 Although this reference to the Normans relates to British imperial forts, it is interesting that the artist William Hodges likened the great fortress at Gwalior to Norman forts in England. William Hodges, *Travels in India in the years 1780, 1781, 1782, 1783* (London, 1793), pp. 136–137.

12 Jan Morris, 'In Quest of the Imperial Style' in Robert Fermor-Hesketh, *The Architecture of Empire* (London, 1986), pp. 10–31.

13 See Chapter 5 below; Anthony D. King, *The Bungalow: The Production of a Global Culture* (London, 1984). For the spread of orientalised styles, see Head, *Indian Style*, Sweetman, *Oriental Obsession* and, particularly in terms of leisure and entertainment, MacKenzie, *Orientalism*, chapter 4.

14 Bernard Porter in 'Cutting the British Empire Down to Size', *History Today*, 62, 10 (October 2012), pp. 22–29.

15 Roderick Graham, *Robert Adam: The Arbiter of Elegance* (Edinburgh, 2009).

16 For England, see John Wilton-Ely, 'The Rise of the Profession of Architect in England' in Spiro Kostof (ed.), *The Architect: Chapters in the History of the Profession* (Berkeley, CA, 1977), pp. 180–208.

17 For a general study of professionalisation at a later period, see Harold J. Perkin, *The Rise of Professional Society in England Since 1880* (London, 1989).

18 The separate Royal Incorporation of Architects of Scotland was founded in 1916.

19 In the 1880s, Cooper's Hill added forestry to its curriculum.

20 The college at Roorkee was later a university and is now the Indian Institute of Technology. One of the characters in Vikram Seth's celebrated novel *A Suitable Boy* (London, 1993) is a graduate of Roorkee. For the later period in India, see Aparajith Ramnath, *The Birth of an Indian Profession: Engineers, Industry and the State, 1900–1947* (Oxford, 2017). The founding of schools of engineering in Canada and Australia can be charted in Tamson Pietsch, *Empire of Scholars: Universities, Networks and the British Academic World 1850–1939* (Manchester, 2013). Schools of Architecture came later since the route into architectural practice was through 'articles' or apprenticeship in existing practices or was sometimes associated with Colleges of Art. Schools of Architecture were founded at Toronto in 1890 and in McGill in 1896, in Australia in Sydney in 1918 and in Melbourne in 1919. The University of Cambridge School of Architecture was founded in 1912. For its history see www.arct.cam.ac.uk/aboutthedepartment/aboutthedepthome (accessed 12 February 2019).

21 For example, James Gibbs published *A Book of Architecture* in 1728, a pattern book designed, as he put it, for those working 'in remote parts of the country'. It was

quickly used in the American colonies and soon became valuable elsewhere in the empire.
22 In the case of Canada, the creation of the Institute emerged from the desire to coordinate architectural practice across the various provinces of the Confederation. The legislation to establish it was bitterly fought since opponents thought there was going to be a 'closed shop' inhibiting the activities of other engineers, architects, surveyors and the employees of companies. Nonetheless the legislation went through (www.raic.org/raic/history). Little historical information is available for the other Institutes. The Australian Institute has 'chapters' in all the states and territories of the Commonwealth.
23 Crinson, *Empire Building*, pp. 109, 177, 196.
24 Peter Scriver, 'The Public Works Department of British India' in Scriver and Vikramaditya Prakash (eds), *Colonial Modernities: Building, Dwelling and Architecture in British India and Ceylon* (London, 2007), pp. 69–92.
25 Appointments in PWDs were invariably handled centrally by the Crown Agents to the Colonies in London. David Sunderland, *Managing the British Empire: The Crown Agents, 1833–1914* (London, 2004).
26 There were also specialisms among the people of the British four nations. If white miners often came from Cornwall, stonemasons were invariably recruited from Scotland, particularly north-east Scotland, since those who were capable of working in granite could cope with almost any kind of stone.
27 In the 1920s and early 1930s African prisoners in Kenya were trained as bricklayers. For the colonial authorities it was convenient to have a (literally) captive student body to acquire building-trade skills important for the construction industry in a relatively new colony (oral evidence from Alexander MacKenzie).
28 Arindam Dutta, '"Strangers within the Gate": Public Works and Industrial Art Reform' in Scriver and Prakash (eds), *Colonial Modernities*, pp. 103–105.
29 Forced labour was commonplace (and legislated for in colonial regulations) throughout African colonies, particularly for road making. There is a considerable literature on colonial forced labour. Lord Hailey's *An African Survey* (London, 1938, a new edition in 1956), pp. 608–635, reveals the manner in which colonial authorities justified forced labour on the basis of communal labour in traditional societies. Such labour was used in public works, in military conscription and in the extension of colonial agricultural practice. Sir Granville St John Orde Browne was the adviser to the Colonial Office on colonial labour in the inter-war years and produced a sequence of reports on the operation of labour regulations, including forced labour.
30 Some recent books on architecture have concentrated on the constructive material effects of empire. These include G.A. Bremner's edited landmark volume *Architecture and Urbanism in the British Empire* (Oxford, 2016), Ashley Jackson's *Buildings of Empire* (Oxford, 2013) and Tristram Hunt's *Ten Cities that Made an Empire* (London, 2014).
31 Additionally, there is the environmental destruction inherent in the foundation and extension of cities and towns in imperial territories, not to mention the exploitation

of raw materials required for their construction, the creation of infrastructures or for the energy requirements of their inhabitants.

32 For visual evidence of such destruction, see John E. Crowley, *Imperial Landscapes: Britain's Global Visual Culture* (New Haven, CT, 2011), p. 60.
33 Ferdinand Mount, *Tears of the Rajahs: Mutiny, Money and Marriage in India 1805–1905* (London, 2015), p. 573.
34 James Fergusson, *History of Indian and Eastern Architecture* (London, 1876), Vol. II, p. 594, quoted in William Dalrymple, *The Last Mughal: The Fall of a Dynasty, Delhi 1857* (London, 2006), p. 459.
35 Ibid., pp. 454–464. Dalrymple derived much of his information from Narayani Gupta, *Delhi Between Two Empires, 1803 – 1931: Society, Government and Urban Growth* (New Delhi, 1991).
36 Jyoti Hosagrahar, 'Negotiated Modernities' in Scriver and Prakash (eds), *Colonial Modernities*, p. 226.
37 Rosie Llewellyn-Jones (ed.), *Lucknow: City of Illusion* (London, 2006), pp. 34–37.
38 Quoted in ibid., p. 89.
39 These are reproduced in ibid., pp. 90–99. Biographies of both Indian and British photographers can be found in an appendix, pp. 248–254.
40 Volker M. Welter, 'Arcades for Lucknow: Patrick Geddes, Charles Rennie Mackintosh and the Reconstruction of the City', *Architectural History*, 42 (11 April 2016), pp. 316–332.
41 Sylvia Shorto, 'A Tomb of One's Own: The Governor's House, Lahore' in Scriver and Prakash (eds), *Colonial Modernities*, pp. 151–168.
42 Ian Talbot and Tahir Kamran, *Colonial Lahore: A History of the City and Beyond* (London, 2016), pp. 18–30.
43 Mark Harrison, *Public Health in British India: Anglo-Indian Preventive Medicine, 1859–1914* (Cambridge, 1994). See also Muhammad Umair Mushtaq, 'Public Health in British India: A Brief Account of Medical Services and Disease Prevention in Colonial India', *Indian Journal of Community Medicine*, 34, 1 (2009), pp. 6–14.
44 Anthony D. King, *Urbanism, Colonialism and the World Economy* (London, 2015), p. 40.
45 These concerns run through Flora Annie Steel and Grace Gardiner, *The Complete Indian Housekeeper and Cook*, new edition edited by Ralph Crane and Anna Johnston (Oxford, 2010). This work, which repeatedly inveighs against the dirt of the Indian domestic environment, proved to be very popular and ran through ten editions between 1888 and 1921.
46 A detailed account of the dispersal of Benin material culture can be found in Annie Coombes, *Reinventing Africa: Museums, Material Culture and Popular Imagination* (New Haven, CT, 1994). See also Frank Willett, *African Art* (London, 1971).
47 This project is being led by National Museums Scotland, largely funded by the Arts and Humanities Research Council. See *History Scotland*, 17, 4 (July/August 2017), p. 31. I have been involved in the planning of this project. An excellent example of a country house is Blair Castle in northern Perthshire, which the then heir to

the Duke of Atholl, the Marquis of Tullibardine, filled with loot from the Sudan campaign of 1897–98. The ballroom is decorated with it, while the crescent (now a copy) from the top of the Mahdi's tomb adorns one of the castle's smaller towers. Many regimental museums contain such material.

48 Winston S. Churchill, *The Story of the Malakand Field Force* (London, 1989, first published 1898), pp. 164–165. Churchill, in justification, wrote that 'the villages are the fortifications, the fortifications the villages'. He also wrote scornfully of the opposition to such policies at Westminster and in the British press.
49 In the early years of British South Africa Company rule in Mashonaland, village burning occurred as reprisals against people who had allegedly attacked passing whites. T.O. Ranger, *Revolt in Southern Rhodesia, 1896–97* (London, 1967), pp. 64–66.
50 The conversion of impermanent villages into permanent ones had the effect of debilitating the land and impoverishing residents dependent on it.
51 James Belich, *The New Zealand Wars and the Victorian Interpretation of Racial Conflict* (London, 1986). See also John M. MacKenzie, *Museums and Empire* (Manchester, 2009), particularly chapters 8 and 9.
52 Ibid., chapters 2 and 3. It is true that wooden carving traditions often assumed natural deterioration and destruction, as did some indigenous building traditions, but the assumption in these cases was that they would be continuously renewed. It was that renewal that often came to an end.
53 James Danschuk, *Clearing the Plains: Disease, Politics of Starvation and the Loss of Aboriginal Life* (Regina, 2004); Sarah Carter, *Lost Harvests: Prairie Indian Reserves, Farmers and Government* (Montreal, 1990).
54 Barry Gough, *Gunboat Frontier: British Maritime Authority and North-West Coast Indians, 1846–90* (Vancouver, 1984), pp. 81–84.
55 Antony Preston and John Major, *Send a Gun Boat: A Study of the Gunboat and its Role in British Policy, 1854–1904* (London, 1967).
56 David E. Omissi, *Air Power and Colonial Control: The Royal Air Force, 1919–1939* (Manchester, 1990).
57 Matthew Hughes, 'The Practice and Theory of British Counterinsurgency: The History of the Atrocities at the Palestinian Villages of al-Bassa and Hallul, 1938–39', *Small Wars and Insurgencies*, 3–4 (2009), pp. 528–550.
58 Christopher Bayly and Tim Harper, *Forgotten Wars: The End of Britain's Asian Empire* (London, 2007), passim.
59 Tom Briggs and Colin Crisswell, *Hong Kong: The Vanishing City*, Vol. 1 (Hong Kong, 1977) and Vol. 2 (Hong Kong, 1978). The photographic collection of the Hong Kong Museum of History reveals the extent of the destruction. See Joseph S.P.Ting and Wong Nai-Kwan, *City of Victoria: A Selection of the Museum's Historical Photographs* (Hong Kong, 1994).
60 Joy Hughes (ed.), *Demolished Houses of Sydney* (Sydney, 1999). This book was published in conjunction with an exhibition at the Hyde Park Barracks Museum, when Peter Watts, the director of the Historic Houses Trust, wrote in his foreword that 'Greed, Greed and Sydney seem to go together.'

61 http://dioceseofegypt.org/explore/egypt/all-saints-cathedral-cairo/history-of-all-saints-cathedral/ (accessed 10 December 2018).
62 Crinson, *Empire Building*, where there are some examples in chapter 7 on Jerusalem.
63 https://khartoum.anglican.org/index.php?PageID=cathhistory (accessed 10 December 2018).
64 Mark Crinson, *Modern Architecture and the End of Empire* (London, 2003), which examines the manner in which modernism and international style have varied in their messages in Britain, West Africa, Hong Kong, Iran, India and South Asia. See Chapter 8 below.
65 Two examples of architectural heritage books are Andrew Gravette, *Architectural Heritage of the Caribbean: An A-Z of Historic Buildings* (Kingston, Jamaica, 2000) and Khoo Salma Nasution and Halim Berbar, *Heritage Houses of Penang* (Singapore, 2009).

2

Militarisation, mobility and the residencies of power

FORTS, BARRACKS AND MILITARISATION

Most if not all historical empires seem to require two primary characteristics to sustain their initial command of alien territory. The first is the opportunity to retreat to, and sally forth from, military redoubts. The second is the capacity for mobility, to be able to move both military and administrative personnel rapidly round conquered lands. This chapter will examine the material presence of both of these, as well as the manner in which a combination of them represented the emergence of another essential element of militarisation, the initial formation of barracks and, in India, cantonments. While the earlier buildings of empire can be identified across a very considerable spectrum from the strikingly grand to the very humble, the essential requirement in the formative stages of modern European empires, as with empires in the past, was the provision of offensive and defensive structures in order to assert and then maintain an initially tentative imperial power. When empires are first established in exotic or alien environments, their initial character is necessarily military, only later commercial and bureaucratic. For this reason, the characteristic primary imperial building is the fortress. Thus, modern imperial rule, no less than all earlier empires, was expressed through the militarisation of the landscape. This is true within Britain itself, where forts and castles represent the consolidation of an ambitious British monarchy, whether in the great medieval castles of North Wales and elsewhere, or in the forts of Ireland (some of them designed against the possibility of Spanish or French invasion[1]) or Scotland. In the latter, some place names retain these origins, as in Fort Augustus, Fort George and Fort William. In the empire, forts were often found in coastal and riverine locations, but soon appeared as imperial nodes of power further into the interior of territories. They were designed, as in historic empires, both to protect against external attack by rival empires and to provide defence against resistant indigenous populations. They were redoubts to which the forerunners of imperial rule could withdraw when threatened. They always had multiple purposes: military in appearance, they might also shelter early trading functions and the people despatched to conduct and command such activity. Thus their spaces were initially often shared by both military and civilians. Some more specifically military forts were located for the defence of harbours or coasts primarily against the naval operations of rivals, as well as to protect trade. Sometimes, even in the late nineteenth century (when they made a reappearance in Africa), they performed the same function in the far interior of continents, although in the Rhodesian (Zimbabwean) case of the 1890s, for example, 'Fort Salisbury' and 'Fort Victoria' were intended more for psychological effect than to indicate the building of genuine forts in the old style.[2]

Forts could be found everywhere in the British Empire, as in other empires. Indeed such forts often went through a continual process of being taken and retaken or exchanged. Perhaps the classic case is the Caribbean and its essential connection with West Africa. The slave trade was conducted from a whole sequence of castles and forts on the West African coast, beginning with the Portuguese in the late fifteenth century, continuing through the appearance of several other European empires, and reaching a climax in the eighteenth, by which time the British were dominant. By the nineteenth century the British commanded nineteen of the coastal castles and forts. Lawrence identified some forty-three such fortified trading posts on the West African coast and, particularly after the British acquired those of the Danes and the Dutch, those held by Britain were in the majority.[3] These may have been trading posts rather than colonies, but they were unquestionably growth points from which colonies could develop.[4] A number of these castles, such as the formerly Danish Christiansborg (now known as Osu), were as magnificent as anything in Europe and, despite the baleful association with the slave trade, this one even became the seat of government and the Government House of the Gold Coast, later the residence of the first president, Kwame Nkrumah. Others included Cape Coast Castle and Dixcove Fort (now known as Fort Metal Cross). All bear the marks of the horrors of the slave trade, with their barrel-vaulted dungeon-like basements for the holding of slaves until their embarkation for the Atlantic middle passage, their tunnels leading to the beach and their iron gates.[5] These West African forts are therefore emblematic not only of intercolonial violence but also of the violence and human degradation of enslavement. At the other end of the trade, in the Caribbean islands, the destruction of indigenous populations and of pre-Columbian natural environments proceeded at enormous speed in what can be seen as an example of explosive imperialism, particularly in the seventeenth century.[6]

Through the labour power of slaves, island colonies of high value and restricted space became prey to the intense competition of the mercantile empires of the seventeenth and eighteenth centuries. To take the example of the island of Antigua, the conflicts of the eighteenth century, the fierce competition for lands producing sugar and other commodities, are expressed in the amazing ring of forts which the British erected right round the island. There were some forty of them designed to keep out the French, with the most impressive overlooking what is still known as English Harbour, the naval base which Nelson famously used in the 1780s to apply the Navigation Acts with such pedantic ferocity as to cause massive irritation to local plantation owners and merchants, as well as the Americans accustomed to trade with them.[7] Many of these forts are now ruinous, for such structures are particularly prone to destruction by earthquakes and hurricanes. On the island of St Kitts, one of the most impressive of all the West Indian fortresses, Brimstone Hill, has survived to offer a particularly notable example of the way in which striking material remains can provide major insights into militarisation and the powerfully competitive forces of mercantilism. This dramatic fortress, formerly known as Fort George, now a tourist attraction, stands as dramatic evidence of the explosive power of sugar (as well as coffee and cotton) and of eighteenth-century colonial competitive warfare. Dating from the late seventeenth century, it developed progressively into one of the most significant fortresses in the Caribbean, covering 40 acres and rising some 230 feet in height from its lower point (itself 550 feet up the hill), with a striking range of bastions, buildings and redoubts, together with a parade ground. It saw action against the French in 1690, 1782 and 1806 and supplemented another fort on the coast below, Fort Charles. It was effectively shut down in 1853 when the garrison was withdrawn to Barbados, thus indicating the confidence the British felt in the security of their Caribbean possessions.[8] The island of Grenada has fortresses protecting the capital and harbour of St George (Fort George), as well as two magnificent forts high upon the hillside (Forts Frederick and Matthew) designed to provide long-range artillery cover to protect against naval attack.[9] The Jamaica National Heritage Trust lists eighteen forts on that island and has visitor notes for several of them.[10] Even the remote island of St Helena in the

The British Empire through buildings

8 Brimstone Hill Fort, St Kitts

middle of the Atlantic was strongly fortified against attack, not least to prevent the escape of Napoleon during his exile there from 1815 to 1821.

Such military redoubts globalised at least two European styles: the medieval curtain-wall type, generally using a hill as part of its defensive arrangements, and the great star-shaped Renaissance form invented by the Italians to defend themselves against the French in the late fifteenth and early sixteenth centuries. It has been suggested that this fort development produced something of a military revolution in terms of a shift from pitched battles to sieges, necessitating the growth of armies. It is a moot point whether its appearance around the world (starting perhaps with its use by the Portuguese) produced similar military transformations, though variants on such forts, built in brick and masonry, were to be found around the modern empires. The presence of so many of them indicated that Europeans imagined that these structures would protect their trading posts and personnel from hostile surroundings, as well as constituting a valuable place of retreat at times of threat. On some frontiers, notably in North-West India, the forts were designed to protect the physical integrity of

Militarisation, mobility and the residencies of power

9 Jamrud Fort at the entrance of the Khyber Pass, Pakistan

the colony itself. On that frontier, always one of the vulnerable places in the British Empire, forts continued in use until the twentieth century, garrisoned by British imperial troops and sometimes with British expatriates sheltering within them.[11]

The two characteristic early buildings of the East India Company (EIC) were the factory (or trading establishment) and the fort. These two reflected phases in the trading relationship and power balance between England and India. The factory, as at the most notable example at Surat in the early seventeenth century, represented the point at which the English were still suppliants in the trading relationship with Indians. The Surat factory, built after the arrival of English traders in 1608, was large and impressive, offering social and cultural defences against its surrounding environment.[12] The traders and their president were able to live in some style within its confines, but essentially its function was more commercial than military. India was, however, traditionally a land of forts. The British encountered such forts almost throughout the Subcontinent, from small redoubts in villages to immense and powerful fortresses at the centre of Indian states.[13] It is symptomatic of the fact that in the early days of Europeans in India they did not represent any major technological changes that their first architectural recourse, after the so-called factory, was also the fort. Indeed in some places, the British would reuse older indigenous forts on the North-West

Frontier.[14] The artillery associated with the fort was also a technology held in common, and many Indian states had their own armouries producing such artillery, sometimes with the help of European mercenaries. The English soon established forts as their first structures in the three most important trading posts and centres of the EIC.[15] The earliest was Fort St George in Madras (Chennai), established by 1644, followed by Fort William in Calcutta (Kolkata), first built between 1696 and 1706 and with the Governor's residence within its walls. It was located directly on the river bank. After the temporary capture of Calcutta and the fort by the Nawab Siraj-ud-Daulah, the fort was massively rebuilt in a different location in a Renaissance star-shape form between 1758 and 1781.[16] The area that later become the maidan was cleared to ensure maximum defensive lines of fire and the original fort briefly became the customs house, although the river bank turned out to be unstable. Fort George in Bombay (Mumbai) came later, in an area where fortifications and military structures already existed, built by indigenous Indian powers and by the Portuguese. The British progressively fortified Bombay between the late seventeenth and mid-eighteenth centuries, with considerable walls on the landward side and with a number of forts to protect the town.[17] All of this was designed against the Marathas (who took the Portuguese settlements of Salsette and Bassein in 1739) and the French, although the EIC was invariably parsimonious about the cost. The major defences of Fort George were completed in 1769, but demolished in 1862 when the fort's military function was no longer required. Instead it gave its name to the central business district of the imperial city.[18] These Indian forts were often built in the Renaissance style, star-shaped with projecting bastions for maximum defence. They were extensive in scale and constituted complete communities, including the barracks, the church and residences of traders and administrators. The forts in Kolkata and Chennai survive and are still in use, the former as a major barracks for the Indian army. It is perhaps something of an exaggeration – at least when looking at India as a whole – to say that, at a time when some great Mughal architecture was being erected in India, the Company 'was celebrated only for the construction of jail houses and courts'.[19]

In North America, where timber was often plentiful, the wooden stockade fort with ditches was generally the norm. Such stockades were to be found everywhere, defending traders against indigenous First Nation or Native American peoples, and in the far north, the Inuit. Such forts continued to provide their military function right down to the later nineteenth century. As in the Caribbean, others were designed for protection against rival imperial powers. The fortifications at

Fort Anne in Nova Scotia, designed to protect the strategic harbour of Annapolis Royal, were begun in 1629 and were repeatedly reconstructed to provide defences against both the French and First Nation peoples.[20] Further north, the great fort and fortified town of Louisbourg in Cape Breton, Nova Scotia, reflects the importance of such structures in the eighteenth century, their role in imperial rivalry, the manner in which they became liabilities when they were considered to have become obsolete, and the way in which they were to become important in modern tourism. The French built Louisbourg between 1720 and 1740, lost it to the British in 1745 during the War of the Austrian Succession and had it returned in 1748, only for it to be taken again in 1758 during the pivotal Seven Years' War, when British power overwhelmed that of the French. The British proceeded to destroy it to prevent it from continuing to be an object of French desire. In the 1960s and 1970s it was partially reconstructed in order to become a major tourist attraction. Indeed it may be said that this characteristic building type of empire has often become more important in modern tourism than it was in military operations of the past.[21] Other examples of fortresses that changed hands and became significant in tourism include the Castle of Good Hope in Cape Town, built by the Dutch in the 1660s and seized by the British in 1795 and again in 1806. Another is the Portuguese Fort Jesus in Mombasa, built in the 1590s, taken by the Omanis of the Arabian Gulf in 1698 and later becoming part of the British colony of Kenya.

Perhaps the best example of existing forts and fortifications being taken over by the British occurs in Malta. There the Knights Hospitallers of St John of Jerusalem had built one of the most extensively fortified sites in the world, designed against their principal enemy, the Ottoman Turks. Their various forts, particularly St Elmo, Ricasoli and St Angelo, were built after the Knights' arrival in Malta in 1530, sometimes based upon earlier fortifications. The strength of these forts was vital to the Knights' success in the Great Siege of 1565 and they were subsequently rendered even more formidable, together with the many bastions and walls of the Knights' new capital at Valletta.[22] The British took Malta in 1800, after a brief two-year occupation by the French, and they soon converted the forts as barracks for troops or as buildings of the great naval base they established there. They even designated Fort St Angelo as HMS *St Angelo*.[23] As elsewhere, the buildings within the forts of Malta performed a whole range of functions: there were parade grounds, barracks, administrative centres, armouries, officers' messes, recreational facilities, even chapels. The British modernised and modified these structures for their own use, but the principal changes made were in the provision of up-to-date armaments and, in the twentieth century, anti-aircraft artillery. In the course of the nineteenth century, Malta became the principal British naval base in the Mediterranean, particularly vital for the security of the route to India after the opening of the Suez Canal in 1869, so further attempts were made to fortify the island. Coastal defences were erected and, most extraordinarily, British military and naval authorities decided to protect the vital southern part of Malta with a combined wall and forts, built in the 1870s and 1880s along a natural escarpment some twelve kilometres long. This followed previous attempts at defensive structures here, both by the Knights and their predecessors. The British version became known as the Victoria Lines or, more jokingly, as the North-West Front or even the Great Wall of Malta. By the twentieth century, within twenty years of its building, it was recognised as being worthless from a defensive point of view.[24] But what this, and many other forts illustrated, was the extraordinary manner in which defensive technologies that were many centuries old continued to be considered as valuable right down to the twentieth century. Modern empires could have an atavistic effect as well as a modernising one.

Another great siege was that of Gibraltar in 1779–83 by Spain and France during the American War of Independence. This was one of a series of sieges which illustrated the highly strategic location of Gibraltar at the Atlantic entrance to the Mediterranean. Held by the British from its capture in 1704 and its cession in the Treaty of Utrecht in 1713, it had become a fortified redoubt, ringed by batteries, bastions and barracks making good use of the physical characteristics of the Rock. Tunnels also played an important part in its defences. Most of these can still be seen on a territory which classically symbolises empire and remains a considerable source of controversy and tension in a postcolonial world.[25] Indeed, 'the Rock' has been so much regarded as essentially a strategic position that until modern times, its governors were always military men.

Further east, the manner in which the building of forts threads its way through colonial history is neatly exemplified by Forts Cornwallis in Penang and Canning in Singapore. The former was built soon after the British acquisition of what they called Prince of Wales Island in 1786, but the latter was only built after 1859 as a result of a perceived threat. The original government house of Stamford Raffles was actually demolished in order to make way for Fort Canning, an unusual and late shift from administration to militarisation. Unlike those in Malta and Gibraltar, these forts became largely irrelevant in terms of warfare, neatly demonstrating that while some fortifications found themselves in the teeth of imperial conflict, many others never fired, or received, shots in anger. Whatever the intentions of their builders, they thus often became more symbolic and psychological than practical. This is true, for example, of Forts Wellington and Henry, which were built on the St Lawrence River to protect Canada against the United States in the war of 1812, while Fort Wellington was actually refortified against the internal radical revolt of 1837. In some places, as in the Hudson's Bay posts of Fort Victoria and Fort Vancouver (just two of literally dozens of such trading centres called forts), the next phase of colonial settlement was symbolised by the dropping of 'Fort' from the name and the disappearance of the physical forts into the fabric of the cities. In some cases, the name survived, as in the town of Fort St John in the far north of British Columbia.

MOBILITY AND TENTS

If forts are intended to be illustrative of military strength and potential dominance, it is paradoxical that many other early structures of empires were frail and sometimes temporary, symbolising the need for mobility in the establishment of imperial rule. Tents, for example, are by their nature impermanent, but they are in a real sense structures, composed of canvas (or other fabrics) and generally wooden poles. They are surprisingly important in the establishment of imperial rule and even in the splendour of its maintenance. They were thus emblematic of empire, and symbolised the apparent ubiquity of new rulers, as well as their command of manpower and the key military manoeuvres of imperial authority. Early travellers and so-called pioneers were nomads and, although they might erect temporary structures out of the natural materials to hand, often in the style of indigenous peoples (and indeed erected with their help), they also invariably brought tents. These could be light, relatively small examples for ease of erection after a day's travelling. Some more settled tented encampments appeared, such as early mining communities (as in the goldfields of the colony of Victoria in Australia), until it became apparent that the mineral or other resource justified more permanent buildings. They could also be used for religious purposes. When Bishop Selwyn arrived in the newly annexed New Zealand in 1842, he commenced his ministry by conducting services in a large tent, 60 feet by 30 feet.[26] It was said to be a reminder of the biblical tabernacle; in a new colony lacking ecclesiastical buildings, it had the great of advantage of being mobile and could be set up with much of the furniture of a cathedral. It could accommodate over 200 people.[27] Although tents were used throughout empires, India was the supreme land of tents. The Mughal emperors and other Indian rulers were always strikingly itinerant and used their command over considerable labour forces to travel with large, luxurious and highly decorated tents, often in very expensive materials (such as silk), and even bejewelled. The British followed them in the form of the progresses of viceroys, governors, commissioners and commanders-in-chief. General G.C. Mundy provided an excellent description of a tented progress when the Commander-in-Chief in India (General Lord Combermere, C-in-C 1825–30, celebrated for his storming of the princely state of Bharatpur) went on a tour of the Upper Provinces in late 1827. He offered the reader what he described as a 'glimpse of the headquarters' camp', 'invariably pitched in the same order'.[28] He went on to describe the main street as 50 feet wide flanked by twenty to thirty large double-poled tents for the Commander-in-Chief, general and personal staff and visiting VIPs ('as symmetrically ranged as the houses of Portland Place'). There were two large marquees at the centre with canopied porticoes (*shemmianas*), 'the private and public, or durbar, tents of his Excellency'. The Quartermaster-General was responsible for preparing the site, and sentries were posted. Ancillary staff were accommodated in rows of tents behind, and beyond were piqueted lines of officers' horses. Beyond was the camp bazaar. A double line of piqueted horses marked the camp of the cavalry escort, matched by a cantonment of the infantry guard at the opposite side of the camp. At the extreme edge were camels and elephants. The total camp population was estimated as 5,000. Mundy continued that western countries would have regarded as luxuries what the Indian camp considered to be necessities. Referring to the Peninsula campaign in the Napoleonic wars, he asserted that 'To those of our party who had experienced the hardships of a Peninsula bivouac, the contrast must have appeared almost antipodean.' As a humble unmarried captain 'travelling on the most economical principles', 'I had a double-poled tent, a small tent, a servants' tent, 2 elephants, 6 camels, 4 horses, pony, buggy, 24 servants, plus mahouts, camel-drivers, and apparently specialist tent-pitchers.'

Emily Eden travelled in even grander circumstances. In her celebrated diaries, she described the huge caravan of people, 12,000 strong, which accompanied her brother, Governor-General Lord Auckland, on his travels in 1837.[29] There were inevitably large numbers of tents and everything took place in them: banquets, dances, ceremonies, church services, even a wedding. Such encampments were so much like a tented town that she referred to the High Street in front of their tent. On another she reported that thieves had been in the tents. She suggested that when the tents got wet, the viceregal party had to remain for a week in one place to dry them out since they became too heavy for the elephants to carry. Thus they could be an impediment as well as a convenience. On one occasion they were invaded by jewellers trying to sell their wares.[30] It is apparent that large numbers of followers were required to erect, maintain and police these tents. The British even took over the Mughal *shamiana* tent, a large open-sided version, ideal for the climate, which was used for ceremonies, weddings and other events involving considerable numbers of people. These often became extensions to buildings or to other tents to provide external and internal spaces. For example, the Viceroy Lytton and his family had a large *shamiana* tent at Peterhof in Simla to house receptions and durbars with Indian princes.[31] This was transported on viceregal progresses in order to accommodate durbars wherever they went.[32]

Given these displays of travelling residences, encounters between British and Indian rulers echoed, or indeed outranked, the 1520 Field of the Cloth of Gold, the celebrated encounter between Henry VIII of England and Francis I of France, which took place in many tents and temporary structures. Because of the ready availability of pack animals and the capacity to marshal large quantities of labour, British officers travelled with immense tents, sometimes with several 'rooms' or at least with inner and outer sections, the latter for the various attendants. In October 1841 Lord William Bentinck, Governor-General of India, met the ruler of the Sikhs, Ranjit Singh, on what one writer has described as the 'Field of the Cloth of Cashmere', a durbar characterised by vast numbers of retainers and troops, with elephants, camels and horses, and hugely opulent tents.[33] Tents were illuminated and there were fireworks. Sometimes vulnerable tents burned down, even at key moments. This happened in 1911 when the great reception tent in the Delhi Fort burnt down during the rehearsal for the state entry when the Viceroy was standing in for the King. A new reception tent had to be obtained.[34] Lord Dalhousie, a later governor-general, described the dimensions of his tent as being 100 feet long, 40 wide and 30 high.[35] Great travelling imperial caravanserai were both practical and symbolic, exercising authority and diplomacy as well as displaying it in dramatically visible forms. Thus even tents could illustrate the notion that empires are never self-effacing, always seeking to display power and authority. They were a very striking instrument of imperial rule. Although the advent of the railways ensured that the rulers of British India (as well as the Indian princes) travelled by train, still these great caravans continued on hunting expeditions and in more remote regions. For example, the Viceroy Lord Lytton travelled across North India with his family and retainers in a great tented progress in 1876, complete with a durbar tent for encounters with Indian rulers.[36] All such meetings between rulers were known as durbars (the word generally used for Indian rulers' courts, together with the administrative activities and meetings that took place within them), but for the British the greatest such events were the Imperial Assemblage organised by Lytton in 1877 and the coronation durbars of 1903 and 1911. All of these took place on the Ridge at Delhi, a place of symbolic significance after the events of the 1857 Revolt. These durbars featured vast tented encampments. It was said that in 1903, 250,000 people were accommodated in around 80,000 and 100,000 tents (so many that an accurate count was apparently impossible).[37] These were arranged in a strict hierarchy from the Viceroy, members of European royal families, down to hotel tents organised for 400 visitors. It was said that Curzon's camp had 1,400 tents and his personal quarters had a drawing-room tent in white and gold,[38] while the Duke of Connaught had to make do with a mere eight tents. Lord Kitchener, Commander-in-Chief, had six large ones with connecting corridors.[39] It was reported that 'Lord Northcote [Governor of Bombay] has glass doors to his tents and English fireplaces, for Delhi in winter has cold nights, and he has the only billiard table in the "city of tents".'[40] In 1911, over 450 camps were listed in the official directory of the Coronation Durbar.[41]

10 Part of the huge tented encampment, Coronation Durbar, Delhi, 1911

Militarisation, mobility and the residencies of power

Lower down the scale, British rulers and the military used tents as part of their everyday work. Captain Albert Hervey, who wrote a memoir of his service in India in the 1830s and 1840s, described how essential it was to possess a tent. These could be secured from the government stores, but the quality was poor and it was cheaper to buy one at an auction of the possessions of an officer who had died or left for home.[42] He obtained his tent in this way at a quarter of its original value. Relatively junior as he was, when he moved with his regiment, he had six bullocks and no fewer than twenty-five Indians serving with him.[43] As late as the 1940s, Ian Scott, an assistant collector in Sind, later Pakistan, went on tour with a large tent to act as his courthouse and office and a smaller one for his living quarters. He also had many Indian followers, which indicates the extraordinary continuity of the labour-intensive business of empire management.[44] While district commissioners and officers in Africa had permanent quarters at their *boma* or office, they went on safari with tents, as did other officials of various kinds.[45] In Bombay, it was said that in the nineteenth century some Europeans slept in tents during the hot weather because they found them cooler than permanent structures.[46] When Elizabeth Grant went to India in the 1820s with her father, appointed a judge in Bombay, she described the manner in which visitors slept in tents when visiting holiday bungalows.[47] Tents were also, of course, associated with leisure and sport. When in the twentieth century large numbers of officials and other residents withdrew to Mahabaleshwar and Poona (Pune) in the hot weather, most had to live in tents, since renting bungalows was extremely difficult. Tent living indeed became part of the experience.[48] It is quite clear that the call for tents in the empire was so great that tent manufacture must have been a major industry, though regrettably it is a little studied phenomenon. No doubt the famous Army and Navy Stores (founded as a co-operative by army and navy officers in 1871, with branches in India) would have been major suppliers of tents to the British, and it is certainly the case that tent manufacture remains a significant sector of the Indian economy.[49]

In addition to being the visible evidence of a grand travelling ruler, whether indigenous or British, as well as more humble officials, tents were also the marker of the British military, both on the move and in settled positions. Very often the great barracks in the military cantonments were preceded by vast tented camps. One army officer referred to the 'canvas streets and squares' of an army encampment.[50] Cantonments often started out as vast tented cities, as in the case of Secunderabad near the Nizam's capital at Hyderabad.[51] When the British set about besieging Delhi in 1857, they established a tented encampment on the ridge to the north of the city.[52] Soon, however, military encampments and temporary cities were replaced by bricks and mortar or stone buildings. Such barracks were invariably of very considerable extent, and although separate from urban areas, were often close to the 'civil lines', the residences of colonial civilians, in order to provide security. In the case of the Indian Empire, such barracks (or cantonments) appeared throughout the Subcontinent, particularly in the aftermath of the 1857 Revolt, each of them developing the particular tone of the regiment which occupied them. Notable examples are the vast Meerut Cantonment in Uttar Pradesh in North India, the Wellington Cantonment near Coonoor in Tamil Nadu, Poona (Pune) in Maharashtra, and others in the Punjab. Such cantonments, often in repetitive and overbearing styles, appeared in many Asian colonies and elsewhere, including, for example, South Africa. Characteristically, they had extensive parade grounds, large barrack blocks, bungalows for the officers, some married quarters, an armoury, a mess building and occasionally a chapel if distant from the local Christian church. As we saw in Chapter 1, the British also had the temerity to build barracks within the great Red Fort in Delhi in the aftermath of the 1857 Revolt. Given that empires could only survive by military force, barracks were among the most important buildings of the British Empire, and very extensive examples appeared in South Africa and elsewhere. In South Africa, great tented encampments, as well as barracks in temporary huts, were inevitably a characteristic of the Zulu and frontier wars, as well as the first and second Anglo-Boer wars. This was also true of the so-called pacification period. There was, for example, a considerable military encampment with tents and huts at Middelburg in the Cape Colony.[53]

There are two key examples of fortified military positions in Canada whose significance survived into the twentieth century. The Citadel in Halifax, Nova Scotia, begun in 1749 and later developed into one of the great redoubts of the British Empire, was both a fortress and a great barracks. It was particularly important since Halifax was a major imperial naval base. Today, it is typically one of the heritage tourist sites of the city, with enactments of the regiments that have been billeted there.[54] The other striking citadel is that of Quebec City. The French had created some fortifications on Cap Diamant, adjacent to the Heights of Abraham, between the 1690s and the mid-eighteenth century, but never built a complete fortress. Once the British had taken Quebec in 1759, there were further proposals for a fortress, mainly designed to protect Quebec from the Americans, particularly after revolutionary forces had seized Montreal in 1775 and laid siege to Quebec. Ironically, the citadel was only built after the American threat had receded, but it functioned as a barracks (as it remains) and also as protection for the residence of the Governor-General of Upper and Lower Canada and the maritime provinces before Confederation.[55] Like so many forts and fortifications, it was never actually required in conflict. The Citadel, fortifications, gateways and terraces of Quebec City were in dire need of renovation by the 1870s, when the Governor-General, Lord Dufferin, resolved to transform the city into 'a Canadian Carcassonne'.[56] His interest would have been stimulated by the fact that the original governor's residence, still used to this day, lies within the Citadel.

RESIDENCIES AND GOVERNMENT HOUSES

The Quebec Citadel is still in Crown ownership and of course the military ultimately represented the theoretical might of the imperial monarchy. This symbolic connection to the king or queen, however distantly located, had a considerable effect upon the architecture of empire. The dispersal of such surrogate, sometimes ersatz, quasi-royal palaces across the world carries us forward through the rest of the imperial period and into modern times. The creation of such palaces and the diversity of their architecture reveals that the British never sought a standard imperial style, even if neoclassical appears to predominate in some places. Nevertheless, for governors and administrators, their residences represented the authority and dignity of the Crown, a centre of administration, ceremonial and therefore, for them, civilisation. They were also intended to convey to settlers, sojourners and indigenous peoples the ultimate control of the iron fist represented in the military buildings examined above. A survey of such buildings has never been attempted before and occupies the rest of this chapter.

In India, the EIC, despite being a commercial concern, came to represent royal power in respect of indigenous princes, including the Mughal Emperor and other rulers. Residents were sent to keep watch over the rulers of these nominally independent princely states, and they provided themselves with grand accommodation to symbolise their authority as advisers and powers behind the throne, eventually assuming virtually executive authority. These residencies could become grander than some of the later government houses. Warren Hastings sent the first resident to the court of the major state of Awadh in 1773. The residency was originally a collection of bungalows, but a more significant three-storey building, conveniently sited and paid for by the Nawab, was constructed by 1786. It was the developed version of this building, together with its lands and outlying structures (including a banqueting hall), which was besieged during the 1857 Revolt, thereby becoming such a resonant structure for the British that they preserved it in its ruined state (and has been so maintained to this day by independent India).[57] The most notable of such quasi-government houses was the classical palace of the resident of the great state of Hyderabad in South India, built in the last years of the eighteenth century by the resident, James Achilles Kirkpatrick, but entirely at the expense of the Nizam of Hyderabad.[58] Almost all such buildings were classical in style, although some did make concessions to the climate by incorporating extensive shaded verandahs around them. Occasionally they also included elements from indigenous architecture. For the British in the eighteenth and early nineteenth centuries, the classical represented civilisational expansion in the manner of Rome. Greek architecture sometimes represented the alleged Greek concepts of democratic freedoms, which the authoritarian British Empire was allegedly spreading to other parts of the world.

Although these residences were located in a middle ground between indigenous and invasive royal authority, empire came to be inseparably associated with royal magnificence and display, a mystique that operated at different levels designed to impress the populations in the mother country, overseas colonial settlers and 'sojourners' or expatriates, as well as supposedly arousing the respect of indigenous elites and, to a certain extent, the populations who offered allegiance to such rulers. Empire set about establishing hierarchies that flowed downwards from the imperial monarchy through the colonial ruling class, a hierarchical pyramid that was constantly re-emphasised in ceremonies, the celebration of specific dates associated with monarchy (like birthdays, later Empire Day, deaths and coronations), in statuary and in buildings (see Chapter 7). Throughout the empire, governors, governors-general and viceroys, as the local representatives of the imperial monarchy, found their status raised from ordinary citizen (although many were drawn from the aristocracies of England, Scotland and Ireland) to that of monarchical representative, the recipient of all the deference due to the monarch – even taking precedence over visiting members of the royal family. Such figures had to occupy appropriately grand buildings, generally known as government houses, and it is not surprising that such residences in many places (though not universally) were consequently raised to the architectural status of palaces or palace-substitutes. Like the monarch, many governors had multiple residences so that they could go on quasi-royal progresses exhibiting

Militarisation, mobility and the residencies of power

their authority by royal association in different parts of their colonial 'kingdoms'. In India, Australia and a few other places, climatic medical theory ensured that viceroys and governors should be able to retreat to cooler hill stations at the hottest time of the year, thus requiring a further 'hot weather' residence. It is true that some early government houses were ramshackle affairs, offices within forts, even tents and huts in the early days of settlement colonies. But through the ever-present flagpole and the flag they generally exuded the temporary authority vested in the person of the governor. This was true of the early settlements in Australia, for example in Botany Bay in the 1780s and 1790s, later in Western Australia in the 1820s or later again in Fort Salisbury in Central Africa in the 1890s. But whatever the period of the initial conquest, new government houses were soon built to represent the dignity of the monarch's representative. Often the size and grandeur of government houses was expanded in order to reflect the growth and economic significance of the colonies in which they were situated.

But government houses were much more than simply the residences of governors. They were also central to the administration of the colony. The ruling governor met his officials and the executive council often convened there. They received visiting dignitaries or members of the royal family. In Asia particularly, indigenous rulers were received in audience and, hopefully, impressed. There

11 Government House, Lagos

were grand dinners, receptions, balls, investitures of honours and medals, all designed to place the governor and his consort at the apex of the colonial ruling hierarchy. That hierarchy included the pyramid of Viceroy, presidency governors, lieutenant governors, commissioners, and so on. In federal dominions, Canada after 1867, Australia after 1901 and South Africa after 1910, governor-generals' authority flowed down through the lieutenant governors of provinces or states. Government houses thus constituted the prime meeting place between the governor and the surrounding society, at least its elite. They were often a visible presence at the centre of colonial and provincial capitals, the central imperial building around which others revolved. A few were more secluded, but their presence was signalled by impressive railings, gates, lodges, protecting guards and hints of the extensive gardens and grounds beyond. Moreover, there was always a tension between opulence and comfort. The functions of government houses, as well as the size of their rooms, the lengths of their corridors or the wildlife of their extensive gardens, ensured that they were sometimes very uncomfortable living spaces for their inhabitants.[59] Governors and their wives invariably requested extra funds to add more convenient rooms or extra space for leisure, as for billiards. For the surrounding population, expatriate, settler and indigenous, they were an inaccessible and brooding presence, symbols of alien rule.

Thus, government houses, as expressions of the dispersal of royal power, emerged as among the most impressive buildings in each colony. Like royal palaces, they were additionally emblematic of class and racial exclusion, while for the colonial elite they represented the hoped-for privilege of inclusion. They also progressively symbolised a constitutional dynamic. Initially, most government houses were the centres of executive authority, but as colonies came to develop forms of responsible and representative government, that is, nascent parliamentary systems, their constitutional significance was altered. In the so-called 'Dominions' they became the markers of a transposed British system in which the constitutional head (or representative) was supposedly separate from the source of political power, vested in a premier or prime minister and ministers responsible to parliaments. There was an attempt later to create this constitutional separation in many of the dependent territories of empire, but its survival after the wave of post-Second World War colonial decolonisation was mixed. India and some Caribbean islands maintained the system, though the resident of government houses often became a figurehead president instead of the representative of the monarch. In many other territories, however, the president took on executive powers, often after a brief period of the preservation of the separation of constitutional and executive authority.

In India in the early nineteenth century, there was no question where power lay, at least in terms of the still expanding territories under British Company authority. Famously, the grandest of all government houses was the one built, at enormous cost, in Calcutta between 1799 and 1803. Before then, the EIC's Governor-General of India had resided in a rented house owned by an Indian. Famously, the Marquess Wellesley (1798–1805) felt that his dignity and power required somewhere much more palatial. India, it was said, should be governed from a palace, not a counting house. This vast building therefore represented a perceived shift from the primary commercial function of the Company towards a display of the considerable political power it had come to exert. But it also reflected a number of characteristics of British imperial architecture. In the absence of professional architects, a military engineer was called on to design the building, though we should never forget that Indian draughtsmen and surveyors were equally important. The building is invariably attributed to Captain Charles Wyatt of the Bengal Engineers,[60] indicative of the manner in which many early colonial structures were designed by the military. This reliance on military engineers was a typical historical phenomenon. Some of the great architects of the past had started life as engineers (such as Sinan in the Ottoman Empire),[61] and in many ways architecture is in some respects the artistic gloss upon what are essentially exercises in engineering. Nevertheless, given limited training and experience, Wyatt turned to an existing palace as his model, in this case Kedleston Hall in Derbyshire. As a result the building was constructed in a European classical style which made no concessions to its Indian context. It was also supplied with extensive grounds and gardens to shield the imperial ruler from the surrounding environment, grounds that were created through the demolition of what William Hickey described as about sixteen 'extensive private mansions', some of them only recently constructed.[62] While these were designed to be like parkland, such grounds and the wildlife within them inevitably took on an Indian form. But the surroundings were certainly designed as a buffer against the indigenous ethnic environment. They were entered through intimidatingly grand gated archways.[63] And finally, the palace was designed for ceremonial, to be conducted in its grand flight of stairs leading to the main entrance, in its throne room and other reception halls, and in its many suites designed to accommodate visiting dignitaries of various sorts. But if this vast building constituted Wellesley's 'Versailles project', a great structure to symbolise state and empire, unlike Louis XIV he did not possess unlimited funds or powers. He was recalled for his gross extravagance. In 1848, Dalhousie found the 'house superb, the furniture disgraceful'.[64] The palace continued in use by governors-general and viceroys until the capital was moved to New Delhi after 1911. It was then taken over by the Governor of Bengal (who left another grand classical building further from the centre of Calcutta), and is now known as the Raj Bhavan, residence and administrative centre of the Governor of West Bengal. The Bengal Government House later became the national library until it moved into a modern building.[65] The governors-general and viceroys additionally had a country retreat called Barrackpore further up the Ganges (also built by Wellesley), to which they invariably transferred themselves by boat, usually at weekends. Dalhousie found Barrackpore to be 'charming', with rooms that were 'large but liveable' surrounded by 'home-like parkland', offering 'relief and refreshment', some recompense for a residence in Bengal.[66]

Government houses appeared in the other presidency cities of Madras and Bombay and later spread all over India to house the governors and commissioners

12 Ballroom of the Government House of Bengal, Calcutta

of the various provinces. Many of these were essentially classical in style, though with the addition of wide verandahs, awnings, screens ('tatties') and fretted shutters (jalousies) to cope with the climate. Government House in Madras famously had a prefabricated cast-iron durbar hall, which was manufactured by the Saracen Iron Works of MacFarlane and Company in Glasgow.[67] In Bombay, the government house was originally in the fort. In 1719 the governor took over a former Portuguese Franciscan friary in Parell as the government house retreat and it was duly converted and extended, in a neoclassical style with extensive verandahs, becoming the principal government house in 1771.[68] Its distance from the centre of town had its advantages: during the hot weather, visitors arrived so exhausted and tired from the drive that little conversation was possible![69] There were various residences on the closer and cooler Malabar Point to the west of Bombay and Government House was transferred there in 1880. Government houses continued to be built as the British adopted the habit of retreating to hill stations during the hot weather. After a succession of more or less makeshift arrangements, Viceregal Lodge, Simla (Shimla) was built as late as 1888 by the architect Henry Irwin in what has been described as a Jacobethan style,[70] and was often despised as incorporating Scottish baronial forms, presumably symbolising its association with coolness and retreat to the hills. Edwin Montague, Secretary of State for India (1917–22), said that it reminded him of a 'Scotch hydro', the large hotels designed as healthy sanatoria, which appeared in Scotland about the same time.[71] Other critics were even more abusive.[72] Residences of some note were also required for the Commander-in-Chief and for the Lieutenant Governor of the Punjab, who also used Simla as a summer retreat. Other hill stations similarly spawned government houses, cool-weather homes supposedly set at the centre of retreats for high-ranking officials and the military. The hill station, Naini Tal, founded in 1841 and now in Uttarakhand, became the summer residence of the Governor of the United Provinces. A grand government house (now the Raj Bhavan) was designed in a powerful Gothic style by the Bombay architect F.W. Stevens, the construction supervised by Sydney Crookshank.[73] At Ootacamund, the Governor of Madras, the Duke of Buckingham and Chandos, abandoned a smaller cottage-style summer retreat and moved into a grander government house.[74]

Government houses duly appeared as central symbols of authority throughout the Asian colonies. The original government house of Penang was Sir Francis Light's own private residence, bought by the EIC after his death. Until 1832, Penang was the capital of the Straits Settlements, but in that year it was transferred

The British Empire through buildings

13 Government House, Madras

to what had become the more significant port of Singapore. There, Stamford Raffles had built his government house on the hill where Fort Canning was subsequently constructed. In the 1860s a new Government House of near-palatial proportions was built for Governor Sir Harry Ord and designed by a military architect. Built on a considerable estate, the extravagance of this building, as with Wellesley's project, was criticised at the time, but as Singapore (a Crown Colony from 1867) boomed as the crossroads of the East it came not only to be accepted, but to receive plaudits as a fine example of the symbolic grandeur of rule. Hong Kong eventually had three government houses, the first built in colonial Renaissance style in the 1850s (completed in 1855) in the central district of the principal town of Victoria Island. In 1900, Mountain Lodge was opened on the Peak to provide respite from the heat, while another came into use in 1934 in the New Territories. The principal government house was remodelled by the Japanese during their occupation in the Second World War, while mountain lodge was destroyed at the end of that war. Rangoon (Yangon) acquired a dramatically grand government house in 1895, built by the architect Henry Hoyne-Fox, then active in Burma, in what he described as a Queen Anne Renaissance style. Many viewed it as overly elaborate, and during the Second World War the British supreme allied commander in South-East Asia, Lord Mountbatten, considered it hideous, even suggesting that he was disappointed that the Royal Air Force had failed to bomb it. Later, it suffered serious earthquake damage in the 1970s and was demolished in 1985 on the orders of General Ne Win, the military dictator of Burma.[75]

Some government houses, however, could be relatively modest, as on Caribbean islands such as Barbados or Tortola in the British Virgin Islands.[76] In the latter the original government house is now a museum with a newer, but also relatively modest, version built next door. But even on a remote island like St Helena, the government house could maintain the dignity of the EIC and of the royal representative.[77] It was built in an elegant Georgian style by the Company in 1791–92 as a summer residence at a time when the government was conducted principally from the castle in Jamestown.[78] Known as Plantation House, it was greatly coveted by Napoleon Bonaparte during his exile on the island, since he regarded Longwood, the house built for him there, as scarcely appropriate to his dignity. The island became a Crown Colony in 1834 and Plantation House eventually became the year-round residence of the Governor.

14 Plantation House, St Helena

As in Asia, these symbols of power passed through a number of architectural phases in the course of the nineteenth century. The interesting group of gubernatorial residences of Australia neatly reflect this progression. In the colony of South Australia, the governor first took up residence in a mud hut in 1837, but very quickly the next governor, George Gawler, sought a grander residence. A new government house was commissioned and largely designed by George Strickland Kingston, a surveyor with some architectural experience. It was completed in 1840, built in a fairly simple neoclassical style and situated on North Terrace, where almost all the notable buildings of the city were constructed. It is still in use, but Gawlor suffered the fate of several governors, recalled for extravagance, only partly associated with the building of this government house. Summer residences were also built in the Adelaide Hills, one completed in 1860 and a grander one in 1880, later burnt down (in 1955) as a result of a bush fire. Several other government houses were created adjacent to botanic gardens, thus offering at the same time a wider landscaped setting while associating them with science and some degree of public access, if only across the fence. This was true of the government houses of Sydney, Melbourne, Hobart and the first one in Brisbane. In Sydney, after Captain Phillip's temporary structure, the first government house was built by a convict builder, James Bloodsworth. It was a relatively modest building which was extended and has been described as an Italianate cottage. There were efforts to replace it by the celebrated Governor Lachlan Macquarie, who was notably ambitious in giving Sydney architectural expression, but the scheme was not approved. Castle-like stables were built and are now part of the Sydney Conservatorium of Music. Later Edward Blore, architect to William IV, supplied plans for a new building to match the growing significance of the colony, and this building was completed by 1845. Unusually for the period, it adopted a Gothic revival style with crenellated roofline and machicolations on top of the surrounding arcading. Similarly crenellated corner turrets continued the sense of a cross between castle and palace.[79]

Melbourne was the capital of the other major early colony, Victoria. Once separated from New South Wales in 1851, the notable governor Charles La Trobe ambitiously sought to create buildings worthy of what was seen as a prosperous future. He, however, lived in La Trobe cottage, which still survives. This was a modest prefabricated building constructed when he was Superintendent of the Port Phillip district. Governors lived in two other buildings between 1854 and 1876, by which time the discovery of gold was producing the necessary funding for a much grander house, built on land of the King's domain and the botanic

Militarisation, mobility and the residencies of power

garden, landscaped by the celebrated botanist Ferdinand von Mueller. This was an elaborate Italianate building, with three wings and a roofline somewhat reminiscent of Victoria and Albert's Osborne on the Isle of Wight. Interior detail of the entrance hall and the major reception rooms followed an elaborate neoclassical style. After the creation of the Commonwealth of Australia in 1901, bringing together the various colonies into states of the new unified country, there was considerable competition between Sydney and Melbourne to supply the capital, thus transforming their government houses potentially into residences of the Governor-General. Both served as such until the building of Canberra as the new capital. The island colony of Tasmania had three modest government houses before the present magnificent one was constructed. After a tent in Sullivan's Cove (the initial landing place of the new colonists on the site of Hobart), the governor inhabited a wooden hut in Barrack Square, Hobart. A more substantial but rather ramshackle replacement survived within the town between 1817 and 1858, when at last the colony acquired a government house matching its pretensions, one of the finest in Australia. This was designed by the Colonial Architect William Porden Kay in a Gothic revival style between 1855 and 1858. It was sited within 37 acres of grounds adjacent to the botanic gardens

15 Government House, Melbourne

and overlooking the Derwent estuary and harbour. Provided with sumptuous interiors, it boasts as many as 73 rooms.

Further west, the first government house in Perth, Western Australia is said to have been a tent, but was replaced by a relatively modest Georgian building. By the time a much grander version was contemplated, in 1859, styles had moved on, though still firmly historicised. Today's surviving government house was completed in 1863 and designed by the Comptroller of Convicts, E.J.W. Henderson, with the help of the government surveyors. This beautifully reflects the ad hoc, non-professional nature of early imperial design and building. It is Jacobean in style, though surrounded by a Gothic arcading and with some interior Gothic elements. Its combination of stone and banded brick, together with striking turrets topped by ogival-shaped roofs, marks it out as dramatically different from its neoclassical counterparts across the empire. The first government house in Brisbane, Queensland was a relatively modest neoclassical building constructed in the early 1860s to a design by the colonial architect. After more than fifty years, it was decreed to be too small and a larger house was bought in the suburb of Paddington. This had been a private residence since the 1860s, progressively enlarged until it had become a grand Italianate mansion. The creation of a new capital for the Commonwealth of Australia at Canberra necessitated the building of a government house for the Governor-General. This resulted in the purchase of a property called Yarralumia, which originally had a modest house upon it. Because of the problems of war and economic recession, this was not enlarged to the full dignity of a government house until the eve of the Second World War. Despite its twentieth-century origins, it avoided all hint of modernism and emerged as a plain Georgian revival or 'stripped classical' (without any elaboration) building. It is interesting that each of these Australian government houses (and there are others for administrators in Darwin and on Norfolk Island) has a website that seeks to make it clear that they are supposedly for the use of all citizens, either for visits or in some cases for rooms that can be hired for functions. Thus there is an attempt to escape from the former exclusivity and elitism of such residences, although they must remain very distant prospects for the great majority of the Aboriginal population of the country.

The government houses of Australia reveal a number of intriguing characteristics of the history and development of this key colonial institution. Elsewhere, government houses could have a chequered existence, repeatedly rebuilt, suffering fire destruction, and reflecting the changing status of the colonies. In New Zealand, the Auckland government house, built in 1856 (Auckland was the capital until

1865), is a typically classical mansion that became the staff common room of the University of Auckland.[80] Government House, Wellington, went through various vicissitudes until a half-timbered Tudor mansion with Arts and Crafts elements was built between 1908 and 1910. Many of the government houses of Canada are Georgian in style, sometimes with a distinct colonial twist, as in Charlottetown, Prince Edward Island (1832–34). The government house of Upper and Lower Canada was located in the Quebec Citadel and is still visited by the Governor-General each year. It stands in an extended Georgian terrace, high above the St Lawrence, which includes the officers' mess of the barracks and the commanding officer's residence, the plain exteriors belying the opulent spaces lying beyond. Government House in Halifax, Nova Scotia, replaced a rotting timber structure in the early years of the nineteenth century, and is located on one of the main streets of the city. The equivalent in Fredericton, New Brunswick, was rebuilt in 1826–28 after its predecessor burned down. Rideau Hall in Ottawa, government house after the Confederation of 1867, combines an extraordinarily severe, barrack-like exterior with more or less sumptuous interiors. Nevertheless, when Dufferin arrived as Governor-General in 1872, he found it 'hideous', tired, cold and dark from the proximity of too many trees.[81] Its counterpart in Winnipeg, Manitoba stands adjacent to the provincial parliament building. It was built in the 1880s and has been described as 'unpretending and nondescript', although it does have a striking mansard central element to relieve its plainness. The government house in Edmonton, Alberta, a Jacobean Revival mansion, is unusual in having been used only from 1913 to 1938, then converted to a variety of purposes, and is now a government conference centre. The Lieutenant Governor lives in a bungalow with office and reception accommodation elsewhere, but a new government house to match the pretensions of the province is being planned. In Victoria, British Columbia, the governor's residence was known as Cary Castle, and had a round tower to match the name. This 1859 structure was burned down in 1899. It replacement, built between 1903 and 1907, suffered the same fate in 1959. The next one was built in a loosely Tudor style with three deep gables in the façade. It is among the most quirky of all government houses. As we shall see in Chapter 7, the building of government houses continued well into the twentieth century in the plans, for example, of the new capitals of New Delhi and of Lusaka, Northern Rhodesia (Zambia).

This chapter has been concerned with the architecture of power and authority. Forts, tents and government houses may seem like disparate and even contrasting expressions of such power, yet their ubiquity across imperial territories reveals some striking truths. Many forts have been more important as statements of an imperial and colonial presence than as working military redoubts. In some 'hot spots' (as on the North-West Frontier of India), forts have been highly significant as emblematic of that presence and also of its weakness. Other forts regularly symbolised trade, including the slave trade, and were often administrative centres. Temporary imperial structures such as tents and sheds have never been given the attention they deserve, and this chapter has set out to redress this balance, indicating just how important temporary structures were in the exercise and extension of imperial authority. They were also vital in displays of the pageantry and ceremony associated with empire, as well as in command over the environment. Empires needed both temporary structures and strikingly permanent ones, as in the provision of government houses, great brooding presences that demonstrated the global dispersal of royal authority. This survey has demonstrated the striking diversity in size and style that such buildings represented. But, as we shall see in the following chapters, there were many other ways of expressing imperial power in buildings.

NOTES

1 As in the case of James and Charles Forts near Kinsale in the south of Ireland. In the 1920s these forts were abandoned as symbolic of British rule and sometimes raided for building materials. Later their heritage and tourist potential were recognised and they were restored.
2 In times of danger, the European invaders usually went into the distinctive southern African form of the *laager*, the ring of wagons creating a defensive redoubt.
3 A.W. Lawrence, *Fortified Trade-Posts: The English in West Africa 1645–1822* (London, 1963), p. 13.
4 P.E.H. Hair and Robin Law, 'The English in Western Africa to 1700' in Nicholas Canny, *The Origins of Empire: The Oxford History of the British Empire*, Vol. I (Oxford, 1998), p. 260.
5 The architectural details are analysed in Louis B. Nelson, *Architecture and Empire in Jamaica* (New Haven, CT, 2016), pp. 20–23.
6 John M. MacKenzie, 'The British Empire: Ramshackle or Rampaging', *Journal of Imperial and Commonwealth History*, 43, 1 (March 2015), p. 110.
7 It is an irony that if Nelson had not won the Battle of Trafalgar, he might well have been vilified in the British West Indies rather than treated as a hero.
8 Victor T.C. Smith, *Fire and Brimstone: The Story of the Brimstone Hill Fortress, St. Kitts, West Indies, 1690–1853* (St Kitts, 1992). St Kitts, like so many other places, has other examples of ruinous or destroyed forts such as one known as St Thomas.

9 There are of course many other forts in both the Caribbean and Atlantic worlds. Forts were built, for example, in Bermuda and the Bahamas, sometimes in the early days of British rule, and then again in a fresh burst of activity in the second half of the nineteenth century. It is ironic that some forts in this hemisphere were damaged more by severe weather or by lightning strike than by combat. The Grenadan forts were damaged, and people killed, in the American bombing and invasion of 1983.

10 www.jnht.com/showcase_forts.php also has visitor notes even for those that have been wholly or partially destroyed www.jnht.com/site_port_royal_forts.php (accessed 5 June 2018).

11 Sir Ian Scott, *A British Tale of Indian and Foreign Service: Memoirs*, edited by Denis Judd (London, 1999), chapters four and five.

12 A useful account of the Surat factory and life within it can be found in Dennis Kincaid, *British Social Life in India 1608–1937* (London, 1938), chapters 1 and 2. See also Philip Davies, *Splendours of the Raj: British Architecture in India 1660–1947* (London, 1985), pp. 17–18.

13 The magnificent fortresses of the Rajput states of Rajasthan are excellent examples.

14 Winston S. Churchill, *The Story of the Malakand Field Force: An Episode of Frontier War* (London, 1989, first published 1898), pp. 63–64 and passim.

15 Sten Nilsson, *European Architecture in India 1750–1850* (London, 1968) contains a good deal of information – and plans – on both British and French forts in India. This pioneering and important book remains a standard source, though its period ensures that it is mainly concerned with neoclassical forms.

16 For the forts in Madras and Calcutta, see Davies, *Splendours*, chapters 2 and 3. For the second Fort William, see also Krishna Dutta, *Calcutta: A Cultural and Literary History* (Oxford, 2003), pp. 71–73.

17 Samita Gupta, *Architecture and the Raj: Western Deccan 1700–1900* (Delhi, 1985), pp. 68–75. The three gates through the walls, Apollo, Church and Bazaar, are names which survive in modern Bombay.

18 St George (Madras) was named after the English patron saint on whose day the fort was supposedly completed; Fort William after William III and George after the Hanoverian kings.

19 C.A. Bayly, *Rulers, Townsmen and Bazaars, North Indian in the Age of British Expansion: 1770–1870* (Cambridge, 1983), p. 59.

20 Brenda Dunn, *A History of Port Royal and Annapolis Royal 1605–1800* (Halifax, NS, 2004).

21 Susan Biagi, *Louisbourg* (Halifax, NS, 1997).

22 Ernle Bradford, *The Great Siege: Malta 1565* (Ware, 1999).

23 Ashley Jackson, *Buildings of Empire* (Oxford, 2013), chapter 3.

24 Significant portions of the Victoria Lines survive, a striking presence in the Maltese landscape. Like so many other imperial fortifications, the wall is now important in tourism, constituting a well-advertised walking route. The best account of the Victoria Lines is to be found in http://maltainsideout.com/13610/the-great-wall-of-malta/. See also www.victorialinesmalta.com/ (accessed 15 June 2018).

25 Stephen Constantine, *Community and Identity: The Making of Modern Gibraltar Since 1704* (Manchester, 2009). There is a considerable literature on the siege. For a popular, illustrated account see Maurice Harvey, *Gibraltar: A History* (Staplehurst, 1996).
26 New Zealand had become part of the British Empire after the Treaty of Waitangi of 1840.
27 G.A. Bremner, *Imperial Gothic: Religious Architecture and High Anglican Culture in the British Empire, c. 1840–1870* (New Haven, CT, 2013), pp. 27–29.
28 General Godfrey Charles Mundy, *Journal of a Tour in India* (London, 1858, third edition), pp. 7–8.
29 Emily Eden, *Up the Country: Letters Written to Her Sister from the Upper Provinces of India* (London, 1978), p. 31.
30 Ibid., pp. 43, 31, 49, 89, 96.
31 Mary Lutyens, *The Lyttons in India: Lord Lytton's Viceroyalty* (London, 1979), p. 45.
32 Ibid., p. 62.
33 Craig Murray, *Sikunder Burnes: Master of the Great Game* (Edinburgh, 2016), pp. 89–92.
34 *The Scotsman*, 6 December, 1911, p. 9 when Reuter reported that 'the magnificent tent in which the King was to receive the Indian princes has burned down'.
35 J.G.A. Baird (ed.), *Private Letters of the Marquess of Dalhousie* (Edinburgh, 1910), p. 182.
36 Lutyens, *The Lyttons in India*, pp. 59–66.
37 *The Scotsman*, 29 December, 1902, p. 8.
38 Valentia Steer, *The Delhi Durbar 1902–3: A Concise Illustrated History* (London, 1903), p. 12. See also *The Scotsman*, 26 December 1902, p. 4.
39 Steer, *Delhi Durbar*, p. 12.
40 *The Scotsman*, 29 December, 1902, p. 8.
41 *Official Directory of the Coronation Durbar, Delhi 1911* (Calcutta, 1911).
42 Captain Albert Hervey, *A Soldier of the Company: Life of an Indian Ensign 1833–43*, edited and introduced by Charles Allen (London, 1988), p. 65. Hervey asserted that this was the only item he ever purchased from such an auction.
43 Ibid., p. 114. His followers included two immediate servants, a horsekeeper (*sic*), grass-cutter, tent-lascar, bullock-drivers and coolies.
44 Scott, *British Tale of Indian and Foreign Service*, p. 40. Scott travelled with sixteen camels, a court clerk, three camel-men, government orderlies, his personal servants, a bearer, a cook, a syce and a sweeper.
45 In Kenya in the 1920s, my father, a technical officer, lived in a tent, though his dining room and kitchen were located in rondavels, known as *banda*.
46 *Old and New Bombay: A Historical and Descriptive Account of Bombay and its Environs*, published in Bombay in 1911, p. 30, quoted in Barbara Groseclose, *British Sculpture and the Company Raj* (Cranbury, NJ, 1995), p. 45.
47 Elizabeth Grant of Rothiemurchus, *Memoirs of a Highland Lady*, edited with an introduction by Andrew Tod (Edinburgh, 1988), p. 267. This was specifically in Satara, where she had gone on her honeymoon in 1829.
48 Kincaid, *British Social Life in India*, p. 260.

49 See, for example, the extraordinary range of tents available from https://dir.indiamart.com/indianexporters/t_tents.html (accessed 16 June 2018). The Army and Navy Stores had branches in Karachi, Bombay, Calcutta, Delhi, Simla and Ranchi.
50 Richard Holmes, *Sahib: The British Soldier in India* (London, 2005), p. xxix.
51 William Dalrymple, *The White Mughals: Love and Betrayal in Eighteenth-Century India* (London, 2002), p. 287.
52 Dalrymple, *Last Mughal*, chapters 7–9.
53 Postcards were issued of these temporary barracks, two of which are in my collection.
54 Its importance is symbolised by the fact that the Duke of Kent, Queen Victoria's father, served in the military there between 1794 and 1800, while his older brother, the future William IV, had also served in the naval squadron based on Halifax.
55 *The Citadelle of Québec: A Living Fortress* (Quebec, n.d.).
56 Andrew Gailey, *The Lost Imperialist: Lord Dufferin, Memory and Mythmaking in an Age of Celebrity* (London, 2015), p. 144.
57 Llewellyn-Jones (ed.), *Lucknow*, chapter 4.
58 Dalrymple, *White Mughals* has an extensive description of the building of the Residency by Kirkpatrick, its surrounding buildings, including the zenana (later demolished by a British Resident who saw the structure as indicative of the loose morals of the eighteenth century) and various bungalows.
59 Mark Bence-Jones, *Palaces of the Raj: Magnificence and Misery of the Lord Sahibs* (London, 1973).
60 At this time, the EIC did have a civil architect, an Italian called Edward Tiretta. In 1789 he was listed as an officer of the Steward's Lodge of the Freemasons in Calcutta. He was also a member of a Roman Catholic Lodge and, on his death, was buried in a cemetery, now disappeared, which bore his name.
61 For Koca Sinan Mimar Aga as carpenter, engineer and architect, see Godfrey Goodwin, *A History of Ottoman Architecture* (London, 1971). Sinan's genius may have been seldom matched in the British Empire, but his progression from artisan to major artist was not unknown.
62 William Hickey, *Memoirs of William Hickey*, edited by Alfred Spencer, 4 vols (London, 1948), Vol. 4, p. 236, quoted in John McAleer, *Picturing India: People, Places and the World of the East India Company* (London, 2017), p. 207.
63 Illustrations indicate that the building was originally more open to its surroundings until iron fences and gateways enclosed it more completely, emphasising its exclusive characteristics.
64 Baird (ed.), *Private Letters*, p. 20.
65 I wandered around this echoing and empty former government house when on a research trip in Kolkata in 2008. Signs bearing legends such as 'Shakespeare' and 'Fiction' still hung from the columns in the ballroom.
66 Baird (ed.), *Private Letters*, p. 21.
67 Davies, *Splendours of the Raj*, p. 169. Various other prefabricated buildings, kiosks, bridges and piers were exported to India. Macfarlane's was always a major exhibitor

at the international exhibitions of the nineteenth century and produced extensive, impressively illustrated catalogues.
68 It is now the Hafkine Research Institute.
69 Kincaid, *British Social Life in India*, p. 148.
70 That is, a hybrid mixture of Elizabethan and Jacobean.
71 Raaja Bhasin, *Simla: The Summer Capital of British India* (New Delhi, 1992), p. 57. Viceroy Lord Lansdowne, on the other hand, was pleased that it felt more English than Indian.
72 Bence-Jones, *Palaces of the Raj*, p. 142. It is now a research institute.
73 Davies, *Splendours of the Raj*, p. 204.
74 Mollie Panter-Downes, *Ooty Preserved: A Victorian Hill Station in India* (London, 1967), p. 103.
75 Sarah Rooney and the Association of Myanmar Architects, *30 Heritage Buildings of Yangon: Inside the City that Captured Time* (Chicago, MI, 2013), p. 127.
76 In 2012, the guard at the gate of the Government House in Barbados rather charmingly took us on a tour of its surroundings and its verandah with two small cannon at the front steps, since the Governor was not in residence.
77 Forts were also built to defend it against covetous rival empires. Its temporary importance is represented by the fact that in 1834 it was reported that 600 ships had called there for fresh water and provisions, more than in Cape Town. Colin Fox, *A Bitter Draught: St. Helena and the Abolition of Slavery* (Elveden, Norfolk, 2017), p. xviii. For extensive consideration of the fortifications and armament of St Helena, see Philip Gosse, *St. Helena 1502–1938* (London, 1990, first published 1938).
78 The castle in Jamestown, which includes the colonial archive, is readily accessible and tourists visit the grounds of government house to see the allegedly 180-year-old tortoise, as I did in 2015. The tortoise lives in a convenient situation for photography of the house. Each governor is terrified that the tortoise will die on his watch (private information).
79 Because of the need to explain these government houses to modern societies, they invariably have exceptionally informative websites, detailing histories and current arrangements for access. It would be tedious to list these websites, but any search for government house in the Australian states or the Canadian provinces usually brings up a wealth of information.
80 I have visited it in this guise.
81 Gailey, *Lost Imperialist*, p. 122. He also found Ottawa to be an unappealing construction site, entirely lacking the historical charms of Quebec City.

3

Cities, towns, civic buildings and hill stations

FORMAL EMPIRE

The speed of urbanisation and of the appearance of buildings on a western model, both in terms of usage and of style, proceeded rapidly and comprehensively in colonial territories. As imperial invaders began to feel more secure, the various activities that had been concentrated in forts and factories began to fan out into the towns and cities which grew up around the original strategic positions. As well as representing the spread of power and security, this dispersal tracked the development of the economic functions of the nodal points of empire as well as the growth of the expatriate community. In addition, particularly in India and African colonies, an indigenous population arrived to take advantage of the new opportunities either in an elective way or because they were forced out of their rural communities by pressures of land appropriation or taxation. The Victorians, however, had an ambivalent approach to urbanism. On the one hand, cities and major towns were viewed as being the location of civilisation (as supposedly in the ancient world), sites for the avoidance of 'going native', for the development of a bourgeois cultural modernity charted in Chapter 4.[1] But they also unfavourably viewed cities as the creation of modern industrialism, as sinks of slums, poverty, social deprivation and disease, even potentially of epidemics. Just as alarmingly, they were therefore the breeding grounds of political and social dissent, even potentially of revolution. These concerns were of course particularly true of the cities of the imperial metropolis, even though such urban centres constituted the driving force of the industrialism which supported economic, military and imperial power. To a certain extent, it is possible to see a division within the empire. The notion that modern cities implied the spread of civilisation was particularly applied to India (already in many respects a significantly urban society) and to the dependent colonies, although the environments of such territories were seen as presenting opportunities for invigorating physical activity on the part of elite whites, in riding, sports and hunting. On the other hand, the notion of rural renewal in the empire, particularly prevalent in the second half of the nineteenth century, mainly applied to the lower-class migrants heading for the settler colonies. These territories were seen as destinations where poor migrants could rediscover rural roots, to find physical regeneration in allegedly health-giving settlement and farming. Of course it seldom happened like that. Rural settlement schemes had a habit of offering migrants no more than brief sojourns before many of them headed for the greater economic and social security of the towns, where the built environment took familiar and comforting forms. This happened, for example, in the case of the 1820 settlers on the Eastern Cape in southern Africa. Originally intended as a rural settlement to consolidate what was seen as a dangerous frontier with the African Nguni people, many of the migrants broke the indentures intended to keep them on the land and moved into Grahamstown and other such centres.[2] This also happened in Canada and elsewhere. But the empire of renewal was not confined only to settlement colonies. Both there and in the wider empire of conquest, the urban poor could find another form of physical, moral and patriotic regeneration (so the elite thought) through the military. Although martial race theory envisaged military recruitment among sturdy rural people, once again reality diverged from theory and most recruits came from metropolitan cities, eager to find steady employment and pay.[3]

In these processes, there was another significant difference between the colonies of settlement and the territories of rule. In Canada, Australia and (perhaps to a lesser extent) New Zealand, indigenous people were generally not welcome in cities and towns, where there was an attempt to maintain a degree of racial homogeneity. Elsewhere, however, indigenous labour was essential: in India (where urban dwelling was traditionally a familiar, if minority, option), South-East Asia, South Africa and other 'dependent territories' elsewhere on the African continent, indigenous urban migrants were a fact of life, even if there was an attempt to make them temporary residents, mainly as male labour migrants, in, for example, South Africa. Hence, while towns and cities in Canada and Australasia largely reflected their European models, those elsewhere were conditioned in their spatial arrangements according to the desire of imperial rulers and expatriates to create the ethnic separation that they saw as essential to their racial exclusiveness and maintenance of health, their mystique as rulers

Cities, towns, civic buildings and hill stations

and their institutional and architectural requirements. Thus, whereas the great majority of indigenous people in Canada and Australia were mainly banished to distant (and largely out-of-sight) reserves, other territories utilised the labour of slaves until 1833, later of freed slaves and indentured and rural migrant labour. Indigenous people were often required for domestic service, sometimes for craft and trading purposes, and certainly for labouring on construction and other projects. In some Indian cities, urban dwellers simply began to work (though far from exclusively) for new white masters. As the planning of urban colonial areas developed, whites insisted that the residential areas of this working population should be separated from their own zones. As railways were laid through colonial towns and cities, such separation often literally occurred 'on the other side of the tracks'.[4] Yet, while these distinctions are important, still there were considerable elements of similarity in the architecture of urban areas across the empire. And the vital and visible military presence was crucial to all of them.

A range of factors influenced the spatial arrangement of colonial cities and towns, including their origins as ports and commercial cities, the development of urban spaces in the interior of territories and the sudden and explosive effects of 'windfall' economic developments. These included opium trading in India and the Far East, gold in Victoria, diamonds in southern Africa, gold there later, or successful pastoralism and intensive agriculture of immensely successful crops like sugar, cotton, jute, indigo, tea, coffee, rubber, cocoa, palm oil, tobacco, and others. Architecture and town planning came to reflect all of these economic and related social developments. An additional factor was the blending of cultures in some places, occasionally European, sometimes indigenous. In eastern Canada, the architecture of the built environment came to reflect some aspects of the French inheritance of Quebec, while at the Cape and elsewhere in southern Africa, Dutch influences continued down to the twentieth century. In some places, European imperial cultures overlaid each other, as in Ceylon (mainly Dutch and British) or the Straits Settlement of Malacca (Portuguese, Dutch and British). In India, western architecture eventually sought some accommodation with the great works of earlier cultures and empires in the Subcontinent, a development which was sometimes exported to other territories where the hybrid styles were less appropriate, as in South-East Asia or East Africa. After the earliest period, when Europeans lived in structures very similar to those of the indigenous population, it is perhaps ironical (or indicative) that architectural styles for public buildings became strongly historicist, harking back to ancient and medieval precedents, even if both the materials, the techniques of building and the detailing were more contemporary. It is true that such historicism was often subject to modification to reflect the needs of climates substantially different from those of northern Europe. Later, the British were more culturally accommodating, perhaps representing a wider intellectual shift which seemed to see architectural eclecticism as part of a modern vision.[5] This movement had its origins in the middle of the century, but it surprisingly developed at a time both of a stronger sense of racial difference, a time when imperial self-confidence began to be eroded by international pressures, imperial competition, incipient economic and military decline, and often a deep sense of foreboding.

A number of key issues have to be considered in examining the form of the colonial built environment in the nineteenth century. Some of these are practical and some stylistic, although debates about the latter naturally involved elements of the former. Among the practical, we have to consider the extent to which so much civilian work was conducted by the military Royal Engineers. Indeed, as we have seen, engineering and architecture were difficult to separate during this period, not least because of the introduction of a whole range of new techniques, including the use of iron and steel in construction. Sometimes engineers and architects collaborated amicably. But, as we saw in Chapter 1, there were tensions. The PWD symbolised a major paradox at the heart of colonial construction: while it was supposed to be an agent of modernity, both promoting and utilising new technologies, it was also forced to use some indigenous methods, including the labour of Indian workers and of artisanal craftsmen, the latter transformed by the British into supposedly key preservers of iconic traditional crafts.[6] The practical builders in the PWD were often more conservative, disinclined to move stylistically with the times, as architects often saw it. Indian princely states also acquired PWDs, supposedly at the behest of the ruler, but actually often acting as the creature of the British. The state of Jaipur was one key example, where the head of the PWD, Colonel Swinton Jacob, a critic of the PWD of British India, became a key figure in the supposed preservation of Indian architectural and artistic forms.

To these controversies we must add the social dynamic of the demands of the bourgeoisie, charted in the next chapter, as well as the requirements of the extraordinary revolution in transport and communications technologies stimulating a new range of building types to service these developments. The fourth was the use of pattern books by the designers of colonial buildings who, the critics unfairly thought, had neither the expertise nor the imagination to create wholly original buildings. Associated with all of this was the familiar struggle between classical styles – originally a fundamental aesthetic of imperial buildings – and the arrival of neo-Gothic interests signalling the turn to the medieval period, for architectural inspiration. This was particularly the case with Christian churches, which moved from the template of James Gibbs's St Martin-in-the-Fields[7] to what were seen as the more appropriate medieval architectural wellsprings of Christianity, albeit in a variety of modified forms (see Chapter 6).[8] But Gothic architecture also spread into secular buildings before giving way to a return to updated forms of both neoclassical and Baroque in the twentieth century. While some believed that the material presence of modern empires was best expressed through classical precedents, others became convinced that Gothic styles reflected the English medieval origins of the perceived notable attributes of the British Empire. The irony is that so much of this Gothic passion was rooted in Venetian and southern European forms of Gothic. Some believed that such Gothic forms, suitably modified, were better adapted to tropical climates, with their characteristic cool loftiness, opportunities for open traceries and colonnades, external staircases and courtyards. In India, it was thought that Gothic could accommodate the exuberance and lively outlines of some Indian forms.

This pursuit of more oriental detail and of dramatically lively architectural profiles had its supreme achievement in the Indo-Saracenic style. In the case of India it produced the third phase in the British architectural response to the Subcontinent. Thus, it constituted a further point in the escape from the stolidity of imperial classical and a supposedly refreshing deviation from the universal and eclectic Gothic. It was a style that was to be much debated, but in certain influential quarters in India was regarded as an architectural form (though one of tremendous diversity) that had the power to bring British rulers and Indian subjects together as well as act, in the case of its application in the princely states, almost as a source of character formation for westernising princes. It represented an effort by British architects (often against the opposition of the PWD) to create a syncretic architectural response to the perceived architectural styles of India.[9] The style was at its height in the 1880s and 1890s, although with some buildings coming earlier and a few later. It produced a riot of eclecticism when western elements were blended with Islamic ideas (from various different regions), sometimes with Hindu, Jain, Buddhist, Rajput and even Egyptian details (though mercifully not all at the same time).[10] Individual architects had favoured different regional models, with some impressed by the blend of Mughal and Hindu architecture to be found in the Rajput states. The prime debate about hybrid styles is whether they encouraged pastiche or led to a deeper engagement, accurate historicism or creative revivalism.[11] Nevertheless, Indo-Saracenic represented (at its best) something wholly fresh, an original eclecticism which produced a new style integrating adapted elements of older ones. Its signature building was Mayo College, Ajmer in Rajasthan, constructed between 1877 and 1885 and designed by Major Charles Mant, with a later wing by Swinton Jacob.[12] Here the architecture reflected in many respects the objectives of the institution, the education of the sons of princes to turn them into modern rulers with a western education. Metcalf argued that the development of the Indo-Saracenic style by the British was intended to demonstrate the manner in which imperial rule had facilitated the growth of religious toleration in India.[13] It can, however, also be seen as a means of ingratiating the British with Indians at a time of increasing political dissatisfaction, though whether it achieved such an ameliorative effect seems dubious.

The positive side of the style, however, was that it was seen as a means of reintroducing Indian craftsmanship into imperial architecture, supposedly mirroring the British Arts and Crafts movement in an empire context. In places it gave opportunities for Indian craftsmen to escape from attempting to emulate foreign techniques and return to a seemingly more familiar idiom. It gave some of them, of whom Bhai Ram Singh was the most celebrated, the opportunity to transform their status from artisan to artist. In Bombay, buildings appeared in what has been described as Gothic-Saracenic, thus adhering to the overall Gothic style of the public areas of the city while adding 'Saracenic' elements. The real apogee of the style was achieved in Madras where a whole range of public buildings running along the sea front were built to reflect it, including the University Senate House, the Board of Revenue (based on an older palace of the Nawab of the Carnatic), Victoria Public Hall, Presidency College and supremely, the Law Courts. Nearby, the Government Museum and the railway station in Egmore were also major examples. Indian princes were sometimes enamoured of the style and often commissioned it for new palaces and other buildings, though some clung to classicism and others were careful to keep it separate from their more traditional private quarters. George Wittet and John Begg were its main exponents in Bombay, William Emerson in Allahabad and elsewhere, Robert Fellowes Chisholm in Madras and Swinton Jacob in Rajasthan, while Henry Irwin and Sydney Crookshank produced buildings in the style in various locations. Calcutta generally avoided it and some cities remained resolutely classical, such as the important cantonment city of Bangalore in South India. Indo-Saracenic spread out of India, making its appearance in South-East Asia (as in the Secretariat and railway station in Kuala Lumpur, Malaya) and even in East Africa. Although Indo-Saracenic was never adopted for church architecture, except in a few specific details, it has been said that the one Indo-Saracenic Christian building was the Roman Catholic Church in Mathura (now Uttar Pradesh), built in the 1870s.[14]

The period when Indo-Saracenic became fashionable, though always relatively limited in its application to major public buildings such as railway stations, public offices, assembly halls, educational buildings and clock towers, may perhaps be seen as the moment when India broke away from the overall imperial styles to be found in various forms across the British Empire. As the era of Indo-Saracenic waned in the twentieth century, classical and 'Edwardian' Baroque made a comeback in many parts of the empire, including India, while new twentieth-century styles embraced European avant-garde movements such as Art Nouveau and Art Deco. Once again, this was an empire-wide phenomenon. In the twentieth century residential homes also became a setting for architectural experimentation. Whereas Canada had initially reacted against American styles (during the period when the United States still presented a threat to Canadian imperial status), American influences began to be more positive from the late nineteenth century and began to affect the style of urban buildings. This was part of a cultural influence which was to spread to other parts of the British Empire in the twentieth century.

Since it is clearly impossible to chart such architectural developments everywhere, this chapter will concentrate on a number of test cases and examples of building types. It will examine the growth of cities and towns with the appearance of their characteristic buildings. This will be followed in Chapter 4 by a consideration of the new bourgeois institutions which spread across the empire as well as the architectural dimensions of the new technologies of the age. Throughout, the stress will be on social and cultural contexts rather than on technical issues of architectural styles and their proponents, although there will be some references to the architectural progression experienced in colonial territories.

BUILDING TYPES

Colonial capitals soon spawned key buildings to reflect developing administrative and legal functions. The central authority of the governor, initially both politically instrumental and ceremonial, was soon bolstered by the need for buildings to house the secretariats where officials laboured to exercise the practicalities of control. The British always insisted that the rule of law was inherent in the nature of their power, and that had to be expressed through generally impressive law courts. Other aspects of central authority might reside in the mint and the treasury, representing the powers of tax-gathering and the issue of forms of currency. It could also be found in the general post office, invariably one of the colony's grandest buildings, representative of the essential connectedness of empire through the posts and later the telegraphs, very much projected as 'royal mail'. Port cities were characteristic of a maritime and extractive empire. Many of them were also colonial capitals displaying many of the buildings necessary for intercontinental and colonial trade as well as the travel associated with it. These included agencies, hotels, and, in terms of the central importance of revenue collection, customs houses.

If all these represented the central authority of empire dispersed into its local manifestations, there were other devolved sources of power. These might include the local authority vested in civic organisations once the scale of urban development justified their existence. Such civic power mirrored its emergence in Britain itself, in social terms the shift from aristocratic to bourgeois authority. It would be expressed in city and town halls, with their associated administrative offices. Such town halls appeared throughout the empire, representing, as we shall see, local politics throughout the colonies and the provinces and states of the federal administrations of the later Dominions. They reflected the economic growth and alleged successes of their communities, providing a structural presence for the developing materialism of their communities. They can be analysed as building types occupying key sites within their urban fabrics and as social and cultural spaces reflecting the key events in the life of the citizenry, though often circumscribed by social, gender and above all racial considerations. Town halls thus became vital public spaces representing bourgeois civil society, albeit invariably with restricted access.[15] They became vested with considerable symbolism, representing pride in urban growth, the dignity of civic authority and the sense of community cohesion (and its opposite), as well as the cultural and even intellectual accomplishments of the local social formation.

There was a major difference between the appearance of town halls in India and elsewhere in the empire. In India, the early town halls invariably preceded the development of civic administrative institutions, partly because of the central authority of the East India Company . Thus town halls in India often reflected a desire for a cultural space, and municipal administration remained

Cities, towns, civic buildings and hill stations

small-scale until the creation of civic institutions in the 1860s. The town halls in Bombay and Calcutta are good examples, both neoclassical buildings of the early nineteenth century and founded by the imperial citizenry to add both status and convenience to their cities. Both are situated in prominent positions, in Calcutta on the Esplanade, in Bombay on Horniman Circle. The Calcutta building was opened in 1814, designed, as was usual at the time, by a military engineer, John Garstin, and intended to be used for social occasions principally by the European inhabitants of the city.[16] It initially had structural problems that led to the suggestion that it was immediately shunned by its potential public, and parts of it had to be reconstructed.[17] In some respects overshadowed by the adjacent Mint building, designed by Major Forbes, it was swiftly turned into a sort of Valhalla of statues and portraits of imperial figures. The Danish botanist, Nathaniel Wallich, created a museum in the building which later became, as it is today, the museum of the history of Calcutta. Moorhouse suggested that 'everything in Calcutta was derivative', by which he meant that engineers designed out of pattern books, but there are some notable exceptions, and the overall effect of the classical buildings in the city has long been considered striking.[18] As in the case of so many town halls, the Calcutta building became a highly contested space. It was used for banquets, balls, dinners, memorial meetings, concerts,

16 Town Hall, Bombay

theatrical performances, exhibitions, examinations and prize and convocation events. Elite Indians were admitted, but the relationship between British and Indian publics became increasingly fraught, notably after the Revolt of 1857 and the legal controversies that followed the Black Acts in 1849 and the Ilbert Bill of 1884.[19] Nevertheless, throughout British rule the Town Hall continued to be used for protest meetings for Indians as well as the British residents, despite some attempts to suppress the former.[20] Further impetus was given to such meetings by the development of Indian nationalism from the 1880s and the proposals for the Partition of Bengal of 1905. By this time there had been various attempts to create spaces in which Indians could congregate, either in privately organised rooms or in the open air. Great protest meetings moved into open public spaces that were no longer part of the built environment. To a certain extent, the town hall resumed its significance in the twentieth century, though only as one of many venues for political activity.

The Bombay town hall (more like the original British equivalents) had occupied several houses, in which courts had constituted an important function, before the nineteenth-century grand version was proposed. This was completed (after a long gestation) in 1833. Funds for its construction were raised from a lottery organised by the Literary Society of the city (the government contributed the major finance required to complete it) and was designed by a military engineer, Colonel Thomas Cowper, who chose a Greek revival style, though the large projecting sunshades of the windows are a significant concession to the climate.[21] Davies considered that 'the end result is magnificent – a composition of power and massive solidity' that reflected the growing authority of the British.[22] It housed a museum and library as well as the Asiatic Society of Bombay. It had a large public space for meetings, a durbar room, and offices used by government departments in the basement. It was also intended from the start to be a sort-of Valhalla for statues of distinguished officials and businessmen associated with Bombay. Its significance as a public site was symbolised by the manner in which Queen Victoria's proclamation after the Indian Revolt of 1857 was read from its grandiloquent flight of front steps. It also became a site for controversy about the constituency of its 'public', Indian elites demanding access both for meetings and for statuary, as was demonstrated over the placing of the statue of Jagannath Shankarset. As such, it did become a 'middle ground' for British and Indian elites until the focus of public space moved on to the new municipality from the 1860s and to other spaces with the development of nationalism from the 1880s and 1890s.[23]

Cities, towns, civic buildings and hill stations

Madras had to wait until later in the century for the building of the Victoria Memorial, or Town Hall, intended for social and public occasions, opened to commemorate the Golden Jubilee of the Empress. It was built in an Indo-Saracenic and Romanesque style by the prominent architect Robert Fellowes Chisholm, and was used as a meeting place by significant Indian politicians and literary figures. A similar multi-purpose town hall had already been built in Karachi, completed in 1865. Known as the Frere Hall (to commemorate Bartle Frere's period as Commissioner of Sind), it was similarly designed for 'public meetings, lectures, balls, concerts, and dramatic performances'.[24] It was designed in an attractive Venetian style by General Henry Wilkins, who would contribute to the Gothic character of Bombay. Given the size and usage of these spaces, it can be said that British town halls in India encouraged Indian nationalism by providing the venues in which many meetings could take place. Another example of a 'cultural' town hall is in Singapore, where the original hall was opened in 1862, replacing earlier assembly rooms. As the wealth of the port increased, further additions were made to it until the complex included a theatre and a concert hall joined together by an imposing frontage and projecting columned wings. It occupies a prime site on Empress Place. An example of a smaller, elegant town hall is that of Penang.

17 Town Hall, Singapore

18 Town Hall, Penang

Elsewhere, town halls became dual-purpose buildings representing both the range of functions required by the growing populations of towns and cities and the need for civic administration. They often accommodated the powers vested in mayors and councils, sometimes in simple structures, invariably in opulent rooms and chambers expressive of civic pride. They also incorporated the offices in which their officials administered the tax-raising powers, the trade, the infrastructures, transport, drainage and sanitation of the urban areas. Importantly, such civic centres also included a major space, a great hall where the community could gather, meetings could be held and entertainments provided. They thus represented the enlargement of the bourgeois public sphere and the global dispersal of civic arrangements that were increasingly important within Britain itself. Among the older surviving town halls, there are excellent examples in Sydney, New South Wales; Melbourne, Victoria and Pietermaritzburg, KwaZulu-Natal. Jenny Gregory has demonstrated the manner in which Australian town halls were, in their planning and construction, often major sources of contention.[25] This was particularly true in Sydney, where the building of the town hall took 46 years from the first selection of the site to its completion, damaging the career or health of several architects. Once completed it became a considerable source of pride, though it continued to stimulate much dispute about the appropriate mix of political and social use. The Melbourne town hall followed two other smaller ones and was rather less contentious in its genesis. One of the grandest of civic buildings created in the British Empire, it perfectly reflects the growth of the economy of the colony of Victoria after the gold strikes. A town hall built on the same site between 1849 and 1854 was swiftly considered to be inadequate and a new town hall was planned. The third grandiloquent version was completed in 1870, designed by the local firm of Reed and Barnes.[26] Built in masonry with a prominent clock tower, it has been described as a 'magnificent collection of classically composed pavilions'.[27] In 1908 an additional administrative block was added. The concert hall was damaged by fire in 1925 and reconstructed in a yet larger form. Gregory has catalogued the rituals of civic ceremonial and public meetings which took place in Australian town halls, including many highly disputed events relating to trade-union and anti-war activity. Town halls have also acted as recruitment centres for the wartime military, as well as much else. They have been places of racial exclusion in which, until modern times, calls for Aboriginal freedoms and greater political involvement were often banned. Moreover, they have been locations for the playing out of tensions between British imperial sentiment, loyalty to the British monarch, and Australian nationalism, not least in the flying of symbolic flags. Thus the controversies surrounding them charted the transition from empire to nation state. The penetration of this building form (and associated community activities) to many Australian towns is perfectly symbolised by the fact that more than 300 of them are heritage listed.[28]

On another continent, Pietermaritzburg's city hall was built in an elaborate Flemish Renaissance style, entirely in brick, in 1893. It was seriously damaged by fire only two years later and subsequently reconstructed. It combines civic offices and council chamber with a concert hall. It contrasts with, and to a certain extent outshines, the nearby old parliament and later assembly buildings, which are stolidly classical with Baroque touches. Although Pietermaritzburg was the capital, Durban was conscious of being the larger city and important port and a new Durban city hall was duly built between 1903 and 1910 in a neo-Baroque style reminiscent of the city hall in Belfast. Whereas Melbourne and Pietermaritzburg town halls stand on street frontages, the Durban version occupies a large and discrete space emphasising the civic pride of the city and its capacity to emulate any British equivalent. The Edwardian Baroque Cape Town City Hall was built in 1905 in a prominent position on the Esplanade. Originally a centre of municipal administration, it later lost this function and is now primarily a centre for cultural events, including orchestral concerts. The grandeur of its concert hall was clearly designed to match the equivalent town halls in, for example, Australia. The Johannesburg City Hall, built between 1909 and 1914, is similarly an Edwardian Baroque structure and was intended to celebrate the emergence of the Transvaal from the Boer War and its reacquisition of civic identity. However, municipal functions have declined and it now contains the Gauteng legislature, Gauteng being the name for the small province carved out of the former Transvaal. Such grand buildings in South Africa are to a certain extent still vested with the taint of apartheid, and have never fully taken on the significance attached to such structures in the former 'Dominions' or even in India. Elsewhere in Africa, a number of factors have militated against the maintenance or renewal of the buildings representing civic authority.[29] Inevitably, such structures, sometimes very modest, are inseparably associated with colonialism. In addition, central government in many territories has usurped the status and authority of municipal authority, while some postcolonial governments have established new capitals supposedly more symbolic of modern indigenous rule. Town halls do however survive in a form that would be familiar in the colonial era, though of course now manned entirely by African staffs and politicians, in such territories as Kenya, Zambia and Botswana.[30] Still, in many places the communities of citizenry in a situation of rapid rural–urban migration and consequent demographic shift have found other informal spaces such that civic materialism has taken up residence in markets, shops, religious establishments, sometimes civic centres, and forms of hospitality and trading associated with tourism.

The built environment of the principal colonial cities was inevitably influenced by constitutional developments in the British Empire. Although colonial assemblies were founded in the late seventeenth and eighteenth centuries, the modern emergence of Legislative Councils dates from the institution of responsible government, the first example being Nova Scotia in 1848. The first assembly in Halifax, Nova Scotia, had been founded in 1758 and met in a modest wooden building. It moved to a relatively plain neoclassical building in 1819, which remains the Nova Scotia legislature to this day. It is striking that this sequence of parliamentary buildings followed the dominant styles of the day rather than any conception that the development of progressive democratic institutions should be reflected in a specific form. Whereas the state capitols and Congress of the United States have a sense of ideological unity about them, the British Empire was wholly eclectic, often following the dominant style of the day. For example, the Georgian Province House in Charlottetown, Prince Edward Island, dates from 1847, while the equivalent building in Fredericton, New Brunswick, was built in the fashionable Second Empire style in 1882. The parliament buildings of Quebec have a complicated and chequered history after the British conquest, with multiple moves and several fires. A modest parliament building in Montreal was burned down by rioters in 1849, symbolic of opposition to the authoritarian governments in Canada which had first broken out in 1837. The capital of Quebec was subsequently moved to Quebec City and eventually a new parliament building, almost inevitably in a strongly Second Empire style, was built there between 1877 and 1886. The building has a prominent central clock tower and is notable for the quantity of statuary associated with it, reflecting the dominant figures of Quebec history and including a First Nation group. This building represents the transition between the relatively modest parliaments of the maritime provinces and the later overblown legislative buildings apparently justified by the considerable growth of provincial economies. After Confederation in 1867, they were built in consciously overbearing styles and it seems clear that they were, to a certain extent, emulating the state capitols of the United States. They came to dominate their urban environments, invariably the grandest buildings of the province. The heavy Romanesque Ontario legislature was opened in Toronto in 1893 and Victoria, British Columbia acquired a massive neo-Baroque (and hybrid) building, with two wings connected by colonnades, built between 1893 and 1898. It continues to dominate the harbour area. Beaux Arts buildings, often highly eclectic in form, appeared in Regina, Saskatchewan, built in 1908 and 1912, and Edmonton, Alberta, in 1907–13, while Winnipeg's equivalent was not completed until 1919, delayed by overspending and the First World War. Even the modern legislature of Newfoundland and Labrador in St John's, completed in 1960, dominates the city, its more contemporary style forming the traditional outline of the earlier legislatures with an upright central section paralleling the older drums and domes.[31]

By contrast with Canada, the legislative assembly buildings or parliament houses of Australia are generally a good deal more modest. They also reflect, to a certain extent, the combination of the architectural history of the relevant colony together with its economic fortunes. The parliament building of New South Wales in Sydney is strikingly restrained. It partly started out as the general hospital, a Georgian building begun in 1811 as part of Governor Lachlan Macquarie's building schemes in Sydney.[32] One wing was converted into the legislature building in 1829 and eventually the legislature and the Mint took over the whole structure, later extended. The parliament house of Victoria in Melbourne, the construction beginning in 1855, is grandly classical, reflecting the flow of funds coming from the gold strikes in the colony a few years earlier. Like Sydney, it stands on a street frontage, lacking the grandiloquent parkland settings of some Canadian equivalents. The parliament house of South Australia also stands directly on its Adelaide North Terrace frontage. Built over a long period from the 1870s to 1939, it is a Greek revival building, constructed in granite and marble, notable for having lost the dome and towers of the original plans for want of funds. The old parliament building of 1843 still stands beside the current parliament and later became a museum. In Hobart, Tasmania, the parliament house was originally built as the customs house in a classic colonial Georgian style, but after the granting of responsible government to the colony in 1856 it was taken over as the assembly building, though sharing the space with the customs house until the beginning of the twentieth century. The equally modest parliament house of Western Australia in Perth was built between 1902 and 1904. None of these buildings dominate their cities in the manner of the later Canadian examples. In fact the grandest of the Australian parliament houses is that of Queensland in Brisbane, built between 1866 and 1868. Though far from vast, its Second Empire/French Renaissance style is more assertive than other Australian equivalents.[33]

The creation of confederations and unions in the white-settler 'Dominions' led to the foundation of capitals and the creation of new parliament buildings. Between 1841 and 1865, the capital of New Zealand was Auckland, and the first parliamentary assemblies met there in the 1850s, occupying a very modest building jokingly known as the 'shedifice'. Once the capital moved to Wellington, a wooden parliament building was constructed, which burned down in 1907. The parliamentary library had been constructed in rendered brick, completed in 1899, and survived the conflagration that destroyed the other buildings. Its Gothic style was intended to complement that of the wooden parliament building.[34] A competition was held for the reconstruction of the parliament and was won by the government architect, John Campbell. Inevitably the new neo-Baroque building had a fraught genesis, given the problems of the First World War. The intention had been to match the parliament with a new library building, but because of the paucity of building materials this never happened, and the older library survived. In 1964, new offices (engagingly known as the 'beehive') designed by Basil Spence completed the strikingly eclectic composition of neo-Gothic, Baroque and modernist.[35] Perhaps the most celebrated of the Dominion parliament buildings is that in Ottawa. The United Province of Canada had been created in 1841 to bring together Upper and Lower Canada and Ottawa was eventually chosen as the capital of this political unit. A new parliament building was required and the prominent Barracks Hill was chosen for its construction. This was begun in 1859 and it was not completed until 1876. By that time the Canadian Confederation had been founded in 1867 and the two provinces were redivided, with Ottawa becoming the federal capital. The new parliament buildings (three of them surrounding a central parade ground) became the grandest in the British Empire, constructed in a Victorian High Gothic style which was supposed to reflect what were perceived to be the Gothic parliamentary traditions of the British as opposed to the overblown republican classical and Baroque of the United States. A complex of Gothic buildings sprouted up on the hill, although a devastating fire in 1916 destroyed the central portion and tower. A new block, with much enlarged accommodation, was built in a striking Gothic Revival style between 1916 and 1922,

19 Parliament building, Ottawa

completed in 1927 with a somewhat ecclesiastical-looking central tower (the Peace Tower, commemorating the First World War) and tapering spire.[36] The principal architect was John Pearson, who sought to combine French and British elements, creating lobbies and entrance halls reminiscent of large cathedral chapter houses. The building was also embellished with many symbolic sculptures and portraits. The forging of Canadian nationalism through the First World War was symbolised by a commemorative chapel in the tower and the lining of the walls of the Senate by eight large paintings of events in the First World War. The British parliamentary tradition is followed closely in both architectural and procedural terms in the Commons and Senate, and the buildings have come to be seen as embodying the vast sea-to-sea continental scale of Canadian national identity.[37]

The Gothic tradition was carried no further. In the case of South Africa, the Union parliament was developed out of the colonial Cape parliament. Responsible government at the Cape was granted in 1853, but the resulting assembly met in various locations for thirty years, including the governor's residence, a masonic lodge and a court building. A dedicated assembly building was a long time in the making owing to financial constraints (despite the discovery of diamonds), political and military upheavals and a faulty and overblown design by Charles Freeman, which would have matched the North American devotion to domes and towers. A simpler neoclassical building was duly completed in 1884, overlooking the government gardens and adjacent to the library. It subsequently became the Union parliament and was extended by Herbert Baker in the 1920s, with a modern extension of the 1980s attempting to match the earlier style with a more contemporary feel. In some respects, the Union Buildings in Pretoria housing government offices are architecturally more interesting. Designed by Sir Herbert Baker and built between 1909 and 1913, they constituted a unique expression of an Edwardian classical style that owed nothing to any of its parliamentary and governmental predecessors. The building was intended to be immensely symbolic, with two wings representing English and Afrikaans speakers and a central colonnaded section, with an amphitheatre symbolising their unity in the new Union. Africans, by far the largest population in the new Dominion, were left out of account. Nevertheless, Baker's composition, on a prominent hill with extensive gardens, close to the city centre, is an acknowledged masterpiece, its original symbolism entirely irrelevant since the start of African majority rule in 1994. Baker famously went on to work on the design of New Delhi.

Cities, towns, civic buildings and hill stations

20 Parliament House, Cape Town

After the declaration of the Commonwealth of Australia in 1901 (proclaimed in the 1880 Exhibition building in Melbourne),[38] the parliament met in Melbourne until 1927. A parliament building was constructed in the new capital of Canberra, built in what has been described as the practical and simple 'stripped classical' style of that city. Like much of Canberra, the building was low-rise, designed by the government architect, John Smith Murdoch, but was also intended to be temporary. A new parliament building, modernist and supposedly reflecting the ethnic and natural characteristics of the country, was built between 1981 and its opening in 1988, described as representing a double boomerang. The contrast between these buildings and Ottawa (or those in Wellington or South Africa) could not have been greater.

If any building should have been emblematic of the British Empire, it should have been law courts. A central aspect of the ideology of empire was its alleged basis in law and its dissemination of distinctively English legal practices to the rest of the world: English because the common law, rooted in the Middle Ages, was so different from the Roman Dutch law of parts of continental practice, as well as of Scotland (the British encountered Roman Dutch law in Ceylon and in South Africa and often turned to Scots to operate what they had inherited). In consequence, it might have been expected that if there was a classic imperial architectural style it would have been used to represent the administration of the law. The architecture of courts was, however, as diverse as other imperial buildings. As usual, it was the style of the period that was more important than ideological presentation of function. This diversity is illustrated by a few examples. High-court buildings in India are among the most striking structures of the three former presidency cities, though they are all very different. Mumbai's is one of the city's notable Gothic buildings, grandly situated on the maidan and built in an Early English style (though with distinctly Venetian elements) between 1871 and 1878, designed by Colonel James Fuller.[39] Calcutta was provided with a building vaguely reminiscent of the Cloth Hall in Ypres between 1888 and 1892, designed by Walter Granville. The Madras equivalent is by far the most flamboyant, almost inevitably following the Indo-Saracenic style of the city, built between 1888 and 1892 and designed by the government consultant architect, J.W. Brassington. By contrast, the high court in Karachi was severely classical. The Palais de Justice in Montreal is a complex of buildings, severely classical in style, with a modernist addition, almost as though Quebec was

21 High Court, Calcutta

Cities, towns, civic buildings and hill stations

22 High Court, Karachi

consciously avoiding the English obsession with the medieval. The Supreme Court of Canada in Ottawa, opened after the Second World War, avoids the Gothic of its neighbours, the Parliament buildings, and adopts what has been described as a 'Châteauesque design with steep copper roofs'. There is Art Deco ornament, together with statues of Louis Saint Laurent, Truth and Justice.[40] It succeeds in conveying a slightly French feel. The High Court in Cape Town is an unpretentious classical building adjacent to the government gardens, while that of Johannesburg is in twentieth-century Baroque. It is however indicative that the grandest courthouse in South Africa was not built by the British at all, but by the Afrikaans government of Paul Kruger. The Palace of Justice in Pretoria, designed by the Dutch architect Sytze Wierda, is in an extravagantly hybrid Renaissance style and became one of the grandest buildings of the city, featuring on many postcards. It was an expression of national independence and pride rather than imperial power, though by the time it was completed the British had taken over. The former British High Court building in Hong Kong, built in the domed classical style of that period, completed in 1912, is one of the few major buildings from the British period to survive. Much more modest is the courthouse in Falmouth, Jamaica, built in 1817, Georgian with a portico and an open arcaded lower floor. Indeed, not all courthouses are domineeringly grand. In Road Town, Tortola, the Supreme Court and the legislative assembly inhabit the same modest building, with arcading on the ground floor and a balcony above.[41] The court in Charlestown on Nevis shares its building with a library on the floor above.[42]

But any consideration of the manner in which imperial power and authority were represented in the construction of grand public buildings requires correctives. Such buildings supremely represented the modernism of the new political dispensation, but towns were largely made up of modest structures, and much early urban and rural construction could be more related to the pre-existing built environment. As we shall see in Chapter 5, colonialists often inhabited frail, quickly erected buildings. We have already seen that tents and huts were among the first residences of early colonists and officials, even governors. The transition to more substantial buildings may have been relatively swift, particularly where the military were involved, but other forms of experimentation took place during the transition period. Nothing more powerfully represented the supposed technical distancing of settlers and sojourners from indigenous people than the use of industrially produced materials. Corrugated galvanised iron, for example, was invented in the 1820s and was soon exported to the colonies for use in construction, mainly as roofing material. This appeared everywhere in colonial territories, although it was often climatically unsuitable, both in transmitting heat and in being intolerably noisy during rainstorms. Soon, entire portable buildings were being transported. The manufacture of prefabricated buildings seemed to offer a considerable opportunity for suppliers in Britain eager to trade with the colonies. Such portable buildings, mainly iron, were developed from the mid-nineteenth century. English and Scottish iron foundries began to produce elaborate, illustrated catalogues of such buildings from the 1850s and they became regular exhibitors at the international exhibitions of the period.[43] We have already encountered a cast-iron durbar hall in Madras, and cast-iron churches, halls, homes and other buildings were also sold to buyers in both formal and informal empire.[44] Such exports, advertised in the catalogues as including stores, warehouses, shops, schools, halls, even a theatre, continued until at least the 1890s. They seem to have been particularly popular in Melbourne, where the gold boom created a considerable demand for such buildings when materials and builders were relatively scarce, so iron houses and a church helped to solve the problem. A complete street of iron housing was erected in Melbourne and survived into the twentieth century.[45] These helped to house people who had been living in tents, given the extremely rapid growth in population of the city. There were, however, problems of erection, which was costly, and of insulation.[46]

Cities, towns, civic buildings and hill stations

One relatively grand iron house, Corio Villa, ordered in the early 1850s from the Edinburgh firm of Charles D. Young and Company, was erected in Geelong in 1856 and survives to this day.[47]

Of greater significance in the creation of a distinctive colonial architecture was the export (and eventually the local manufacture) of highly decorative cast-iron railings, gates, balconies, verandahs, balusters and balustrades which became almost ubiquitous in colonial shops and houses. This became a major fashion from the mid-nineteenth until the early twentieth century, still apparent throughout the Caribbean, Australia, India, South Africa, other African colonies and New Zealand. Balconies and verandahs framed by iron were particularly suited to hot climates, offering open spaces, supplementary to internal rooms, on the upper storeys of buildings and verandahs around homes or covered walkways (as in rows of shops) at the ground floors. Squares and public parks in both Britain and the colonies were seldom without fountains, kiosks and bandstands (of varying sizes), all manufactured in prefabricated cast iron. These were also characteristic of coastal resorts (where iron might also be used in the provision of piers) and hill stations. These public structures and ornaments were indicative of leisure, of open-air socialising and public entertainment (often provided by military bands). As public 'furniture' they constituted a link with the civic pride of the metropolis while also representing the economic and social elevation of settlers with their opportunities for such leisure. Indeed the use of such iron became so ubiquitous, not least in cities like Melbourne and Adelaide, that they became characteristic of colonial style, now often subject to civic preservation regulations. The export of such decorative iron features from British companies (at least six manufactured such wares in Scotland) became a major colonial trade of the second half of the nineteenth century.[48]

However, many colonial/imperial buildings were not the product of military engineers, surveyors or amateur and later professional architects. Farmhouses throughout the empire, sugar and cotton plantation houses and ancillary buildings in the West Indies or on indigo, jute or tea plantations in India and Ceylon, rubber plantations in Malaya or cocoa, palm oil, tobacco and coffee plantations in various African colonies were often a matter of 'do-it-yourself' design and construction.[49] Necessity was indeed the mother of invention. Colonists and expatriates in such situations may have followed visual precedents, but generally they set out to create structures that answered to their practical requirements.[50] If they designed and marked out the footprint of such structures, they were always dependent on local craftsmen and labourers to build them. Many were sufficiently well built that they survive to this day, 'informal builds' that were nonetheless practical and effective. Such informal construction often responded to the needs of the environment.[51] Throughout African, Asian and island territories in the Caribbean, Indian Ocean and South Pacific the menial tasks and sometimes the building 'trades' were performed by locals or immigrants. Slaves and indentured labourers have to be numbered among this army of workers. This dependence on indigenous people was also true of Christian mission stations and churches. Many missionaries had to turn themselves into builders, as many did in Africa and elsewhere, including David Livingstone before he started his travels. Brickmaking became an essential economic activity of many such mission stations (no doubt also of farms and plantations). At one African mission station, so many Africans were co-opted into the processes of brickmaking that other Africans began to refer to them as 'the bricks'. Indeed bricks came to be seen as much more than simply the building blocks of structures. They constituted the essential geometry of imperialism, symbolising as they did the rectangles that, when placed together, created the disciplined straight lines of the buildings of the dominant culture.[52] Missionaries additionally saw themselves as the builders of roads, canals, even telegraph lines, all made possible by indigenous labour. The felling and milling of timber was clearly important, and in some environmentally appropriate places the quarrying of stone and aggregates.

Thus, when we look at an imperial or colonial building, small or large, public or commercial, secular or religious, or at modifications to the environment, we should remember the indigenous workers who constructed them, carpenters, bricklayers, stonemasons, plasterers, glaziers and many unskilled labourers, sometimes supervised by European artisans, but often struggling to bring (in India, say) older methods to bear on new structures or to learn wholly fresh techniques. Often there were Indian contractors in India, or Chinese in South-East Asia, a few of whom made fortunes out of their imperial clients, but such indigenous entrepreneurship was relatively rare across the empire. But both they and their white counterparts were entirely dependent on large numbers of poor artisans and labourers. Imperial cities expanded mightily as migrants moved in from the rural areas to work on such construction projects, as well as on commercial and manufacturing enterprises.[53] Meanwhile, some at least of the older crafts of India continued to be practised in the bazaars, for local, white and tourist customers. Some craft skills, for example in sculpture, were often adapted to the requirements of new building types, particularly under the influence of Europeans in the new western-inspired schools of art.[54] In the territories of settlement, such services were principally supplied by European immigrants until indigenous crafts and carving traditions were revalued, mainly in the later twentieth century.

INFORMAL EMPIRE

As we saw in the previous chapter, trading posts, factories and fortresses in the early days of empire invariably incorporated all functions within them, commercial, administrative, military and religious. These buildings largely preceded the imposition of direct imperial power. In informal empire, where direct colonial administrations were never established, despite a powerful western economic presence, this early multi-use character of buildings was often re-created. Wherever British (and other European) economic influence became dominant, areas of port towns and specific buildings reflected the spread of commercial power. Good examples can be found in the Middle East and the Far East. In Istanbul, centre of the Ottoman Empire, for example, westerners established themselves in areas where they could pursue business and create a familiar cultural and political environment. The area of Beyoglu, across the Golden Horn from the old city of Istanbul, came to be partly given over to westerners.[55] Consulates and embassies, containing a variety of functions, were built there, as well as hotels, an opera house, and Christian chapels of various denominations once the Sultan liberalised prohibitions on the creation of non-Muslim institutions. This area supposedly became the engine for the modernisation of the empire and its orientation towards Western European powers, notably Prussia (later Germany), France and Britain. The buildings were consequently (at least initially) in western styles.

Territories in the Levant and North-East Africa became protectorates and mandates in the British Empire in the twentieth century, but they were never fully-fledged colonies. Egypt was clearly exceptionally important on the route both to India and as a staging post up the Nile into the interior of Africa. Although from 1882, after the British invasion and defeat of the nationalist Urubi Pasha, it was known as the 'veiled protectorate' of the British Empire, ruled by the British in all but formal name, it was officially proclaimed a protectorate only between 1914 and 1922. Nevertheless, a significant British community established itself there and inevitably created the buildings expected of an imperial territory, not least one that combined key economic and strategic functions with tourism, including clubs, hotels, barracks, hospitals, schools, cathedrals and churches.

These appeared in the major cities of Cairo and Alexandria, as well as other significant settlements like Port Said, Port Suez and Luxor. To some extent they became hot spots of resistance, since nationalist politicians and the public who supported them often seemed keen to destroy the structures that symbolised alien rule and influence.

In the first half of the nineteenth century, the Egyptian ruler Muhammad Ali was sufficiently anxious to 'modernise' his country along western lines in order to protect its independence, unrealistically as it turned out, that he permitted westerners to occupy their own areas and buildings in Alexandria. One square of the city (the Maydan al-Tahrir) was laid out to achieve these objectives. The British were far from being alone; indeed the buildings were often designed by Italian and other European architects and sometimes both supervisory and artisan expertise was imported. In the Islamic world, alien multi-use structures were known as *okelles*. According to Crinson, such *okelles* might have 'a café, a theatre, a hotel, shops, and a European post office'.[56] Commercial activities would be pursued on the ground floor, with hotel and other residential spaces on the upper floors. With growing self-confidence, or an increasingly permissive approach on the part of rulers, such functions would eventually move into separate buildings. Plans for a British consulate in Alexandria went through a whole sequence of design proposals, but it was never built since it was realised that the centre of gravity was moving to Cairo.[57] Cairo then became the main site of western buildings, not only consulates, but also hotels, clubs, sporting provision, Christian churches, the opera house and other structures associated with the familiar comforts of western expatriates. Soon consulates of the various European powers spread across the Middle East and invariably contained the complete requirements for expatriate communities, including, for example, a post office, a chapel, residential and reception areas, as well as a court and jail cells to deal with aspects of territoriality. Europeans were also penetrating Palestine and in particular Jerusalem and were soon negotiating to build churches and hospitals, in this case for cultural and evangelical reasons rather than commercial ones. As well as evangelising efforts to convert Jews, 'Holy Land' tourism was becoming increasingly significant, particularly as developed by Thomas Cook after 1869.[58] Other denominations and elements of the 'four nations' of the British Isles also became highly active, with a greater range of Protestant churches, missions and hospitals being established.[59] The Scottish Mission to the Jews, for example, planned to create a new Christian Israel in the Middle East, founding missions in Istanbul and the Levant. By the 1880s, however, the Scots had abandoned missions in Damascus, Aleppo and Beirut and were concentrating on Palestine with missions in Galilee, establishing a notable hospital in Tiberias. By the inter-war years, as detailed in Chapter 6, there was a Presbyterian church in Jerusalem commemorating Scottish soldiers killed in the region during the First World War.

In the Far East, both China and Japan had westerners, their commercial functions and their buildings, forced upon them. The 'treaty ports' were established in China after the Treaty of Nanking that concluded the first Opium War in 1842 and more were later conceded after 1860. There were also small leased territories to Russia, Germany, France and Britain. The most famous treaty port was Shanghai, where the area along the river bank, the Bund, became celebrated for its western buildings, commercial headquarters, customs offices, banks and other such structures. There were also concessionary areas for the residences of the westerners. In Japan, the treaty ports were established after the Americans forced open the country to western trade in the 1850s. The most celebrated of these became Nagasaki, the southern port where the Dutch had been permitted to maintain their 'factory' on Deshima Island during the closure of the country to westerners between the late seventeenth century and the mid-nineteenth. Nagasaki, despite the American atomic bomb (which missed the harbour area), has the best-preserved buildings of the international settlement, complete with the surviving former British consulate, the original branch of the Hong Kong and Shanghai Bank and the home of Robert Blake Glover (as well as many other residences and related buildings) in the 'Glover Garden'. Westerners in China and Japan made no concessions whatsoever to local styles and simply planted resolutely western buildings, sometimes classical in style, in this largely alien environment.

HILL STATIONS

Hill stations were somewhat unreal environments, semi-urban zones that were socially and racially exclusive. Wholly new towns designed for bourgeois and upper-class enjoyment, they were supposed to provide intimations of home through softer climatic conditions. They offered rest and recreation supposedly insulated from the environmental conditions of the colony in which they were situated. They were generally established from scratch, with no pre-existing indigenous settlement or economic rationale, at least initially. Yet hill stations were not unique to the British Empire. The Dutch had established Buitenzorg

(Bogor) as a hill station in Java as early as 1808 (it had earlier origins in the mid-eighteenth century), while the Spanish in the Philippines had created a sanatorium at La Trinidad.[60] After the Spanish-American war of 1898, the Americans decided to establish a hill station at Baguio in the Philippines in the early years of the twentieth century, building an exceptionally expensive road to access it as well as a mansion for the Governor-General.[61] About the same time, the French set about creating a hill station at Dalat (Da Lat), 1,500 metres above sea level, in Vietnam. Bogor, Baguio and Da Lat have all become extensive urban settlements, in the case of Bogor with a population of almost a million. It has even been suggested that Srinagar in Kashmir was in effect a hill station for the Mughals.[62]

In the Anglophone world, hill stations are principally associated with British India, where Simla and Mussoorie dated their origins to 1819 and 1826 with a large number developed from the 1840s, but they existed in many other colonies and imperial territories, including Ceylon, Malaya, West Africa and Australia. Even the Peak in Hong Kong[63] and the higher suburb of Bukit Timah in Singapore[64] functioned as quasi-hill stations, as did higher and cooler spots in southern and eastern Africa. The leading historian of Indian hill stations, Dane Kennedy, has seen them as 'sites of refuge and sites for surveillance', where the British were able both to 'engage with and to disengage from' their alien empire in India.[65] Simla and Ootacamund (both at altitudes of almost 7,500 feet) and the other hill stations offered an escape from discomfort, illness and homesickness, 'an opiate for the pressures of rule'.[66] This was soon justified by the formulation of what have been called ethno-medical theories suggesting that the British were constitutionally unsuited to life in the heat of the plains (although many perforce had to endure conditions there). The hill stations were places which subverted the normal demographics of India, such that European women often predominated over men, while whites at least appeared to be in a majority compared with Indians. If the theories particularly applied to women (notably when pregnant), they were also significant for children such that hill stations became the locations of many schools and orphanages.

Often starting out as sanatoria, places where imperial rulers and members of the military could escape the medical dangers of plains and cities for the restoration of health (an ambition not always fulfilled, as the local cemeteries indicate), they became centres of hot-weather government and destinations for sport and recreation, not least in intense socialising. A few remained primarily military in their tone while others were used by white plantation workers in, for example, tea-planting regions in Sylhet and Assam, in North-East India, the one area where there was a significant economic rationale. They therefore combined official and private functions. They were intended to be a picturesque quasi-cantonment at a higher altitude, designed particularly for European occupation. Their visitors pursued a model of dual residence (common among the wealthier classes in Britain) in order to mitigate a profound sense of exile. Intended for social–recreational objectives, they often became places in which significant government functions, meetings and diplomatic encounters took place as a result of the arrival of governors and their retinues of officials. But as always, racial 'disengagement' was never fully possible since imperial whites required servants as well as institutions and modes of transport that would employ indigenous people in a variety of menial capacities, including of course the provision of rickshaws (drawn by human motive power) and tongas (light carriages drawn by ponies). Large numbers of messengers and also a police force were required for the comfort, activities and protection of the white inhabitants. Given those opportunities for employment, an indigenous population was soon encouraged to arrive, generally creating their own living quarters as well as the inevitable trading bazaar. Hill stations were designed to be places of temporary residence during the hot season, but a more permanent white population settled in order to run hotels, the post and telegraph office, club, church, town hall and library as well as places of entertainment. The larger hill settlements would boast a printing press and a local newspaper. In India, there were four principal regions of hill stations: the North-West, with a long line in the Himalayan foothills stretching from Murree (now in Pakistan) through the modern states of Jammu and Kashmir and Himachal Pradesh; those in the North-East, of which Darjeeling is the most celebrated, and some of them in Bangladesh; those in Maharashtra serving Bombay, notably Matheran and Mahabaleshwa; finally, the group in the South, in Tamil Nadu and Kerala, including Ootacamund.[67] The major hill stations, Ootacamund and Simla being the most celebrated, combined most of their key institutions and characteristics.

Ootacamund or 'Ooty' was the first to be identified as a potentially healthy upland sanatorium between 1819 and 1821 when the Collector of Coimbatore, John Sullivan, visited the area and recognised its potential. Sullivan became its entrepreneur, urging on the building of bungalows, of a hospital and the development of English gardens. It occupied a site only slightly lower than Simla, but was regarded as particularly English because of its softly rolling hills and the opportunities it afforded for hunting of jackals with dogs and for riding on the downs. In 1826, the Governor of Madras, Sir Thomas Munro, visited and shortly afterwards it was officially declared a sanatorium. Very soon Ooty began to acquire standard hill-station characteristics with the opening of a botanic garden (a gardener travelled there from Kew), the building of St Stephen's Anglican Church, Gothic with pinnacles, in 1831, and of course a club. The building of the church was initiated by the Governor, Stephen Lushington, who inhabited a porticoed mansion built by a wealthy businessman from Hyderabad, Sir William Rumbold.[68] This building later became the club, indicating how important this ubiquitous institution was in any imperial settlement. A grand mansion for the Governor of Madras was begun in 1877, with its later portico allegedly modelled on Stowe in Buckinghamshire, the English home of the Governor, the Duke of Buckingham and Chandos. When the Viceroy Lytton visited Ooty with the Duke, he initially had a poor impression because he had a headache and it was pouring with rain. But when the sky cleared on the following day, he proclaimed it 'to be paradise. The road was muddy, but such beautiful English mud. Imagine a combination of Hertfordshire lanes, Devonshire downs, Westmorland lakes and Scottish trout streams.'[69] The railway reached Ooty in 1902, rendering it readily accessible, including to modern tourists.[70] Ooty developed a different social tone from Simla, although the Governor of Madras did withdraw there for several months of the year. It was felt, for example, that Simla was rather too high and mighty for a mere district officer or Collector to partake of its physical and architectural charms.[71] They preferred Naini Tal or Darjeeling, where they could feel more socially at ease.

As part of their restorative, therapeutic function, hill stations were intended to offer reminders of 'home', in their architecture, their gardens, their flowers and their public institutions. The irony is that this could embrace an immense assortment of architectural styles, including Gothic, Renaissance, Jacobean, Swiss and Bavarian mixed with both colonial and Himalayan forms. Some of the flowers supposedly reminiscent of home were in fact exotica that had arrived in Britain (rhododendrons are a good example) from the Himalayas. All this was intended to maintain the identity of the imperial overlords and yet it was impossible to avoid the fact that they were distinctively Indian, in their stunning scenery, their flora and fauna (such as deodar trees, ubiquitous monkeys, sambar and other deer, even bears), and of course in the presence of so many Indians generally performing menial functions. The somewhat overheated social life of hill stations became notorious, as satirised by Kipling through his leading character, the meaningfully named Mrs Hauksbee, in *Plain Tales from the Hills*.

Nevertheless, at least as a young man, Kipling liked Simla, which he described in 1885 as offering 'as much riding, waltzing, dining out and concerts in a week as I should get in a lifetime at home'.[72] It is not surprising that Simla was liked and loathed in equal measure. It had in effect been founded in the early 1820s by the Agent to the hill states, Captain Kennedy, when he decided to build a house there, and visits by senior officials soon followed. The Governor-General, Lord William Bentinck, came in the 1830s (and Bentinck Castle was built as his residence),[73] as did his successor Lord Auckland, on a visit famously described by his sister Emily Eden. Such visits tended to be intermittent and informal until it was officially declared to be the summer capital of British India in 1864. After that the Viceroy withdrew there for six months of every year, causing the migration of hundreds of officials into the hills to keep the wheels of administration turning. It also became the summer capital of the Lieutenant Governor of the Punjab. Once Simla had reached this official status, there was inevitably a considerable building boom. By that time there was a fairly strict separation between the European houses on the higher ground above the ridge (which became the celebrated promenading mall), with its shops and public buildings, and the Lower Bazaar, cascading down the slopes where Indians lived and traded. Indeed, major clearance had occurred in order to create this racial separation. The British were also not very keen on the notion that Indian princely rulers might also use Simla, and banned sales of major houses to them on two occasions. Nevertheless, by the 1920s, that battle had been lost and wealthy and aristocratic Indians had arrived in some numbers. Throughout the British occupation of Simla, its 'otherworldliness' was mitigated by the manner in which the security of the area continued to be a priority. No fewer than three military cantonments were built within easy reach: Jutogh in 1843, Dagshai in 1847 and Solan in 1861.

The early buildings in Simla were built in what became known as 'Simla style', largely of a wooden frame, packed with earth and gravel, a technique known as *dhajji*.[74] Roofs were invariably of corrugated iron. Later, the public buildings came to be built of imported iron and of locally produced concrete. Until the later years of the century, all these buildings were created by either military or PWD engineers. They had to use their engineering skills to cope with very difficult sites and uneven ground. Christ Church, the Anglican church dominating the end of the Mall,[75] designed in a Tudor style by Major Boileau, a military engineer, was built between 1841 and 1856, when it was taken over as a government building. The clock tower and porch were added in succeeding decades.

Christ Church and the open ground outside it became vital to British imperial rituals, military church parades and other ceremonies. Government buildings such as the Secretariat and the army headquarters were soon constructed, and an impressive bank and post office, the latter with balconies, were located on the Mall. A vast town hall was built in a Gothic style in 1887–88 near the church. It was strikingly multi-purpose, containing spaces for a variety of functions such as meetings, balls, dinners, receptions and exhibitions, as well as a masonic hall, a police station and a library. Famously, the town hall's architecture was not admired and when it became structurally unsound few regretted its dismantling before the First World War, although the Gaiety Theatre survived.[76] It had been designed by the engineer Henry Irwin, who was appointed superintendent of works of the Simla area and proceeded to design many of the principal buildings, including the Viceregal Lodge of 1888.[77] Once the full panoply of telegraphic communications reached Simla in the 1880s, there was a wooden telegraph office, also by Irwin, later dismantled, when John Begg, consultant architect to the government of India, designed a grander telegraph building. The completion of the Kalka–Simla railway (the lines had reached Kalka some years earlier) in 1903 greatly facilitated the transport of people, mails and other goods. As Simla became increasingly busy, there was yet another holiday home used by the viceroys, the Retreat at Mashobra, just a few miles away.[78] Railways reached Darjeeling (1881) and the Bombay hill station, Matheran (1907).

In Sri Lanka, the traditional capital, Kandy, was regarded as having a much more agreeable climate compared with the coast, but the British chose Nuwara Eliya, at over 6,000 feet, as a hill station. Its potential was first spotted by Samuel Baker in 1846 and it became known, like so many others, as 'Little England', developing the usual buildings such as the governor's residence, the hill club, the golf club and course, the church, post office, public park and many hotels and bungalows. Today it is used by Sri Lankan visitors and people from the Gulf states seeking somewhere cooler to take a holiday. Further east, the colony of Malaya, its economy driven by rubber plantations and tin mining, eventually produced several hill stations. The first is often said to have been Penang Hill, which became a nearby place of retreat soon after the annexation of Penang by Francis Light in 1786. The British built summer homes, often grand in scale, and were eventually joined by wealthy Chinese businessmen. Access was made even easier by the building of a funicular railway opened in 1923. Other hill stations included Maxwell Hill, founded around 1884, Fraser's Hill (which, despite its Scottish name, was known as 'Little England') and the Cameron Highlands, which was surrounded by tea estates. These were all characterised by summer homes, hotels and the inevitable club, some of them half-timbered in an English style and with such characteristic additions as clock towers (in Fraser's Hill still standing on a roundabout). Intriguingly, as in India, these hill stations have been taken over by Malaysians in modern times, and a new hill station was created at the Genting Highlands, close to Kuala Lumpur, as late as 1971. Hill stations, with their cooler weather, cloud, mist and rain, have become chic, pleasant recreational retreats for a postcolonial Malaysian bourgeoisie.

To a certain extent, this is also true of Myanmar/Burma, which had its own celebrated hill stations. In a strikingly hot country, these were again places of retreat for the British, from the Commissioner, later Governor, downwards, seeking cooler temperatures during the hottest months. The two principal hill stations (there were several others) in Burma were Maymyo (now Pyin Oo Lwin, though most locals still call it Maymyo) and Kalaw, both in the Shan Hills. Maymyo is at a height of 3,500 feet above sea level while Kalaw is somewhat higher, at over 4.200 feet, according to the sign at the railway station. These two hill stations bear most of the marks of the equivalents in India and Ceylon: railway lines to access them, hotels, appealing holiday homes, churches, educational institutions, hospitals, military sanatoria and gardens (in the case of Maymyo a strikingly attractive national botanic garden, partly laid out by Turkish prisoners during the First World War). In Maymyo, the horse-drawn carriages which contributed to the atmosphere of the town remain active, partly as a tourist attraction, although it would seem that the opportunities for various entertainments so prized by the British have largely disappeared. There are striking survivals of colonial houses (including one with the very Scottish name of Candacraig, formerly owned by one of the Wallace brothers, president of the Bombay Burmah trading corporation) and public buildings in both towns. In Maymyo, the governor's summer residence has been rebuilt, having been damaged during the war by locals, either as a nationalist statement in defiance of the British or to frustrate the Japanese.[79] It was built in 1903 and was used by the Commissioner, then the Governor, for three months each year. The Centre of Maymyo has a striking clock tower, built in 1934–35, donated by a lawyer from Mandalay called Purcell, concerned to see that his imperial patriotism (and sense of discipline) should be given tangible form. Nan Dar Street was formerly Downing Street and the Chief Secretary lived at number ten, which must have caused some amusement in colonial times. As elsewhere, the atmosphere of the colonial hill station undoubtedly survives.

23 Candacraig, Maymyo, Burma

On another continent, there was a hill station above Freetown in Sierra Leone, which boasted the inevitable club as well as colonial houses raised on stilts, presumably to protect them from termites and to permit the circulation of cooling winds.[80] The higher altitudes of Kenya and Southern Rhodesia were regarded as particularly suitable for white settlement, while additional resorts in these territories were established in Naivasha (almost 1,500 feet higher than Nairobi) and in the (now Zimbabwean) Eastern Highlands close to the Mozambique border. Mineral-spring spas were regularly advertised as health resorts for whites in South Africa.[81] One example is Caledon in the Cape, founded in 1811, where the white and Coloured (mixed-race) populations still (2019) constitute a considerably higher proportion than in the country as a whole. Other places regarded as high-altitude resorts include Ifrane in the Middle Atlas Mountains in Morocco (founded by the French),[82] Jos in Nigeria, Fort Portal in Uganda and Troodos and Platres in Cyprus.[83] In Jamaica, the military sanatorium of Newcastle in the Blue Mountains was founded in 1841, when General Gomm was horrified at the numbers of deaths of troops in the island. It has remained a military base to this day.[84] However, although there was a coffee plantation there, the station did not develop into a civilian settlement as other military hill stations tended to do.

Meanwhile, the ruling, professional and commercial elites of Australia also decided that a retreat in the hot weather would reduce the discomforts of living at lower altitudes near the coast, where the principal cities and colonial (later state) capitals were located. The Australian colonies had a number of connections with India, through trade, horse breeding for the extensive demands of the Indian cavalry regiments and as a place of retirement. They consequently created hill resorts that were, in effect, modelled on the Indian predecessors. These included Mount Macedon and Upper Macedon in Victoria, a retreat from Melbourne, founded in the 1870s with a number of grand homes, some in Arts and Crafts style, and extensive gardens. In South Australia, Mount Barker and Stirling in the Adelaide Hills and Mount Lofty nearer the coast offered retreats from Adelaide. In 1876–79 the Governor, Sir William Jervois, a Royal Engineer more famous for designing military fortifications, decided to build a summer retreat at Marble Hill, 2,000 feet higher than Adelaide itself. This was built in Scottish baronial style and survived until destroyed in a bush fire in 1955, after which it was abandoned.[85] Katoomba in the Blue Mountains and a few spots in the Southern Highlands in New South Wales performed the same function. Once again, the 'stations' came to boast grand residences, gardens and a few public buildings. In Queensland, the equivalent was Toowoomba in the Darling Downs.[86] Elsewhere, as in many hot parts of the world, altitude was invariably the prerogative of social status. In Mauritius, 'no one lives in Port Louis who is rich enough to have a house in the surrounding hills'.[87] Hill stations were thus a climatic and architectural phenomenon in many parts of the British Empire (as well as other empires), offering opportunities for residences that adopted styles that were reminiscent of 'home', even if in Asian-inspired bungalows with concessions to both climate and, in some places, local indigenous forms. They were distinctive settlements because they were often founded from scratch in relatively uninhabited areas. In some places, indigenous people were simply dispossessed. Many were creations of state authorities in order to afford comforts (and the restoration of health) for their troops and administrators. In all of them, the built environment was supplied with the requisite structures to achieve these ends, including barracks, hospitals, schools, hotels, homes for administrators and other visitors as well as opportunities for obsessive recreation. Originally intended as white enclaves with indigenous servants and other supporting staff, they have now been largely taken over by indigenous populations, both as permanent residents and as holiday (mainly elite) visitors.

NOTES

1 Both E.G. Wakefield and John Stuart Mill thought in these terms. See Duncan Bell, *Reordering the World* (Princeton, NJ, 2016), p. 219.
2 The settlement was arranged by the governor in a manner appropriate to the British origins of the settlers, with Scots in the north! John M. MacKenzie with Nigel R. Dalziel, *The Scots in South Africa: Ethnicity, Identity, Gender and Race, 1772–1914* (Manchester, 2007), pp. 48–59.
3 Heather Streets, *Martial Races: The Military, Race and Masculinity in British Imperial Culture 1857–1914* (Manchester, 2004). Martial race theory allegedly embraced both Europeans and indigenous in an environmental synergy. As Kipling's Private Mulvaney remarks in the short story 'With the Main Guard' (1888), 'Scotchies an' Gurkys are twins' (i.e. Scotsmen and Gurkhas).
4 As an example, in Salisbury, Southern Rhodesia (Harare, Zimbabwe), the white areas lay to the north of the city centre; the African to the south on the other side of the railway tracks and station.
5 G.A. Bremner, '"Some Imperial Institute": Architecture, Symbolism and the Ideal of Empire in late Victorian Britain, 1887 – 1893', *Journal of the Society of Architectural Historians*, 62, 1 (March 2003), pp. 50–73.
6 Arindam Dutta, '"Strangers at the Gates": Public Works and Industrial Art Reform' in Peter Scriver and Vokramaditya Prakash (eds), *Colonial Modernities: Building, Dwelling and Architecture in British India and Ceylon* (London, 2007), pp. 93–114.
7 James Gibbs (1682–1754), a Scottish Catholic, was influential in creating an architecture which represented a mixture of Baroque and Palladian elements. He designed a large number of churches and public buildings, as well as city and country houses. His *A Book of Architecture*, published in London in 1728, contained plans of churches, and there were many other pattern books which became influential in designs in the British Empire.
8 G.A. Bremner, *Imperial Gothic: Religious Architecture and High Anglican Culture in the British Empire, c. 1840–1870* (New Haven, CT, 2013).
9 An introduction to Indo-Saracenic can be found in Philip Davies, *Splendours of the Raj: British Architecture in India 1660–1947* (London, 1985), chapter 8, 'Saracenic Dreams'. See also chapters 3 and 4 of Thomas R. Metcalf, *An Imperial Vision: Indian Architecture and Britain's Raj* (London, 1989); Preeti Chopra, 'South and South-East Asia' in G.A. Bremner (ed.), *Architecture and Urbanism in the British Empire* (Oxford, 2016), particularly pp. 303–310.
10 Jan Morris with Simon Winchester, *Stones of Empire: The Buildings of the Raj* (Oxford, 1983). Morris brings an ironic and typically eccentric tone to bear on Indo-Saracenic.

11 Thomas Metcalf called it 'mix and match' architecture, a matter of manipulation rather than re-creation. Metcalf, *Imperial Vision*, p. 86.
12 Bindu Singhal, 'Glimpses of Indo-Saracenic Architecture', *Architecture and Design*, 17, 5 (Sept./Oct. 2000), pp. 98–101. Charles Mant also designed, among other buildings, the palace at Kolhapur.
13 Metcalf, *Imperial Vision*.
14 Ibid., pp. 100–101.
15 Swati Chattopadhyay and Jeremy White (eds), *City Halls and Civic Materialism: Towards a Global History of Urban Public Space* (London, 2014), introduction.
16 Geoffrey Moorhouse, *Calcutta: The City Revealed* (Harmondsworth, 1974), pp. 241–242.
17 Davies, *Splendours of the Raj*, p. 70. Davies suggested that the building was scheduled for demolition, but this does not appear to have happened. See http://noisebreak.com/heritage-buildings-colonial-calcutta-town-hall/ (accessed 20 March 2018).
18 See, for example, J.P. Losty, *Calcutta, City of Palaces: A Survey of the City in the Days of the East India Company, 1690–1858* (London, 1990).
19 These were concerned with aspects of legal equality, as between Europeans and Indians.
20 Swati Chattopadhyay, 'Politics, Planning and Subjection: Anticolonial Nationalism and Public Space in Colonial Calcutta' in Chattopadhyay and White (eds), *City Halls*, pp. 199–216.
21 Davies, *Splendours of the Raj*, p. 100. See also www.victorianweb.org/history/empire/india/99.html (accessed 20 March 2018).
22 Davies, *Splendours of the Raj*, p. 100.
23 Preeti Chopra, 'The Bombay Town Hall: Engaging the Function and Quality of Public Space, 1811–1918' in Chattopadhyay and White (eds), *City Halls*, pp. 158–176.
24 Hamida Khuhro and Anwer Mooraj (eds), *Karachi: Megacity of Our Times* (Oxford, 2010), pp. 48–49.
25 Jenny Gregory, 'Town Halls in Australia: Sites of Conflict and Consensus' in Chattopadhyay and White (eds), *City Halls*, pp. 115–135.
26 http://vhd.heritagecouncil.vic.gov.au/places/813/download-report (accessed 10 February 2018).
27 Philip Goad, *Melbourne Architecture* (Sydney, 1999), p. 41.
28 Gregory, 'Town Halls', p. 115.
29 Garth Andrew Myers, 'Moving Beyond Colonialism: Town Halls in Sub-Saharan Africa's Postcolonial Capitals' in Chattopadhyay and White (eds), *City Halls*, pp. 237–254.
30 In 2013, at the time of the bicentennial of the birth of David Livingstone, I delivered a lecture in the council chamber of the Livingstone Town Hall, Zambia, a town hall much like any British one.
31 There are now legislatures in Nunavut and the Yukon, in contemporary styles.
32 The State Heritage Register of New South Wales indicates that when the governor failed to secure funding for his hospital in London, he raised the money from three businessmen who were given the right to import rum into the colony. The resulting

building was then known as 'the Rum Hospital'. www.environment.nsw.gov.au/heritageapp/ViewHeritageItemDetails.aspx?ID=2423805 (accessed 28 July 2018).

33 www.parliament.qld.gov.au/explore/history/parliament-house/new-parliament-house (accessed 9 February 2018).
34 It had a chequered building history, being started by Thomas Turnbull, who resigned when the plans were changed, and completed by John Campbell, the government architect. The New Zealand Register of Historic Places describes it as 'one of New Zealand's architectural treasures'. www.heritage.org.nz/the-list/details/217 (accessed 8 February 2018).
35 www.heritage.org.nz/the-list/details/223 (accessed 8 February 2018). The New Zealand Register of Historic Places regrets the lack of architectural coherence of the ensemble, but sees the building as reflecting the emergence of the new Dominion (announced only a few months before the fire) and matching the neo-Baroque buildings to be found elsewhere in the former British Empire. It cites Alberta, New Delhi and Canberra.
36 The parliament buildings are closing in 2018 for major renovations, perhaps for as long as a decade.
37 John McQuarrie (ed.), *The Hill/ La Colline* (Ottawa, 2015). See also Anthony Waldron, *Exploring the Capital: An Architectural Guide to the Ottawa-Gatineau Region* (Vancouver, 2017), pp. 6–9.
38 This building still stands and is a UNESCO World Heritage Site. The proclamation by the Duke of York, the future George V, is commemorated in a striking painting by Tom Roberts.
39 Christopher W. London, *Bombay Gothic* (Mumbai, 2002), pp. 52–54.
40 Waldron, *Exploring the Capital*, pp. 13–14.
41 The Legislative Assembly meets on the ground floor and the Supreme Court above, which runs contrary to the concept of the Assembly handing down the laws.
42 Joyce Gordon, *Nevis: Queen of the Caribees* (Oxford, 2005), p. 12.
43 The Great Exhibition building of 1851 was itself a triumph of iron and glass, to which it owed the speed of its erection.
44 Paul Dobraszczyk and Peter Sealy (eds), *Function and Fantasy: Iron Architecture in the Long Nineteenth Century* (Abingdon, 2016). See chapters 5–8 by Jonathan Clarke, Lucia Juarez, Elizabeth Pigou-Dennis and Anne Warr, dealing respectively with iron building exports to Argentina, Jamaica and Australia. See also Lucia Juarez, 'Trading Nations: Architecture, Informal Empire and the Scottish Cast Iron Industry in Argentina', *Architecture Beyond Europe*, 13 (2018), which deals with three Scottish iron foundries, Carron, Saracen and Lion; and Juarez, 'Documenting Scottish Architectural Cast Iron in Argentina', *Architecture Beyond Europe, 5 (2014)*.
45 Andrew Hassam, 'Portable Iron Structures and Uncertain Colonial Spaces at the Sydenham Crystal Palace' in Felix Driver and David Gilbert (eds), *Imperial Cities* (Manchester, 1999), pp. 174–175. Three of these survive in the care of the National Trust for Victoria. See www.nationaltrust.org.au/places/portable-iron-houses/ (accessed 14 May 2019). One of these was by the major company E.T. Bellhouse of Manchester.

46 E. Graeme Robertson and Joan Robertson, *Cast Iron Decoration: A World Survey* (London, 1977), pp. 56–64.
47 It was sold for a considerable sum as recently as 2012, exciting a number of articles in the Australian press.
48 The Glasgow Saracen works, for example, continued to be active throughout the inter-war years of the twentieth century, but went into steep decline after the Second World War, as a result of the loss of empire trades and of major changes in fashion.
49 An ex-tea planter once forcibly pointed this out to me during a lecture on imperial architecture.
50 A good example comes from the experiences of the Scottish tea planter, James Taylor, in Ceylon. See Angela McCarthy and T.M. Devine, *Tea and Empire: James Taylor in Victorian Ceylon* (Manchester, 2017), p. 99. Taylor was given plans from which to construct his own bungalow, but he cheerfully deviated from these in order to build something more to his liking. He commented on the extreme simplicity of the workers' accommodation on the plantation, contrasting with the more commodious planter accommodation.
51 Taylor, for example, brought various ideas with him from Scotland, in the building of dry-stone dikes or in creating water channels for irrigation. McCarthy and Devine, *Tea and Empire*, p. 107. It is also thought that Taylor may have constructed a fireplace and hearth on the model that he was used to in the Mearns area of Scotland. Ibid., pp. 188–189.
52 For development of these ideas, see John M. MacKenzie, 'Missionaries, Science and the Environment in Nineteenth-Century Africa' in Andrew Porter (ed.), *The Imperial Horizons of British Protestant Missions, 1880–1914* (Grand Rapids, MI, 2003), pp. 105–130, particularly 115–116.
53 The effects of such migration on the city of Lahore have been charted in Ian Talbot and Tahir Kamran, *Colonial Lahore* (London, 2016).
54 Julius Bryant and Susan Weber (eds), *John Lockwood Kipling: Arts and Crafts in the Punjab and London* (New Haven, CT, 2017), the catalogue of an exhibition at the V&A Museum, London and the Bard Graduate Centre, New York. See especially chapters 4–8 and 16–17.
55 Mark Crinson, *Empire Building: Orientalism and Victorian Architecture* (London 1996), chapter 5.
56 Ibid., p. 173.
57 Ibid., chapter 6. Crinson's conclusions about difficulties of building in the region and the length of time taken in construction relate only to larger and more prestigious structures, particularly religious ones. Other buildings, including for example hotels, seem to have been less problematic.
58 Cook invariably combined tours to Egypt and up the Nile with visits to Palestine. Piers Brendon, *Thomas Cook: 150 Years of Popular Travel* (London, 1991), chapter 7.
59 Crinson's work is Anglocentric, but see also Michael Marten, *Attempting to Bring the Gospel Home: Scottish Missions to Palestine, 1839–1917* (London, 2006). The Scottish Mission to the Jews was active over a long period. See also George Adam Smith, *The*

Historical Geography of the Holy Land (London, 1901) and W.P. Livingstone, *A Galilee Doctor: Being a Sketch of the Career of Dr. D.W. Torrance of Tiberias* (London, 1923).

60 Pamela Kanwar, *Imperial Simla: The Political Culture of the Raj* (New Delhi, 1990), p. 35.
61 Anthony D. King, *Colonial Urban Development* (London, 1976), p. 41.
62 Ibid., p. 158.
63 The governor of Hong Kong had a residence there from the late 1860s, and many of the wealthy businessmen of the colony built homes above the hurly-burly of the city and harbour of Victoria.
64 Bukit Timah Hill was first recognised in the 1840s and came to have high-value residences, many educational institutions and the Singapore racecourse.
65 Dane Kennedy, *Magic Mountains: Hill Stations and the British Raj* (Berkeley, CA, 1996), p. 1.
66 Raaja Bhasin, *Simla: The Summer Capital of India* (New Delhi, 1992), p. xii.
67 Vikram Bhatt, *Resorts of the Raj* (Ahmedabad, 1998) provides a useful map, pp. 10–11. This book also contains some beautiful modern photographs. Bhatt includes 91 hill stations, though Kennedy suggests only 65, excluding cities. King numbers 80 at elevations over 4,000 feet. J.E. Spencer and W.L. Thomas identified a total of 115 hill stations in Asia. Spencer and Thomas, 'The Hill Stations and Summer Resorts of the Orient', *Geographical Review*, 38, 4 (1948), pp. 637–651.
68 Mollie Panter-Downes, *Ooty Preserved: A Victorian Hill Station in India* (London, 1967), p. 33.
69 Lytton's description comes from a letter to his wife, Edith. Mary Lutyens, *The Lyttons in India: Lord Lytton's Viceroyalty* (London, 1979), p. 112.
70 Now known as Udagamandalam.
71 Dennis Kincaid, *British Social Life in India 1608–1937* (London, 1938), p. 223.
72 Bhasin, *Simla*, p. 64.
73 Bentinck also visited Ootacamund and in 1834 received his new legal adviser to the Governor-General's Council, Thomas Babington Macaulay, who disliked the place. Staying between June and September of that year, he found it dull and complained of incessant rain. Panter-Downes, *Ooty Preserved*, pp. 62–63.
74 This and later building techniques are described by Kanwar in a valuable afterword in *Imperial Simla*, pp. 296–301.
75 The original church was located in a billiard hall.
76 Kanwar, *Imperial Simla*, pp. 61–62 and 112–116.
77 Viceregal Lodge is now known as Rashrapati Niwas, occupied by the Indian Institute of Advanced Study. Raaja Bhasin, 'Viceregal Lodge and the Indian Institute of Advanced Study', pamphlet (Shimla, 2009).
78 Illustrations of some of the principal buildings of Simla, including the Retreat and the bazaar areas, can be found in Pat Barr and Ray Desmond, *Simla: A Hill Station in British India* (New York, 1978). Simla became a favourite subject of photographers working in India, including the celebrated Charles Bourne.
79 It was bought by the Htoop Foundation (which also owns the botanic gardens) and restored in 2005. See Chapter 8.

80 The hill-station railway closed in 1974 and the club and other buildings were damaged during the civil war and subsequent climatic disasters.
81 The *Union-Castle Line Guide to South and East Africa* (1911–12 edition), p. 219, and still being advertised in the *Union-Castle Line Guide to South and East Africa* (1948 edition), p. 173.
82 Ifrane is now a ski resort, frequented by the king, who has a royal palace there, and other members of the Moroccan elite.
83 For the significance of Troodos in the British administration of Cyprus, see Andrekos Varnava, *British Imperialism in Cyprus, 1878–1915: The Inconsequential Possession* (Manchester, 2009), pp. 210–211 and passim.
84 www.jdfweb.com/newcastle-base/ (accessed 10 February 2019).
85 Now part of a private estate and vineyard, the residence and its stables are being restored under a Heritage Agreement after sale by the National Trust of South Australia in 2009. The Duke and Duchess of Cornwall and York visited Marble Hill on their empire tour in 1901.
86 Andrea Scott Inglis, *Summer in the Hills: The Nineteenth-Century Mountain Resort in Australia* (Melbourne, 2007), based on a University of Melbourne Ph.D. thesis (2004), 'Claiming the Higher Ground: The Nineteenth-Century Hill Station in Australia as a Manifestation of Empire'.
87 Donald Mackenzie Wallace, *The Web of Empire* (London, 1902), p. 336. The royal party visiting in 1901 retreated to the Governor's residence in the hills, Le Réduit. Originally built as a fortress by the French in the mid-eighteenth century, it underwent many changes by the British and emerged in a neo-Georgian style.

4

Institutions of the bourgeois public sphere and new technologies

The principal social characteristic of the British Empire in the nineteenth century was the emergence and phenomenal growth of the bourgeoisie. From the point of view of whites in both the territories of settlement and in the dependent colonies, empire became essentially a middle-class phenomenon, brought into being by the growth of the capitalist world economy. If some, but by no means all, governors were aristocrats, as were some at least of the senior military officers (particularly before the Cardwell reforms of the 1870s promoted a more meritocratic system), the great majority of the growing cadre of officials, professionals and business people were bourgeois, people whose status was invariably acquired not through family background but through education and professional or commercial success. They translated to the empire the expectations they had developed in respect of the cities and towns of Britain. Indeed, it may be said that the combined effects of the industrial revolution and the resulting growth in commercial activity caused the bourgeoisie to expand in numbers so rapidly in Britain that the empire represented a necessary 'overspill' region for its activities. It was a class which serviced commercial and extractive industries throughout the colonies.[1] It may even be said that British universities, particularly the Scottish ones, were producing more graduates than could be employed in the metropolis, promoting graduate migration and the resulting growth in the professions. In imperial territories, the bourgeoisie soon became, at least partly, self-sustaining. This inevitably occurred initially in the settler territories, but also became a characteristic of Indian social change in the second half of the nineteenth century. These processes transferred to the West Indies and to West Africa in the twentieth century. At least for whites, this common adherence to a social class and its cultural affinities helped to create the networks which were important in exchanges of administrative, commercial and cultural forms.[2]

Family networks were also significant in developing these military and bourgeois connections across the empire, as illustrated in a number of recent works of 'microhistory' (mainly relating to the eighteenth century) which often illustrate 'macro' phenomena.[3] Such networks, connected through the key institutions and training within Britain, were also significant in the promotion of classic bourgeois professions such as architecture and engineering in relation to the built environment.[4]

Increasingly, the public sphere came to embrace what has been called 'the cultural apparatus of the bourgeoisie'[5] in the provision of libraries, museums, public parks and botanic gardens, public sporting and games provision, possibly zoological gardens, art galleries and halls for meetings, concerts, dances, dinners, exhibitions and other events, as well as the Christian churches surveyed in Chapter 6. To these we can add schools (with more buildings as primary education, at least for whites, became compulsory around the empire), universities and hospitals.[6] At the strictly gendered end of such provision we find the exclusively masculine clubs and masonic halls. Some of these building types within the fabric of towns and cities had emerged in the thirteen colonies of North America and in the Caribbean islands at an earlier date,[7] but they became the essential component of any self-respecting city and town in the colonies during the nineteenth century. Obviously, all of these had architectural expressions, often grand ones in the capitals and larger cities of empire, although they also appeared in more humble form in many smaller towns. The colonial middle class, far from being anti-intellectual, aspired to these key markers of status, without which no colony could feel that it had fully entered the modern world. While sports may have been seen as important for the preservation of health, class status and camaraderie, museums and libraries in particular were institutions that reflected the conferring of a mantle of learning, scientific modernity and culture to compete with the European world the colonial bourgeoisie had left behind. It is impossible to examine all of these in this chapter, but it will consider those that seemed to be most important for a colonial bourgeoisie.

Such buildings neatly represent the notion of the social production of the built environment as well as the dynamic in which 'built environments both represent and condition economies, societies and cultures'.[8] Nevertheless, such cultural productions in the built environment, together with the centres of civic power, were socially reconfigured in the imperial and colonial setting. It may be that in their original manifestation they were seen primarily as places of limited access by the male bourgeoisie. In the colonies that remained true, though the additional factors of race joined those of class and gender such that ritualised modes of behaviour were initially defined as racially exclusive. However, both social and racial exclusivity were broken down in an ideologically charged process of growing accessibility. In Britain, the engine for this was the notion of rational recreation, the belief that the working classes should be dissuaded from frequenting more rowdy pastimes in favour of forms of 'amusement' that would ultimately have an educational and improving character. To a certain extent this became true, in racial terms, in the colonies. There were of course many events, both social and cultural, that remained racially exclusive, sometimes almost throughout the colonial era, even if in many places there was limited access for indigenous people, particularly those from ruling groups or those who had achieved a western-style education. In a limited way, this became true of the bourgeois institutions, although private clubs and subscription libraries invariably maintained racial separation.

LIBRARIES AND MUSEUMS

The founding and development of libraries offered a key example of the growth of the public sphere in the bourgeois desire for the civilised institutions that would match (or outdo) the metropolitan world. Together with museums they symbolised the growth of science and learning, essential components of modernity, in colonial settings. They confirmed the emergence of significant cities with the full panoply of cultural bodies enshrined in notable buildings. Occasionally, the British took over an existing library, as they did in Valletta, Malta. There the Knights had been collecting books between the sixteenth and eighteenth centuries. A project to build a neoclassical library building was developed in the 1780s and was completed by 1796, though its opening was delayed by the French invasion. The British eventually (1891) placed a statue of Queen Victoria outside it, and the square became known as Piazza Regina.[9] The Library was thus located in a handsome (pre-British) building on a significant site of Malta's capital. Similarly, in Quebec there were libraries associated with religious and private institutions before the British conquest, but the development of public libraries in both Quebec and Ontario was very much associated with the appearance of mechanics' institutes.[10] There was a private subscription library located in Elmsley House in York (the original name of Toronto) from 1810, but this was clearly only available to an elite.[11] The association of libraries with private institutions was common. The Literary and Historical Society of

Quebec, an expression of Anglophone cultural dominance after the conquest, was founded in Quebec City in 1824, under the influence of Governor-General Dalhousie and prominent citizens. It was later associated with Morrin College, an Anglophone outrider from McGill University of Montreal, and moved into a former prison building (in an elegant Georgian style) opposite St Andrew's Church, where it exists, after many vicissitudes, to this day.[12] Many of its finest rare books and the documents the Society collected were passed on to other libraries or the Archives of Quebec, and the contents of its museum were also dispersed.[13] The York Mechanics Institute was founded in 1830, complete with library, changing its name to Toronto MI in 1834. By 1867 it had occupied an impressive building on the corner of Church and Adelaide streets, but by then there were local mechanics' institutes in other suburbs and towns of Ontario. There seems to have been a concentration on this localisation of library provision rather than the founding of grand central libraries, as in Australia. It was not, however, until 1882 that a Free Libraries Act was passed by the Ontario Legislature. This represented the relatively late development of free public libraries, funded by provincial or local governments in Canada.

Elsewhere, libraries often had similarly informal origins. While India had significant precolonial libraries, modern library provision is usually dated from the foundation of learned societies in the British period, including the Asiatic Society of Bengal, founded in 1784. This library still functions at 1 Park Street in Kolkata and is the forerunner of the modern library service throughout Bengal. Another survivor is the Library of the Bombay Asiatic Society, still to be found in the severely classical building of the old Town Hall. The founding of Indian universities in the late 1850s led to the creation of academic libraries, of which the grandest is perhaps the great Gothic building in Bombay. Since hill stations were intended as places of leisure, libraries were naturally founded in them, originally for the use of Europeans. The Simla library was in the old town hall, while that in Ootacamund, opened in a Gothic-style brick building in 1869 (though founded earlier), has become celebrated for its echoes of the colonial period.[14] Elsewhere, the founding of mechanics' institutes around the colonies of settlement continued to propagate the concept of the lending library. As in Ontario, these were often established in some of the smaller settlements, in Australia for example, as well as the larger cities.[15] As the need for libraries developed with what may be called the cultural maturity of the territory, significant governors and prominent local citizens were vital in founding them. An excellent example is the State Library of Victoria (as it is now). This library was effectively founded at the suggestion of Lieutenant Governor La Trobe and the judge Sir Redmond Barry (together with other leading citizens who formed the trustees).[16] Barry was also instrumental in the founding of the museum, the university and other Melbourne institutions. The library was proposed in 1853 and first opened in 1856 on one of the most important sites in the centre of the city. Its architect, Joseph Reed, also designed many of the other important buildings of the rapidly growing city. As the income from the Victoria goldfields flowed in it was greatly extended, acquiring a magnificent Corinthian portico in 1879 and a reading room under a dome in 1913, the latter accessed by a grand staircase of Sicilian marble. The classical frontage, with its wide flight of steps, was clearly intended to echo the façade of the British Museum in London's Bloomsbury, still at that time containing the most significant library in the empire. The domed reading room again echoed the old British Museum reading room, although in a more modern octagonal style, with exposed balcony floors almost giving the appearance of a theatre, perhaps a theatre of learning.[17] The message was clear, one that Melbourne rejoiced in issuing, that this new city in the southern hemisphere could match anything in the imperial northern metropole.[18]

The state library of New South Wales had a rather more chequered history, though by the early twentieth century it had become a major institution. It claimed to be the oldest library in Australia, tracing its origins to a private subscription library set up in 1826.[19] It declined to open itself up to a wider public and ran into severe financial difficulties. In 1869 it was purchased by the Government of New South Wales and established in a relatively modest building, albeit with a central position on the corner of Macquarie Street and Shakespeare Place. From there it grew, notably as a result of inheriting the major collections of David Scott Mitchell. The new building, opened in 1910 and designed by Walter Liberty Vernon, had an impressive presence overlooking the Royal Botanic Garden in a building with a dominant ionic portico and neoclassical wings, a style which seemed to have become the language of learning. It subsequently acquired another major collection, mainly of pictures and manuscripts, donated by Sir William Dixson. The South Australian library was actually conceived in London at the time of the planning of the colony in 1834 and the first collection of books was sent out in 1836.[20] This eventually became the Adelaide, then the State, Library and moved from the founding institute into its own building (originally also containing the museum) in 1884. By then building styles had changed and this was constructed in a banded neo-Romanesque, French Renaissance style, complete with a mansard roof containing an extra floor, with decorative window surrounds and ironwork on the ridges. In Perth, Western Australia, where such developments were often somewhat later than in earlier colonies, the major public library was eventually opened as a Jubilee project in 1887. In 1897 it moved into a building shared with the Museum and Art Gallery, later acquiring its own premises.[21]

The South African Library in Cape Town dates its origins to 1818, when the Governor Lord Charles Somerset imposed a wine tax, some of the proceeds of which were to be devoted to the establishment of a library. In 1761, a Dutch inhabitant of the Cape, Joachim Nicolaus von Dessin, had already left his major library to the Dutch Reformed Church to form a public collection, and this was later donated to the projected Somerset library in 1820. The library later flourished with the governorship of Sir George Grey. Grey had a remarkable career as a governor, in South Australia, the Cape and New Zealand, and as a politician in the latter colony. He was concerned to establish intellectual and cultural institutions in all these colonies, and when he left the Cape in 1861 he handed over 5,000 volumes of his own library (he later donated another collection in New Zealand). Under his direction, a building intended to contain both the library and the museum was designed by W.H. Köhler, supposedly based on the architectural model of the Fitzwilliam Museum in Cambridge. This was another example of a metropolitan model being used to indicate the cultural sophistication of a colony. Completed in 1859 in a choice position overlooking the Government Garden, it was opened in 1861 by Prince Alfred, Duke of Edinburgh. A statue of Grey was unveiled in front of it in 1864.[22] Very soon, the founding of universities and colleges produced further library provision, at least for the use of students and academics. Parliamentary libraries were founded in many of the colonial assemblies, initially for the use of parliamentarians, but often later opened to the public. In the case of the Gothic parliament building in Ottawa, the library was opened in 1876. The libraries of the legislatures of Upper and Lower Canada had originated in the 1790s, later amalgamated in 1841. But libraries were known to be vulnerable. In 1849, the legislature and library in Montreal had been burned down by rebels, destroying all but 200 of the holdings of 12,000 books. Perhaps it was because of this that, in a far-seeing arrangement, the new Ottawa library was placed in a separate structure at the back of the main parliament building. The first librarian, Alpheus Todd, insisted that it should have a metal fire door. It was built in a high Gothic style with buttresses over the terrace by the river, once again round like the British

Museum, with mezzanine stacks and with a white marble statue of Queen Victoria in the centre. When the parliament building was burned down in the disastrous fire of 1916, the library survived unscathed.[23]

One of the greatest fillips to the foundation of libraries in the British Empire came from the philanthropy of the Scottish-American industrialist Andrew Carnegie. Carnegie's setting aside of funds for libraries began in the 1880s and ended in 1919, although the greatest push came in the first two decades of the twentieth century. In that period, Carnegie money provided over 2,500 libraries worldwide. In the British Empire, no fewer than 125 were built in Canada, 111 in Ontario.[24] Eighteen were donated to various towns in New Zealand, twelve in South Africa, six in the Caribbean, four in Australia, one in Mauritius and another in the Seychelles. From these statistics it can be seen that the territories of white settlement were by far the biggest beneficiaries of the Carnegie largesse, but the reason for this is that communities had to apply for funds and had to agree to Carnegie's conditions (including agreement that the community would take on the costs of running and maintenance once the building had been supplied, and ensure that access to the library would be free). The libraries were generally, but not exclusively, built in a neoclassical style, usually from local materials.[25] In Ontario, New Zealand and South Africa, it is apparent that the Carnegie philanthropy was influential in the provision of library facilities in smaller settlements (sometimes in suburbs of the larger cities), and that his libraries partially influenced the architectural style of the colonial bourgeois sphere.

As in the case of Carnegie, many of the institutions of the public sphere were privately funded rather than publicly financed: they were founded by societies and sometimes by wealthy individuals, successful in colonial business. Museums constitute excellent examples of these developments. Their architecture can be seen as representing for Europeans the global march of the rational, of understanding of the natural world and of global cultures and ethnographies.[26] They became, in effect, archives of natural history and of human cultures (increasingly concentrating on the local as time went on). They invariably occupied choice locations in imperial and colonial cities and became closely connected with the foundation of universities (whose professors often maintained research connections with the museums). It was a development which took place across all parts of the British Empire. Calcutta's museum had its origins in the scholarly ambitions of the Asiatic Society of Bengal in the 1790s. The Society, its library and its museum moved to premises in Park Street, and after many vicissitudes it was decided that a grand imperial museum was required, built in the 1870s (opened in 1878) on Chowringhee Road, the principal thoroughfare facing the Maidan. In keeping with the overall form of the city, it is built in a neoclassical style with a strongly projecting porte cochère. The Literary Society of Madras (Chennai) was influential in proposing the foundation of a museum, partly to house its own collections, in 1851. It moved to its extensive site in Egmore in 1854 and progressively acquired a complex of buildings including the semicircular pantheon and several other structures, built in the Indo-Saracenic style which became characteristic of Madras in the period under the influence of Robert Fellowes Chisholm. These also housed a library, theatre and art gallery. Thus, the great collection of cultural institutions was gathered on one site, with a zoo developed in the grounds. In Bombay, the Victoria and Albert Museum (now the Bhau Daji Lad), looking like a fine neoclassical mansion, was opened in Byculla (originally an important area of the city) in 1872. Later, Bombay acquired the partly Indo-Saracenic Prince of Wales Museum (now the Chhatrapati Shivaji Maharaj Vastu), with a dome based upon one in Bijapur, completed during the First World War and opened in 1922. Its Scottish architect George Wittet was also working on the Gateway of India, the grand harbour arch commemorating the visit of George V and Queen Mary in 1911. Other museums were opened throughout the Subcontinent, including that in Lahore, originally founded in the 1860s and moved to its important location on the Mall in 1894, in a Baroque building with some concessions to Indian hybridity, designed by Ganga Ram. It is now the largest museum in Pakistan.

Many Indian princes also aspired to the creation of museums in their states, often significant buildings in their rapidly modernising capitals. This ambition reflected the manner in which the princes were keen to secure the approval of the British by adopting the supposedly socially improving institutions like museums, colleges and libraries, perhaps imagining that they were preparing their populations for a global technical and cosmopolitan modernity. One of the most striking of these is the extraordinary Albert Hall Museum in Jaipur. The foundation stone for this building was laid by Albert Edward, Prince of Wales, on his visit to India in 1876. Initially, the purpose of the building was subject to debate, including the possibility of its becoming a town hall. But eventually agreement was reached, enthusiastically endorsed by the Maharajah Sawai Madho Singh, that it should be a museum. The British doctor associated with the Maharajah's court, Dr Thomas Hendley, was a keen collector with an interest in crafts and in museums. He was ambitious to encourage the arts

The British Empire through buildings

24 Albert Hall Museum, Jaipur

and manufactures of Jaipur and held exhibitions to display these for the inspiration of craftspeople and the edification of visitors. By the time the museum opened in 1887, its purpose was clear. It was to display the arts of Jaipur in the context of those of other parts of India, and there would also be an attempt to contextualise them within the great civilisations of world history.[27] It would exhibit, for example, the products and craftsmanship inspired by the Jaipur Art School, one of the many educational reforms of the Maharajah, which he had opened in 1866.[28] Its creator was Sir Samuel Swinton Jacob, chief engineer of the Jaipur PWD, and his experience of designing the museum prompted him to initiate *The Jeypore Portfolio of Indian Architectural Details*, published in twelve volumes between 1890 and 1913. This was part of his desire to resurrect Indian craftsmanship, though it was a revival entirely seen through the eyes of the British. It may be that this publication served to turn such craftspeople into copyists rather than creators, quite the opposite of what he intended.[29] Nevertheless, the Jaipur Museum constitutes a striking example of Indo-Saracenic architecture.[30] It occupies a notable location at the end of an avenue leading from one of the

The bourgeois public sphere and new technologies

gates of the city. The museum was immediately popular with the people of Jaipur and remains so to this day.[31] Another example is the Napier Museum in Travancore, built by Robert Fellowes Chisholm in what he suggested was a suitably Travancore, Malabar Coast, style.[32] It was opened in 1880.

Ceylon was unusual in having a governor, Sir William Gregory, who was interested in museums (he had been a trustee of the British Museum), and he encouraged the creation of a museum in Colombo, an Italianate building with cooling open arcades on all sides, completed in 1876 and opened the following year. Museums soon proliferated throughout South-East Asia. The Singapore Museum was founded in 1877 and opened in a magnificent domed building, designed by the colonial architect Henry McCallum, in 1887. It has now been renovated and much extended as the national museum.[33] Most of these museums celebrated the sculpture, architecture, archaeology and arts of India and other Asian states, although the Madras Museum amassed one of the greatest collections of Roman artefacts outside Europe.

Museums were founded in the principal cities of Canada, with the Royal Ontario Museum eventually emerging as one of the most notable, perhaps the only one in the British Empire to aspire to the scale of the great museums of Europe. Its foundation was based upon the remarkable growth of Toronto

25 Colombo Museum, Ceylon

from a population of no more than 10,000 in 1834 to a great city of 375,000 in 1911. This growth was mirrored by the rapid emergence of scientific societies and educational institutions and to a certain extent its collections were helped by the series of exhibitions held in the city. Most colonial museums came to display principally local cultures, once their global aspirations had been curbed, but the Royal Ontario had wider ambitions, embracing displays of ancient, European and Asian materials. In this it was helped by its relative proximity to Europe, by the presence of a wealthy business class in the city, and by a buccaneering collector-curator, Charles Trick Curelly. It was opened in its new building on the present site in 1914 and later grew with many additions, including a recent one by Daniel Libeskind, which makes no concessions at all to the original architecture, yet opens up the museum to the city. Australian cities similarly produced museums and art galleries, such as the neoclassical museum at Hyde Park in Sydney, first opened in 1852 and extended in 1867. In Melbourne, the museum started its life in the university and only moved into the centre of town in 1905, eventually becoming a major presence behind the great Exhibition Building of 1880. In Adelaide, the bourgeois spirit was most effectively illustrated by the manner in which so many significant buildings in the city were arranged along North Terrace, on the edge of the slopes leading to the River Torrens. These eventually included the railway station, Government House, the old and new parliament buildings, the Institute, the state library and art gallery, the museum, the original campus of the university and the botanic garden. Few cities had such an agglomeration of political and cultural buildings strung out together. Several of these institutions were influenced by the founding of mechanics' institutes, the Adelaide Philosophical Society in 1853 and the Adelaide Institute. The latter classical building was opened in 1860 and originally contained a museum, art gallery and library before they moved out into their own buildings. Institute, museum and library all influenced, and their histories ran parallel to, the University of Adelaide, founded in 1874.[34] Whereas the Melbourne Museum moved from the university into the centre of town, the University of Sydney maintained its own museums, one of them of natural history, the other emphasising the importance of the university's archaeological collections. In Auckland, New Zealand, the museum moved out of the centre of town to the Domain, where it was housed in a robustly neoclassical building in 1929, named the War Memorial Museum. Once again, the museum (originally founded in 1852) had its origins in the combination of a mechanics' institute, a book society and the Auckland Philosophical Society of 1867, later the Auckland Institute. Although mechanics' institutes attempted to draw in self-educating, improving members of the working classes, it was usually the middle-class associations like the Auckland Institute which made the key moves in the creation of museums and other cultural bodies.

In Africa, notable museums, with striking architectural presences, were founded in Cape Town and elsewhere. The importance of these institutions was generally exemplified by the central locations in which they were built. The Cape Town museum was built facing the government garden, with the governor's residence nearby, directly opposite the earlier library on the other side of the gardens. This museum had been founded in 1855 and the collections were moved from the neoclassical library into its own separate building, the architecture of which now had a strong hint of Dutch influence in 1895. The Grahamstown museum on the Eastern Cape was more Dutch in appearance, given the prominence of its Dutch-style gables, and was opened in 1900 (the architect of these two museums was J.E. Vixseboxse). The museum on the East African island of Zanzibar is a particularly interesting example of a colonial museum, the history and architecture of which have been revealed in a highly sophisticated analysis by Sarah Longair.[35] This museum was designed by a colonial administrator, John Houston Sinclair, who had received architectural training in the office of the distinguished London architect J.L. Pearson. Although he never qualified, Sinclair put his training to good effect once he became a colonial official, illustrating perhaps the degree to which imperial architecture was often produced on an ad hoc basis. Arriving in Mombasa in 1895, he was roped into designing an Anglican cathedral for this formerly Swahili and Omani port.[36] After moving to Zanzibar, where he eventually became the Resident and Chief Secretary to the Government of the Protectorate, he was involved in designing the residence of the Agent (later renamed the Residency), the High Court and finally the museum, which came to be known as the Beit al Amani or House of Peace when it opened in 1925. This building translated elements of the Indo-Saracenic style to East Africa, where Sinclair was committed, as in all his buildings, to creating what he thought would be suitably eastern-influenced forms for a coast that had been closely connected to the Arabian Gulf.[37] Like most visitors he was intrigued by the history and theatricality of Zanzibar, notably in the trading and residential old town known as Stone Town, and sought to re-create the sense of a great emporium, a crossroads of the Indian Ocean and the African continent. The contents of the museum were similarly conceived as reflecting these cultural interchanges. Some thought it had a mosque-like religious air, as though intended, like so many other museums, to convey a reverence for learning.

Originally, it was supposed that such museums would emulate the great institutions of Europe in making global natural histories and world civilisations available to people, not least the young, in the colonies. However, it was later recognised that such intentions were hopelessly ambitious, and generally colonial museums, with one or two exceptions, came to concentrate on the native phenomena, cultures and artefacts of their own territories. In these respects, these institutions invariably reflected the turning of the imperial gaze upon the natural products of their regions as well as the peoples among whom Europeans had settled. They developed, at least for a period, a genuinely developmental function, in helping to understand the indigenous resources of colonies, in their geologies, soil types and flora and fauna, a role that was soon taken over by university research institutes. As they came to concentrate mainly on the local, both natural and ethnic, they unquestionably began to contribute to a sense of national identity. Another way to do so was to showcase immigrants and local heroes in the emergence of identities that were increasingly national rather than imperial. One excellent example is the commemoration of the radical politician and journalist William Lyon Mackenzie in Ontario. Mackenzie was an immigrant from Scotland who founded and edited the newspaper, *The Colonial Advocate*, and was a member of the legislative assembly and mayor of Toronto.[38] He took a leading role in the 1837 rebellion against the Ontario social and political Establishment. When the rebellion failed, he fled to the United States to avoid arrest and possible execution (some associates were subjected to the death penalty). When he returned to Canada in 1849, after a royal pardon, he resumed his journalistic and political ambitions, later becoming one of the great heroes of Canadian history. His home in Toronto, bought for him by public subscription and a plain late Georgian building, was declared a historic site in 1936 and became and remains a museum, as did his printing shop in Queenston, Ontario, now described as 'Canada's largest operational printing museum'.[39]

CLUBS AND MARKETS

The institutions and their buildings examined so far were generally bourgeois public foundations, mainly designed for public use and instruction, for an inclusive rational recreation and for developmental and surveillance purposes, serving to bring the members of the bourgeoisie together in associated societies, and later contributing to dominion and colonial nationalisms. We should however remember that there were also private institutions in the bourgeois sphere which were intended to create and maintain a degree of exclusivity. These were essential for the formation of connections, in an empire in which networking and social bonding were crucial to the operation of the military, the administration and business. Such networking took place in various different settings, particularly cultural and ethnic societies, as well as through freemasonry and, perhaps above all, the club. Although clubs were always masculine institutions, women attended some dinners and balls, and in consequence they also became locations for marriage-broking. Indeed, political and commercial bonds might additionally be formed through family connections. Another function of clubs was to provide accommodation for military and civilian personnel either when arriving at a new posting or when travelling. To facilitate this and movement within the empire, many clubs provided reciprocal and short-term memberships. Clubs were more or less ubiquitous, attempting to emulate the traditions of London clubland, both in social and in architectural terms. In Canada, Australia and India, indeed, the founding of clubs was virtually coterminous with the appearance of the most famous London examples. There were of course many types of club, including sporting ones of various sorts, but here the main concern is with those which were primarily social, though they often added facilities for sports if the necessary amount of land was available. In the territories of white settlement, such clubs were places of elite white-male socialising designed for the promotion of political causes and the maintenance of business contacts. Their membership in the nineteenth and twentieth centuries reads like a list of the respective colonial 'movers and shakers' of their times, a reflection of their significance in the economic and political development of their respective territories. In the absence of a major study of colonial clubland, these effects are not fully understood. Their parallel foundation across the empire represents a striking phenomenon. The Toronto Club, Canada's oldest, was founded in 1837; the Halifax, Nova Scotia Club in 1862, later inhabiting an impressive neo-Baroque building in a prime location. The Vancouver Club appeared later in 1889 with Edwardian Baroque premises opening in 1913, while the Mount Royal Club in Montreal was founded in 1899 when the city was 'at the apex of its power and influence', regarded as 'the financial, social and commercial capital of the Dominion'.[40] Formerly exclusively male, it now admits women to membership. Both the Melbourne Club and the Australian Club in Sydney date from 1838. The Melbourne Club is in a classic Renaissance-palace club building, located in a prime position in Collins Street, while the Australian is on Macquarie Street, both standing as symbols of a British social heritage, elitist and exclusive.[41] Both retain men-only membership with women only admitted as guests. Hobart, Tasmania boasts both the Tasmanian Club of 1861, located in a neo-Georgian former bank building since 1873, and the Athenaeum, founded in 1889 and moving into an Edwardian Baroque building in the early twentieth century. The Cape Town Civil Service Club of 1858 and the City Club of 1878 eventually amalgamated, inhabiting traditionally wood-panelled rooms in an Edwardian Baroque building, appropriately enough in Queen Victoria Street. A portrait of Cecil John Rhodes still looks down upon the dining room, although the club, clearly formerly exclusively white, now delicately announces that it welcomes people of 'all cultures'. The Durban Club was founded in 1854 as the economy of that colony was expanding rapidly on the strength of sugar growing and coal mining. Durban, though not the capital, was the significant commercial and port centre. It occupied two premises until it set about the construction of the kind of dignified building to which its membership aspired. This was an Edwardian Baroque structure, once described as 'one of the Town's most exquisite'.[42] In more recent times, it has proved to be too large, despite the abandonment of its former racial exclusiveness, and it has now been reduced to leasing one section, having sold the building off.[43] In Auckland, New Zealand, the Auckland Club was probably in existence by 1853. This club was notorious for not admitting Jews. Its rival was the Northern Club (which did admit Jews), apparently founded in 1867, and was already sufficiently financially secure (with 120 members) by 1859 to be able to buy the Royal Hotel, an Italianate building on Princes Street, where it became celebrated for being covered with Virginia creeper. Its classic slogan is 'relax, network and be entertained'.[44] Some clubs have had problems in modern times, and the Auckland Club merged with the Northern in 2010, its chairman declaring that it had been killed off by the decline in corporate business memberships, the ending of long lunches, and drink-drive laws.[45]

Clubs had a different tone in India and the dependent colonies. There they represented racial exclusivity even more profoundly than in the settlement territories, marking them out as spaces where the colonial elite sought security from the surrounding ethnic and to a certain extent natural environment. Often surrounded by gardens that evoked a different climate and geographical context, they provided a psychological, if not realistic, protection, which helps to explain the intensity of the controversies about the admittance of even aristocratic and elite Indians. They existed in almost every colonial town and city, a place in which whites could socialise, network, and plan aspects of policy and development, as well as just 'let their hair down' in more relaxing surroundings than the formal offices of administration and the military. Although there were sporting clubs in India in the eighteenth century, the Bengal Club was founded in 1827 by East India Company officials. It inhabited various premises before settling on the prestigious Chowringhee in 1845, in a building owned by an Indian – highly ironic, since it was racially exclusive. Of the original 141 names of members, most were high-ranking administrators and military personnel, with just a few medical professionals and only six merchants or bank directors. With growing membership it was able to build large premises in the traditional Calcutta neoclassical style. According to its own website, Indians were only admitted in 1959, twelve years after independence, and women only appeared in the membership in 1990.[46] By that time, it had inevitably encountered problems of maintaining membership and therefore income, and had withdrawn to an annexe of the building on Russell Street.[47] The controversies over racial exclusion were worked out in the founding of many clubs in India. The Calcutta Club was founded in 1907, supposedly at the behest of the Viceroy Lord Minto so that he could entertain an Indian prince. It soon inhabited a grand neo-Georgian building on the Lower Circular Road, and maintained its rule of alternating British and Indian presidents right down to the 1970s.[48] The Tollygunge Club on the edge of Calcutta was founded as a sports and country club in 1895, occupying 100 acres, formerly owned by the Sultan of Mysore.

A similar racial history occurred in Bombay, where the Byculla Club was founded in 1833, with a rather grand neoclassical palace constructed in the 1840s.[49] In 1850 this club had 570 members, of whom 352 were military, 80 civil, 43 medical and over 90 merchants and others. But the history of the Byculla Club presents an object lesson in the transformation of a city. While the fort survived, Byculla was an important area beyond this militarised heart. With the demise of the fort and the consequent freeing-up of large quantities of land, the centre of gravity shifted. Byculla became an area of industrial mills and of working-class housing.[50] Even the racecourse had to move closer to the coast, and the club was left isolated. It could no longer compete with those nearer the harbour such as the Royal Bombay Yacht Club, founded in 1846, with its magnificent clubhouse at the Apollo Bunder, or the Bombay Gymkhana founded in the 1870s to bring various sporting clubs together.[51] Because these clubs were racially exclusive, the governor of Bombay, Lord Willingdon, insisted on

The British Empire through buildings

26 Tollygunge Club, Calcutta

the founding of a non-racial club in 1918.[52] The Madras Club was founded in 1832 and by 1862 had no fewer than 3,000 members, occupying premises in a 'garden house'. It became celebrated for entertaining several members of the royal family at grand balls in the 1870s and the early years of the twentieth century. A rival Adyar Club appeared in 1890. These are, however, among the most celebrated of examples. There were clubs in almost every town in India and in many other colonies, which is why they have always featured so powerfully in colonial literature (such as George Orwell's *Burmese Days*, Paul Scott's Raj Quartet or accounts of the 'Happy Valley' set in Kenya).

Clubs were also an important feature of hill stations, as in Ootacamund.[53] Another hill club was the famous Planters' Club in Darjeeling, founded in 1868 to serve the tea plantations of the Dooars and Terai regions, as well as British officials and army officers.[54] Because of the problems of travel in that area of North-East India, particularly during the monsoons, there were local clubs for almost all the planter districts. Occasionally such clubs became less racially exclusive in the imperial period, permitting membership to high-status bourgeois

The bourgeois public sphere and new technologies

27 Royal Bombay Yacht Club

Indians, such as doctors. The smaller clubs were also more likely to admit women. Some of the social restrictions of these clubs were experienced by the young women who arrived in the so-called 'fishing fleet'. The Maharajah of Mysore could be found in the Madras Gymkhana Club but never in the racially exclusive Adyar Club. The Club of Western India in Poona (Pune) allowed women in only once a month.[55]

An interesting example of the formation of a club which set out to overturn the racial exclusiveness of British colonial clubs can be found in Ceylon. The Orient Club was founded in Colombo in the early twentieth century with a membership which was to be all male, entirely Ceylonese and specifically excluding Europeans. A photograph of the members indicates the extent of westernisation of those who had joined such that while they made a racial and political point they remained closely aligned (not least in gender exclusivity) with the colonial culture that had produced such clubs.[56] Elsewhere in Ceylon, the Hill Club in Nuwara Eliya remains an impressive building and an active social centre, as it was throughout colonial times in Ceylon.[57] The Selangor Club in Kuala Lumpur was founded on the *padang* (an open space like a maidan) in

1884, interestingly with a grant from the government. Having started out in a thatched hut, it was eventually housed in a mock-Tudor, half-timbered range contrasting strongly with the Orientalist architecture of the nearby government offices and railway station. Known as 'the Dog', it admitted 'affluent and well educated' representatives of all races from the start. Its own history describes it as having been central in the development of Malaysian sports, as well as the arts and theatre. Having survived fire and floods, it was given the title of 'Royal' by the Sultan of Selangor in 1984 and regards itself as an icon of the Malaysian nation.[58] In such a manner has an essentially colonial institution been appropriated and adapted by a postcolonial elite. On the other hand, the magnificent wooden building of the famous Pegu Club in Yangon stands empty.

The exclusive character of all of these clubs was emphasised by the manner in which travelling members of the royal family so often visited them for social events, invited by local governors and senior officials. They were, after all, invariably housed in the grandest of buildings, often second only to the major public institutions and government houses themselves. In the case of India, it is intriguing that large numbers of clubs have survived because of the rapid growth of an Indian bourgeoisie in recent decades, seeking the 'prestige and status' conferred by club membership. Formerly a symbol of British power and racial dominance, they have now become evidence of upward social mobility and new wealth. Thus an 'increasingly affluent middle class' seeks a 'coveted status symbol', a 'style statement' within a 'visionary space'.[59] They have substituted social exclusivity for racial. In Africa, the city of Livingstone (the original capital of Northern Rhodesia before Lusaka was created in the inter-war years) acquired what became the Royal Golf and Country Club, royal on account of the visits of the Duke and Duchess of Connaught in 1910 and the Prince of Wales in 1925. These events are still commemorated in the clubhouse, erected in 1908 in a typical colonial style with an extensive verandah and a Dutch gable. It still displays its 'honour boards' of presidents and trophy holders.[60] Similar clubs appeared throughout the African colonies, all performing the same functions. One of the most celebrated, or notorious, was the Muthainga Club, some miles out of Nairobi and the haunt of settlers of the White Highlands and 'Happy Valley' set. Founded in 1913, it survives as an exclusive club to this day, the barrier to membership now being wealth rather than race.

Another bourgeois institution that was originally designed to be exclusive later became highly inclusive. These were those extraordinary temples of commerce, the great markets of imperial cities, invariably developed around the

The bourgeois public sphere and new technologies

same time, 1870, as the bourgeoisie sought better shopping facilities. They were also designed to improve hygiene and therefore promote health through centralisation and inspection, arrangements that in India were to benefit the European population much more than the Indian.[61] Perhaps the greatest of these was the Crawford Market, located just north of Victoria Terminus, in Bombay. Designed by William Emerson in a predominantly flamboyant Norman polychromatic style with some Flemish flourishes, this was in use by 1870. An octagonal clock tower, the usual symbol of imperial discipline, rises from the roof of its main building. The design was highly controversial, but soon became one of the architectural sights of the city.[62] The Sir Stuart Hogg Market in Calcutta's Lindsay Street (now the New Market) was originally intended to be a place where the European population could shop free from the hustle of the Indian bazaars which had preceded it.[63] Designed by Richard Roskell Bayne, the architect of the East India Railway, it was constructed in the early 1870s (opened in 1874) in a red-brick Gothic style, with a grand clock tower added as late as the 1930s. Europeans invariably sent their servants to these markets to buy foodstuffs,

28 Crawford Market, Bombay

but they later became great inclusive emporia with literally hundreds of stalls, and Europeans often visited them with a guide to their labyrinthine aisles and a porter to carry their purchases. The Moore Market in Madras has had a less happy history. Construction of a brick, strongly Indo-Saracenic building by the architect R.E. Ellis began in 1898, and it became an important commercial centre of the city. In 1985, however, it was destroyed by fire and became the site of the Chennai suburban railway system and headquarters. The Karachi equivalent was the Empress Market, built in 1884–88 and designed in a commercial Gothic style, with a grand clock tower, by the municipal engineer, James Strachan.[64] The surviving markets remain among the busiest and liveliest places in their respective cities. Perhaps the most striking of such markets outside India is the Central Market in Adelaide, celebrated as one of the grandest in Australia, the original building dating from 1870 (in wood and iron), with later additions and reconstruction in more permanent materials. It is now a red-brick structure with a chunky four-square tower, situated on Gouger Street in a central location of the city. The Victoria Market in Melbourne likewise dates from the same period and also replaced several earlier markets. All these markets are now promoted as significant tourist attractions.

NEW TECHNOLOGIES

Another major conditioning factor in the development of imperial buildings (as throughout the world) was the requirement of the new technologies of the nineteenth century.[65] These were interlocking, often dependent on each other, and can be identified as the portals of the worldwide posts and telegraphs, the explosive arrival of the railways and their need for railway stations, as well as other structures such as engine sheds, maintenance workshops, freight yards, offices and much else. The workshops and other aspects of railway employment invariably influenced the layout of towns further, since suburbs were created to accommodate the thousands of workers required for the maintenance and operation of the railways. In addition to all of this, the arrival of steamships created a demand for the development of major harbours and shipping company headquarters. Sailing ships could, with difficulty, be manoeuvred alongside quays, particularly once steam tugs became available, but the age of sail had seen such ships often anchoring offshore with goods and passengers being transferred to the land by smaller boats. This could even happen through dangerous surf, as famously in Madras. But the size and manoeuvrability of steamships meant that they could be berthed in rivers and harbours with greater ease, thus enabling people and freight to pass to dry land with far greater speed and comfort, additionally ensuring faster turnaround times. With the manufacture of cranes, larger items could be carried than had been possible before (including the steam engines required for the railways). Quays in turn demanded sheds and warehouses, some of them for customs, others for the 'processing' of arriving immigrants, as at Pier 21 in Halifax, Nova Scotia, which dealt with immigrants between 1928 and 1971 and is now an immigration museum. Once passengers had landed and been checked though customs and immigration, they required (where appropriate) passenger stations to transfer them to the trains for the next part of their journey. All this has to be organised by harbour and dock administration and pilotage offices with, in some large ports, control towers for the marshalling of shipping. Thus a much expanded or entirely new architectural portfolio of buildings was required to service the new technologies. Such buildings became amongst the most characteristic construction projects of imperial ports in territories around the world, particularly in the second half of the nineteenth century. In passing, it may be said that they also appeared in territories of 'informal empire' invaded by the commerce, personnel and products of a globalised West. To take but one example, the harbour of Buenos Aires on the River Plate in Argentina was developed in the late nineteenth century by the businessman Eduardo Madero, who commissioned a British design precisely modelled on the docks of Liverpool.[66]

These technological changes and their material presence in the cities and towns of empire had a deeper significance than just the transformation in speed, regularity and reliability of communications. White colonialists and settlers began to see them (together with perceived advances in western science and medicine) as symptomatic of their dominance, as convincingly demonstrating both their cultural superiority and their right to rule others supposedly incapable of such striking developments.[67] They became a measure of human achievement, a means to the dispersal of the civilising mission while at the same time justifying, promoting and protecting this mission and its adherents. It is striking that the 'bard of empire', Rudyard Kipling, had a fascination with technology, with the engines of naval vessels, with railways, and with engineers and their activities as 'bridge builders'.[68] Kipling would surely have recognised that the buildings emerging to service these technologies were much more than simply neutral structures associated with the utilisation of modes of communication: they were symbols of European technological 'progress', the principal ideology of empire. Yet some at least of these buildings (notably railway stations) became the means by which indigenous people could utilise modern technologies, opportunities for access exploited with considerable alacrity. These buildings therefore encapsulated within them an imperial view from above and an opportunist perspective from below, providing opportunities to exploit such modernity by facilitating travel and speeding up journeys of pilgrimage (principally an Asian phenomenon) that reflected long-standing cultural desires.

Of all the imperial cities, perhaps Bombay is the quintessential city of these new technologies. It is also, arguably, the city with the greatest collection of Victorian neo-Gothic and eclectic buildings in the world.[69] Moreover, it is one where its key modern development reflects the influence of one governor. This was the career imperial official Sir Henry Bartle Frere (1815–84), who first arrived in India in 1834 as an East India Company writer. From 1850 to 1859 he was Commissioner of Sind and developed an interest in agriculture, postal systems and communications. The development of the port city of Karachi was at least partly attributed to his time as Commissioner.[70] Appointed Governor of Bombay in 1862, he immediately made a crucial decision. He proposed that the old fortifications should be dismantled, freeing up large amounts of land for a major building programme. He was also convinced that such a programme should follow neo-Gothic architectural forms, which were increasingly considered to be much more appropriate to the Indian cultural and climatic environment than the neoclassical style of Calcutta and of a few of the early public buildings of Bombay. Significantly, the 1860s were to be a boom decade in Bombay, fuelled by the considerable growth in cotton production and export from western India, the indirect consequence of the American Civil War. The development of the railway network out of Bombay was already a major phenomenon. All this was to reach its climax with the opening of the Suez Canal in 1869, which ensured that henceforth Bombay would be the principal gateway to British India and not, as in the past, Madras and Calcutta. Whereas Madras and Calcutta had originally been ports of sailing vessels, Bombay was the port of steam. Frere's vision for the reconstruction of the city to perform this significant new role was put into practice by the appointment of a Ramparts Removal Committee and the presence and later arrival in India of men eager to promote his ideas. These included the engineers Henry Conybeare, John Fuller and Henry Wilkins,[71] all of whom designed significant buildings, and the architects John Adams, Sir William Emerson, George Molecey, Walter Paris and F.W. Stevens. Celebrated architects like William Burges and George Gilbert Scott were also involved, as were artists and sculptors like Owen Jones and John Lockwood Kipling. There was also an influential Indian architect, Cowasjee Khan Bahadur Murzban, while the clerks of works supervising construction were invariably Indians. Moreover, wealthy Parsi merchants like Sir Jamsetjee Jeejeebhoy and Sir Cowasjee Readymoney were active in helping to finance some of the institutions. The result was that 'there is no other city with so many buildings erected in similar style, with so few modern insertions', ensuring that 'the grandeur and completeness of the undertaking is breathtaking'.[72]

The project was helped by the fact that open ground, presumably for defensive reasons, had been left to the west of the ramparts, spaces that became a sequence of four maidans, Azad, Oval, Cross and the Cooperage. These became the settings for the buildings, ensuring that the architectural impact of many of them could be heightened. Almost all of them were characterised by climatic adaptations, including exposed open stairwells, balconies, arcades, deeply shading eaves, sizeable portes cochères and internally wide corridors, high atriums, large rooms and airy circulation zones. They were invariably further enhanced by gardens and fountains. They reflected a mix of English, French and Venetian Gothic elements, using various local stones to create a polychromatic effect. They usually had striking profiles with domes large and small, clock towers and spires. They were further embellished by a large number of sculptures, statues and other decorative items, usually furnished by Lockwood Kipling and the students of the Jamsetjee Jeejeebhoy (or JJ) School of Art (founded in 1862, its own building completed 1878). The Elphinstone High School, the David Sassoon Library and the University Convocation Hall and Library (the latter two by G.G. Scott) were other educational institutions, while such major buildings as the Secretariat, the PWD Building, the Magistrates' and the High courts, as well as the later Bombay Municipal Building, were devoted to the increased scale of administration and construction in the city. All of them reflected the new engineering, building and economic technologies while the General Post Office, the Telegraph Office, the great railway station (the Victoria Terminus, described by Davies as 'an architectural sensation' and 'one of the architectural treasures of India'),[73] the magnificent headquarters of the Bombay, Baroda and Central India Railway, and buildings nearer the harbour such as the British India Steam Navigation Company headquarters entirely reflected the transforming technologies of the age.[74] Some of these were built by private enterprise, though on land provided by the government, but there can be little doubt that bringing the entire ensemble together would not have been possible without the autocratic command of imperial rule.

If Bombay illustrated dramatic growth under the influence of the new technologies in the space of a few decades between the 1860s and the beginning of the twentieth century, elsewhere technological changes also produced significant architectural results. The general post offices of all the most significant colonial and imperial cities were often among the grandest buildings, as they were in British cities. They were freighted with all kinds of symbolic significance as well as the highly practical business of the imperial posts. They represented literacy and global communications, conducted by the latest transport technologies, as well as the multiple connections with the metropole, other colonies and territories outside the immediate imperial nexus. They therefore symbolised a sort-of nervous system of empire (and of globalisation) which held together political, military, cultural, commercial, press and private functions of the imperial body politic, all connected by the royal mail ships subsidised to carry the posts.[75] The military significance seemed incalculable, ensuring that the existence of unrest and revolt could be readily communicated, stimulating the necessary military responses. This had seemed to be the lesson of the use of the telegraph in signalling the early manifestations of the Indian revolt of 1857. It was even thought that the existence of these technologies could lead to various forms of closer union or federation in empire.[76] In the most important centres, the telegraph office was a separate building, often another impressive and extensive one, with large numbers of operators dealing with government, administrative, business and commercial press 'wires' as well as the private business and family concerns of individuals. These buildings represent the material expression, often but not exclusively in classical forms, of one of the great technological developments of the age, telegraphic communication over considerable land distances as well as undersea cables progressively connecting the entire globe.[77] From the indigenous point of view, posts and telegraph offices soon came to enhance the search for western forms of literature and learning, as people posted applications to educational institutions or alternatively communicated, in English or the vernacular, with other scholars. Later they provided the means of communicating with fellow nationalists at home and abroad. In lesser centres, telegraph offices were conveniently situated close to the incoming landlines, vulnerably carried on poles, at railway stations. In Durban. Natal, there was a particularly grand post office, formerly the town hall until an even bigger one was completed in 1910.[78]

The bourgeois public sphere and new technologies

29 Telegraph Office, Calcutta

Of all the architectural expressions of these new technologies it was the railway station which became the most ubiquitous and the most prominent.[79] These ranged from vast buildings in the large cities and colonial capitals through middling examples in mid-sized towns, to a multiplicity of smaller ones in lesser centres, even villages. The railway station encapsulated multiple messages through its presence. It expressed the power and pride of the railway companies in providing the most important infrastructural development holding colonies together. It represented nodal points in global communications, not least in its function in handling freight and mails. Beyond its central function of the reception and despatch of trains, often on multiple tracks and platforms, the larger stations were associated with a whole gamut of travel arrangements including ticket offices, telegraph offices, various refreshment and resting rooms, waiting rooms and facilities all reflecting the social hierarchies of colonies transferred into the grading of accommodation on the trains themselves. There might also be an integral or adjacent hotel and facilities for the large staffs employed. In many significant centres, the national or regional headquarters of the railway might be housed in a separate building. For indigenous people, stations offered not just employment opportunities, but also the chance of setting up small businesses in supplying tea, snacks and street food. Stations and the railways they served reflected the strict hierarchies of class and race in their employment practices, perhaps most complex in India, where the driving and maintenance of engines became the preserve of Anglo-Indian (mixed-race) people. Segregated facilities, notably in Africa and Asia where class was massively complicated by race, provided, at least in theory, protection for travelling colonial elites with zones of separation. Such distinctions were less pronounced in Canada, Australia and New Zealand.

Railway stations were, however, buildings which opened up a striking ambivalence. On the one hand, stations reflected the new technology which facilitated imperial power through the swifter extraction of products and the movement of goods, as well as of colonial peoples and, above all, the military. Some even looked like forts, like the great railway station in Lahore, opened in 1860. They therefore represented both the tight grip and the economic dynamic of colonial and settler rule, particularly when the arrival of the line and the building of a station galvanised the development of towns. Yet, unlike so many other imperial buildings, they were generally not exclusive in terms of race and class. Of all colonial buildings, they became available to all, regardless of racial or social status, in order to maximise ticket sales, since in India and a few other places the sheer scale of indigenous travel became a vital contributor to the profits of the railway companies. They also presented opportunities for people (often indigenous) to seek employment as porters, cleaners and newspaper sellers and to carry out various other services, official and unofficial, required by travellers. For some, their enclosed and covered spaces could become temporary residences or shelters for the underprivileged. Stations were thus public spaces where the different classes and races encountered each other in closer proximity than in many other places, heightening the need for aspects of separation both for elite comfort and their perceived personal security. The railways facilitated the movement of indigenous labour, for example to the mines in southern Africa and elsewhere, but they also provided opportunities for trade-union activity, and in India and Africa for the movement of nationalist leaders and the development of resistance to colonial rule. Few buildings represented the extraordinary combination of modernity and of the social and political dynamics of imperial rule better than railway stations. Stations seemed to offer limitless imperial opportunities, but they also presented choke points, points of vulnerability that could be exploited by resisters.[80] These included opportunities for passive resistance in twentieth-century nationalisms as well as tense personal encounters between the races, rulers and ruled. While this might be less true of the settler

The bourgeois public sphere and new technologies

Dominions and some African dependent territories, still stations represented vulnerable points in the technological armoury of imperial people.

There were also built-in weaknesses in the new technologies. In Africa and Asia, telegraph lines could readily be cut, which might be a political act or simply an opportunistic one to secure copper wire for other purposes.[81] Railways offered almost unlimited supplies of iron, for example in the ties that secured the tracks to the sleepers, and the removal of such ties became a source of an important metal resource right down to modern times.[82] Freight yards often provided opportunities for theft. Moreover, imperial elites often seemed vulnerable when undergoing the stresses of travel. Even among Europeans in the Dominions, classes would mix at stations and poorer, unemployed people might resent the style and opportunities of the better-off observed at stations.[83] They could also represent a portal to leisure, as at the coast or in hill stations and mountain resorts, and for some people a means for pilgrimage. They greatly facilitated the sports of empire, enabling teams to travel to fixtures and those seeking opportunities for shooting and fishing to come closer to their destinations. Horses could also be accommodated in travelling to race meetings or polo matches. In more remote areas, the railway station was emblematic of a sense of connection into the imperial system. Symbolically, some stations in India were supplied with coffins for whites who died while travelling, clearly intended to protect the dignity of imperial people, but ultimately representing the death knell of the imperial system.

Although stations were a new building type added into many existing colonial towns and cities, the companies building them usually succeeded in bringing the lines into the urban centres, thereby ensuring that the stations built from the mid-point of the nineteenth century generally occupied highly significant locations in the existing plan. Good examples include the great Union Station in Toronto and the famously magnificent Victoria Terminus (long known to all as VT, but now officially Chhatrapati Shivaji Station) in Bombay.[84] As in Europe, the major cities might have multiple major stations. Elsewhere, stations were located close to transport hubs and topographically strategic points, as at ports or river crossings (like Howrah Station in Calcutta). Those that were a little to the edge of the city centre were nonetheless built on important streets in the network offering ready access to other parts of the urban plan. Examples would be Sydney, New South Wales, Melbourne, Victoria or Wellington, New Zealand. While the functions performed by stations and incorporated into their structures were universal, there were unquestionably no rules as to styles.

The British Empire through buildings

Some stations, as in Toronto, were built in severely classical or Renaissance manner, representing adherence to an apparently atavistic style even in the representation of striking technological modernity. This was also true of some stations in Australia (for example in Sydney) and South Africa (Cape Town, now demolished). Occasionally a particular architect would set his stamp upon the railway stations in a specific colony. An example is the role of the Scottish architect, Alexander Troup, in the development of stations in New Zealand. The 'Flemish Renaissance' Dunedin Station of 1907 is an excellent example (see p. 15 above).[85] Smaller stations adhered to a more simple colonial style, often basically bungalows with verandahs on the platform side, sometimes on each side. Railway stations lay at the emotional heart of the imperial condition. In imperial Britain itself, they were the scenes of departures on long journeys to the territories of settlement and to worldwide colonies. In colonial territories they represented arrivals to settle or to take up posts as expatriates. Their extraordinarily emotive significance might be stressed, for example, in sending children off to school or home to Britain. They were often the settings for ceremonial, ritualised arrivals and departures for senior figures in colonial politics and administration, as well as nationalists drawing large crowds. Bourgeois tourists flaunted their ready access to the technologies of communication and travel as a marker of their class and affluence. Nineteenth-century guidebooks invariably offered tours that fanned out from railway stations.[86] In all these ways, particularly in the twentieth century, the strategic position of stations was political, social and military, as well as economic.

BANKS, COMMERCIAL BUILDINGS, HOTELS AND CINEMAS

While posts, telegraphs and railways created a vital and imposing range of buildings throughout the empire, more comfortable methods of travel ensured that the later nineteenth century was also the period when other economic interest groups set about expressing their significance for the colonial economy within the built environment. Banks were perhaps particularly important here, seeking to assert their economic significance through architecture. Notable banking buildings can be found in cities and towns throughout the former British Empire, generally strongly neoclassical or Baroque in style. The great banking companies, such as the Hong Kong and Shanghai, Standard and Chartered in southern Africa, Grindlays in many places, and the Bank of Montreal in Canada invariably built for themselves magnificent headquarters and branches in central positions in

The bourgeois public sphere and new technologies

the principal cities with other outlets in many towns. All of these were designed to indicate the dignity and stability of the bank. An excellent example is the domed and columned temple headquarters of the Bank of Montreal in the Place d'Armes of that city. In many port cities, it is still possible to see the magnificence of company headquarters, shipping offices and agencies, industrial units and other buildings associated with the growth of the imperial economy. To take just a few examples, the great shipping, trading and travel agency, Mackinnon Mackenzie Ltd, had grand buildings in all the ports eastwards from Bombay to Japan. Founded in 1847, this agency controlled a large proportion of the trade of the East. The surviving Mackinnon Mackenzie building in Bombay was built on the Ballard estate adjacent to the docks during the First World War and opened in 1920. In Sydney, New South Wales, the headquarters of the significant coastal and South Pacific shipping company, Burns Philp, founded in 1883, can still be seen on Bridge Street. Built in 1901 to a design by Arthur Anderson of the firm McCredie and Anderson, it has a highly assertive entrance with masonry coat of arms and banners above, with a columned central element flanked by striking oriels on two floors. The New South Wales Office of Environment and Heritage describes it as a building of aesthetic and historical significance in the

30 Bank of Montreal, Montreal

conservation area of Sydney.[87] In Yangon, the headquarters of the Irrawaddy Flotilla Company, in its day the largest and perhaps most significant river trading company in the world, can still be seen on Pansodan Street (formerly Phayre Street). A late classical building with a row of twinned Corinthian columns along its façade, this was built in 1933 and is now appropriately the headquarters of the Inland Waterways Department.[88]

The greater comfort of modern travel was reflected in the new imperial hotels which appeared round the empire. Many of these survive and are now seen as significant heritage buildings, reflecting a different age. Of course there were inns and hotels at an earlier period, but many of these were establishments that the imperial elite chose to avoid, often preferring to reside in the newly developing clubs or live with relatives or friends in private homes. Those of the appropriate status might well gain access to the residences of governors and high-ranking officials. But by the end of the nineteenth century, a remarkable chain of hotels had been established across the empire, as well as in staging posts outside it. All of them were built as impressive palaces, major symbols of western dominance as exhibited by their clients, the better-heeled citizens of European empires. An example of an imperial hotel outside the British Empire is the celebrated Reid's in Madeira, a significant staging post on shipping routes to West Africa, the Caribbean, South America and South Africa. The Scot William Reid had been renting out farmhouses on the island for some time before he ambitiously decided to create a grand hotel. Designed by G.S. Clarke and J.T. Micklethwaite, the building dominated a headland with views over the Atlantic to the west of Funchal, but Reid died before it was opened in 1891. As Reid's it became known as one of the great hotels of imperial networks.[89] Another Scot who created a notable imperial hotel was Sir Donald Currie, the shipowner who had masterminded the development of the Union-Castle Line as the premier shipping line serving South Africa. In 1890 he purchased the Nelson property in Cape Town, north of the Government Gardens under Table Mountain and commissioned the hotel which opened in 1899, designed initially for first-class passengers on his ships. Currie also commissioned a hotel in the Canary Islands from the Arts and Crafts Architect, James Maclaren, as a stopping-off place for his Union-Castle passengers. Among other great imperial hotels were those of the Canadian Pacific Railway (CPR) company, which included the Royal York in Toronto, directly opposite Union Station, the Banff Springs in the Rockies, the Vancouver Hotel in British Columbia and the Empress in Victoria.[90] Shepheard's in Cairo was one of the most celebrated places for those heading east to have

The bourgeois public sphere and new technologies

31 Empress Hotel, Victoria, British Columbia

a stopover or for those visiting the antiquities of the Nile.[91] It featured in many fictional and travel accounts, not least because of its significance during the two world wars of the twentieth century. A symbol of western imperialism, it burnt down in 1952 during the Egyptian revolution. The Norfolk in Nairobi, the Galle Face in Colombo, the Taj Mahal in Bombay, the Connemara in Madras, the Grand in Calcutta and the Peninsula in Hong Kong created a great chain of hotels for elite imperial travellers, all of them supplying the comforts and conditions that such people expected. Inland, Faletti's Hotel in Lahore was opened in 1880 and is still marketed for its 'heritage' character.[92] Other colonial port cities were well supplied with hotels. Mombasa constituted the gateway to East Africa, with its harbour at Kilindini and the start of the celebrated railway line which ultimately reached Uganda. By the First World War, it already possessed a number of sizeable hotels, including the Metropole, the Cecil and the four-storey Palace, all its rooms leading off verandahs that wrapped around each of its floors. In South-East Asia, the Eastern and Oriental in Penang, Raffles in Singapore and the Strand in Rangoon were regarded as peerless imperial hotels. Many of

The British Empire through buildings

32 Midland Hotel, Castlemaine, Victoria, Australia

the survivors stress their colonial pasts as part of their marketing strategies. In these ways, the explosive building of imperial institutions throughout the empire marked the combined expression of both corporate and civic presence.

By the inter-war years of the twentieth century, some hotels were developing Art Deco features, and this represented the manner in which a modernist international style began to invade imperial territories. Art Deco in the service of residential architecture will be examined in Chapter 5, but in the public sphere Art Deco made its appearance in company headquarters, club buildings and above all in the architecture of entertainment. Across the empire, cinemas began to replace theatres as the principal structures of urban entertainment. Many such cinemas adopted Art Deco as the architecture that most fitted a new technology of entertainment, bringing together an opulent style with a source of the exciting projection of other worlds and sometimes different times. Art Deco offered an elaborate stylistic escapism to go with the escapism on the screen and cheap ticket prices meant that the medium was open virtually to all – in ways that clubs, upmarket hotels and many other buildings were not. Cinemas were demotic 'palaces' where the bourgeois and other classes could mix in the same building, if in differently priced seats and exclusive floors. Bombay is noted as having developed an extraordinary collection of Art Deco buildings, among them several very large cinemas.[93] It is indicative of the changing requirements of succeeding ages that while F.W. Stevens is celebrated for designing a great railway station and other notable public structures, his son Charles Frederick Stevens designed Bombay's Art Deco Regal Cinema which opened in 1933. There are Art Deco cinemas and other buildings in Calcutta, Madras and other Indian cities, as well as in many urban locations in the former British Empire, though many are less well-preserved than those in (as it is now) Mumbai, partly because Mumbai has had heritage regulations in place since 1995.[94]

The buildings of the imperial and colonial bourgeois sphere are many and varied both in functional type and in style. Ironically, it is sometimes those which date from the heart of the imperial period which are better preserved than those of more recent provenance. But they remain highly recognisable as a product of the globalising effects of the British Empire. More particularly, the urban landscape was a reflection of the great social changes that took place within the British world. If the cities and towns of colonial territories were connected into both a local and worldwide web of commerce embracing industrial goods, agricultural and mining production, they were also interwoven through cultural forms. The institutions of the bourgeois cultural sphere were created out of global cultural relationships with parallel forms reflected in the English language, common religious and masonic rites, imperial ceremonial, journals, books and sports, as well as theatrical and musical performances of all sorts.[95] They were additionally connected by the royal tours (facilitated by the new technologies) which, from the 1860s, became a regular performance of the imperial relationship. Increasingly frequent travels of the children and descendants of Queen Victoria became a prime source of manipulation by functionaries, settler politicians and members of the bourgeoisie as one of the most potent symbols of an overarching British culture. This was reflected in extensive coverage in newspapers (both in Britain and overseas), engravings, photography, and later, moving film and even theatrical performances. Manipulation, of course, cuts two ways, and there is little doubt that indigenous peoples (generally through their rulers), governors and settler politicians also set about manipulating such events for their own purposes.[96] All of these bourgeois interests constituted the social and cultural glue which helped to hold together, at least for a period, the central economic relationships of empire.

NOTES

1 For the globalisation of commodity networks, see Jonathan Curry-Machado (ed.), *Global Histories, Imperial Commodities, Local Interactions* (Basingstoke, 2013).
2 David Lambert and Alan Lester (eds), *Colonial Lives Across the British Empire: Imperial Careering in the Long Nineteenth Century* (Cambridge, 2006); Alan Lester, *Imperial Networks: Creating Identities in South Africa and Britain* (London, 2001); Gary B. Magee and Andrew S. Thompson, *Empire and Globalisation: Networks of People, Goods and Capital in the British World, c. 1850–1914* (Cambridge, 2010).
3 Stephen Foster, *A Private Empire* (Millers Point, NSW, 2010); Emma Rothschild, *The Inner Life of Empires: An Eighteenth-Century History* (Princeton, NJ, 2011); Alexander Charles Baillie, *Call of Empire: From the Highlands to Hindostan* (Kingston, Jamaica, 2017); Alistair Mutch, *Tiger Duff: India Madeira and Empire in Eighteenth-Century Scotland* (Aberdeen, 2017). Another example is the Inglis family of Edzell in Angus, successful middle-class people who migrated to different parts of the British Empire. See Jean Smedley, *Inglis Memorial Hall and Library* (Edzell, 2015).
4 The rise of the middle classes has stimulated a considerable literature. See, for example, Leonore Davidoff and Catherine Hall, *Family Fortunes: Men and Women of the English Middle Class, 1780–1850* (London, 1997); Simon Gunn and Rachel Bell, *Middle Classes: Their Rise and Sprawl* (London, 2011); Simon Gunn, *The Public Culture of the Victorian Middle Class* (Manchester, 2000); Robert W. Stern, *Changing India: Bourgeois Revolution on the Sub-Continent* (Cambridge, 1993); Henning Melber, *The Rise of Africa's Middle Class* (London, 1988).
5 Swato Chattopadhyay and Jeremy White, 'Introduction' in Chattopadhyay and White (eds), *Civic Halls and Civic Materialism: Towards a Global History of Urban Public Space* (London, 2014), p. 8. Here Chattopadhyay and White reference the terminology of Jürgen Habermas and Michael Mumford.
6 Little has been written about the architecture of schools and hospitals, so they will be omitted from this survey.
7 Daniel Maudlin and Bernard L. Herman (eds), *Building the British Atlantic World: Spaces, Places and Material Culture, 1600–1850* (Chapel Hill, NC, 2016). See also some of the contributions to G.A. Bremner (ed.), *Architecture and Urbanism in the British Empire* (Oxford, 2016).
8 Anthony D. King, *Urbanism, Colonialism and the World Economy* (London, 1991), p. 1.
9 Now Republic Square or Piazza Repubblica.
10 See the article on libraries by Margaret Beckman, Moshe Dahms and Lorne Bruce, online Canadian Encyclopedia, www.thecanadianencyclopedia.ca/en/article/libraries/ (accessed 2 February 2018).
11 In the American war of 1812, boxes of books were looted, but some were returned.
12 Louisa Blair, Patrick Donovan and Donal Fyson, *Iron Bars and Bookshelves: A History of the Morrin Centre* (Montreal, 2016). In pursuing research in this library, I am grateful for the help of the volunteer librarian, Shirley Nadeau. The Morrin Centre was

named after Dr Joseph Morrin, prominent Scots doctor and mayor of Quebec City, who was influential in developing the library and founding the college.
13 In a striking piece of ethnic neighbourliness, the Francophone cultural centre and library, originally founded in 1848 to withstand Anglophone influence, now occupies the former Wesley Church next door. Despite this the Morrin Library retains the statue of General Wolfe formerly placed in a niche in a building on a street corner nearby.
14 Mollie Panter-Downes, *Ooty Preserved: A British Hill Station in India* (London, 1967), p. 49.
15 See the example of Western Australia, as revealed in an article by Jan Partridge in Jenny Gregory and Jan Gothard (eds), *Historical Encyclopedia of Western Australia* (Perth, 1909), pp. 563–564.
16 Harriet Elquist, *Building a New World: A History of the State Library of Victoria, 1853–1913* (Melbourne, 2013). There is a considerable literature on the history of the library.
17 The various sections of the library, in their different building periods, do not make a coherent architectural whole, as was pointed out in an article in 1951. J. Alex Allan, 'The Melbourne Public Library', *Australian Builder* (March 1951), pp 138–141. An ambitious scheme to expand the library on to its full site in the late nineteenth century was never executed.
18 The municipal pride of Melbourne is well revealed in Asa Briggs, *Victorian Cities* (Harmondsworth, 1968), chapter 7, 'Melbourne: A Victorian Community Overseas'.
19 History of the Library: State Library of New South Wales, www.sl.nsw.gov.au/about-library/history-library (accessed 20 September 2018).
20 For the state library see Carl Bridge, *A Trunk Full of Books: The History of the State Library of South Australia and its Forerunners* (Netley, South Australia, 1986).
21 See the article by Alison Gregg on the history of the library in Gregory and Gothard (eds), *Encyclopedia of Western Australia*, pp. 530–1.
22 John M. MacKenzie, *Museums and Empire: Natural History, Human Cultures and Colonial Identities* (Manchester, 1909), pp. 85–86.
23 John McQuarrie (ed.), *The Hill* (Ottawa, 2015), pp. 92–101.
24 There is a great deal of information about Carnegie libraries on the web. Many of the publications on the libraries relate to the United States, but see Burton J. Hendrick, *The Life of Andrew Carnegie* (London, 1933), pp. 550–556. The more recent biography, David Nasaw, *Andrew Carnegie* (London, 2006), contains surprisingly little on the libraries.
25 Theoretically, the local community chose the architectural style, but in practice it was often influenced by the administrator of the scheme, James Bertram.
26 These paragraphs are based upon MacKenzie, *Museums and Empire*.
27 There are mural scenes of European, Egyptian, Chinese, Greek and Babylonian civilisations. Part of a gallery is even devoted to the arts of medieval Europe. For the conception and construction of the Albert Hall Museum, see Vibhuti Sachdev and Giles Tillotson, *Building Jaipur: The Making of an Indian City* (London, 2002), pp. 102–108.

28 Ibid., p. 99. See also Thomas R. Metcalf, *An Imperial Vision: Indian Architecture and Britain's Raj* (London, 1989), p. 134.
29 Vikramaditya Prakash, 'Between Copying and Creation: The Jeypore Portfolio of Architectural Details' in Scriver and Prakash (eds), *Colonial Modernities*, pp. 115–125.
30 Jacob was assisted by a local architect and builder, Mir Toojoomool Hoosein.
31 Though now little visited by overseas tourists, it was thronged with locals when I visited it in November 2017.
32 Paul Walker, 'Institutional Audiences and Architectural Style: The Napier Museum' in Scriver and Prakash (eds), *Colonial Modernities*, pp. 127–147. Napier was a Governor of Madras who had his own theories about appropriate architecture.
33 MacKenzie, *Museums and Empire*, pp. 246–259.
34 For the foundation of universities around the British Empire, see Tamson Pietsch, *Empire of Scholars: Universities, Networks and the British Academic World 1850–1939* (Manchester, 2013).
35 Sarah Longair, *Cracks in the Dome: Fractured Histories of Empire in the Zanzibar Museum, 1897–1964* (London, 2015).
36 Mombasa was intermittently dominated by the Portuguese in the sixteenth and seventeenth centuries until they were ejected by the Omanis after the siege of Fort Jesus in 1698.
37 It is perhaps not surprising that Sinclair retired to Tangier, Morocco.
38 Chris Raible, *A Colonial Advocate: The Launching of his Newspaper and the Queenston Career of William Lyon Mackenzie* (Creemore, Ont., 1999).
39 Nancy Luno, 'The Mackenzie Homestead: A Brief History from 1858 to Present Day' (Toronto, 2000). For the printing museum, see https://mackenzieprintery.wordpress.com/ (accessed 26 July 2018).
40 *Montreal Times*, 18 April 2014.
41 Philip Goad, in *Melbourne Architecture*, p. 40, describes the Melbourne Club as the city's 'oldest institution', built in 1858–59 by Melbourne's specialist in neo-Renaissance, Leonard Terry.
42 Denis Radford, *A Guide to the Architecture of Durban and Pietermaritzburg* (Cape Town, 2002), p. 20.
43 www.durbanclub.co.za/club-history/ (accessed 2 July 2018).
44 https://northernclub.co.nz/the-club/ (accessed 2 July 2018). I paid a visit to this club in November 1998.
45 *National Business Review*, 27 January 2010: www.nbr.co.nz/article/auckland-club-forced-sell-mulls-northern-club-merger-117587 (accessed 25 June 2018). The Officers' Club had already amalgamated with the Northern in 2007.
46 www.thebengalclub.com/a-brief-history/ (accessed 25 June 2018). See also Purchottam Bhageria with Pavan Malhotra, *Elite Clubs of India* (New Delhi, 2005), pp. 19–22.
47 There is an amusing account of the 1970 auction in which many of the possessions of the club were sold off in Geoffrey Moorhouse, *Calcutta: The City Revealed* (Harmondsworth, 1974), pp. 259–260.

48 www.calcuttaclub.in/newclub/claclub/history/ (accessed 25 June 2018). Bhageria with Malhotra, *Elite Clubs*, pp. 47–50.
49 Samuel T. Sheppard, *The Byculla Club, 1833–1916: A History* (Bombay, 1916). This book is available on the Internet Archive. Interestingly, the original invitation to found the club, in 1832, introduced an element of competition by mentioning the fact that a club had just been founded in Madras.
50 Gillian Tindall, *City of Gold: The Biography of Bombay* (Hounslow, 1982), pp. 240–242.
51 The Byculla Club closed and was sold off in the 1920s. A British India Line ship's captain entertained me to lunch in the Gymkhana Club in 1982, when entering its portals was like walking into a colonial time warp.
52 Ironically enough, this club has now become the most socially exclusive in Mumbai, its membership lists closed.
53 Panter-Downes, *Ooty Preserved*, pp. 33 and 59.
54 It retains its status as a club, but is now also a two-star hotel.
55 Anne de Courcy, *The Fishing Fleet: Husband Hunting in the Raj* (London, 2012), pp. 162 and 275.
56 Anoma Pieris, 'The Trouser Under the Cloth' in Scriver and Prakash (eds), *Colonial Modernities*, p. 211.
57 At least it seemed so when I visited it in 2011. See www.hillclubsrilanka.lk/ (accessed 25 June 2018).
58 www.rsc.org.my/royal-selangor-club-history-3.aspx (accessed 25 June 2018). The club now has 6,000 members.
59 Ibid., preface.
60 https://thebestofzambia.com/orgs/livingstone-royal-golf/ (accessed 25 June 2018). I visited this club in 2013 while attending a bicentennial conference on David Livingstone in his eponymous town. The clubhouse was empty of guests, but not of staff, at that time.
61 Madhu Kelkar, 'The Sanitary Crusader, Arthur Crawford and the Politics of Sanitation in Bombay', *South Asian Journal of Multi-Disciplinary Studies*, 2, 2 (2016), pp. 1–15.
62 Christopher W. London, *Bombay Gothic* (Mumbai, 2002), pp. 62–66. See also Tindall, *City of Gold*, pp. 236–237. Arthur Crawford was the municipal commissioner of Bombay. It may be that his concern with improved sanitation and clean water supplies helped to promote the racial apartheid of the city.
63 Sir Stuart Hogg was the chairman of the Calcutta City Council at the time.
64 Karachi has had some difficulties maintaining architectural heritage, perhaps not surprising for a city which had under a million population in 1947 and now has over 18 million. https://widerimage.reuters.com/story/from-raj-to-architectural-riches (accessed 20 July 2018).
65 The significance of these new technologies, including railways, the steamship, advances in tropical disease control and weaponry in their relationship with modern imperialism was first surveyed by Daniel R. Headrick in *The Tools of Empire: Technology and European Imperialism in the Nineteenth Century* (Oxford,1981), but the significant architectural expressions of these technologies has never been fully explored.

66 A wall plaque on one of the buildings of the port refers to Liverpool as the model, to emphasise the port's modernity and global significance (personal observation in Buenos Aires in 2000).
67 Michael Adas, *Machines as the Measure of Men: Science, Technology and Ideologies of Western Dominance* (Ithaca, NY, 1989).
68 Christopher Harvie, '"The Sons of Martha": Technology, Transport and Rudyard Kipling', *Victorian Studies*, 20, 3 (spring 1977), pp. 269–282. Harvie attempts to draw a contrast between Kipling's view of race and empire and his technological interests, but it may well be that there is in fact a synergy between them. See Adas, *Machines*, pp. 235–236. There is a considerable literature on these aspects of Kipling's life, writing and thought.
69 Two Mumbai architects, Abha Bahl and Brinda Gaitonde Nayak, founded heritage walks in 1999. These have been greatly admired as helping to unveil the architectural glories of the city. https://bombayheritagewalks.com/ (accessed 30 July 2018).
70 Hamida Khuhro, 'The Making of a Port' in Khuhro and Mooraj (eds), *Karachi*, pp. 34–35. The outbreak of the Revolt of 1857 enhanced the potential significance of Karachi as a port of strategic significance.
71 Both Fuller and Wilkins later became generals in the Royal Engineers.
72 London, *Bombay Gothic*, p. 37. For the architectural transformation of Bombay into Mumbai, see Pauline Rohatgi, Pheroza Godrej and Rohul Mehrotra (eds), *Bombay to Mumbai: Changing Perspectives* (Mumbai, 1997). This magnificently illustrated book is dedicated to J.R.D. Tata to celebrate his support for Marg on its Golden Jubilee.
73 Davies, *Splendours of the Raj*, p. 175.
74 The BISN building had some Scottish baronial characteristics, reflecting the origins of its founders.
75 The general post office in Singapore was grand enough to be converted into a hotel, the Fullerton. Located near the Esplanade Bridge, this is one of the striking buildings of the waterfront. Built between 1919 and 1928, as an earnest of the inter-war faith in the Singapore economy, it was opened as a hotel in 2001. See Ilsa Sharp, *The Fullerton Heritage: Where the Past Meets the Present* (Singapore, 2011).
76 Duncan Bell, *The Idea of Greater Britain: Empire and the Future of World Order, 1860–1900* (Princeton, NJ, 2007).
77 Daniel R. Headrick, *The Invisible Weapon: Telecommunications and International Politics, 1851–1945* (Oxford, 1991). Headrick also deals with the beginnings of the international use of the telephone and the radio at the end of the nineteenth century.
78 Radford, *Guide to the Architecture of Durban and Pietermaritzburg*, p. 7.
79 Jeffrey Richards and John M. MacKenzie, *The Railway Station: A Social History* (Oxford, 1986), particularly chapters 3, 6, 7, 8 and 9. See also Steven Parissien, *Station to Station* (London, 2001).
80 This is well represented in John Masters's novel *Bhowani Junction* (and the famous film based on it), as well as in other novels like Paul Scott's 'Raj Quartet'.
81 In Africa, this sometimes occurred in order to supply Africans with copper for bangles and other pieces of jewellery.

The bourgeois public sphere and new technologies

82 In India, it is still possible to be held up on a train because some of the ties have been removed by local people, as was explained to me by an engineer when on a journey from Delhi to Bombay in 1982.
83 During the era of the Great Depression in the 1930s, the unemployed in Canada, and perhaps elsewhere, would clandestinely 'ride the rails' on freight trains, the comforts of the stations and passenger trains denied to them by poverty. Canadian uncles described their riding-the-rails exploits to me in the 1960s.
84 It featured in the film *Slumdog Millionaire*.
85 This replaced earlier smaller stations. Richards and MacKenzie, *Railway Station*, p. 88.
86 For example, the Murray Guides to India.
87 www.environment.nsw.gov.au/heritageapp/ViewHeritageItemDetails.aspx?ID=5045720 (accessed 20 June 2018).
88 This is now regarded as one of the heritage buildings of Yangon. See Sarah Rooney, *30 Heritage Buildings of Yangon* (Chicago, 2013), pp. 86–88.
89 For this and other celebrated hotels, see Elaine Denby, *Grand Hotels* (London, 2002).
90 The Duke and Duchess of Cornwall and York stayed in Banff in their journey across Canada in 1901 and the diarist of their tour was particularly complimentary about the excellence of the CPR hotels. Banff was a 'sanatorium' and 'charming summer retreat', created by the CPR. Donald Mackenzie Wallace, *The Web of Empire* (London, 1902), pp. 393 and 407.
91 Nina Nelson, *Shepheard's Hotel* (Bath, 1974) provides a chatty account of the visitors to Shepheard's.
92 Ian Talbot and Tahir Kamran, *Colonial Lahore* (London, 2016), p. 16. http://falettishotel.com/ (accessed 14 February 2019).
93 Navin Ramani, *Bombay Art Deco Architecture: A Visual Journey 1930–1953* (Delhi, 2007) identifies five major Art Deco cinemas in the city. The Regal by Stevens is at pp. 204–209.
94 www.gounesco.com/chennais-vanishing-art-deco-architecture/ (accessed 26 July 2018).
95 These aspects of the cultural connections of the British Empire will be explored in another book. For the earlier period, see the extensive and varied work of Holger Hoock, *Empires of the Imagination: Politics, War and the Arts in the British World, 1750–1850* (London, 2010); the pioneering and highly regarded work on India is Bernard S. Cohn, *Colonialism and its Forms of Knowledge: The British in India* (Princeton, NJ, 1996).
96 Charles Reed, *Royal Tourists, Colonial Subjects and the Making of a British World* (Manchester, 2016); Robert Aldrich and Cindy McCreery (eds), *Royals on Tour: Politics, Pageantry and Colonialism* (Manchester, 2018).

5

Domestic residences and city improvement

The history of domestic residences in the British Empire embraces a great range from the very grand to the extremely humble, from the mansion house to the shack, the self-confident urban bourgeois residence to the slum. In all cases, the architecture of the homes of both colonial and indigenous people reflects the economic conditions of specific colonies as well as responses to particular environmental contexts. Among bourgeois residences, many had the stamp of empire upon them, in the sense of being adapted to tropical and subtropical climates as well as to the presence and work of servants. Thus appropriate colonial styles were invented, sometimes adopting characteristics from traditional architecture, often creating what became in effect the foundation of a distinctive national form. They also demonstrate the manner in which builders in different colonial possessions, even on very contrasting continents (in environmental, social and economic ways), influenced each other. As the major architectural phenomenon of a global empire, such domestic residences have received some attention from architectural historians. There have been long-standing discussions of the standard colonial form, the bungalow, as well as of the appearance of striking new styles of bourgeois residence, as in Singapore, and the extensive survey of residences of all sorts in Jamaica. The residences of the poor have also been considered in relation to some colonial cities.[1] This chapter will consider various types of residences throughout the empire, both on settler territories and other types of colonies. But all colonies had in common the extraordinary urban growth of the late nineteenth century, with considerable consequences for the living quarters of migrant workers. As a result, colonial officials began to consider the threat of what they considered to be unhealthy and insanitary structures, and these anxieties led to the development of ideas of city improvement in the twentieth century.

Domestic residences and city improvement

It should be remembered that many types of domestic architecture are temporary in their nature. It is obvious that hunting and gathering peoples in many parts of the British Empire, notably in Australia and Africa as well as a few parts of Asia and North America, constructed temporary shelters as they followed their hunted prey or seasonal plants and fruits. But settled agriculturalists also built essentially temporary residences, albeit larger in scale. Easily exhausted soils ensured that 'transhumance', the movement to new lands as a result of the depletion of nutrients after a variable period of years, led to the reconstruction of villages of thatched wattle-and-daub huts. This abandonment and relocation of villages also had advantages in terms of health and sanitation. Imperial authorities, however, found such mobility unacceptable. It offended their desire to map settlements and enumerate people in order to administer and tax them. Moreover, in areas of white settlement, notably in southern, Central and East Africa, Africans were moved into reserves where they were intended to be settled in more permanent habitations. Alternatively they found themselves (sometimes temporarily) living on what had become white-owned land, where they were expected to supply labour or other services to the new landlords. This historically and ecologically unsuitable permanence ensured the impoverishment of soils and of their inhabitants, often resulting in the fact that those living on 'reserves' or tenancies on white-owned land were forced into labour migration in order to survive. Modern states, the inheritors of imperial modes of administration, surveillance and financial controls, also prefer population stability.

In societies where white settlers predominated (in the case of South Africa and some African colonies in terms of power rather than numbers), indigenous peoples generally lived in relatively simple dwellings (unsophisticated in the eyes of settlers) that were well adapted to the environment. In some places, these could display magnificent carving traditions, particularly among the Maori of New Zealand and the First Nation peoples of Canada. In the early days of the white arrival, the need for the rapid provision of shelters ensured that the early homes of whites were often not particularly distant in style and materials from those of the surrounding indigenous. But while the structural and material gap among the different levels of indigenous societies, almost everywhere except India, was relatively slight, immigrant whites soon introduced a growing, and eventually considerable, social and racial gulf, strongly reflected in architectural terms. Even poorer whites attempted to live in homes which cut them off crucially from the people round about them, particularly in urban areas which, when indigenous people were attracted to them, were swiftly zoned to ensure that class and racial differences were spatially and structurally emphasised. By the end of the nineteenth century urban growth in many places ensured the emergence of peri-urban poor dwellings, including shanty towns, where amenities of all sorts, including clean water, sanitation and refuse collection, were unknown. In India and to a lesser extent in other Asian territories there had always been a great architectural gulf between the wealthy and the powerful on the one hand, and ordinary people on the other. This was now reasserted through the appearance of the new rulers and above all through the development of their cities. Carefully laid-out and spacious 'white towns' or civil and military lines contrasted strikingly with the dense and chaotic 'black towns' or quarters, later suburbs of indigenous residents.[2]

PLANTATION ECONOMIES

Ironically, as we saw in an earlier chapter, imperial officials and settlers often valued the opportunities for mobility presented by the use of tents. There were other ways of creating residences that could be moved about. In Barbados and other islands in the West Indies, 'chattel houses' were homes (often used by 'free blacks' in the days of slavery and a wider social grouping after abolition) which could be readily erected and moved because their owners usually did not own the land on which they were situated.[3] They were wooden homes, built on blocks and generally without nails so that they could be easily deconstructed to be reassembled elsewhere. They invariably comprised two rooms in a symmetrical frontage with a door in the centre, with their windows distinctively shaded by 'bell awnings' (rounded canopies) or other forms of shelter from the sun or with 'jalousies' (pierced screens) designed to permit the free flow of air. These can still be seen in the Caribbean, though they have now sprouted extensions and in some cases, verandahs.[4] They have become more permanent because of the requirements of modern life in the provision of mains electricity, water and sewerage (or in the latter case septic tanks). In Barbados, they are now regarded as historic architectural features, though many residents have to be dissuaded from substituting breeze blocks to avoid the trouble and expense of regular replacement of the wood when it deteriorates. Another residential type which has been seen as temporary and sometimes as mobile is the log cabin. Log cabins are of course the classic home of pioneers in North America, although their basic construction has ensured that they have been a common building type since the ancient world, in Europe particularly common in Scandinavia and the eastern territories. In Canada, the ready availability of woodland, often requiring to be cleared for agriculture, ensured that log cabins were used across the continent. Constructed of logs placed horizontally on each other, often with interlocking cog joints at each end and with corners resting on large stones, they were finished with different roofing structures and materials. Most were abandoned once more sophisticated homes were available, but some do survive and have become holiday rentals, given the cultural and emotional significance of the type in North American history. Throughout Canada, many later houses were built of board frames and were regarded as potentially mobile. Such wooden homes were often built on substantial service basements (later accommodating central heating boilers), with the principal rooms on a floor above and sometimes bedroom dormers above that. They were often capable of being moved to new sites, a striking phenomenon for European visitors seeing a complete house being conveyed through the streets on a large 'low-loader' truck. In New Zealand, the ready availability of wood ensured that all early migrant habitations were wooden, but not in the log-cabin style. It has been suggested that Scottish migrants, for example, followed styles that would be familiar at home, and later attempted to introduce Scots architectural characteristics into their more substantial dwellings.[5]

In the Caribbean and elsewhere in plantation economies, domestic architecture spanned an extraordinary range in terms of scale and quality. In towns, this embraced grander structures for officials and merchants to more modest residences for free blacks. Many places in the West Indies, as elsewhere in the British Empire, had 'shop houses' with retail outlets on the ground floor and homes (originally for the shopkeepers) above, the latter projecting outwards in order to create an arcade for pedestrians and shoppers to be shielded from the sun. This form, which to a certain extent was derived from British practice, was common in, for example, South-East Asia, notably in Singapore and Penang. In the plantations, the powerhouse of Caribbean economies, the range was even greater, from the most basic accommodation for slaves through somewhat better structures for privileged or artisan slaves, to the residences of overseers, finally to the often grand mansion for the plantation owner. The plantations were, however, as much industrial as agricultural sites given the need for boiling houses, trash houses (in which to store the residue of the canes after crushing) and molasses and rum making. All of these required buildings, sometimes quite extensive, together with either windmills or later, watermills, to power the

33 A 'native home', Trinidad

processes (animal or steam power were also used). Sometimes, concerns about the continuing economic value of slaves led to the building of hospitals. The slaves were usually instructed to build their own structures of wood and thatch with earth floors, and there has been some debate among historians whether they followed the familiar precedents from West Africa or simply responded to the requirements of fast and temporary construction in parallel ways, given the materials available to them.[6] Heat was a common environmental factor in both West Africa and in the West Indies, but hurricanes were unique (and by no means universal) in the latter. The frequency of hurricanes and the immense damage they caused induced variations in architectural practice, including efforts to create the least resistance by building with low profiles and with gently rather than steeply sloping roofs. Nevertheless, merchant houses in the port cities were often double-storied, while the major plantation houses could even reflect aspects of British architectural styles.[7]

Indeed, many architectural styles in the Caribbean not only reflect social and racial history, but also cultural interaction with Britain.[8] There was additionally an inheritance from predecessor Spanish practice, particularly in the inclusion of the piazza in domestic architecture and townscapes.[9] The piazza can be

Domestic residences and city improvement

defined as a mixture of the open gallery in front of or around houses, and the arcade or loggia along streets. The piazza has elements of the verandah once that feature, and the word, were learned from Indian practice. It was designed as an intermediate space between house and garden, a space for living to catch cooler breezes, particularly in the evenings, but also a space in which to conduct business, and, on the plantations, from which to exercise surveillance over the workers, the cultivation and its processes. In a great town house, such as the Hibbert House of 1755 in Kingston, Jamaica, an essentially Georgian style was combined with front and rear piazzas, the rear possibly used for trading in slaves who were marshalled for sale in the courtyard. Its materials were brick, masonry and wood, a mixture not uncommon in the West Indies. The Jamaican National Heritage Trust describes it as 'the most beautiful house in Kingston'.[10] Humbler buildings might also be constructed with masonry bases and wood frames above, partly to cope with hurricanes (wood often surviving better than masonry), and to facilitate rebuilding. Excellent examples of such a mixed masonry and wood construction can be seen in the streets of Basse Terre in St Kitts.[11]

34 Shops and homes in Fort Street, Basseterre, St Kitts

The British Empire through buildings

So far as the great plantation houses are concerned, they adopted various styles, such as the Jacobean of St Nicholas Abbey on Barbados, built in the mid-seventeenth century.[12] Still privately owned, this house has inevitably become a heritage site, with some of its industrial outbuildings surviving.[13] But in the guide to the house, the modern tourist is largely shielded from the reality of slavery.[14] Many later plantation residences developed distinctive Caribbean styles with long façades, 'piazzas' on one, two or three sides, central flights of steps at the front, and sometimes a second storey of bedrooms. Examples include Mount Plenty great house in Jamaica, Fairview estate house and Romney Manor on St Kitts, or on a smaller scale, Hamden or Winefields in Jamaica.[15] Intriguing changes over time have been identified in the building of estate mansions. As slave revolts became more common in the eighteenth century, plantation residences adopted the style of defensive structures, 'Castles of Fear', as Nelson called them.[16] These were often built with corner towers (offering surveillance of the walls), with loopholes for firearms, and sometimes with defensive walls around their gardens or courtyards. Examples (many of them

35 St Nicholas Abbey, plantation house, Barbados

Domestic residences and city improvement

36 Fairview, plantation house, St Kitts

now ruined) include Stewart Castle, Stokes Hall and Colbeck Castle, which have been linked architecturally to examples in Ireland and Scotland. Further social changes induced other architectural developments beyond these various cultural legacies and responses to local environmental, economic and social conditions. In the later eighteenth century, many of the wealthiest plantation owners chose to be absentees, perhaps in response to fears of revolts or of hurricanes, moving to Britain and leaving their West Indian estates to be run by overseers. It may even be the case that this was encouraged by the migration of literate and numerate Scots to the West Indies ready and willing to take these overseer positions.[17] The return of Caribbean plantation wealth could stimulate transfers in materials and even style features, for example mahogany for panelling and staircases, in the British homes of such plantation owners. Sculptural features on both private residences and, in particular, on public buildings, might also reflect West Indian origins.

In the same period, the numbers of free blacks and mulatto (mixed-race) people grew considerably, creating architectural responses in the growth in numbers of residences to accommodate these expanding population groups.

Such homes were often scaled-up versions of the original two-room structures inhabited by free blacks, buildings with piazzas, a larger footprint and number of rooms, and invariably an outside yard constituting, in effect, further living space. The quality of construction and materials also improved, with wooden flooring and the provision of windows. Such residences have sometimes been called examples of Creole architecture.[18] To a certain extent the abolition of slavery thus produced further changes, though invariably continuing to reflect the great poverty of the former slaves. They received no compensation at all for their years of enslavement, although the former owners were compensated, sometimes in staggeringly high amounts, by the British Government.[19]

The plantation houses of the Caribbean are well documented, but there were many other plantations in the British Empire, all revealing the social hierarchy from plantation owner or manager to a large and exploited labour forces. Almost all plantations consequently exhibit the same spectrum in size and quality of buildings, from the great house to the basic, sometimes flimsy accommodation for slaves and free workers, with industrial buildings for storage and processing. The essential socioeconomic character of all plantations is to be highly labour-intensive and in the post-slavery era, new solutions had to be found, as for example indentured labour of Indians, the 'new system of slavery'.[20] In the case of tea, the labour force was largely made up of poorly paid women. In the Cape, the vineyards boasted grand houses, often in a Dutch style, many dating from the seventeenth and eighteenth centuries.[21] Tea plantations in Ceylon and in North-East India, jute and indigo plantations in Bengal, sugar plantations in Indian Ocean Island such as Mauritius, as well as rubber plantations in Malaya, also created large estate houses.[22] Many of these were in the classic extended bungalow style, with long verandahs and, if a second storey, equivalent balconies, usually with considerable awnings to offer shelter from the sun. Many such plantations also required industrial buildings with extensive machinery, requiring accommodation for the operatives.[23]

Where white settlers acquired extensive lands in East, Central and southern Africa, whether for agricultural production or for cattle ranching, many again supplied themselves with grand bungalows that came to be associated with landownership by a small minority.[24] In areas of extensive tobacco production, notably in Southern Rhodesia (Zimbabwe), large barns were used to dry and cure the tobacco. Such large-scale agricultural establishments projected the contrast between the grand white residence at the centre of the estate and the workers' huts in the village or villages that used a portion of the land on the periphery

Domestic residences and city improvement

(sometimes workers were permitted to cultivate on their own behalf). Large-scale sheep farmers, particularly in New South Wales and Victoria, similarly inhabited large bungalows to reflect their status. In all these ways, strikingly alien buildings appeared in many areas of colonial rule. Plantation economies also established their architectural presence in grand pavilions, often Orientalist in style, in the great exhibitions in Europe (and elsewhere) of the late nineteenth and first half of the twentieth centuries.

URBAN RESIDENCES AND THE BUNGALOW

Very grand houses were also a characteristic of Indian colonial cities. Calcutta famously became the 'City of Palaces' with major residences in Chowringhee Road and elsewhere.[25] Moreover, around Calcutta there were mansions which symbolised the interpenetration of the rural and the urban in the manner in which they were used as weekend retreats, as the residences of zamindars (the feudal landowners underpinned by the Permanent Settlement system in Bengal), Bengali elites and wealthy British businessmen and senior administrators. Such residences were to be found on the garden reach of the Hooghly, in Barrackpore, Dumdum and other parts of the environs of the city. They were all marked by 'conspicuous consumption of nature' in their extensive gardens, orchards and other lands which became part of their cultural presence for weekend parties and events.[26] Grand houses used alike by British imperial figures and elite Indians were also a feature of Delhi and other cities, where they displayed a degree of ambiguity in their cultural hybridity and even reuse of original Mughal structures.[27] There was a parallel development in Ceylon, where elite Sinhalese and Europeans alike built grand houses, often with extensive gardens, in the appropriately named affluent area of Colombo, Cinnamon Gardens. These houses often adopted a variety of European styles, but those owned by the wealthy local elite came to reflect a degree of dynamic cultural hybridity which became increasingly nationalist in the twentieth century, involving the inclusion of Buddhist and other eastern motifs, as well as changes in the taste and clothing of their inhabitants.[28]

If plantation houses were often notable for their scale and opulence, there were many castles and major houses created by wealthy capitalists in the empire. Such figures were consciously trying to demonstrate their capacity to match the spending power and architectural ambitions of their equivalents in Europe, while at the same time demonstrating the economic opportunities of the new

The British Empire through buildings

Dominions and opportunities for upward social mobility. A few examples of such buildings that have survived (and are now open to the public) would include Larnach Castle near Dunedin in Otago, New Zealand. This strange confection has a powerful masonry structure with a machicolated tower, but looks distinctly colonial because of its verandahs and balconies with their iron balustrades. It was built in the 1870s by a wealthy banker, William Larnach, who had succeeded in capitalising on the considerable economic growth of Australia and New Zealand at the middle of the century. James Horne Stewart, who had inherited the Mount Pleasant estate in Bathurst, New South Wales, from his father, General William Stewart, set about building in the 1870s a mansion in what has been described as the romantic, picturesque style, with both Georgian and Victorian elements. He was determined to outrank all the other grand homes in the colony. Originally called The Mount, it was later renamed Abercrombie.[29] In the far west of Canada, Robert Dunsmuir, a successful coal baron, built himself a Scottish baronial castle with the appropriate name of Craigdarroch between 1887 and 1890.[30] It has an aura of the Scottish Highlands, but proclaims itself

37 Craigdarroch, Victoria, British Columbia

to be a Canadian alternative. In Toronto, Sir Henry Pellatt used his wealth from stockbroking to build one of the most astonishing residences in the dominions, the vast Casa Loma, Gothic Revival, and sufficiently eclectic that it has many European resonances. This was constructed between 1911 and 1914.

If these somewhat megalomaniac residences were generally one-off statements of wealth and success, it is apparent that by far the most widespread residential type in the British Empire was the bungalow. King's classic work has the subtitle 'The Production of a Global Culture'.[31] This perfectly encapsulates the manner in which an Indian residential style, the *bangla* or *bangala* from Bengal, swept the world in many different forms and sizes during the imperial period.[32] *Hobson-Jobson*, the Anglo-Indian dictionary of 1886, has a valuable definition of the bungalow:

> The most usual class of house occupied by Europeans in the interior of India; being on one story [sic], and covered by a pyramidal roof, which in the normal *bungalow* is of thatch, but which may be of tiles without impairing its title to be called a *bungalow*. Most of the houses of officers in Indian cantonments are of this character. In reference to the style of the house, *bungalow* is sometimes employed in contradistinction to the (usually more pretentious) *pukka house*; by which latter term is understood a masonry house with a terraced roof.[33]

The dictionary goes on to explain that bungalow can also apply to a garden structure or one on the roof of a larger house for sleeping in. Having covered the etymology of the word and the spread of the type to Bihar and Upper India, the editors then examine the several different variations of Bengali bungalow, before demonstrating from quotations that the word was coming into use by European travellers in India from the early eighteenth century. Their next definition was to describe the functions of the 'dawk' or 'dak bungalow', the rest-houses for travellers in British India. What they did not know was the extent to which word and building would effect a worldwide dispersal.

Hobson-Jobson thus captured the essence of the bungalow, the single storey,[34] the relatively unpretentious nature of the structure, the tight arrangement of rooms, and its convenience as a standard building type across the colonies. Scriver considers that the PWD had a conservative and deadening effect upon the built environment of British India by creating standardised approaches to various public buildings, military and civilian, as well as in respect of the countless bungalows built across the Subcontinent in order to create residential accommodation in cantonments for officials and military officers.[35] Standardised plans were also produced for such structures as officers' messes and for the accommodation of railway employees. Bungalows were graded according to the rank of the various officials inhabiting them. After the 1857 Revolt and the creation of direct imperial rule in India, the demand caused by the rapid growth in the numbers of such imperial employees ensured that accommodation (and the various other structures required) had to be supplied with some speed. In a situation of such urgency, standardisation was almost inevitable. In any case, cityscapes everywhere invariably display a combination of the banal and the self-consciously grand public and religious buildings required by the population.

Such standardisation was not unique to India. Almost everywhere, bungalows were thrown up for colonial officials, generally sprouting that other feature of Indian origin, the verandah. This liminal zone between the domestic interior and the environmental surroundings became a key space for socialising and drinking, notably in the early evening. In Africa, all officials and others in government service, as well as most expatriate inhabitants of towns, lived in bungalows. In the Northern Rhodesian (Zambian) town of Ndola there were parallel streets of them, built by the PWD. The standard layout was an entrance via the verandah, which had a front door opening directly into a living room, with the dining room, kitchen and other utilities on one side, bedrooms on the other.[36] The roof was often of corrugated iron, noisy in heavy rains and hot when subjected to strong sun, although this was mitigated somewhat by internal ceilings. Each bungalow was detached in its own plot, often an acre, with outbuildings for servants located on what was known as the 'sanitary lane' running along the back between two rows of bungalows. Some examples were often larger, occasionally smaller than the one described in this paragraph. Bungalows were produced in portable, prefabricated versions, sold through catalogues, in wood with galvanised corrugated iron, lined inside with what was described as matchboarding, all standing on a light brickwork foundation and with windows glazed in 21-ounce sheet glass (priced at £220–£240). Another larger version was described as a shooting lodge, of similar construction and priced at £440.[37] While these appear to have been manufactured for the domestic British market, similar prefabricated buildings could be exported around the world. They appeared regularly in Ideal Home exhibitions in the twentieth century and in newspaper advertisements.

It may be, however, that it is possible to identify another variation, the California bungalow, which appeared in Los Angeles in the late nineteenth century and rapidly spread through the state. Many of its features were similar to the

Domestic residences and city improvement

Indian and imperial version, though it was generally built in wooden shingles and was simple and rustic in form. About the time of the First World War, it was transferred to Australia, where it was built in brick and was developed as ideal for hotter climes.[38] If it can be seen as influential in Australia, still it is possible to see this US West Coast model as ultimately derived from the *bangla*. Whether we can identify one or two origins, it is certainly the case that the bungalow spread throughout the British colonies in Asia, as well as appearing in variants in Africa, Australia and New Zealand. Photographic evidence certainly reveals the popularity of the bungalow in Australia and New Zealand.[39] Such global influence continued well into the twentieth century and occasioned the provision of pattern books.[40] The bungalow also became the key instance of an imperial style which became influential in the metropolis. Bungalows became a favoured (if sometimes denigrated) building type in seaside resorts, suburban developments throughout Britain, particularly in the inter-war years of the twentieth century. Despite their severely practical and agricultural origins, they became particularly associated with leisure and recreation, appearing in hill

38 Classic colonial bungalow in Lyttelton, South Island, New Zealand

stations and seaside resorts, symbolising release from the worlds of industry, business, commerce and labour. Even the Arts and Crafts movement approved of the bungalow and considered it an appealing building as a country home on mountain or in valley.[41] Its full potential is revealed in the manner in which it was adopted as a useful residential type for aspirant Africans (replacing the round hut with the rectangular structure supposedly representative of civilisation) and as the ideal home for residents of new capitals such as Canberra, New Delhi and Lusaka, on three different continents (see Chapter 7). The bungalow had been assimilated into the hierarchical structures of the imperial social pyramid to such an extent that the grandest and most elaborate of versions seemed to bear little relationship to the prototype *bangla*.

Nowhere was this more true than in colonies like Penang and Singapore. The earliest residences of Europeans in Prince of Wales Island (Penang) in the late eighteenth century and of Singapore from the 1820s tended to follow the *bangla* type while blending with certain elements from the Malayan context, particularly the raising of structures on stilts and the provision of *atap* thatch roofs (that is, thatched with the leaves of a nipa palm), sometimes pyramidal in style, sometimes hipped. Indeed, residential buildings in Penang reflected the extraordinary history and ethnic hybridity of the place. Before the British acquired it in 1786, the island already occupied a key position in the trades of the East. In the late eighteenth and early nineteenth centuries it experienced a phenomenal growth as a free port, connecting the trades of India, the Malay Peninsula and the Far East. Cloves, nutmeg, cinnamon and pepper were all grown nearby and the opium trade was serviced there, while the development of tin mining in Malaya and later the rubber trade produced wealthy merchants and entrepreneurs (many of them Chinese) who sought to live there. The result was an ethnic and cultural melting pot of Chinese, Malays, some Indians, Eurasians and Europeans. The architecture came to reflect this in extraordinary ways. As the capital George Town grew in size, thousands of shophouses were built, producing covered street arcades.[42] Penang was remote from indigenous authority and this ensured that efforts to maintain cultural homogeneity were lacking. It enjoyed an architectural free-for-all, out of which emerged 'Straits Eclectic', at the same time both style and non-style.[43] This combined elements of the vernacular with colonial mercantile, of Anglo-Indian structures with European detailing, sometimes even classical pediments. Bungalows were transformed by a climatic awareness of the significance of the raised post-and-lintel Malay style, then combined with imported materials such as roof tiles, decorative ironwork (for verandahs and balconies) – often from Scottish producers like Glasgow's Saracen Iron Works – and encaustic tiles from the English potteries – hence 'pluralistic Penang'.[44] Europeans came to demand more substantial residences, two-storey bungalows, with verandas and with masonry or brick bases and external stairs. Meanwhile, better-off Chinese created courtyard houses with central airwells and much Chinese decoration on the basic Straits Eclectic bungalow style. This style developed from the late eighteenth century during the astonishing period of economic growth up to the 1860s, after which it became in some respects more internationalised and, in the case of the grander homes, subject to the work of professional architects and engineers. These hybrid structures, many still to be seen in Penang, were filled with artefacts from China and Europe, often purchased from the incoming colonial stores such as Whiteaway, Laidlaw and Company. During the later period, architects and engineers working in Singapore, such as Stark and McNeill and Swan and Maclaren, began to supply larger Straits Eclectic houses for Europeans and wealthy Chinese, sometimes incorporating 'Chinese rusticated Arts and Crafts', Art Nouveau elements (particularly in stained glass) and later Art Deco. By the twentieth century, western-trained Chinese architects were also designing buildings in Penang and Singapore. Few places in the world reflect ethnic, economic, colonial and international histories in its architecture as strikingly as Penang. Meanwhile, on Penang Hill, grand houses were built, sometimes in masonry.[45]

In Singapore, after the initial period of settlement, Europeans began to demand more substantial residences, so Anglo-Indian bungalows appeared, though in rapidly modified styles. In Singapore as elsewhere in the Straits Settlements and the Malay Peninsula, these were often of two storeys, even adopting neoclassical elements. Such structures passed through many variations in the course of the nineteenth century, but from the later 1890s a distinctive form appeared that was to last into the inter-war years of the twentieth century. This has been called the black-and-white house, a 'singular architectural tradition', made up of 'an amalgam of western and local' elements.[46] This type of residence was in its prime from the end of the nineteenth century to the inter-war years, but it continued with an 'afterlife' of various identifiable variants down to the Second World War. While it had affinities with the Indian bungalow, it was also adapted to a Malayan/Singaporean environment through the provision of 'stilts' of masonry or brick to raise the main rooms from the ground, a convenient arrangement to allow the flow of air underneath, a defence against termites and protection from flooding. But the style took on elements of the Arts and

Crafts, as well as the 'mock Tudor' which became popular in Britain at the same period. This was made up of half-timbering (painted black) and white render on brick (painted white). Wide overhanging eaves provided shelter for verandahs, which often ran round four sides of the building, while a porte cochère was generally prominent on the front (to allow Europeans to alight from rickshaws or horse-drawn vehicles in heavy rain). A sitting area or extension to a living room was usually positioned above this porch. The houses were sometimes symmetrical, sometimes L-shaped, and the style was also adapted for clubs, messes and other larger public buildings. The roofs were frequently high and steeply pitched, once again to provide a free flow of cooling air. It has been suggested that its remarkable hybridity was some two centuries in the making.[47]

Dozens of these houses were built throughout Singapore as the original town rapidly expanded in a number of directions in response to the economic booms which occurred in the years before and after the First World War. They were built by the private sector, by the PWD, by the military, the navy and later the air force, particularly during the era when Singapore was developed militarily in the 1930s in the face of expected Japanese aggression. These various providers ensured that the black-and-white house was adapted to satisfy an extensive hierarchy. The PWD built houses to match the official status of occupants. The private sector built to commissions by notable businessmen, bankers, commodity brokers, shipping managers and financiers of the island, as well as for the better-off professionals like doctors and lawyers. When the armed forces began an extensive building programme, the houses were designed to match the ranks of the officers who were to live in them. Gradually the style changed, passing through phases that have been dubbed tropical Edwardian, late Arts and Crafts, and finally a more modernist Art Deco. The latter style responded to the plasticity possible in the shift from masonry, brick, timber and stucco to reinforced concrete, permitting the classic rounded forms, simple lines and flat roofs of the international style. These Singapore houses were also marked by the plots of land they occupied, often extensive gardens with tennis courts, permitting them to be surrounded by lush tropical vegetation. All of this was of course made possible by the fact that their inhabitants enjoyed the services of a number of servants, once again according to status.

Servants would also have been readily available in South Africa and this affected the provision of comfortable homes for whites in Cape Town, Johannesburg and other cities. Cecil Rhodes insisted on the use of a Dutch style and of local craftsmanship (that is, by whites) for his home Groote Schuur at the base of

Domestic residences and city improvement

39 Groote Schuur, Cape Town

Table Mountain. Formerly a barn, it was transformed into the opulent quasi-Dutch homestead of his imagination, with the help of his favourite architect, Herbert Baker. This derivative style was reinforced after it was burnt down in the mid-1890s and had to be rebuilt. Baker was later implicated in a movement which linked politics to architecture when he contributed to a journal run by the followers of the High Commissioner, Alfred Milner (the group known as the Kindergarten), in insisting that the Cape Dutch style was a vital constituent of the cultural identity of a future Union of South Africa.[48] Despite such an assertion, the Cape Town suburbs were larded with very English names like Kenilworth, Claremont, Goodwood, Kensington and the more local Constantia, where substantial bungalows were built with only the southern African stoep (not much different from verandahs elsewhere) to locate them culturally and geographically. They were generally in single plots well sheltered by trees and hedges (now often with high fences and gates) to protect them from the surrounding natural and ethnic environment, and remain a marker of status. This is true of many other places in South Africa, including the well-heeled Johannesburg suburb of Parktown and other suburbs further from the city centre. There was a major building boom here in the aftermath of the Anglo-Boer War from 1902, with large numbers of homes designed by Baker to house the officials and professionals of the new imperial regime. Once again the large bungalow type was the norm, all of them with the southern African stoep, as it was among the small minority of white settlers in Southern Rhodesia and a few other places in Central Africa. All of these homes contrast dramatically with the ubiquitous huts and shanties of the black population.

URBAN TERRACES

The more opulent Singapore and South African houses were as far as could be imagined from the urban terraced house, always a significant characteristic of British residential architecture. This again spanned a considerable social range from the great terraces of London squares, with town houses of aristocrats, wealthy entrepreneurs and leading politicians, to the celebrated Georgian terraces of Bath or Edinburgh, and on down the social scale to peri-urban working-class terraces, including the seemingly endless brick terraces of Lancashire and elsewhere in the north of England and the Midlands. Terraces duly appeared in colonial cities, before the ready availability of land ensured that suburban detached houses on single plots became standard in cities and towns in the territories of settlement. In an era of primitive public transport, the desire to live close to places of work ensured that colonial terraces, some of considerable aesthetic distinction, were built in many places in Australia, notably in Sydney (in the Rocks area and in Paddington), Melbourne (for example, Royal Terrace and Tasma Terrace) and Adelaide (with examples on North Terrace).[49] These terraces, however, were adapted to the climate in the provision of verandahs or first-floor balconies, often ornamented with typically colonial wrought-iron balusters and details. Fine terraces also appeared in the principal New Zealand cities, of which Stuart Street, Dunedin is a good example. In South Africa, some of the most attractive terraced houses can be found in the Bo Kaap or Malay quarter of Cape Town, and other examples include a magnificent terrace in Port Elizabeth on the sloping Donkin Street by the Donkin Reserve, and again the attractive university town of Grahamstown. In Canada, given the climate, the style is very different, but terraces in Toronto include a short one in Berkeley Street in what is known locally as the bay and gable design, and Clarence Terrace on Clarence Square.[50] Of course the provision of such terraces depends entirely on the availability of land, ownership arrangements and the predilections of developers. Moreover, such housing had a tendency to start out as reasonably high status, but as suburbs became more fashionable, inner-city terraces often moved down the social scale, particularly if divided into multiple residences. In recent times, they have sometimes become gentrified again and indeed, the renewed desire for tighter living space and ready access to town centres has ensured that the concept of the terrace has been developed in modern architectural styles.

Many surviving terraces have been turned into office accommodation or have become highly fashionable residences, but some of the older ones had become inner-city slums at the end of the nineteenth and beginning of the twentieth centuries. Most cities in the Anglophone world received major inward migration, such that the residential stock was wholly inadequate to house the press of people. The result was overcrowding, dilapidation, unsanitary conditions and frequently epidemics of disease. Sydney in New South Wales was so afflicted by such inadequacies that a Royal Commission reported on its problems in 1909. In 1910, New South Wales acquired its first Labor government and the colonial secretary John Rowland Dacey wrote that 'The day is past when free Australians were content to be herded together in terraces of mere dog boxes.'[51] He recommended the building of a garden suburb to alleviate the problems. This was the first public housing scheme in Australia and perhaps anywhere in the empire, with construction beginning in 1912. Although Daceyville, as it was called, was never completed, it has survived despite several attempts to demolish it. Almost inevitably, it consisted largely of small bungalows on individual plots. After the First World War it supplied homes for returning soldiers and war widows. Located about six kilometres from the city centre, it was part of the major movement of suburbanisation which turned Sydney into a 'city of suburbs' and produced its greatly spread-out urban plan to be seen today.[52] Yet Melbourne may be even more suburbanised than Sydney. The Encyclopedia of Melbourne lists literally dozens of suburbs and describes it as 'the most self-consciously suburban of Australian cities'. By the end of the nineteenth century it was 'one of the most extensive areas of low-density urban settlement in the world', with an extraordinarily high level of individual ownership of detached properties.[53] Wide-open spaces, together with inhabitants' preference for living on their own plots of land, ensured that Australian settlements became megacities in surface area. Sometimes, there was a class banding effect to this suburban growth. In Melbourne, for example, it has been suggested that the working-class suburbs were closer to the centre, with the middle classes seeking grander homes on larger plots.[54] While it is difficult to establish a fully accurate like-for-like survey, nevertheless a few statistics reveal the extraordinary spread-out character of these cities, a reflection of the nature of their housing stock. Sydney, with a population just over five million, covers over 12,300 square kilometres, while Melbourne, with just under five million, occupies almost 10,000 square kilometres. By contrast, and as an indication of much greater density of housing stock, Mumbai has a population of over 18 million and covers an area of just over 600 square kilometres. In the case of Toronto, the greater city has a population of almost 6 million and a surface area of 5.9 million square kilometres.

TRANSPORT SYSTEMS, URBAN GROWTH AND CITY IMPROVEMENT

None of this urban expansion would have been possible without developments in transport systems. Horse-drawn buses and trams were limited in their scope, but from the electrification of tramway systems, starting in the 1890s, the conveyance of people to places of work in the cities became easier. Networks of trams and buses developed further in the twentieth century (also necessitating the building of large depots) and were supplemented by suburban railway systems. In some places, suburbs were stimulated into development by the arrival of a railway line and a convenient station, some highly attractive in appearance. By such means cities were also able to open out into rural areas or towards seaside resorts. In the case of great harbour cities like Sydney, Auckland or Hong Kong, ferries were vital in transporting people from home to work or city-centre attractions. In Hong Kong, the opening of the Peak Tramway in 1888 was important in developing the Mid-Levels and the Peak for European elite housing to catch the cooler breezes. In the years before the First World War, the first cars began to appear in colonial towns. Often the arrival of the first car was almost as much a source of celebration as the opening of railway lines had been in the past. By the inter-war years, cars had become commonplace, as had commercial applications of internal combustion engines for buses and trucks. All of these inevitably had effects on the layout of towns, cities and suburbs. Thus, developments in transport technologies interacted with economic and residential zoning in promoting the geographical spread of cities, forces which city planners sometimes tried to control, but which often controlled them. These expansive imperatives resulted in the eating up of surrounding areas of the natural environment.

Such dramatic urban growth was occurring throughout the empire and everywhere it was bringing major problems in its wake. Henry Beveridge of the Bengal Civil Service,[55] and father of William, Lord Beveridge (generally regarded as one of the founders of the British Welfare State), wrote in a letter in August 1899:

> I feel sure that our native towns in Bombay, Calcutta and Madras are a disgrace. We choose the best sites, put grand buildings on them and huddle up all the rest. As if the body politic could flourish if any extremity thereof be left in dirt and squalor. The European quarter is like the electric light. It only throws into deeper shadow the un-lighted places.[56]

Although Beveridge was specifically writing about India, the same could be said of British cities (even in the twenty-first century) and of many other places in the British Empire.

By the early twentieth century, soon after Beveridge's acute observation, there was a growing realisation among British imperial administrators and planners that the old laissez-faire approach to the growth of imperial cities had become outmoded. Major problems of the social and environmental conditions of residential areas were becoming apparent everywhere. Class and racial distinctions were invariably zoned in cities of the Dominions as well as in India and the dependent colonies. In non-white territories, Anthony King has proposed the concept of enclavism for racial separation in the sociocultural space of cities,[57] although, as indicated in the Introduction, the need for servants, many of whom lived on site, meant that some members of different races lived in close proximity. Such a servant class, and their living conditions, were however subject to the surveillance of their employers, necessitating possibly superior arrangements from those of 'native quarters' which, from a European point of view, were left alone and largely out of sight, at least metaphorically. There can be little doubt that part of the concern with the housing of the lower classes was stimulated by the anxieties of bourgeois settlers and sojourners, that overcrowding, decaying and inadequate buildings, and above all lack of sanitary arrangements promoted a danger to the health of the inhabitants and were therefore potentially threatening through cross-contagion to white inhabitants in adjacent or even more distant housing areas. The problems associated with contaminated water supply and inadequate sewage disposal were well understood long before the development of the germ theory of disease and the emergence of microbiological studies relating to insect vectors and bacteria transmission towards the end of the century.

Such problems were far from being unique to the tropical imperial territories. They had become apparent in British cities during the nineteenth century, even when precise causation was still not fully understood. Outbreaks of cholera and typhus remained relatively common until the last decades of the century. In Glasgow, there were several cholera epidemics between 1831 and 1853, as well as repeated epidemics of typhus (transmitted, for example, by body lice and fleas), which caused major increases in death rates in a population living in considerable squalor and much debilitated by respiratory diseases. 'By the 1830s the once elegant city had acquired the unenviable reputation of being the filthiest and least healthy in Britain.'[58] Efforts to improve conditions in Glasgow culminated in the provision of a clean water supply from Loch Katrine in 1859, borne to the city through a combination of aqueducts and tunnels some forty miles long, and also through the surveys of the Glasgow City Improvement Trust from 1866. These surveys examined the closes and alleys of the city, the building stock, the arrangements for refuse and sewage disposal and much else. They led to efforts to improve the quality of housing after the demolition of the worst of the slums.[59] This background is important for an understanding of equivalent problems in the British Empire. Improvement trusts on the Glasgow model were created in Bombay (1898), Calcutta (1911), Rangoon (1920), Singapore (1927), Lagos (1928) and Delhi (1936–37).[60] What had started out as a highly discriminatory class order of residential accommodation, water supply and sanitation had become a racial one overseas.

By the twentieth century, the Colonial Office and various colonial administrations had become more interventionist, commissioning reports that would guide these efforts at 'improvement' of the environment of colonial cities. There was, for example, a Report on the Sanitary Conditions of Singapore in 1907.[61] The Calcutta Improvement Trust appointed a chief engineer, Edwin Percy Richards, a founder of the town planning institute, who produced in 1914 a major (492-page) Report on the Condition, Improvement and Town Planning of the City of Calcutta and Contiguous Areas.[62] This recommended the building and widening of roads, slum clearance and improvement, legislation and suburban planning. It was accompanied by extensive charts, photographs and maps.[63] Such reports and the related improvement trusts significantly increased the twentieth-century concern with data, particularly in relation to hygiene, city layouts and housing quality in tropical and subtropical contexts. Censuses, mapping, photography, building conditions and regulations were all marshalled in this search for 'improvement'. Theories were developed about the need for the circulation of air, for the provision of adequate open spaces and lanes between houses, as well as for the provision of cottage-style residences for workers and sometimes flats (see below) for 'blue-collar' and other upper working-class categories. These efforts were at times hindered by powerful property-owning classes in Asia and elsewhere, as well as by the inevitable diversion of energies during the First and Second World Wars. Moreover, as Richards discovered in Calcutta, there were also entrenched administrative interests. He criticised past practice and the officials who controlled it, which inevitably made him unpopular with these permanent (and perhaps hidebound) figures. Thus there was a variety of brakes upon such efforts at improvement. Nevertheless, the economic cycles of the inter-war years and the resulting trade-union activity and 'public order' problems of the period seemed to render the improvement in living conditions all the more urgent. Chang has postulated that the increasingly interventionist activities of these decades leading up to decolonisation were driven by the development of environmental and climatic 'technoscience' promoted by increasing professionalisation of these movements for urban improvement.[64] Such professionalisation promoted the creation and interaction of empire-wide networks, the founding of building research stations to develop and supposedly standardise approaches to colonial housing types. All of this was characterised by an increase in publications relating to these movements as well as the promulgation of reports on housing.

As we saw in a previous chapter, there was a close interdependence between the supposedly modernist elements of Asian cities, notably in India, that is, the 'civil lines' and 'cantonments' and the old towns that serviced them. Development of the former inevitably stimulated migration into the latter, with consequent overcrowding, social deprivation and the degeneration of the built environment. This led to haphazard construction, with property owners maximising income by subdividing or building unregulated extensions, the whole becoming very difficult to supervise and survey by imperial authorities. In the case of Delhi, the creation of the 'New' section of the city with its post-1911 status as the capital stimulated a renewed flood of migration into the city. The censuses indicate that in 1911 Delhi's population was just under 414,000. By 1941, it had more than doubled to nearly 918,000. In the 1930s, the rate of increase was over 44 per cent for the decade.[65] Partly as a result of this growth, the old walled town became, in British eyes, a hopelessly congested, overcrowded, unsanitary and unhealthy zone urgently requiring attention. At this late date in British imperial administration, the Improvement Trust set about the reconstruction of the old town and the creation of new 'overspill' areas. Jyoti Hosegrahar has described the extraordinary ethnocentric ways in which the British planners set about these objectives, with slum clearance and new roads, planning new areas of housing that would satisfy, as they thought, the requirements of a threefold class hierarchy: upper, middle and lower class.[66] Different layouts, architectural forms and densities were organised for each. They set about this by pursuing what they regarded as the scientific rationality of data collection and the laying out of statistical tables of appropriate densities, cubic living space and the like, often adopting norms that were inappropriate to both the climate and the heterogeneous character of the population, not to mention its religious and social requirements. Moreover, they pursued a model in which work and living accommodation would be separate, with transportation supposedly appropriate to a commuting society linking the two. This flew in the face of the fact that the old arrangements had harboured 'cottage' industries. These efforts at rational planning were frustrated by the resistance of the population, the landowners and recourse to legal efforts to hold up compulsory purchase and other planning tools. There was some reconstruction, but the demolition of properties and the eviction of their residents led to more 'informal' living arrangements, often in shanties. The resulting dislocation had not been satisfactorily overcome when the British left India in 1947.

In this same inter-war era, in many cities apartment blocks became a preferred mode of urban living across a range of social classes. Multi-storey buildings had already become a characteristic of lower-class housing in the major Indian cities, often rapidly becoming slums. The development of railway and tram lines encouraged the spread of such buildings far into suburbs. But in the inter-war years, middle-class and even aristocratic residents looked to more upmarket apartment blocks as a convenient means of urban living. By the 1930s and 1940s these became supreme expressions of Art Deco in the architecture, notably of Bombay.[67] Apartment blocks appeared on reclaimed land and on sea frontages, for example on Back Bay and Marine Drive, where the lights of the apartment blocks at night are still known as 'the Queen's Necklace'. This international style, originating in Europe, was enthusiastically taken up by architects in India, some British but mainly Indian, with one of the world's greatest collections of Art Deco buildings appearing in the city. The opportunities afforded by steel and concrete construction created an architecture of flowing lines, curving balconies, faceted façades, striking rooflines (sometimes marine in inspiration,[68] sometimes ziggurat in appearance) and 'eyebrows' (projecting shade elements over windows), all decorated in the motifs characteristic of the style, with the sunburst, the frozen fountain and geometric patterns, and often with sculptures, some of them featuring Indian deities and mythical figures. Art Deco forms also appeared in striking ways in interiors, in magnificent terrazzo floors, glasswork, jazzy patterning, lift shafts and the flowing lines of stairwells and railings. Here was an international modernist style which lent itself to an imperial city on the edge of independence. While it might not be regarded as a truly imperial style, still its presence in empire contexts became important in many territories, not least in public buildings, places of entertainment and clubs.

Putting the more upmarket apartment developments to one side, there are various ways of interpreting the developments in efforts at the improvement of urban housing. They may be seen as indicative of an acceleration of concepts of 'progress' and 'improvement'. But they have also been interpreted as evidence of an increasing tendency to colonial surveillance and regulatory control of the lives of the colonised, including tighter hegemony over their bodies, their living conditions and aspects of their social and cultural lives. The protection provided by the wholly different environments, building stock and social arrangements of the enclaves of white sojourners (as well as the upper classes in the towns and cities of the settler territories) was certainly an important motivation, though to suggest that it was the sole one may be going too far. On the other hand, although these activities appeared to be suffused with an air of idealism, from the point of view of the colonisers, the fact is that they were often only effective at the margins. Massive social and environmental problems continued to be the main characteristic of colonial urbanisation, particularly as the movements of populations from rural contexts to towns and cities accelerated during the twentieth century (and continued to do so with even greater speed after decolonisation). Some districts and a few building types were improved. There were some efforts at supplying purer water and better sewage disposal, but problems ultimately overwhelmed colonial rulers, for whom constraints of finance, of personnel and also of will presented insuperable obstacles. In any case, 'experts' often produced 'solutions' which simply created new problems. They invariably paid too little attention to indigenous knowledge, to the perceived requirements of urban dwellers themselves, and to social and cultural qualities of life which were too often missed by the eager proponents of 'technoscience'.

NOTES

1 Jiat-Hwee Chang, *A Genealogy of Tropical Architecture: Colonial Networks, Nature and Techno-Science* (Abingdon, 2016), chapter 4; Swati Chattopadhyay, *Representing Calcutta: Modernity, Nationalism and the Colonial Uncanny* (London, 2005), passim.

2 Gillian Tindall, 'Existential Cities' in Robert Fermor-Hesketh (ed.), *Architecture of the British Empire* (London, 1986), pp. 74–103 is a useful analysis of the morphology of imperial cities.
3 For slave and chattel houses, see Andrew Gravette, *Architectural Heritage of the Caribbean: An A-Z of Historic Buildings* (Kingston, Jamaica, 2000), pp. 117–118.
4 But see note 9 below on 'piazza'.
5 Brad Patterson, Tom Brooking and Jim McAloon, *Unpacking the Kists: The Scots in New Zealand* (Dunedin, 2013), pp. 214–215.
6 For this debate, see Louis P. Nelson, *Architecture and Empire in Jamaica* (New Haven, CT, 2016), pp. 73–77. In some places, generally at a later date, slaves were accommodated in 'barracks'.
7 Other celebrated larger residences in hybrid styles were the celebrated *kothis* of Lucknow. Rosie Llewllyn-Jones (ed.), *Lucknow: City of Illusion* (Munich, 2003), pp. 168–190.
8 Nelson, *Architecture and Empire*.
9 In this usage, piazza is different from the Italian word for 'square'.
10 This house was used for meetings of the legislative council after the colonial capital relocated from Spanish Town to Kingston. In 1814 it was bought by the West Indies Regiment and became the office and residence of the military commander. Bought by the government in 1872, it became the seat of the Jamaican legislature and the office of the colonial secretary (second to the governor), and since 1983 the headquarters of the Jamaican National Heritage Trust. See www.jnht.com/site_hibbert_house_headquarters_house.php (accessed 20 July 2018).
11 Most of the great houses on St Kitts' neighbouring island Nevis are in ruins. Joyce Gordon, *Nevis: Queen of the Caribees* (Oxford, 2005), chapter 3.
12 When I visited St Nicholas in 2012, there was almost no evidence at all of the baleful past of slavery associated with it. One of the very few indications was a list of slaves pinned to a wall, each one identified according to his or her value.
13 The architectural incongruity of this and other derivative houses in the West Indies, such as Drax Hall in Barbados (1650s) and the Georgian Rose Hall, Montego Bay, Jamaica (1770s) is explored in Harold Kalman and Louis P. Nelson, 'British North America and the West Indies' in G.A. Bremner (ed.), *Architecture and Urbanism in the British Empire* (Oxford, 2016), p. 254.
14 See the tourist literature associated with the Abbey – the 'tour guide, history' and tour map available to visitors.
15 Both Fairview estate house and Romney Manor are much-restored tourist attractions. Romney is quite a modest house with origins in the seventeenth century. Fairview is larger, with both single- and double-storey elements and impressive gardens.
16 Nelson, *Architecture and Empire*, chapter 2. See also Sophie Drinkall, 'The Jamaican Plantation House: Scottish Influences', *Journal of the Architectural Heritage of Scotland*, II, 1 (1992), pp. 56–68.
17 Douglas Hamilton, *Scotland, the Caribbean and the Atlantic World, 1750–1820* (Manchester, 2005). Famously the Scottish national poet, Robert Burns, very nearly emigrated

to the West Indies to become an overseer and was saved by the success of his Kilmarnock edition of poems.
18 Creole, like Anglo-Indian, is a complex and challenging word to define. Originally it meant whites who were born in the West Indies, while later it came to mean cultural and genetic admixture.
19 The father of the later prime minister, John Gladstone, received £110,000, an enormous sum for the time, amounting to millions today. He was already a very rich man. www.ucl.ac.uk/lbs/search/ (accessed 4 February 2019).
20 The classic work is Hugh Tinker, *A New System of Slavery: The Export of Indian Labour Overseas, 1830–1920* (Oxford, 1974).
21 Excellent photographs of many of these can be found in Doris Jansen and Kay Lereschke, *Exploring the Cape Winelands* (Middletown, CA, n.d.).
22 For tea, see Erika Rappaport, *A Thirst for Empire: How Tea Shaped the Modern World* (Princeton, NJ, 2017); for indigo (where the plantations were relatively closely situated to the Indian imperial capital of Calcutta), see Swati Chattopadhyay, 'The Other Face of Primitive Accumulation: The Garden House in British Colonial Bengal' in Peter Scriver and Vikramaditya Prakash (eds),), *Colonial Modernities: Building, Dwelling and Architecture in British India and Ceylon*, pp. 184–187.
23 Tea 'factories' and extensive machinery can still be seen in Sri Lanka and North-East India. Most such plantations required engineers to be able to look after, repair and reconstruct machinery. For excellent descriptions of this, see the memoir by Rod Brown, *Tea and Me, One for Tea: A Country Boy Becomes a Man on an Indian Tea Estate* (Cirencester, 2015).
24 Dane Kennedy, *Islands of White: Settler Society and Culture in Kenya and Southern Rhodesia, 1890–1939* (Durham, NC, 1987).
25 J.P. Losty, *Calcutta, City of Palaces* (London, 1990). A catalogue of an exhibition, this contains many illustrations of such 'palaces'. Swati Chattopadhyay, *Representing Calcutta* closely examines the character of such residences, the social and ethnic range of their ownership and their transformation over time.
26 Chattopadhyay, 'The Other Face of Primitive Accumulation' in Scriver and Prakash (eds), *Colonial Modernities*, pp. 169–197.
27 Sylvia Shorto, *British Houses in Late Mughal Delhi* (London, 2018), which deals with the EIC period between 1803 and the 1850s.
28 Anoma Pieris, 'The Trouser Under the Cloth: Personal Space in Colonial-Modern Ceylon' in Scriver and Prakash (eds), *Colonial Modernities*, pp. 199–218.
29 www.victorianweb.org/art/architecture/australia/poc3.html (accessed 25 July 2018).
30 Terry Reksten, *Craigdarroch: The Story of Dunsmuir Castle* (Victoria, BC, 1987).
31 Anthony D. King, *The Bungalow: The Production of a Gobal Culture* (London, 1984).
32 There is a useful discussion of the complexities of the bungalow in Charles Allen, 'A Home from Home' in Fermor-Hesketh (ed.), *Architecture of the British Empire*, pp. 57–67.
33 Henry Yule and A.C. Burnell, *Hobson-Jobson: The Anglo-Indian Dictionary* (Ware, 1996, first published 1886), pp. 128–129.

34 Multi-storey 'bungalows' were more common in some places in Asia.
35 Peter Scriver, 'Empire Building and Thinking in the Public Works Department of British India' in Scriver and Prakash (eds), *Colonial Modernities* (London, 2007), pp. 69–92.
36 My home in the 1950s was just such a bungalow, perhaps a lower one in the PWD hierarchy, in Ndola, Northern Rhodesia. At other times, I lived in a Glasgow tenement, a building type that appeared in a different form in the larger Indian cities, though generally not exported elsewhere in the empire.
37 These appeared in the Boulton and Paul of Norwich catalogue in 1889. See King, *Bungalow*, p. 109.
38 Graeme Butler, *The Californian Bungalow in Australia* (Port Melbourne, 1992).
39 See the striking examples illustrated in King, *Bungalow*, nos. 132–134 between pp. 238 and 239.
40 Douglas Meadows, *Modern Eastern Bungalows and How to Build Them* (Calcutta, 1931).
41 Ibid., p. 134.
42 For examples of rows of shophouses, see Khoo Su Nin, *Streets of George Town, Penang: An Illustrated Guide to Penang's City Streets and Historic Attractions* (Penang, 2007), pp. 51 (Bridge Street) and 62 (Carnarvon Street).
43 Khoo Salma Nasution and Halim Berbar, *Heritage Houses of Penang* (Singapore, 2009).
44 Ibid., p. 18.
45 For colonial architecture elsewhere in Malaysia, see A. Ghafar Ahmad, *British Colonial Architecture in Malaysia, 1800–1930* (Kuala Lumpur, 1997).
46 Julian Davison with Luca Invernizzi Tettoni (photography), *Black and White: The Singapore House 1898–1941* (Singapore, 2006), p 1. See also Julian Davison, *Swan & Maclaren: A Story of Singapore Architecture* (Singapore, 2019). The Swan and Maclaren practice was based principally in Kuala Lumpur, but also had offices in Penang, Singapore and Bangkok. For studies of British and more particularly Scottish architects working in the Far East and South-East Asia, see Hideo Izamida, 'A Study on British Architects in East and South-East Asia, 1830–1940', *Journal of Asian Architectural and Building Engineering* (January 2003), pp. 131–136, in which Izumida identifies 70 qualified British architects, members of RIBA, working in the Far East and South-East Asia in the nineteenth and early twentieth centuries. Also Hideo Izumida, 'Scottish Architects in the Far East, 1840–1870', *Journal of the Architectural Heritage of Scotland*, II, 1 (1992), pp. 99–103. The Editorial by Deborah Howard introducing this special issue on Scottish architects overseas, pp. 1–2, points to the importance of Scottish architects in British and imperial architecture.
47 Andrew Ballantyne and Andrew Law, 'The Genealogy of the Singaporean Black and White House', *Singapore Journal of Tropical Geography*, 22 (2011), pp. 301–313.
48 Peter Merrington, '*The State* and the "Invention of Heritage" in Edwardian South Africa' in Andrea Bosco and Alex May (eds), *The Round Table, the Empire/Commonwealth and British Foreign Policy* (London, 1997). *The State* was a monthly journal, published in English and Dutch, designed to forward either the Federation or Union of South

Africa. Andrea Bosco, *The Round Table Movement and the Fall of the 'Second' British Empire, 1909–1919* (Newcastle upon Tyne, 2017), pp. 138–141. Baker's designs for the Union buildings in Pretoria, however, owed nothing to the Cape Dutch style.
49 For the Melbourne examples, see Philip Goad, *Melbourne Architecture* (Sydney, 1999), pp. 29 and 50.
50 Patricia McHugh, *Toronto Architecture: A City Guide* (Toronto, 1989), pp. 41 and 51.
51 Article by Samantha Sinnayah (2011), https://dictionaryofsydney.org/entry/daceyville (accessed 20 June 2018). It is said that Sydney now has 658 suburbs.
52 Article by Paul Ashton (2008), https://dictionaryofsydney.org/entry/suburban_sydney (accessed 20 June 2018).
53 See articles in www.emelbourne.net.au/biogs/EM00022b.htm (accessed 20 June 2018).
54 Benjamin Wilkie, *The Scots in Australia, 1788–1938* (Woodbridge, 2017), pp. 128–130.
55 Henry Beveridge (1837–1929), born in Scotland and educated in Glasgow, Edinburgh and Belfast, joined the East India Company service in 1857. He was a collector and sessions judge in Bengal and president of the Asiatic Society in 1890–91. His wife was a scholarly linguist and translator.
56 Lord Beveridge, *India Called Them* (London, 1947), p. 354.
57 Anthony D. King, *Colonial Urban Development* (London, 1976).
58 W. Hamish Fraser and Irene Mavor, 'The Social Problems of the City' in Fraser and Mavor (eds), *Glasgow*, Vol. II: 1830–1912 (Manchester, 1996), p. 352.
59 Matthew Withey, 'The Glasgow City Improvement Trust: An Analysis of its Genesis, Impact and Legacy and an Inventory of its Buildings, 1866–1910' (Ph.D. thesis, University of St Andrews, 2003). Available at file:///C:/Users/JOHNMA~1/AppData/Local/Temp/MatthewWitheyPhdThesis.pdf (accessed 22 January 2019).
60 Each of these trusts required legislation to put them into effect.
61 Jiat-Hwee Chang, *A Genealogy of Tropical Architecture; Colonial Networks, Nature and Techno-Science* (Abingdon, 2016), chapter 4.
62 Ibid., p. 144. In an intriguing slip Chang renders 'contiguous' areas as 'contagious'. Edwin Percy Richards (1873–1961) was the son of the borough engineer of Warwick and had experience in several English cities before moving to India to work initially in Madras (1908–11). As engineer to the Calcutta Improvement Trust, he toured European cities looking at developments in town planning and sanitation arrangements. It is indicative of the problems thrown up by the world wars that he left India for military service in 1914. After the war he became the city engineer of Singapore. See his obituary in *Proceedings of the Institute of Civil Engineers*, 2, 3 (November 1962), pp. 540–541. www.icevirtuallibrary.com/doi/pdf/10.1680/iicep.1962.10888 (accessed 6 February 2019).
63 The Report was republished on its centenary by Routledge in 2014.
64 The years after the First World War became the era of the rise of the 'expert' in agricultural, zoological, forestry and other incipient sciences. Labour relations and anthropological and sociological studies also became susceptible to the activities of this new breed of expert commentators, who made themselves felt throughout the empire.

65 In 2011, the population of the city was at least 16.787 million, depending on the definition of its area.
66 Jyoti Hosagrahar, 'Negotiated Modernities; Symbolic Terrains of Housing in Delhi' in Scriver and Prakash (eds), *Colonial Modernities*, pp. 219–240. See also Jyoti Hosagrahar, *Indigenous Modernities: Negotiating Architecture and Urbanism* (Abingdon, 2005), particularly chapters 1 and 7.
67 Navin Ramani, *Bombay Art Deco Architecture: A Visual Journey 1930–1953* (New Delhi, 2007).
68 Art Deco was particularly important in the design values of ships in this period and, in turn, elements of marine architecture were influential in the appearance of buildings. An important exhibition on ocean liner design took place at the V&A Museum in London in 2018, later the opening exhibition of the new V&A in Dundee.

6

The buildings of ritual: religion and freemasonry

In the nineteenth century, the leaders of the distinctively post-Reformation British denominations of the Christian Church realised that they had the opportunity to create world churches with a truly global reach. This challenge was presented by the combination of the expansion of empire with its growing number of settlers and the rise of evangelicalism, not least in respect of the urge to convert indigenous people. Ultimately these ambitions were not confined to empire since such churches came to be built wherever the British settled to trade, including key positions in Europe, the Middle East and the 'informal' empire in South America and the Far East. The Roman Catholic Church had developed such ambitions with the world expansion of the Spanish and Portuguese empires from the late fifteenth century onwards. Mission churches had been established in Central and South America while the Jesuits had commenced their missionary endeavour in Asia, famously in the case of Francis Xavier. Indeed Iberian expansiveness had in a sense been supervised by the Pope in Rome, as reflected in the Treaty of Tordesillas of 1494. Britain on the other hand ended up with two Protestant national churches, the Church of England and, after the settlement associated with the 1707 Act of Union, the Church of Scotland. The Anglican Communion had the associated Churches of Ireland and Wales, as well as the Episcopal Church of Scotland, but after the struggles of the seventeenth century, Presbyterianism, with church governance based on lay kirk sessions, presbyteries, synods and general assemblies, emerged as the acknowledged Scottish national church.[1] But other nonconformist or dissenting churches also developed within the Protestant communion, including Wesleyan Methodists, Baptists and Congregationalists. The Presbyterians produced several schismatic churches in the eighteenth century, two of which later coalesced into the United Presbyterian Church (1847), while the 'Disruption' of the Church of Scotland in 1843 spawned the immensely energetic and successful Free Church of Scotland.[2] A number of these churches were to create a material and spiritual presence around the world in territories both within and outside the empire. The Anglicans were to be the most significant of these, but the Church of Scotland fought its own corner in the built environment. Denominational and cross-denominational missionary societies also created distinctive buildings in many parts of the world. As a result, enormous numbers of churches were built in all five continents, and some might suggest that this global reach, combined with aesthetic values, could make them among the most significant buildings of empire. They were certainly among the most visible and therefore the most intrusive in what were often wholly alien environments, climatically and culturally. It may be that it was these religious buildings which most explicitly conveyed in material form the sense of an expanding European imperial culture.

Leaving aside the intriguing range of churches built in the North American colonies,[3] the earlier examples of British religious architecture in the empire (once beyond the earliest phases of the tent or the hut) generally followed the pattern of London churches by Wren and Gibbs, with a tower (sometimes with a clock) and spire to distinguish them from secular buildings with similar classical porticoes with multiple columns.[4] The great expansion of Anglicanism is surveyed below, but there were some intriguing beginnings and stylistic debates. From the 1840s, the standard form of Christian churches began to move in new directions, passing through various phases of inspiration from different periods of medieval church architecture.[5] In the case of the Anglican Church there were a number of significant conditioning factors. The first was the establishment of colonial bishoprics, first of all in North America (Nova Scotia in 1787 and Quebec in 1793), then in India, the West Indies and Australia, expanding considerably after the creation of the Colonial Bishoprics' Fund in 1841.[6] Bishops were then consecrated for new sees in India, New Zealand, Australia and South Africa. The second was the shift from a Low Church to a High Church and evangelical position, with a renewed emphasis on appropriate liturgies and associated theological positions.[7] These were largely based on the various tracts of 1833–41, the adherents of which became known as Tractarians, members of the Oxford movement.[8] New forms of disciplined piety were extolled and ordinands for the colonial priesthood were expected to bring physical strength (the sporting attributes of muscular Christianity) to their calling in unfamiliar climates and environments. Many of these priests themselves became interested in architecture, as were the new bishops. One or two of them, such as Bishop Broughton in Sydney, had received architectural training. In the case of the first bishop of Cape Town, Robert Gray, it was his wife Sophia (or Sophy) who had a considerable interest in church architecture and was said to have been influential in the design of over forty churches in the diocese, which helps to indicate just how architecturally 'explosive' the provision of Christian churches could be in the colonial world. Some of the priests designed churches themselves, having been under the influence of societies in Oxford and Cambridge which were concerned with an appropriate ecclesiology. In the nineteenth century this came to mean the architecture, layout and interior arrangements and furniture of the churches. The debates and publications which the members of these societies indulged in now seem almost impossibly arcane, often placing issues of form over the essentials of function, although to the practitioners of ecclesiology form and function were integrally intertwined, necessarily so for what they conceived to be the essential pursuit of their religious objectives. Thus, the spiritual functions of churches could be dispensed more effectively if the material and architectural surroundings were appropriate to the Anglican confession and liturgy.

Two other debates by ecclesiologists about the architecture of their churches were important, one ideological and the other environmental. The first may now be described as an essentially subjective concern with the projection of cultural identity, the sense that Anglican architecture should at least attempt to convey Englishness through the global extension of the national church. Thus it ought to be apparent to the onlooker that the church was aesthetically suitable in character for an Anglican diaspora, such that these buildings should make cultural and political as well as religious statements. The other was the more objective interest in the architectural forms that would suit climates that were often very different from those of England. This produced considerable debate about the architecture that would be comfortable in exceptionally cold climates like those of Newfoundland and northern Canada and, more frequently, what would be appropriate for hot sunny climes. This involved discussions about window size, about the depth of walls, the circulation of air, and other ways in which churches could be kept tolerably warm or cool in a pre-air-conditioning age. The effect of these debates, including the more recherché concerns with appropriate architectural envelopes and furniture for the mysteries of the liturgy, was to produce a worldwide aesthetic effect on the design and appearance of churches of the Anglican Communion around the world. They also may have had some effect on the appearance of Scots kirks and of nonconformist churches, although the adherents of such preaching-based, largely lay-controlled congregations would probably not have liked to admit to any such influence.

But many seemed to agree that the old mixed styles with Baroque–Palladian and neoclassical elements would no longer do.[9] They represented variations on the architecture of what were described as the pagan Greeks and idolatrous Romans. Later European forms more in keeping with Christian history had to be revived. In some colonies, after the initial reliance on tents, canvas cathedrals, huts and even boats (as on the coast of Labrador, in the South Pacific and on African lakes), it was thought that a relatively simple style, easier to construct, possibly even more in keeping with indigenous forms, could be found in Norman architecture. Small-scale, relatively unsophisticated churches in this Norman style appeared in both New Zealand and Australia, but soon Gothic became the preferred form, initially in a late medieval perpendicular style, later in what came be'regarded by the ecclesiologists as the most appropriate thirteenth-century Middle Pointed period, commending itself as being distinctively English. Churches in these styles, particularly the latter, rapidly appeared throughout the colonies of settlement and elsewhere, sometimes receiving a subsidy from public funds (though some bishops turned this down to maintain their freedom of action). An additional great debate was about materials. Should imperial churches follow the European precedent of being generally built of masonry, or should the architectural cloth be cut according to what was available in the colonies? Would brick, whether bare or rendered, be appropriate? Since Gothic architecture with its multiple interior columns was often likened to a forest, would it not be a good idea to use timber, particularly where it was plentiful, as in Canada or New Zealand? Would the process of church building for new and perhaps small communities be helped by prefabrication, in wood or even in iron ('tin tabernacles')? And what material would most effectively withstand the force of hurricanes, where they existed? All these issues lay behind the provision of the remarkable numbers of churches throughout the empire. But as we shall see, in the late nineteenth and early twentieth centuries, some Anglican churches occasionally broke away from what had become the conventional Gothic. Other historicist styles returned and some degree of cultural eclecticism was even introduced into cathedral and church buildings.

ANGLICAN CATHEDRALS AND CHURCHES IN THE EMPIRE

The first Anglican cathedral in Canada was founded in Quebec City in 1793, built in the Palladian St Martin-in-the-Fields style, and constructed between 1800 and 1804 (designed by Captain Hall and Major Robe of the Royal Engineers), claiming to be the first Anglican cathedral built outside Britain.[10] After the initial foundation of Anglican bishoprics noted above, new sees rapidly spread across the Empire, in the Mediterranean, Canada, India, New Zealand, Australia, Africa and elsewhere. This precipitated discussions about the building of cathedrals for each diocese, an ambition which often preceded the provision of multiple parish churches as settlement expanded. Some thought this an unnecessary extravagance, but for an episcopal church cathedrals were deemed essential for proper church governance and for acts of ordination, consecration and other significant ceremonies. Cathedrals duly appeared throughout the empire, stimulating in each case considerable debate about financing and appropriate architecture. However, they did take a wide variety of forms and were designed in different ways. In Calcutta, St Paul's Cathedral was built (between 1839 and 1847) in a prime position on the edge of the maidan by a Scottish military engineer, Major (later Major General) W.N. Forbes, in a style that came to be known as Commissioner's Gothic.[11] It contrasted strongly with the earlier St John's Church, a neoclassical building built between 1784 and 1787 with a powerful portico and a columned arcading along the side wall, designed to keep out the power of the sun. Materials contrasted, too. St John's was built in stone taken from the medieval ruins of Gour, but St Paul's was constructed in brick faced with *chunam*.[12] St Thomas's Cathedral, Bombay has an extraordinary history. The foundation stone for an Anglican church was laid as early as the 1670s, but services there only started in 1718. It was raised to the status of a cathedral in 1837 and a tower and clock to match its dignity were added in 1838.[13] St George's, Madras, a grandly classical (though unusually shaped) building, was designed by the East India Company engineer, J.L. Caldwell, and opened in 1815. It was raised to the status of cathedral in 1838. The grandest of Baroque cathedrals is St George's in Kingston, Ontario, built between 1825 and the 1840s, when a dome was added.[14] Originally built as a parish church, it replaced a wooden predecessor of 1792 and was raised to the status of cathedral in 1862.

Elsewhere some of the most prominent British Gothic architects of the nineteenth century were active in submitting designs for Anglican cathedrals (and sometimes churches). However, they did not visit their imperial projects, their designs were often modified (not least by resident supervisory architects) and they did adapt them to local circumstances, financial, aesthetic and environmental. These included Sir George Gilbert Scott (1811–78), who designed the Cathedral of St John the Baptist, St Johns, Newfoundland (1847–1905), Christ Church Cathedral, Christchurch, New Zealand (built 1862–1904)[15] and Holy

40 St Paul's Cathedral, Calcutta

Trinity, Shanghai (1868–70)[16] and contributed to St Michael and St George at Grahamstown at the Cape (1861–1912), later completed by his son J.O. Scott. Other notable architects were William Butterfield (1814–1900), designer of St Peter's, Adelaide (built 1868–78) and St Paul's, Melbourne (1880–91); John L. Pearson (1817–97), Brisbane Cathedral (1906–2009); George Frederick Bodley (1827–1907), St David's Cathedral, Hobart (1868–1936); William Burges (1827–81)[17] and William Emerson (1843–1924), All Saints' Cathedral, Allahabad (1870–87), which Bremner has described as a particularly successful example of tropical pointed architecture, not least in its recognition of the requirements of the environment.[18] In Wellington, New Zealand, St Paul's Cathedral was built entirely in timber, designed by the priest/architect Frederick Thatcher in 1865–66. It constitutes 'a master-class in adapting timber to the formal requirements of the Gothic style'.[19] In some of these buildings a greater degree of eclecticism was incorporated as the century wore on, including in the sculptural decoration which came to include images of local flora and fauna. It should also be remembered that they would often have been built by indigenous craftsmen and labourers (for example in New Zealand and in India), who inevitably left their marks on their work, both literally and figuratively, as in the Middle Ages. Another example of a church transformed into a cathedral is in Sierra Leone. There the Gothic St George's Church had been built between 1817 and 1828 for the Church Missionary Society with funds provided by the government (reflecting Sierra Leone's role as a colony for freed slaves). A muscular Gothic building, it was upgraded to the cathedral of the diocese in 1852 and only ceased to be publicly funded in 1898.[20] Subsidies to churches reveal the extent to which imperial and colonial governments saw the activities of Christian denominations as instilling loyalty to the imperial authorities. In addition to the professional architects, we have already seen that Bishop Broughton in Sydney was capable of being his own architect, as was Bishop Armstrong in Grahamstown at the Cape, and Bishop Medley in Fredericton, New Brunswick.

The connections between cathedral building and the extension of empire are neatly illustrated in Rangoon.[21] The Anglican cathedral there was designed by Robert Fellowes Chisholm, the notable Consulting Architect to the Government of Madras. Although he was most celebrated for his Indo-Saracenic buildings in that city and elsewhere, the cathedral, built between 1886 and 1895, is Gothic, though with appropriate climatic features.[22] Its remarkably elongated spire and tower open out into a large covered space at its base in order to provide shelter for worshippers at times of heavy rains. Its foundation stone was laid by the Viceroy of India, the Marquess of Dufferin, on his visit after the conclusion of the third Anglo-Burmese war. It can therefore be seen almost as a symbol of the completion of the British conquest, prominently positioned beside the Scott Market (now Bogyoke Aung San Market). The Roman Catholic Cathedral of St Mary in Yangon was built between 1895 and 1911 (replacing an older cathedral) and was situated on land given by the colonial government adjacent to the Catholic St Paul's School. The design was originally by the consulting architect to the Government of Burma, H. Hoyne-Fox, and was to have been in a Byzantine style. However, the land was marshy and the plan was abandoned. A Dutch priest with architectural training, Hendrick Janzen, took over and the twin-towered Gothic building was completed in 1911.[23]

The British Empire through buildings

41 Anglican cathedral, Rangoon

In the later period, eclecticism became more acceptable in church and cathedral building, though it had precedents in informal empire. St Mark's Anglican Church in Alexandria (now a pro-cathedral) was built by the architect James Wild at one end of the Mayden al-Tahrir, the principal centre of the expatriate community there, in the 1840s.[24] Both its exterior and interior combine Islamic and other North-East African elements with some Christian forms. Its eclecticism represented a degree of sensitivity to its cultural and climatic environment.[25] A later example is in Mombasa, Kenya, completed in 1905. It was probably designed by the colonial administrator, John Houston Sinclair, who had some architectural training.[26] It is often described as being mosque-like, an impression given by its dome, its Islamic-style arches and its short towers. On the other hand, the cathedral designed by Herbert Baker for Salisbury (Harare) in Southern Rhodesia

The buildings of ritual: religion and freemasonry

(Zimbabwe) follows his Pretoria Cathedral precedent in being constructed of powerful masonry in a Romanesque style. A plan to include a round tower along the lines of the one at Great Zimbabwe was never executed, a pity, since this would have been a rare example of the adoption of a local African architectural motif into a Christian cathedral. Baker's other contribution to ecclesiastical architecture occurred after the Anglo-Boer War. When the Johannesburg suburb of Parktown was laid out, he was commissioned to supply an Anglican church. Built of masonry in a robust Romanesque style, St George's, Parktown was first opened in 1904 with a powerful tower added later.

Among colonial churches, a particularly elegant example is the first Anglican one in South-East Asia, St George's in Penang, built between 1816 and 1819 and designed by Captain Robert N. Smith of the Madras engineers in the neoclassical style.[27] It was originally built with what was known as a Madras-style flat roof, changed into a pitched one in 1864. It was restored in the 1940s after a good deal of destruction wrought by the Japanese occupation. Sometimes, early churches took unusual forms. A striking case is St James's or Skinner's Church in Delhi, an Anglican church started in the 1820s and completed in 1836.[28] It is classical in form, with three porticoes and an octagonal central element, possibly designed by two officers of the Bengal Engineers, Major Robert Smith and Captain de Bude. Much damaged in the revolt of 1857, when all its early records were lost, it has recently been restored.[29] Wesleyan Methodists were also active in India, sometimes at the behest of the Wesleyan mission to indigenous people, sometimes because of the requirements of Methodists among the soldiery. Thus notable Methodist churches were founded in Bangalore and in Madras, as well as throughout India and the rest of the empire.[30]

Churches and cathedrals thus became more than religious statements. They also laid down powerful ethnic, cultural and political markers that deeply embedded them in the whole business of imperial expansion and rule. But they never secured the status of being an imperial established Church, as enjoyed in England itself. Throughout the British Empire, governors generally took an even-handed approach to the various denominations, offering subsidies and payments for chaplains in each. This included the Roman Catholic Church, whose adherents had secured emancipation in Britain in 1829. The result was to create often intense competition between Catholic and Anglican, as well as among the various other Protestant churches in many colonies. But they also made statements about the four nations of the British and Hibernian isles, Pocock's Atlantic archipelago.[31] It may be, as David Armitage has suggested, that the fractured

42 St James's (Skinner's) Church, Delhi

Christian denominations in the British Empire were never able to present the unified imperial theory of the Catholic Church in other empires, but theory aside, multiple denominations made a pluralistic and strikingly apparent contribution to the built environment.[32] In the nineteenth century, the competing churches, including those from Scotland, were seized by a remarkable energy which infused their missionary activity.[33] They also operated in a period characterised by an extraordinary growth of print culture through which they could propagate their activities to a metropolitan population that was often highly receptive, at least among particular social classes at specific periods.[34]

While the episcopate and their cathedrals separated the Anglicans from the Scottish and so-called nonconformist denominations, all the clergy of these churches felt themselves to be swept up into an extraordinary historic moment. Their evangelical activities rendered them akin to the early Christian fathers, like St Augustine, St Columba or St Ninian, broadcasting the faith in new lands. In some of these territories, the principal objective was to create spiritual homes for the settlers and expatriates, still predominantly British in composition, who had

The buildings of ritual: religion and freemasonry

settled in these vast territories. The welcome afforded to indigenous people in these churches varied according to the racial context (as contemporaries would have seen it). Some Christian churches remained exclusively European, as in the slave islands of the West Indies (though slaves were admitted to some non-Anglican churches such as Methodist and Baptist in the era of reform before abolition) and in settler territories, even if indigenous people were theoretically welcomed. Those in Asia, however, generally expected Indian, Burmese, Malay or Chinese Christians to be able to attend. But the activities of missions were of course specifically directed towards the conversion of indigenous peoples.

IMPERIAL COMMEMORATIVE CHURCHES

The British also required consecrated land in which to bury their dead, and such land either lay around their churches or in separate cemeteries. The dead were always prominent in imperial churches, whether in impressive monuments both inside and outside the churches, in memorials on their walls or indeed in the very fabric of memorial churches, such as the Afghan Memorial Church in Colaba, Bombay (one of the earliest and most striking examples of Gothic in India), built by the city engineer Henry Conybeare between 1847 and 1858 after a design sent from Britain had been rejected on grounds of cost.[35] Another was the Cawnpore Memorial Church (originally known as All Souls' Cathedral), commemorating the deaths of Europeans in the siege during the Rising of 1857.[36] Consecrated in 1875, it was designed by Walter Granville, architect to the East Bengal Railway, in a Lombardic Gothic style, though in polychromatic (predominately red) brick. Yet another, outside the British Empire, though in decidedly empire-related contexts, is the Crimea Memorial Church in Istanbul, built between 1858 and 1868. This was originally designed by William Burges, but his exuberant eclecticism went too far for his clients and he was replaced by the noted architect G.E. Street (1824–81).[37] Empires invariably set about commemorating what they perceived to be their heroic dead in dramatically imposing ways. Turning to Africa, another example is Christ Church Cathedral in Zanzibar. This has all sorts of resonances. In a sense, it constituted a commemoration of David Livingstone, who began his East African explorations and his subsequent propaganda against the Swahili slave trade in Zanzibar. The Anglican Universities' Mission to Central Africa, which built the cathedral, was founded after his speech in the Senate Chamber in Oxford in 1858. To emphasise this commemorative function further, the cathedral was built between 1873 and

The British Empire through buildings

43 Memorial Church, Cawnpore

44 Christ Church Cathedral, Zanzibar

1880 on the site of the former slave market. It is a remarkably eclectic building, distinctively relating to its location through Islamic and African elements while still maintaining the appearance of a Christian cathedral. It integrates itself even more through its materials – it is built of chunks of coral reef with a rough mortar render.[38] As noted in Chapter 3, Scots also provided Jerusalem with a Presbyterian Church, designed to commemorate the sacrifice of Scottish soldiers in the campaign against the Ottoman Empire (there were also Presbyterian churches in Jaffa and Safad).[39] The Jerusalem church was first proposed at the end of the war and the public fundraising was led by Ninian Hill, a shipowner.[40] The church and its adjacent guesthouse, built in an eclectic style, were built on the edge of the Hinnom Valley in 1927 and consecrated in 1930. While there was a considerable Scots community in Jerusalem during the mandate period, this departed with the war and the independence of Israel in 1947–48. But the church still survives, despite the turbulence of recent Israeli history.

SCOTTISH CHURCHES

In the West Indies, where Scots settlers, plantation owners and managers had been active for some time, Presbyterianism arrived characteristically late.[41] A Scottish minister only arrived in Jamaica in 1800 and it was not until 1814 that a meeting of prominent Scots plantation owners and merchants in the Court House in Kingston set out to raise funds for the establishment of a Presbyterian chapel (there had been a failed attempt twenty years earlier). A total of £8,000 was subscribed, but attempts to secure legislation for the legal establishment of the church and a subsidy from the House of Assembly caused considerable controversy, with the colony's Council at one point reversing a decision of the Assembly.[42] One member asserted that it was an 'English, not a Scotch colony' and that the Anglican church should take precedence,[43] a conflict which was to emerge elsewhere. The resulting church was built in a neoclassical style, with several columned porticoes. It was destroyed in the Jamaican earthquake of 1907 and replaced by a smaller and lower, presumably less wind-resistant, building. Presbyterian churches duly appeared on other Caribbean islands, such as Grenada, later destroyed in Hurricane Ivan in 2004, reflecting the seismic and climatic problems so many colonial buildings had to face.[44]

The struggles between the English and Scottish national churches were to be played out in the EIC's possessions in Asia. Before the early nineteenth century, Presbyterian practice was little observed among Scots in India. It may well be that the efforts of Scots to make money as fast as possible, as well as their propensity (in common with all European sojourners) to adopt liaisons with Indian women, sometimes promiscuously, constituted a bar to the acknowledgement of Presbyterian principles. All this changed when the new wave of evangelicalism responded to the religious opportunities initiated in the renewals of the Charter of the EIC in 1813 and 1833. The Scottish established Church was by now determined to assert equality with the Anglicans, winning an agreement in the 1813 charter renewal that the Company should subsidise the building of Scots churches in the three presidency cities of Calcutta, Madras and Bombay and help pay for their chaplains. There ensued considerable conflict over the amounts of such subsidies, as well as over the building of steeples on the buildings, since Anglicans insisted that as an established Church (forgetting that they were not the only one) they alone had a right to build spires. Steeples thus carried highly symbolic resonance. But very soon, Scottish Presbyterianism had a powerful visual presence in the three cities. Both the St Andrew's churches of Calcutta and of Madras were opened in 1818, each built in a style reminiscent of St Martin-in-the-Fields, so influential throughout the empire.[45] This neoclassical style suited Presbyterian forms of worship very well. The Calcutta church was

45 St Andrew's Church, Calcutta

The buildings of ritual: religion and freemasonry

built in Dalhousie Square, close to the EIC Writers' Building.[46] The Madras equivalent, designed by two Madras engineers, was also located in a prominent position. Both churches were probably copied, with modifications, from a pattern book. The Bombay Scottish Church was built in a central position opposite the Lion Gate of the dockyard. In the 1833 Charter renewal, Scottish chaplains and their supporters won the right to joint church establishment.[47] All three churches thus made a strong ethnic statement, built in a distinctive style that distanced them from the later predominantly Gothic buildings.

After the 1843 Disruption, Free churches appeared remarkably quickly in India, including St Columba's in Bombay, near the maidan. Free churches also appeared in Madras and Calcutta, the former founded in 1845 and still known as the Anderson Church after its founder. The Calcutta example had a turbulent start. Designed by Captain Henry Goodwyn, it was built in 1846, but the roof collapsed as a result of weakened walls; however more money was raised and it was rebuilt, its Gothic architecture contrasting sharply with St Andrew's.[48] It has prominent roof pinnacles and hooded windows to reduce sun and glare. Such churches ministered to imperial sojourners and helped to maintain a sense of Scottish identity, as well as asserting the ubiquity of the Christian imperial presence. Soon they were closely involved with the educational and medical endeavours of related missions in both cities and rural areas. Famously, three Scottish ministers, Alexander Duff, John Wilson and John Anderson, founded Scottish missions respectively in Calcutta, Bombay and Madras and all were committed to educational provision, including at tertiary level, founding colleges in 1830, 1832 and 1837. These further architectural statements were to be significant in the development of higher education in India since all three became part of the universities later founded in those cities. These were major urban missions, but, as we shall see, missions were perhaps principally influential in spreading Christianity into rural areas.

In this extraordinary outburst of building, Scottish churches for settlers and expatriates were founded in imperial cities throughout the Empire.[49] On another continent, the Presbyterian congregation in Quebec City was founded soon after the British conquest of New France in 1759, initially resulting from the presence of troops from the Fraser Highlanders, but it soon became more civilian in character, with a neoclassical church built between 1807 and 1810.[50] There may also have been a Scottish congregation in Montreal from as early as 1787 formed by the sizeable Scottish mercantile community on the St Lawrence.[51] St Andrew's Church was not, however, opened until 1810 and another Scots kirk was founded there by the middle of the century. They united in 1918. The presence of Scottish stonemasons building the Rideau Canal in Bytown (now Ottawa) ensured that a Scots church appeared there in the late 1820s, built by the masons when the canal experienced a delay. Originally regarded as the established church, it was provided with a glebe to help fund it. A Gothic replacement was built in 1872.[52] A Free Church congregation was formed in 1844 and built a church soon afterwards, though the current Knox Presbyterian Church is a replacement of 1955, built in a muscular Gothic style, external masonry over modern reinforced concrete.[53] In Toronto, the first Presbyterian church was a wooden hut with a minister from Northern Ireland. A Scots Presbyterian congregation, formed in 1830, created St Andrew's in a simplified St Martin-in-the-Fields style. The original church was replaced by an impressive Romanesque Revival building opened in 1876.[54] The architect of this building, W.G. Storm, called the style Norman Scottish, and it was located in a prime position opposite Government House.[55] As in Ottawa, the 1843 Disruption led to a large portion of the Toronto congregation breaking away to form the Knox Free Church.[56] By 1882, there were no fewer than twelve Presbyterian churches in Toronto. During the same period, Presbyterian churches, as well as those of Catholic and other Protestant denominations, were appearing in cities and towns throughout Canada. The scale of such building reveals the manner in which this constituted a Christian architectural colonisation of Canadian urban and rural landscapes.

Similar developments took place in South Africa. In Cape Town, the first St Andrew's Scottish church, in a severe Greek Revival Doric style, was opened in 1829. A Free Church existed only briefly in the city between 1846 and 1851, but a second Presbyterian church emerged from a Sunday School created to serve the expanding (white) population further north near the foot of Table Mountain. From 1894, this eventually became the Gardens Church, with a new Gothic building opening in 1903.[57] In a remarkable burst of expansion, Presbyterian churches were founded throughout the Western Cape and on the Eastern Cape frontier, with others appearing in the coastal cities.[58] A Presbyterian church was built in a Gothic style in Pietermaritzburg, Natal, between 1851 and 1854, on land granted by the government. Interestingly, it has been suggested that the government decreed that it should have a clock tower, imposing time discipline through a religious building.[59] In 1879, during the Zulu War, it became a place of refuge. Denominational rivalry was particularly acute in New South Wales. The Revd John Dunmore Lang arrived in Sydney in 1823 and founded the first

The buildings of ritual: religion and freemasonry

46 Presbyterian Church, Grahamstown, Eastern Cape, South Africa

Scots church, which was opened in 1826, but was demolished in the twentieth century to make way for the approaches to the Sydney Harbour Bridge. Lang was a radical polemicist, a republican, a long-standing member of the Legislative Council of New South Wales and a sectarian controversialist.[60] He was fierce in his insistence on Presbyterians securing equality with Anglicans and Catholics in the colony and in the 1820s inaugurated a conflict with the Governor, Sir Thomas Brisbane (an Ayrshire-born Scot), to secure official funding (he later repudiated the concept of official funding). In Victoria (as it became), the first Scots church was founded at a meeting in Melbourne in 1830 and eventually a grand Gothic building was constructed in a prominent position between 1871 and 1874. Its spire was supposed to be the highest structure in the city in the late nineteenth century. Presbyterian churches duly appeared, along with those of other denominations, across Australia.[61]

Presbyterianism was equally active in New Zealand. The central Presbyterian Church was opened in Auckland in 1850, initially a plain rectangular hall, with the later addition of a portico and tower to bring it into line with the St Martin-in-the-Fields template. In Wellington, the Glasgow-born architect Thomas Turnbull built (among other buildings) St Peter's Anglican Church (1879) and St John's Presbyterian (1885), both in timber and replacements for earlier smaller churches.[62] Although Christchurch was specifically founded as an Anglican settlement in 1850, it had a Presbyterian church by 1857, its timber construction facilitating several extensions.[63] The province of Otago and its capital Dunedin were founded as a Scottish Free Church settlement in 1848 and, inevitably, Presbyterian churches appeared there very quickly. The First Church moved from a weatherboard hut built within months of the settlers' landing to a stone building in 1850, which also served as school and public hall. Two Scottish architects dominated the design of the Victorian buildings of Dunedin, Robert Lawson (1833–1902), who learnt his Gothic at the practice of James Gillespie Graham in Edinburgh, and David Ross (1828–1908), who studied with a firm in Aberdeen.[64] Lawson designed both the First and Knox Presbyterian churches (respectively 1873 and 1874–76) in a Puginesque late Gothic.[65] The First Church is grand in scale, making good use of the falling-away of the land to give its apsidal east end and towers a particularly impressive appearance.[66] As with the building of so many cathedrals, some complained of the cost, arguing that the provision of churches in smaller towns was more important, but the original minister of the settlement, Revd Dr Thomas Burns (nephew of Robert, the poet), insisted that such grandeur was essential at the centre of the settlement. Lawson designed many other churches and commercial buildings in Otago, including the Trinity Wesleyan in 1869. Scott was also highly prolific and he and Lawson dominated the design of the architectural fabric of both city and province.[67] If there ever was an attempt to make Otago an exclusively Scots and Presbyterian settlement, it was doomed to failure through the arrival of all the other denominations.[68]

MISSION STATIONS

If the full range of Christian denominational places of worship could be found in the leading towns and cities of colonies, mission stations designed to proselytise among indigenous populations were created in many rural areas, some of them distant from the European-dominated towns. In southern Africa, for example, Church of Scotland missions, together with those of Congregationalists, Anglicans and others, became significant in many areas occupied by indigenous populations, colonising the region in striking ways. Among these,

The buildings of ritual: religion and freemasonry

Lovedale was a classic example among several missions on the Eastern Cape. It developed a major community with a significant school, technical education and printing press, and ultimately fed into the nearby Fort Hare College (later University).[69] The architecture of its several buildings, many surviving, must have made a dramatic statement upon the landscape. Similar developments can be identified in missions to First Nations peoples in Canada and throughout Australia.[70] They reveal yet again the manner in which the rivalry among Christian denominations helped to press forward expansion. Indeed, it has been suggested that missionary rivalry and desire for particular territories to extend proselytisation could occasionally lead to a missionary 'scramble' for parts of Africa and elsewhere.[71] In rural areas of many colonies, it would have been the presence of a mission, with its church, schools, perhaps a printing establishment and other workshops, hospital (sometimes), and residences for missionaries, teachers, artisans, doctors, nurses and also for their indigenous adherents, which would constitute the principal architectural manifestation of both an alien religious culture and an imperial presence. Modernity and imperial connectivity were often symbolised by a posts and telegraph establishment, while church spires and clock towers imposed western concepts of time and discipline in highly visible ways. This was true, for example in the remarkable mission stations of the Established and Free churches of Scotland in Nyasaland

47 Lovedale Mission, Eastern Cape, South Africa

(Malawi), respectively in Blantyre and Livingstonia.[72] Missionaries, in creating these missions, theorised the significance of the straight line, in architecture and European-style residences, in the layout of the stations, even in the arrangement of the productive (and sometimes experimental) mission gardens.[73] Thus the architecture and grid form of missions were seen as symbolising the appearance of western science and sensibility, mixing rational modernism with religious faith. In these ways, the missions created complete communities, theocratic towns separate from colonial settlements and the centres of economic activity. In all of this, missionaries were often their own architects. A stunning example is the Church of St Michael and All Saints in Blantyre, Malawi, an extraordinarily hybrid confection with Norman, Gothic and even Moorish elements (the dome and some window shapes, perhaps), designed, and with construction overseen, by the missionary David Clement Scott between 1888 and 1891. Scott had no architectural training, but his strangely intriguing church is still very much in use today. These different mission communities were, however, inseparably interlinked through the provision of literate workers to service the middle levels of the colonial capitalist economy. This mission-educated class became the necessary auxiliaries in the full range of workplaces, from plantations to mines, or moved into the capitalist towns to work in commercial businesses, port installations or infrastructure developments such as the railways. Missions thus satisfied the demand for literate 'blue-collar workers' for the capitalist enterprises of the imperial economic nexus. They also reproduced western gendering, not least in their classes for girls in domesticity and supposedly feminine activities like sewing and cooking.

The missions thus contributed to the tremendous outburst of Christian church building around the world, producing literally thousands of churches in colonial territories on all five continents. Almost everywhere, this alien architectural incursion occurred in areas where there were significant non-Christian religions – notably Islam in Africa, the Middle East and throughout Asia, as well as Hinduism and Buddhism, not to mention the religious systems of indigenous peoples outside these world religions, whether in North America, Africa, the Pacific islands, Australasia and some parts of Asia. The range of Protestant denominations also intruded church buildings into European and South American contexts where Catholicism or European Protestantism (like Lutheranism) had predominated. Both Anglicans and Catholics exported their church hierarchies, dioceses and cathedrals, including metropolitan ones constituting the centres of provinces presided over by archbishops. A striking example of prolific building can

The buildings of ritual: religion and freemasonry

be found in New Zealand, where it is said that the highly active Robert Lawson designed some forty churches,[74] while David Ross was involved in the building of at least eight, including Roman Catholic, Anglican, Presbyterian, Wesleyan and Congregational.[75] They were just two architects practising in Australasia, but their careers help to indicate the plethora of Christian churches prompted by the rivalries among Christian denominations stimulating energetic responses to each other. Both these architects also designed many of public buildings which became standard in the imperial bourgeois public sphere.

Not all churches have survived as places of worship. In Quebec City, the former Methodist Church is now the French cultural centre and library, while the former St Matthew's Anglican Church has become a municipal library. Conversion into a library seems to be one of the preferred options for reused ecclesiastical buildings. In Fort William, Kolkata, the former Anglican Church, St Peter's, designed in a Gothic style with four corner turrets (famously painted by William Prinsep in the 1830s), is now a library for the Indian troops garrisoned in the fort.

FREEMASONRY

If the Christian churches were generally, but not exclusively, built in a Gothic style, the lodges and temples of another widely dispersed and highly ritualised imperial institution, freemasonry, were almost always classical.[76] Freemasonry had a lengthy history, but became particularly important in the eighteenth century (often dated to 1717) when several different 'rites' or constitutions emerged.[77] In some respects it constituted a reaction to Christian religion, trying to create an international brotherhood dedicated to social inclusion, cosmopolitanism and benevolent works. As freemasonry was non-sectarian, there are also examples of non-white people being admitted to its rites in the early period. In this guise it had links to the Enlightenment and attracted many celebrated figures of the age, including the radical Scottish poet Robert Burns and the Austrian composer Mozart. Masons were prominent on both sides of the American War of Independence and were also active within the Irish ethnic and religious divide. However, the masons were put to the test by the Napoleonic wars, after which they became both more nationalist and to some degree more elitist, to a considerable extent losing their eighteenth-century radical urge. In this form, freemasonry spread across the globe through empire, borne by the dispersal of the military and colonial administrative and commercial elite, while still

215

claiming a degree of social inclusion. As it became increasingly imperial in its ideology, it took on a predominantly Protestant and royalist form, with senior members of the royal family among its adherents. From now on the masonic hierarchy of master and grand masters often reflected the social pyramid of each colony. It had become an organisation much favoured by the great naval, military, political and imperial figures of the age, including Nelson, Wellington, later imperial generals like Wolseley, Roberts and Kitchener, and many colonial governors and viceroys, including Dalhousie and Elphinstone in India and Lachlan Macquarie in New South Wales, as well as a great range of politicians and literary figures from the prime minister and foreign secretary Lord Salisbury to Rudyard Kipling.[78] It has been said that freemasonry was a vital 'connective force of empire', facilitating 'the circulation of men, information and ideas' and thus constituting one of the essential global and imperial networks.[79]

Throughout, of course, freemasonry remained exclusively male. Yet the masons used the metaphor of female family members to identify their 'mother' and 'sister' lodges. It has been said that its history has illustrated the essential tension between inclusion and exclusion, mirroring the political and social life of empire itself.[80] Freemasonry arrived in India in EIC days and lodges were built throughout the Subcontinent, one of the first having been Lodge Harmony of 1834 in Cawnpore (Kanpur). The secrecy of the rites led the lodges to be known to many of the general populace as 'houses of magic'.[81] A significant lodge in Calcutta was built in a severely classical style at 19 Park Street, along the road from the Asiatic Society Library. An official directory of Bengal indicates that there were some six lodges in Calcutta in 1789 and, given the numbering, there could have been more in the presidency as a whole.[82] One of the striking characteristics of masonic lodges was the complexity of the hierarchies of their officials, reflecting imperial gradations of civil and military officers. Nevertheless, by the later nineteenth century, the Freemasons were increasingly keen to include elite Indians in their membership, notably Indian princes, great entrepreneurs like the patriarchs of the wealthy Tata family, and lawyers such as Motilal Nehru, the father of Jawaharlal, independent India's first prime minister. Kipling indeed was anxious to demonstrate that his admission had been sponsored by Indians. Nowadays, most of the brethren are Indians, and the 1860s controversy about whether Hindus could be admitted at all seems far in the past.[83] Today, some of the halls have taken on some of the characteristics of community centres. But however much they maintained the privacy of their rites, the imperial masons were always a highly public organisation. They often paraded in public and large numbers of people turned out to see them in their regalia. They were a standard constituent of all foundation stone-laying ceremonies, when the ritual adopted was that of the masons themselves. They always processed before such ceremonies, as they did for funerals of their brethren. In many places across the empire they also marched and feasted on St John's Day, either that of St John the Baptist or St John the Evangelist (the latter particularly in the case of the Scottish rites). Thus they made a public declaration of their existence, of their networks and common characteristics across the colonial scene, even if their rites remained more secretive. They were a part of the often spectacular ceremonial that seemed to be a visual necessity for the empire. As Harland-Jacobs put it, 'Freemasonry was thus a prominent feature of the public landscape of the British Empire' from the later eighteenth century onwards.[84]

Another highly public aspect of their presence and rituals was the architecture of their lodges. It would have been difficult to find an imperial city (and also many towns), whether in Canada, South Africa, India, Australia, New Zealand, colonies in West, East and Central Africa, as well as in many islands of the Caribbean and the Indian Ocean which lacked a masonic lodge and, in the case of the larger cities, a grand lodge or temple. Whether in Montreal, Quebec or Brisbane, Queensland, in Winnipeg, Manitoba or Adelaide, South Australia, Cape Town in South Africa, Calcutta in India or Singapore, such buildings made a powerful statement about the social tone and wealth of the Masons. The predominantly classical style of such buildings was often combined with Egyptian or other Orientalist details. Within each of these buildings there would normally be a grand central chamber, again sometimes Orientalist in tone (because of the alleged relationship between masonic rites and the East), in which the Masons would conduct their more private rituals. An intriguing example of a notable masonic lodge is that in Cape Town, the Goede Hoop Temple, situated at the very administrative heart of the city, near the Government Gardens, the President's residence and the Parliament building.[85] It was built in 1804, the architect described as Brother Thibault helped by two other brethren. A visiting Mason in the early nineteenth century described it as being a place of 'elegance, strength and beauty' with numerous brethren constituting the 'respectable part of the inhabitants'. The visitor was equally complimentary about the attractiveness of the interiors, the lodge being one of the southern division lodges making up the Grand Lodge of South Africa. Inevitably, the brethren were all white males, but the Masons apparently held a ball and supper for the ladies. Along with many white ethnic associations (of which the Scots were perhaps the most prominent),

48 Masonic Hall, Canning Place, Singapore

the social and other clubs of empire were vital places for networking and probably making political, commercial and other financial relationships. They were also a powerful physical statement of the connections of a particular group which operated within the specific colony, but which also transcended that individual territory to form a horizontal global relationship with the metropolis, yet also forming, just as importantly, transcolonial connections across the empire itself.

There were other lodges, generally known as the Friendly Societies. An early twentieth-century postcard portrays the members of the Manchester Unity of Oddfellows (founded in 1810), a benevolent and charitable body, in Freetown, Sierra Leone.[86] There are at least fifty of them. All are wearing masonic aprons and other aspects of the regalia, most in top hats, and all are Africans. The flight of stairs may be at the entrance to their lodge. On the royal tour of 1901, such friendly societies paraded in several Australian and New Zealand cities. In Wellington, they included the Sons of Temperance, the Druids, the Oddfellows, Hibernians, Rechabites and Foresters, 'some of them dressed in quaint costumes'. Some will certainly have had 'halls' or other headquarters,

The buildings of ritual: religion and freemasonry

49 Manchester Unity of Oddfellows, Freetown, Sierra Leone

as would the craft guilds and trade unions which also regularly paraded. There were additionally deputations from all the Christian denominations, as well as ethnic associations such as 'Highlanders, Cornishmen and Chinese'.[87] Thus, of all the architectural 'explosions' of formal and informal empire, few were as significant or as prominent as that involving Christian churches and organisations like the masons and related friendly societies. Churches, missions and other buildings associated with European spirituality and rituals appeared everywhere, often revealing the importance of examining the 'four nations' of the United Kingdom, both in terms of the variety of denominations reflected in their buildings, but also in the associational and mutually supportive societies that appeared throughout the world. As we have seen, the material expressions of the Christian religion ensured their prominence in both urban and built environments across the empire and beyond. Masonic lodges were also universal, present in every imperial city and most towns.

NOTES

1 Enshrined in the Protestant Religion and Presbyterian Church Act, 1707 (act 5, Anne, c. 8). There were also Presbyterians in Ireland and elsewhere in the United Kingdom.

2 The United Presbyterian and Free Churches amalgamated in 1900 as the United Free Church and the larger part of this church rejoined the Church of Scotland in 1929.
3 For some account of these, see chapters 4, 5 and 6 of Daniel Maudlin and Bernard L. Herman (eds), *Building the British Atlantic World: Spaces, Places and Material Culture, 1600–1850* (Chapel Hill, NC, 2016).
4 Before the first churches were built, divine services were held in whatever reasonable space was available. In Calcutta in the mid-eighteenth century, services took place in the customs house. Dennis Kincaid, *British Social Life in India 1608–1937* (London, 1938), p. 92.
5 G.A. Bremner, *Imperial Gothic: Religious Architecture and High Anglican Culture in the British Empire, c. 1840–1870* (New Haven, CT, 2013). This book contains little on the extra-urban Gothic churches of the dispersed mission stations, perhaps not surprising given the vast nature of the subject.
6 The diocese of Calcutta was founded in 1813, Madras in 1835 and Bombay in 1837. A bishop arrived in the West Indies in 1825 and the diocese of Australia based on Sydney was founded in 1836, later separated into several sees in 1847. The diocese of Toronto was created in 1839. For these developments, see Rowan Strong, *Anglicanism and the British Empire, c. 1700–1850* (Oxford, 2007).
7 Bremner has also pointed to the influence upon architecture of the 'corporate' character of Anglican organisations like the Society for the Propagation of the Gospel in Foreign Parts, the Church Missionary Society and the Society for the Propagation of Christian Knowledge. Bremner, 'The Corporatisation of Global Anglicanism: Architecture, Organisation and Faith-based Patronage in the Nineteenth-century British Colonial World', *Architecture beyond Europe*, 2 (2012), online. He illustrated this with early churches in New South Wales, New Zealand and Labrador.
8 It should be remembered that at this period almost all Anglican clergy, certainly the influential ones, were products of Oxford and Cambridge.
9 However, they did survive in the West Indies, as the cathedrals in Bridgetown, Barbados and St John's, Antigua seem to indicate. The latter is sufficiently Baroque that it could be mistaken for a church in the Catholic dominions.
10 To symbolise this fact George III gifted the cathedral a magnificent set of 27 pieces of silver church plate and other accessories, created by the royal silversmiths and now known as Le Cadeau du Roi. This is exhibited in a secure glass cubicle in an aisle of the cathedral.
11 Damaged in earthquakes in 1897 and 1934 it was remodelled, including the demolition of its spire.
12 A rough lime plaster regularly used in India (notably in Madras) and elsewhere in the British Asian Empire. For its composition, see Bremner, *Imperial Gothic*, p. 168.
13 Vijaya Gupchup, edited by T. Thomas, *St Thomas' Cathedral, Bombay: A Witness to History* (Bombay, 2005). This beautifully illustrated book is available in the cathedral, which is filled with extraordinary sculptural monuments. The presence of this church contributed the name of Churchgate and its railway station.

The buildings of ritual: religion and freemasonry

14 St George's was raised to cathedral status in 1862. The architect appears to have been William Coverdale.
15 Christ Church Cathedral was severely damaged in the earthquakes of 2011, including the collapse of its spire and tower. Since then there has been a major controversy as to whether to renovate Scott's design or to build a new cathedral.
16 This was variously known as church and cathedral. Its spire was removed during the Cultural Revolution and it was subsequently used for secular purposes.
17 Burges produced a design for Brisbane Cathedral.
18 Bremner, *Imperial Gothic*, p. 140.
19 Ibid., p. 160.
20 *Sierra Leone Telegraph*, 4 May 2017. www.thesierraleonetelegraph.com/sierra-leones-oldest-church-st-georges-cathedral-celebrates-its-two-hundred-years-history/ (accessed 20 May 2018). Several postcards were issued of the cathedral, copies of which are in the author's collection.
21 The Society for the Propagation of the Gospel had arrived in Burma in 1854 and a separate Anglican diocese was created in 1877 in the province of Calcutta. A survey of colonial architecture in Yangon can be found in Chapter 8.
22 It is still a working cathedral and contains many memorials and British regimental connections. Its organ was destroyed during the Second World War. Personal knowledge, visited January 2016.
23 https://en.wikipedia.org/wiki/St._Mary%27s_Cathedral,_Yangon. Personal knowledge, visited January 2016.
24 Mark Crinson, *Empire Building: Orientalism and Victorian Architecture* (London 1996), chapter 4. Crinson suggests, p. 189, that Wild's eclecticism was not so ideologically charged as Indo-Saracenic styles in India.
25 http://dioceseofegypt.org/explore/egypt/st-marks-pro-cathedral-alexandria/ (accessed 13 January 2019). St Mark's is one of thirty-seven episcopal (mainly formerly Anglican) churches in Egypt and the Horn of Africa.
26 Sarah Longair, *Cracks in the Dome: Fractured Histories of Empire in the Zanzibar Museum, 1870–1864* (Farnham, 2015), pp. 76–81 and 98–99.
27 Smith also painted early views of Penang. Khoo Su Nin, *Streets of George Town Penang: An Illustrated Guide to Penang's City Streets and Historic Attractions* (Penang, 2007), p. 87. Francis Light, who annexed Penang for the British, is commemorated in a structure in the grounds of the church.
28 Though its progenitor, Colonel James Skinner, was of Scottish and Rajput parentage.
29 I am grateful to Mr Shunil Joseph, elder and treasurer of the church, for his information about its history and its restoration under the supervision of INTACH, the Indian National Trust for Artistic and Cultural Heritage. It is gazetted as a Grade 1 heritage structure and is virtually a memorial to the British killed in 1857. See the pamphlet *A Living Witness*, published by the church.
30 In the case of India, these churches have now been subsumed into the churches of North and South India.

31 J.G.A. Pocock, 'British History: A Plea for a New Subject', *Journal of Modern History*, 47 (1975), pp. 601–621; reprinted in Pocock, *The Discovery of Islands: Essays in British History* (Cambridge, 2005), chapter 2, pp. 24–43.
32 David Armitage, *The Ideological Origins of the British Empire* (Cambridge, 2000), p. 63, note 8.
33 David Fitzpatrick has argued that Presbyterianism was so 'volatile and fragmented' that it cannot be seen as a unifying factor for Scots (in comparison with the Roman Catholic Church for the Irish and others), or as a contributing feature to Scottish identity. This seems hard to sustain. David Fitzpatrick, 'What Scottish Diaspora?' in Angela McCarthy and John M. MacKenzie (eds), *Global Migrations: The Scottish Diaspora since 1800* (Edinburgh, 2016), p. 257.
34 This print culture included missionary periodicals, biographies of famous missionaries, materials for children, postcards and much else, often distributed through missionary exhibitions.
35 Captain Tremenheere of the Royal Engineers became the consulting architect after 1850 and modified the building, while William Butterfield made contributions to the interior design. Christopher W. London, *Bombay Gothic* (Bombay, 2002), pp. 16–19. Bremner, *Imperial Gothic*, pp. 295–297.
36 The church is inevitably filled with memorials to those killed in the so-called Mutiny, and there is also a memorial garden nearby.
37 For a detailed account of the debates surrounding the Crimean Memorial Church, particularly in respect of the style appropriate to its location in Constantinople (Istanbul), see Crinson, *Empire Building*, chapter 4.
38 Bremner, *Imperial Gothic*, pp. 172–175. One of its designers was the Revd Edward Steere, the third bishop of Zanzibar. It was supplied with a narthex, an ante-chamber to the nave for non-communicants to observe the Anglican rites, an ethnic arrangement which paralleled its architectural eclecticism.
39 John M. MacKenzie, 'Scottish Orientalists, Administrators and Missions: A Distinctive Scots Approach to Asia?' in T. M. Devine and Angela McCarthy (eds), *The Scottish Experience in Asia, c. 1700 to the Present; Settlers and Sojourners* (London, 2017), pp. 51–73; John M. MacKenzie, 'Presbyterianism and Scottish Identity in Global Context', *Britain and the World*, 10, 1 (March 2017), pp. 88–112.
40 The church's website contains valuable historical information: www.standrewsjerusalem.org/history/ (accessed 13 January 2019). For other architecture by the British in the mandate period, including government house, the post office and hotels, see Lili Eylon, 'Architecture of the Mandate Period', https://mfa.gov.il/mfa/mfa-archive/1999/pages/focus%20on%20israel-%20jerusalem%20-%20architecture%20in%20the%20b.aspx (accessed 13 January 2019).
41 Douglas J. Hamilton, *Scotland, the Caribbean and the Atlantic World, 1750–1820* (Manchester, 2005).
42 A member of the House of Assembly who proposed some of these arrangements was John Shand, later the owner of the Burn House near Edzell in Kincardineshire.

43 *Jamaica Royal Gazette,* 12 November 1814, Supplement, p. 17; *Jamaica Royal Gazette,* 4 February 1815, Supplement, p. 10; www.jamaicanfamilysearch.com/Samples2/PresbyteriansJamaica.htm (accessed 24 July 2016).

44 St Andrew's Church in St George's, Grenada was built at the behest of stonemasons and other Scottish workmen living on the island. It was constructed between 1830 and 1833 in a Gothic style, surprisingly early for Presbyterians. Andrew Gravette, *Architectural Heritage of the Caribbean: An A-Z of Historic Buildings* (Kingston, Jamaica, 2000), p. 187.

45 The prominent location of St Andrew's, Calcutta is explained by the fact that it was built on the site of the old courthouse, which was demolished when a new one was built.

46 The opening of St Andrew's Church was swiftly followed by the creation of the Scottish cemetery further along South Park Street from the celebrated earlier one. Scots in death seem to have wished to be in their own cemetery, perhaps to ensure that Scottish ministers could officiate at funerals there, or alternatively to avoid the costs of being buried in the English cemetery. Volumes of burial records in the graveyard have been found in the former Scottish kirk in Dalhousie Square. The graveyard has recently become subject to a project to restore and renovate it associated with the Kolkata Scottish Heritage Trust. https://scottishcemeterykolkata.wordpress.com (accessed 23 July 2016). The interest in family history has done a great deal to make records available. A significant example is the Kabristan Archive publications, which include the burial records of the Scots Kolkata cemetery. http://kabristan.org.uk/kabristan-publications/india/15-publications/kabristan-archives-publications/1390-the-scots-cemetery-calcutta-burial-records (accessed 23 July 2016). For the Presbyterian cemetery in Mumbai, see www.cwgc.org/find-a-cemetery/cemetery/70823/Bombay%20Church%20Cemetery. The Presbyterian cemetery in Chennai is now derelict and overgrown. http://wiki.fibis.org/index.php/Madras_Cemeteries.

47 The struggles of the Scottish Church to gain establishment status in India were revealed in Joseph Sramek, 'Empire, Religion, and Scottishness in Nineteenth-Century Colonial India', paper delivered at the 'Religion and Greater Scotland' conference, University of Aberdeen, 3–4 June 2016. I am grateful to Joe Sramek for permission to draw on his paper to inform this passage about the Scots churches in India. I have myself visited the St Andrew's churches in Kolkata and Mumbai, the latter the church of St Andrew and St Columba, representing a union which took place in 1938. See *Times of India,* 24 May 2015, http://timesofindia.indiatimes.com/city/mumbai/In-its-200th-year-Mumbais-Scottish-Church-meets-its-first-reverends-descendant/articleshow/47402091.cms (accessed 4 February 2018).

48 Brian Paul Bach, *Calcutta's Edifice: The Buildings of the Great City* (New Delhi, 2006), p. 589. I am grateful to Hauke Wiebe for this reference. After the two Scottish churches united, this church was handed over to the Jesuits in 1969, now the Church of the Lord Jesus.

49 For this global expansion of Presbyterianism, see Esther Breitenbach, 'Scots Churches and Missions' in John M. MacKenzie and T.M. Devine (eds), *Scotland and the British*

Empire (Oxford, 2011), pp. 196–226; MacKenzie, 'Presbyterianism and Scottish Identity'.
50 George W. Crawford, *Remember All the Way: The History of the Chalmers-Wesley United Church, Quebec City* (Montreal, 2005). This book deals in detail with the creation of a Free Church rival to the Church of Scotland and the building of its Gothic church in the early 1850s. Shirley Nadeau and the caretaker of St Andrew's Church in Quebec City provided information and the opportunity to see these churches in April 2018.
51 www.standrewstpaul.com/our-history.php (accessed 30 May 2018). This website of the Scottish Church of St Andrew and St Paul in Montreal has a useful section on its history.
52 Andrew Waldron, *Exploring the Capital: An Architectural Guide to the Ottawa-Gatineau Region* (Vancouver, 2017), p. 12.
53 Ibid., p. 58. These churches both remained aloof from the United Church and remained Presbyterian. I am grateful to Vivian, office administrator of St Andrew's, for opening up the church.
54 www.standrewstoronto.org/discover/history.html. See also Patricia McHugh, *Toronto Architecture: A City Guide* (Toronto, 1989), p. 49.
55 The other corners of this junction were occupied by government house, Upper Canada College and a tavern, so that it was known as the junction of Legislation, Education, Damnation and Salvation. St Andrew's Church is associated with the 48th Highlanders of Canada regiment and contains the regimental museum.
56 Andrew Hinson, 'A Hub of Community: The Presbyterian Church of Toronto and its Role among the City's Scots' in Tanja Bueltmann, Andrew Hinson and Graeme Morton (eds), *Ties of Bluid, Kin and Countrie: Scottish Associational Culture in the Diaspora* (Markham, Ont., 2009), pp. 119–133.
57 The Governor and High Commissioner at the Cape, Sir Henry Loch, himself a Scot, was involved with the founding of this church. I am grateful to its former minister, Revd James Patrick, for hospitality and information.
58 MacKenzie with Dalziel, *Scots in South Africa*, pp. 174–182.
59 https://en.wikipedia.org/wiki/List_of_heritage_sites_in_Pietermaritzburg (accessed 3 July 2018).
60 D.W.A. Baker, 'John Dunmore Lang (1799–1878)', *Australian Dictionary of Biography*, National Centre for Biography, Australian National University (accessed 11 August 2017). He was never averse to inflammatory language, referring for example to 'papal chains' in his anti-Catholicism.
61 There is also a Welsh-language church in Melbourne which still holds services in Welsh from time to time.
62 Chris Cochrane, 'Turnbull, Thomas', *Dictionary of New Zealand Biography*, Vol. 2 (1993) (accessed 11 August 2017).
63 In 1887 it was cut into three portions and moved to a new location. In the earthquakes of 2011, it survived, whereas the brick Knox Presbyterian Church collapsed.
64 See the online Dictionary of Scottish Architects for entries on these two architects. For Scott, www.scottisharchitects.org.uk/architect_list.php?asnme=Ross%2C+David&ass

tr=&astwn=&ascnt=Dunedin&asctr and for Lawson, www.scottisharchitects.org.uk/architect_full.php?id=200587 (accessed 10 May 2018).
65 Lawson only avoided the long chancels, unnecessary in Presbyterian services.
66 Jonathan Mane-Wheoki, 'Lawson, Robert Arthur', *New Zealand Dictionary of Biography*, Vol. 2 (1993) (accessed 12 August 2017).
67 For Scott, see the valuable blog article by David Murray, https://builtindunedin.com/2013/01/05/david-ross/.
68 Donald Mackenzie Wallace, the Scottish chronicler of the royal empire tour of the Duke and Duchess of Cornwall and York in 1901, described this as an 'invasion' and the 'Episcopalians' as having the 'audacity' to demand the finest site for their cathedral. Wallace was assistant private secretary to the duke, the future George V. Donald Mackenzie Wallace, *The Web of Empire* (London, 1902), p. 285. St Paul's Anglican Church had been founded in 1862–63 in the central octagon of Dunedin. The separate diocese was created in the 1860s and received its first bishop in 1871. St Paul's was rebuilt and extended as the cathedral after 1915.
69 MacKenzie with Dalziel, *Scots in South Africa*, pp. 104–108 and passim. For the foundation of the mission and early photographs, see James Wells, *Stewart of Lovedale: The Life of James Stewart* (London, 1909).
70 See the excellent and extensive website of the Griffith University project: http://missionaries.griffith.edu.au/introduction (accessed 12 July 2018).
71 Roland Oliver, *The Missionary Factor in East Africa* (London, 1952); Anthony J. Dachs, 'Missionary Imperialism – the Case of Bechuanaland', *Journal of African History*, 13, 4 (1972), pp. 641–658.
72 John McCracken, *Politics and Christianity in Malawi, 1875–1940: The Impact of Christianity in the Northern Province* (Cambridge, 1977).
73 Robert Laws, *Reminiscences of Livingstonia* (Edinburgh, 1934); W.P. Livingstone, *Laws of Livingstonia: A Narrative of Missionary Adventure and Achievement* (London, 1921); John M. MacKenzie, 'Missionaries, Science and the Environment in Nineteenth-Century Africa' in Andrew Porter (ed.), *The Imperial Horizons of British Protestant Missions, 1880–1914* (Grand Rapids, MI, 2003), pp. 106–130.
74 https://teara.govt.nz/en/biographies/2l5/lawson-robert-arthur (accessed 16 July 2018).
75 www.scottisharchitects.org.uk/architect_full.php?id=203010 (accessed 16 July 2018). Dictionary of Scottish Architects.
76 James Stevens Curl, *The Art and Architecture of Freemasonry* (London, 1991) deals exclusively with European and American freemasonry.
77 The most important recent study of imperial freemasonry is Jessica L. Harland-Jacobs, *Builders of Empire: Freemasonry and British Imperialism, 1717–1827* (Chapel Hill, NC, 2007). See also P.J. Rich, *Chains of Empire: English Public Schools, Masonic Children, Historical Causality and Imperial Clubdom* (Washington, DC, 2015). There was a pioneering look at imperial freemasonry in Ronald Hyam's durable book, *Britain's Imperial Century 1815–1914: A Study of Empire and Expansion* (third edition, London, 2002, originally published in 1976), particularly chapter 5.

78 In India many of the governors-general from Cornwallis and Wellesley were associated with freemasonry, while Lord Moira helped to establish it as a significant force. The Scots Dalhousie and Elphinstone were particularly enthusiastic. Elphinstone, when governor of Madras, became provincial grand master in 1840. The government granted a building site for a grand temple and Elphinstone laid the foundation stone. The Madras brethren enjoyed an annual ball with the ladies. Harland-Jacobs, *Builders of Empire*, p. 175.
79 Simon Deschamps, 'From Britain to India: Freemasonry as a Connective Force of Empire', *Revue Electronique d'études sur le monde Anglophone,* put online 15 June 2017 (accessed 5 June 2018).
80 This comment was in an endorsement by Mrinalini Sinha to the book by Harland-Jacobs.
81 Charles Allen, 'A Home Away From Home' in Robert Fermor-Hesketh (ed.), *Architecture of the British Empire* (London, 1986), pp. 69–70.
82 *The Bengal calendar for the year 1789: including a list of the Hon. and United East-India Company's civil and military servants on the Bengal establishment, &c. including also those at Madras, Bombay, Fort Marlborough, China, and St. Helena.* [London]: Calcutta printed; London re-printed: for John Stockdale, Piccadilly. MDCCLXXXIX. Entered at Stationers-Hall, [1789] Great Britain England London. The British Library. Among the officers of the Provincial Grand Lodge listed was one John Mackenzie, who had been the former deputy grand master. There do not seem to have been any Indians listed, although only the officers were named.
83 The Scottish Masons had been interested in opening up freemasonry of the Scottish rite to Indians from the 1830s. A Parsi considered that the Scottish lodges in India 'thoroughly represent the noble principles of Masonry in refusing to make distinctions of caste or creed'. Other lodges, however, followed as the century progressed, always of course assuming that the new brother was of appropriate social status or wealth. Harland-Jacobs, *Builders of Empire*, pp. 220–238, the quotation on p. 232. A photograph on the same page shows the large number of Indian brethren in the Lodge Rising Star of Western India (Scottish constitution) in 1903.
84 Harland-Jacobs, *Builders of Empire*, p. 57.
85 www.grandlodge.co.za/de-goede-hoop-temple-cape-town-3/ (accessed 7 June 2018).
86 This lodge may owe its founding to the special origins of Sierra Leone as the evangelical freed slaves colony.
87 Wallace, *Web of Empire*, pp. 266 and 272.

7

Colonial cities: Valletta, Rangoon and new capitals

The explosive growths and resultant buildings of many of the great cities of empire in the second half of the nineteenth century have been examined by a number of historians. In the case of Melbourne, for example, there is the classic essay by Asa Briggs.[1] The historian James Belich placed cities like Melbourne and Toronto into his category of mega-cities and their architecture has received a good deal of attention.[2] Representative buildings in these cities have been mentioned earlier in the book, but this chapter seeks to assess the buildings of two contrasting smaller and less well-known colonial cities. The focus will be on the development of architectural forms in the key colonial fortress of Malta and the rapidly developing colonial capital city of Burma, Rangoon. In the second part of the chapter the creation of new capitals of Australia in Canberra, India at New Delhi and Northern Rhodesia at Lusaka will be examined to determine their meanings for the later imperial period.

THE CASE OF VALLETTA

Malta was a vital strategic Mediterranean colony where British building reflected the architectural debates and struggles of the time, between what were seen as pure styles and elements of hybridity, as well as between neoclassical and Gothic. Underlying all of this there was another tension, between the dominant and historic Roman Catholic Church of the Knights Hospitallers and the new Protestant rulers. The development of the built environment according to what the British thought were appropriate styles began soon after the island was taken from the French (at the invitation of the islanders, who had rebelled against the occupying Napoleonic forces) in 1800. The first Commissioner, Alexander Ball (who returned in 1802 for a longer stint), was determined to transform the island through architecture, the development of gardens, scientific horticulture and the design values (including furniture) that he considered appropriate to what was to become a British Crown Colony.³ Malta was to some extent a special case (although there are parallels elsewhere in the empire), since it was in effect a fortress writ large. All building projects, particularly around Valletta, had to be submitted to the government to ensure that they did not interfere with the extensive bastions and walled defences. There were repeated reports on the ways in which the islands could be defended in time of war, and these took into consideration both the built environment and food and water supplies.⁴ The architectural and monumental history of the island colony also reflects the fact that it seemed ripe for the development of a Romantic approach, given its key position in the Mediterranean close to the lands of the ancient empires of Greece and Rome. The development of these ideas owed a great deal to the influence of military engineers in the early days of colonialism, as well as the civilian engineers who doubled up as architects. Colonel George Whitmore took on major civil engineering public works (eventually being paid separate

50 Victoria Gate and bastions, Valletta, Malta

Colonial cities: Valletta, Rangoon and new capitals

51 Fort St Elmo, Valletta, Malta

fees for them) and transformed the appearance of the harbour by laying out the Upper Barrakka Gardens, with terraced arches that were to become a Valhalla of monuments and tombs, with the matching Lower Gardens containing the Greek revivalist monument to Alexander Ball. Whitmore also designed the massive Greek revivalist Bighi Naval Hospital on the other side of Grand Harbour. He was even employed to design and build the governor's 'palace' in Corfu and exported both stone and craftsmen from Malta to accomplish this.[5] William Scamp, a former clerk of works at the restoration of Windsor Castle and sometimes described as a naval engineer, designed the new Anglican pro-cathedral (consciously distancing itself from the Catholic Baroque of the island)[6] in the early 1840s, financed by the Dowager Queen Adelaide, as well as the enormous naval bakery in Vittorioso mixing classical form with hybrid local touches.

These engineers-as-architects were obviously influenced by styles at home and by their earlier experience, but nonetheless they were alert to the particular historical and environmental context of Malta. The shift to Gothic started to take place as a result of a request from the Free Church of Scotland to build a church appropriate to their Presbyterian form of worship. There is a certain paradox here because Presbyterian churches often clung to classical styles after they had gone out of fashion. This was partly to distance themselves from Catholicism, partly to emphasise the fact that it was a preaching church and not a liturgical one like the Church of England. But in Malta in the 1850s, the Free Church decided to build in a Gothic style, either to distance itself from the Anglican classical pro-cathedral or because of the predilection of the architect. The Catholic Archbishop of Malta strongly objected to the building of the church, considering that one Protestant building was enough, and insisted that if built it should have neither tower nor spire. This was parallel to similar struggles that took place at an earlier period in India where the conflict was between Anglicans and Scots.[7] The governor, Major General Sir William Reid (a Scot from Fife), rejected the Catholic objections, insisting that it was a fundamental tenet of the British Empire to offer freedom of worship to all religions.[8] St Andrew's Presbyterian Church was duly built, completed in 1865, and remains active today.[9] Its architect was an engineering draughtsman, Giuseppe Bonavia, a member of a local family of *periti*, the Maltese term for surveyors who worked in the engineering department. Other Gothic structures followed, including a Methodist church and chapels in new cemeteries of the 1860s, one of them Catholic.[10] A striking, predominantly Romanesque (with Gothic elements) memorial chapel was built in the Ta-Braxia cemetery in memory of Lady Gordon and completed in 1896.[11] It was designed by J.L. Pearson, a well-known late Victorian eclectic architect in London.

Gothic did not, however, displace neoclassical. At the same time as the Scottish church was being built, the garrison church was constructed in a neoclassical style near the Barrakka Gardens (moving from God to Mammon, it is now the Bourse). Other neoclassical buildings included the Corradino prison, the lunatic asylum (as it was called then) and the Palladian chapel of the charitable hospitals. Indeed the coexistence of the two styles was neatly symbolised by the fact that a pumping station (at Gzira) was built in a Gothic style while the seawater distilling station at Sliema was distinctly neoclassical. The grandest classical project of the time was the major Opera House. The governor of the day (Sir John Gaspard Le Marchant) actually considered that this would be a means of social control, helping to avoid 'dissipation and gambling'.[12] The Opera House was built in the 1860s since it was felt that the eighteenth-century Baroque Manoel Theatre (already extended and refurbished by the British) was no longer adequate and that opera was a very popular attraction. It was designed by E.M. Barry (son of Sir Charles) and was a strikingly monumental building, the original chaste ionic Greek revivalist style of Malta replaced by elaborate Corinthian columns embracing the whole structure. After a chequered existence (including being burnt down and rebuilt) it was destroyed by bombing during the Second World War and its ruins stand adjacent to the new parliament building. From 1869, Malta became even more important, with the opening of the Suez Canal and the further development of the steamship. The colony was now a vital strategic point on routes from West to East, although it had already become significant from the establishment thirty years earlier of the 'overland route' using Egypt as a land bridge.

COLONIAL RANGOON[13]

It has been suggested that Rangoon (Yangon) was 'a foreign city erected on Burmese soil ... a mimeograph of dozens of port cities scattered throughout colonial South and Southeast Asia'.[14] Yet, while there were indeed some resemblances to Singapore or Penang, it nonetheless developed its own distinctive character.[15] Its rapid urban growth is a striking case of an emergent imperial city, both in terms of spatial arrangements and in respect of its striking architecture. Yet it is little known within the historical literature. There are several reasons for this. First, the long period of post-independence military rule (1962–2011, only theoretically concluded in recent years) ensured that there has been little research relating to Rangoon's status as a great colonial city.[16] On the other hand, the lack of dramatic economic change during that time means that many buildings have survived where they might have been swept away by either nationalist cultural fervour or new commercial and industrial developments. Indeed, there has been a good deal of restoration after the destruction wrought during the Japanese occupation, although many notable buildings in the city centre survived that period. Moreover, the capital of Myanmar (Burma) was moved inland to Naypyidaw or Nay Pyi Taw, two hundred miles north of Yangon, between 2006 and 2012. The official reason for this was that Yangon had become too crowded and there was therefore insufficient space for the expansion of government offices.[17] This move might again have had a conservationist effect. Finally, remarkable preservationist activities have been conducted by a combination of the Yangon Heritage Trust and the Association of Myanmar Architects. The Heritage Trust was founded in 2013 by Dr Thant Myint-U, among others, to preserve Yangon through what was felt would be sensible planning arrangements, since 'Yangon boasts one of the most spectacular and diverse urban landscapes.'[18]

Burma was conquered by the British in three nineteenth-century wars. The provinces of Arakan and Tenasserim were taken after the first Burmese War in 1824; Lower Burma in 1852 after the second, and Upper Burma after the third in 1885. A major centre was developed after each war: Moulmein in the Tenasserim panhandle (now Mawlamyine), Rangoon on the Rangoon river, one of the arms of the delta of the Irrawaddy (now Ayeyarwaddy), and Mandalay in the north.[19] The British transformed these three into significant colonial cities, overlaying, but not entirely obliterating, indigenous settlements as they did so. The former Moulmein, capital of the British Colony from 1824 to 1852, in its striking setting on the banks of the Salween River, is in many respects still a colonial town, with surviving administrative buildings, Christian churches and hints of the former harbour, though most traces of a European population have now disappeared.[20] The original Mandalay was seriously damaged, in many respects almost destroyed, during the Second World War, and is now mainly a modern Myanmar city, with surviving Buddhist monasteries, including the hill overlooking the town, and fragments of the former royal palace (including some elements of rebuilding), its great moat and walls providing hints of past glory. Rangoon was the capital from 1852 until the British were ejected by the Japanese in the Second World War, returning post-war for a brief period before independence in 1948. During this time, there was some reconstruction, for example the rebuilding of the railway station, destroyed by the British (like many other installations) in the face of the Japanese advance. The new station, an impressively large structure in the nineteenth-century tradition, which still functions, was provided with pagoda-like towers to emphasise its Burmese location.

Some colonial contemporaries regarded Burma as a Scottish colony because so many of the commercial companies involved in its development were Scottish or founded by Scots.[21] These included the Paddy Henderson company, the main shipping concern connecting Rangoon to Europe and other Asian territories,[22] the British India Steam Navigation Company, which was formed by the Scottish shipowner Sir William Mackinnon in 1856 to connect India to Burma,[23] though it later developed in many other directions, and the smaller shipping company, J & F Graham. The Irrawaddy Flotilla Company (which possessed in its heyday the largest river fleet in the world),[24] the Bulloch Brothers' company, priding themselves as being the largest rice milling establishment in Asia,[25] the Bombay and Burma Trading Corporation, the powerful mercantile house Finlay, Fleming

Colonial cities: Valletta, Rangoon and new capitals

52 Rebuilt railway station, Rangoon

and Company and the Burmah Oil Company were all either registered in Glasgow or were founded by Scots. In addition, there were many Scottish personnel involved in the running of the colony, which was a province of India until 1937. In this respect, it should be remembered that the capitals of the provinces of India were often grander than the capitals of 'dependent' colonies elsewhere: this was certainly true of Rangoon.

After the conquest of 1852, the British superintendent military surgeon was Dr William Montgomerie, who had already had experience of town planning and municipal organisation in Singapore, where he had been working for thirty years.[26] He recognised the proposed location as an ideal port site and suggested a major road along the river bank, where quays would be developed, with a grid plan of streets beyond. The task of planning the city was taken over by Lieutenant Alexander Fraser of the Bengal Engineers (both Montgomerie and Fraser were Scots), and he developed Montgomerie's ideas, with the grid of streets running from the Pazun Daung creek to the east to the great bend of the main river to the west. Buddhist pagodas and monasteries would be respected and survive, but the rest of the indigenous community would be swept away. The Sule and Shwedagon pagodas ironically became both the symbols and the subsidiary nodal points of the city, in many respects the exotica curiously contrasting with and validating the modernity round about. Many visitors seemed, for example, to send postcards of the pagodas (in preference to modern buildings) home to indicate the nature of the fascinating colony in which they were living.[27] However, complete freedom of action for the new city was initially constrained by the creation of a great military cantonment to the north of the grid plan and, although this was later moved to the edges of the city, this division influences the layout to this day. The white suburb was established, somewhat offset from the grid plan, to the west of the Kan Dawgyi Lake, gradually extending northwards to the area of the Inya Lake, which became a significant centre of recreation. Other lower-value suburbs developed towards the east, later across the creek and also upriver and on the other side of the Rangoon River. A map of 1910/11 shows the layout and all the principal buildings very clearly.[28] Both Montgomerie and Fraser were thus alert to the need for the grand buildings required in a colonial capital as well as the racial separation required (in the imperial mind) for the security and health of the white inhabitants.

To emphasise these Scottish connections, it has even been suggested that there is a 'Glasgow–Yangon Architectural Axis', that some of the buildings in Rangoon bear some resemblance to Glasgow buildings of the same period.[29] This effect did not, however, emerge until later in the nineteenth century. Forty years earlier, very soon after the laying out of the city, key buildings began to appear on Strand Road. At that point, many of the city's buildings would have reflected eclectic Victorian styles, fairly nondescript and, in terms of architects and contractors, usually anonymous. An example surviving from the earlier period is the now derelict Burma Railways Company headquarters of 1877. The Pegu Club of 1882 was magnificently built in teak and is an extraordinary survivor from colonial times, now standing empty.[30] Its wooden construction and roofline give it a distinctive Burmese feel, although its interiors and the social life that was pursued within it would have been distinctly British and imperial. However, from the end of the century the appearance of professional architects on the scene, together with a tremendous economic boom, created a city with real pretensions and with what has been described as a 'more cohesive aesthetic'[31] – although the buildings are so diverse that such an idea cannot be taken too far.

Colonial cities: Valletta, Rangoon and new capitals

53 Pegu Club, Rangoon

This extraordinary growth of the Burmese economy, rendering it highly significant in the British eastern empire, occurred partly because of the annexation of the north, but principally through the growing exports of rice, teak, minerals and later oil. This boom is perfectly symbolised by the large number of bank buildings that appeared at this time, often very impressive structures. As a result of all this construction activity, which continued from the 1890s to the inter-war years of the twentieth century, most of the earlier structures were replaced.[32] The city that emerged had a sequence of grand imperial buildings on Strand Road, Phayre Street (now Pansodan Street), Sule Pagoda Street, Merchant Road (which was the banking quarter) and Dalhousie Street (Mahabandoola Road). The buildings were often in red brick, giving the city an overall rosy effect, or alternatively in light-coloured masonry or stucco. Colonial classical elements predominated, although the vast, rambling Secretariat building of 1889–1905 was described as 'bureaucratic Byzantine'. It was designed by Henry Hoyne Fox, an engineer rather than an architect who had a penchant for over-elaborate designs, exemplified in his much-derided government house.[33] In 2016 the Secretariat still stood in a derelict state, displaying many of its Romanesque elements. It was built slightly to the edge of the main centre, no doubt to find a site sufficiently large

The British Empire through buildings

for its vast scale. Some of the other major colonial buildings, such as the High Court (1905–11, red-brick Romanesque with a hint of Indo-Saracenic), Rowe's department store (1908–10) and the Custom House (1912–15) had clock towers, emblems of modernity and imperial discipline.[34] Some of the buildings of the new aesthetic were designed by the Scottish architect John Begg (1866–1937), who seized the opportunities for holding official architectural appointments in the British Empire. He was for a period a government architect in South Africa before becoming the Consultant Architect to the Government of Bombay in 1901 and then Consultant Architect to the Government of India from 1908 to 1921, after which he returned to private practice in Edinburgh. As consulting architect he had the opportunity to design some significant public buildings himself as well as considering and influencing the designs of others. He seems to have believed in a certain degree of eclecticism. In Rangoon, he designed the Government Press Office (1908–12) and Central Telegraph Office (1913–17), as well as the prominent Custom House (1912–16). The Custom House was inevitably located on Strand Road and a collection of other significant buildings

54 High Court, Rangoon

Colonial cities: Valletta, Rangoon and new capitals

were strung out along this river bank. These included commercial headquarters, such as that of Bulloch and Company (1908, now the General Post Office[35]), J & F Graham shipping, its Rangoon branch founded in the 1890s (1898, now the British Embassy), the Strand Hotel (1901) and the Imperial Bank of India (1914, now the Myanmar Economic Bank), as well as public buildings such as the Port Authority (1928), the Currency Department (*c.* 1900, now the Divisional Court), and the Yangon Division Office (1927–31). Most of these buildings are hybrid colonial in style, mixing classical, Renaissance and other elements, but paying little attention to their Burmese context. The Yangon Division Office, originally designed as new law courts by Thomas Oliphant Foster, is truly monumental, a steel-framed structure with a massive three-storey Ionic colonnade running along Strand Road for a considerable length. All these buildings of the former Rangoon create a dramatically colonial, 'heritaged' feel to the centre of modern Yangon. Most of them have been taken over for other purposes, while the streets have become settings for a variety of forms of trading (including in books), food stalls and many other social and economic uses which indicate

55 Strand Hotel, Rangoon

the predominance of the Burmese ethnicity in the present population. Perhaps few are outstanding in architectural terms, though they are clearly valued by indigenous architects. The most striking are perhaps the former Irrawaddy Flotilla Company offices, now the Inland Waterways Department; the New Law Courts, now the Yangon Divisional Office Complex; the Reserve Bank of India, now the Myawaddy Bank; the Custom House; the City Hall and the riotously eclectic State Fine Arts School. These more hybrid styles emerged particularly after the end of the First World War. The State Fine Arts School was, in effect, a large mansion built in an extraordinary blend of classical and (perhaps not entirely relevant) Chinese elements. The City Hall, overlooking the large central square and gardens, was built between 1925 and 1940, designed by a combination of European and Burmese architects. It has striking Burmese elements, including intriguingly unusual arches in its elevation, with a stepped-back central roof element and towers capped by pagoda-like structures.

The British Empire was a highly cosmopolitan phenomenon. As well as European migrants, other peoples were attracted by business or labour opportunities. In the case of Burma, such people were mainly of Indian or Chinese ethnicity, although some came from the Middle East. We must assume that the early buildings of Rangoon and elsewhere in the colony were built by local labour, with informal architect and contracting arrangements. The precise people involved are not always apparent from the records. By the end of the century, however, not only had architecture been professionalised, but major construction companies had become active in securing contracts. In the case of the vast Secretariat building, the contractor was an Indian who was known under the name of Baboo Naitran Rambux. His father had come from northern India and was involved in building the first wing before he was killed by a train in 1894. His son took over and built the rest, developing the company into one of the most significant in construction in Burma, employing thousands of workers. He became a wealthy and respected member of Burmese colonial society and secured the contract for the Jubilee Hall, a Gothic cathedral-like structure built to commemorate Victoria's Jubilee in 1897, which became the major social and entertainments centre for colonial society in Burma until demolished in the early 1990s. Other Indian contractors included Bagchi and Company, which built the High Court and the Yangon General Hospital (1904–11, still in use). The Strand Hotel, whose architect was John Darwood, was built by a Turkish Armenian contractor T.J.N. Catchatoor. By the end of the century, there was so much work in Rangoon that several contractors from Britain were also active, including Clark and Greig,[36] Robinson and Munday,[37] and Arthur Flavell and Co.,[38] among others.

This cosmopolitanism also extended to the clients for a few of these buildings. The Rander Building on Phayre Street was commissioned by a group of Surti Indian traders who came from Rander near Surat in Gujarat, western India. They had arrived in Burma during the reign of King Mindon, but they swiftly moved to Rangoon with the arrival of the British. One of these was a Muslim called Moola Hashim, who built the first mosque in Rangoon. Originally constructed in bamboo, this was rebuilt in masonry and stands to this day. Sofaer's building was constructed as a department store (much favoured by Burmese customers) for Isaac Sofaer (1867–1926), a Baghdadi Jewish businessman who became one of the most prominent members of the Rangoon Jewish community. There were some 2,100 Jews in the early twentieth century, most of them traders from the Middle East, who worshipped in a synagogue which survives. Sofaer's sons were educated at St Paul's School, with its impressive buildings built with additions from 1885,[39] and they also became successful traders in the city. Sofaer's building remains a striking presence on the corner of Pansodan Street and Merchant Road. Closer to the river, the Strand Hotel became one of the most celebrated buildings in the city. The start of the Burma boom in the late 1880s aroused the interest of the Armenian Sarkies brothers, who had become the most prominent hoteliers in South-East Asia. Descended from a family of merchants in Calcutta in the early nineteenth century, they had seized the opportunities presented by the British annexation of Singapore in 1819. They soon owned several trading houses there and in Jakarta and they also extended their operations to Penang.[40] In 1884 four Sarkies brothers opened the Eastern Hotel in Penang (later combined with the Oriental next door).[41] In 1887 they inaugurated Raffles Hotel in Singapore, which arguably became the most famous hotel in the East.[42] The famous butterfly building, designed by the most competent architect in Singapore at the time, R.A.J. Bidwell, opened in 1899. Turning their attention to Rangoon, the 60-room Strand was opened in 1901, entering imperial lore almost as strongly as Raffles itself. It was then perfectly positioned directly opposite the quays of the ships arriving in the river. Despite changes of ownership and many vicissitudes, including damaging occupation by the Japanese, it has been fully restored and remains one of the best-known hotels in the city.[43]

The cosmopolitan nature of Rangoon was not of course restricted to elite merchants and entrepreneurs. The population of the city was dramatically transformed from being predominantly ethnic Burmese in the early days of British rule to a melting pot – or 'pressure cooker' as one historian has suggested[44] – of other Burmese ethnicities (both permanent migrants and short-term workers) from Upper Burma, and of both Indian and Chinese immigrants. By 1921, Indians strikingly constituted the majority of the population of Rangoon while by that time there were 21,000 Chinese in the city. Indians, for example, became the docks' stevedores, accepting lower wages than the Burmese.[45] This produced serious communal tensions, which sometimes broke out into rioting, as well as social deprivation and problems of crime, gambling and sexual exploitation (the majority of the immigrant population was male). It also placed heavy pressure upon the fabric of the city and the availability of cheaper accommodation for low-paid workers. These continued, with attendant sanitation problems, through the 1930s Depression period (when social tensions were at their height) and into the 1950s. There were, however, some striking immigrant success stories among Indians and Chinese, including the Chinese businessman Chan Mah Phee, who became a wealthy trader and landowner, succeeded by his son who had been educated at St Paul's RC School.[46] There was a certain degree of fluidity in Rangoon society, where at times money seemed to speak louder than race. Some of the most successful immigrants became involved in the sporting and club life of the city. These activities, so important to a global 'imperial imaginary', will be examined in another work, but it can be noted in passing that Rangoon acquired the full range of sporting and cultural activities associated with a variety of clubs. They often had a built presence in pavilions, sports grounds and the racecourse.

NEW CAPITALS: CANBERRA

One of the most extraordinary of the urban manifestations of the British Empire was the creation of new capitals, particularly as it developed to its highest point in the inter-war years of the twentieth century. This phenomenon helps to give the lie to the notion that empire was effectively killed off in the trenches of the First World War. Historians' inescapable thraldom to hindsight often provides them with a heightened conviction in the importance of key turning points of history. It is true that by the end of the First World War, the British position in Ireland had become tenuous; the Indian nationalist situation had already become more or less critical (though some in India still thought the Raj would endure), while the Dominions would rapidly head towards greater independence, if within the British Empire. Nevertheless, there is much evidence from some economic indicators – the cultural history of empire, the scale of migration, recruitment to the colonial service with more professional training, increasing faith in environmental policies and in the role of experts – that empire seemed to be alive and well, particularly in the so-called dependent empire.[47] To a certain extent the creation of new capitals seems to reflect this. The notion of their foundation (a historic phenomenon throughout the history of empires, not least in India) had been around in the British Empire since the nineteenth century. As we have seen, Ottawa emerged from the tiny lumbering village of Bytown and became respectively the capital of Upper and Lower Canada in 1857 and of the Canadian Confederation after 1867. Although Pretoria was the capital of the Transvaal, the new Union buildings of Sir Herbert Baker, built on the raised site of Meintjeskop between 1910 and 1913, gave the appearance of being part of a new capital. Some capitals of planned new colonies, such as Adelaide in South Australia, were carefully laid out with environmental and social factors in mind. We have just encountered the creation of Rangoon as a new capital almost from scratch. This chapter will examine the process in the three planned capitals of Canberra, New Delhi and Lusaka. Most space will be devoted to Lusaka, since it is strikingly revelatory of both colonial segregation practice and also imperial ideology. Although Lusaka has been discussed by geographers and town-planning specialists, historians have paid surprisingly little attention to its history.

After the declaration of the Commonwealth of Australia in 1901, Melbourne became the temporary capital, holding this status until 1927. The emergence of Canberra as the new capital had an exceptionally convoluted and lengthy history.[48] After some discussion, it was agreed that a planned capital should be created on neutral territory, thus sidestepping the rival claims of Sydney and Melbourne to be the premier city of the Commonwealth. Just as Ottawa had emerged as a compromise between Ontario and Quebec, there does not seem to have been any doubt that it would be sited in the original south-eastern corner of the vast new country. The search for a site started in 1902 and by 1908 no fewer than eleven possibilities were in contention. From these Canberra emerged as the front-runner. It was located in an area where there had been significant indigenous settlement over many centuries (the Aboriginal name was Canberry, meaning meeting place, though Aboriginal people played no role in the original decisions and associated ceremonies). Some European stockmen already possessed farmsteads in the area. It appeared to have good water supplies and some attractive natural features, including several hills, of which Mount Ainslie was the most prominent. There was an Anglican church there, St John's, which had been built in a simple Gothic style between 1841 and 1845, still Canberra's most significant older building, centrally located close to Anzac Parade.[49] Once selected in 1908, the area (about 150 miles south-west of Sydney) was ceded by New South Wales in 1909. The Australian Commonwealth Territory was duly declared in 1911 and the Governor-General named the capital Canberra in a ceremony in 1913. Responsibility for the design was won by the American Walter Burley Griffin, together with his architect wife, Marion Mahony Griffin, who seems to have drawn the plans.

Like so many other places in the British Empire, Canberra had its beginnings in tents. There is a photograph of a group of tents of the survey team led by the Government Surveyor, Charles Scrivener, which surveyed the site between 1909 and 1915. The Griffins duly submitted their highly complex plan which suggested a large central lake and a road network consisting of concentric circles, triangular features and grid-plan areas set at angles to each other. Overall, the concept of the city was partly influenced by the planning of Washington, DC, by developments in Chicago, and even by concepts of the British picturesque. But Canberra was to have an exceptionally rocky road to fruition as a national capital. International events like the First World War, the Great Depression after the Wall Street Crash of 1929 and then the Second World War, severely impeded its progress. Australian officials and politicians had disputes with the Griffins, who resigned in 1920. When the Prince of Wales (later Edward VIII) visited the non-existent capital in that year, it is perhaps not surprising that the chronicler of his imperial travels wrote that it was a city which 'consisted largely of foundation stones, but its importance was not to be judged by its incompleteness' and the Minister of Works explained that with victory in the war, construction would now forge ahead.[50] He was being sanguine. In 1928, Griffin accused the Federal Capital Commission (one of many such commissions) of having 'violated the aesthetic, social and economic principles [of his original plan] in almost every act'.[51] The real push to complete it only came in the 1950s, largely after the National Capital Development Commission was created in 1957, while some of the major national institutions, like the National Museum (2001) and the National Portrait Gallery (2008), only appeared in the twenty-first century.[52] Some impression of this slow emergence is provided by population figures. In 1911, the population of the area was 1,714. By 1957, this lingered at 39,000. But by 2011 it had reached 356,000 and Canberra had at last emerged as a fully-formed capital city.

Various stages reflect this slow gestation. A railway branch line for freight was opened to Queanbean in 1914, and a passenger station constructed by 1924. The Royal Military College was founded at nearby Duntroon in 1911. The Cotter Dam was constructed between 1912 and 1915, with other dams following in the 1960s. An internment camp for 'enemy aliens' was created towards the end of the First World War and was soon reused as a workers' camp. Major earthworks for the roads and building sites took many years to complete and the early public buildings only appeared in the 1920s. These included the temporary parliament building of 1927 and the Albert Hall of 1928. One of the first actions of the parliament was to repeal the alcohol prohibition which had been set in place in 1910. At that point many of the officials and the ministries remained in Melbourne. In 1941, one of the city's only architecturally conservative buildings appeared in a key location at the end of a grand avenue opposite the parliament building. This was the Australian War Memorial, built in a late Edwardian Baroque with grand dome and arcades, later to emerge as a national war museum. This acknowledged the central role of war in the formation of Australian identity. By this time, officials occupied bungalows in the early suburbs and high commissions and embassies were to arrive from the 1930s. The Federal Highway reached Canberra in 1931 and the beginnings of an airfield were constructed in 1936. An important development was the founding of the Australian National University in 1946. This had first been proposed early in the century and a site had been incorporated into the Griffin plan at the foot of the Black Mountain. Originally a postgraduate institution, it added undergraduate students in 1960 and brought large numbers of academics and students to swell the population. Meanwhile, work on the serpentine Lake Burley Griffin (some eleven kilometres long and different from Griffin's original plan) only fully began in the 1960s with the damming of the Molonglo River. The National Library opened in 1968, the High Court in 1980 and the National Gallery in 1982. The Parliament House, at last replacing the Provisional Parliament House of 1927 (still standing as the Old Parliament House, now the Museum of Australian Democracy), was only completed in 1988. All of these buildings are modernist, largely unlike any of their imperial predecessors. Canberra has had its problems, not least the destruction wrought by bush fires in 2003 and the difficulties with blue-green algae in the lake. It remains a spread-out city, difficult for pedestrians to get around, except by taxi, and with a surprisingly small airport for a capital. Visitors often feel ambivalent about the place and it is alleged that Paul Keating, Australian prime minister in the 1990s, regarded it as a 'great mistake', while others have dubbed it a 'good sheep station spoiled'.[53] On the other hand, many residents enjoy living there.

NEW DELHI

If the gestation of Canberra was lengthy and tortuous, the creation of New Delhi was rather more rapid, while that of Lusaka (admittedly somewhat smaller) was accomplished very quickly. New Delhi was one of those major historical developments that occurred as a by-product of other events. Calcutta had been the principal administrative centre of the East India Company and after 1858 the imperial capital, but by the twentieth century it had become one of the main centres of Indian nationalism. The British had long been suspicious of the Bengali intelligentsia and it has generally been considered that Curzon's autocratic decision to partition Bengal on the alleged grounds of administrative expediency was designed to create a division between the Hindus and Muslims of the province. His viceregal successor, Minto, accepted the demand of the newly founded Muslim League that there should be communally based electorates in order to protect the Muslim minority. The announcement at the Delhi Durbar in December 2011 that the partition of Bengal would be revoked while the capital of India would be moved to Delhi seemed to be designed to spike Bengali-led nationalism, the more extreme wing of which were adopting violent techniques. At the same time it was designed to please the British princely allies of northern India as well as respecting the great heartland of the predecessor Mughal Empire. Thus, as David A Johnson has put it, it was 'a symbol of coercion and consent'.[54] Moreover, Delhi had been a city of considerable historical resonance to the British, through the actions of the 1857 Revolt and the symbolic use of the Ridge above Delhi (where the army had camped before recapturing the city) as the setting for the Assemblage of 1877 and the durbars of 1903 and 1911.

These considerations were crucial at a time when the British were obsessed with a strong sense of political unease (almost amounting to panic), paradoxically combined with a passion for historical contexts and alleged traditions engendered by the Durbar. With hindsight, however, it may also be argued that the British no longer saw the necessity of conducting administration from a great port and commercial centre. Delhi was certainly nearer the centre of the Subcontinent such that railways could access many parts of the country more easily, also facilitating troop movements in the maintenance of security. The coming technology would, in any case, be air power, and by the time New Delhi was being constructed it was apparent that air communications would be important from this central position. The first Delhi airfield was laid out in 1930. None of this played any part in the decision, but it must have become apparent as the new capital was being constructed. Moreover, whatever the intentions of the British, there can be no doubt that the location and design of New Delhi proved to be important for independent India. It remains one of the most grandly conceived capitals anywhere.[55] It has also become a major 'heritage' hot spot for international tourists, as the many coaches and taxis on Raisina Hill testify. This is the ceremonial route to the President's residence, the former Viceroy's palace, now the Rashtrapati Bhavan. It is also a magnificent backdrop for Indian ceremonial, such as the annual Republic Day celebrations on 26 January, when the military display on the Rajpath (formerly Kingsway) matches anything the British could produce.[56] Moreover, if there is any suggestion of redevelopment of original areas (like the Lodi estate of official bungalows) of New Delhi, there is an immediate outcry from heritage lobbies.[57] The Indian National Trust for Art and Cultural Heritage has indeed called it 'a synthesis of Indian and European architectural and civic ideas'.[58]

Historians have paid a great deal of attention to the planning and building of New Delhi and generally its layout and buildings have received a good press as the work of two major twentieth-century architects, Edwin Lutyens and Herbert Baker.[59] Lutyens was a testy figure who seems to have been particularly dismissive of historic Indian architecture, yet nonetheless succeeded in producing an extraordinary fusion of West and East (in that order) in the Viceroy's palace. His appointment, together with that of Herbert Baker, fresh from designing the Union buildings in Pretoria, ensured that the architecture would be a variant on the neo-Georgian revival. Consequently, the suggestion by E.B. Havell (former principal of the Calcutta School of Art and prolific writer on Indian art and architecture) that the new capital should adopt Indo-Saracenic styles was comprehensively rejected. Havel's hope that considerable opportunities would be offered to Indian craftspeople in the production of buildings in this style was also a non-starter. The hybrid style seemed to have run its course and, for Lutyens, Baker and their supporters, a great new administrative capital required to be inspired by the dignity of at least some derivation from Roman precedents.

Nevertheless, Lutyens was induced to include Indian elements in the viceroy's palace, notably the shape of the dome, the *chujjas*, or deep overhanging eaves, and *chattris* (small pavilions) that adorn its roof, ensuring that its Palladianism is culturally adulterated and clearly located in India. Famously, Lutyens and Baker fell out over the approach to the palace. Baker insisted that the Secretariat buildings should be on the hill, which necessitated the moving of the Viceroy's palace further back. The effect of this was to ensure that the palace failed to dominate the whole area as Lutyens wished. The slope of Raisina Hill meant that its dome and details would rise like a mirage as they are approached. Inevitably, Lutyens wanted the slope to be evened out and held Baker responsible for the obscuring of the palace. Fortunately, there was neither money nor time for such earthworks and the dramatically striking effect survives.[60]

New Delhi was also, to a certain extent, given the garden-city treatment, with extensive tree planting on all of the avenues and sizeable grounds for most of the bungalows, while the palace was provided with vast gardens, partly as an echo of the predilections of Mughal predecessors. The whole area is now a relative haven of space and peace in a city of almost twenty million (2019), where air pollution is a daily problem. Whether this insulates legislators and civil servants from the realities of India may be a moot point. Despite the scale of the conception, and in contrast with Canberra, the entire scheme was completed in twenty years and the new capital was inaugurated in 1931. This included the general layout, Baker's north and south blocks of the Secretariat buildings that seem to guard the approach to the palace, the circular Council Chamber building (now the Parliament), the various monumental structures, such as the war memorial arch, the many bungalows for civil servants (carefully graded according to rank), Connaught Place for shops and offices, and other ancillary buildings. Of course, the speed and grandeur of construction, built by an Indian contractor, were greatly helped by the fact that it was paid for out of Indian revenues. The extraordinary sense of space and the fact that it was a typically British creation are enhanced by the presence of the 220-acre golf club and the 27 acres of the Delhi Gymkhana Club, very much part of Lutyens's conception and both located in the heart of the new capital. The Club, that essential attribute of any imperial city, was designed by the architect Robert T. Russell (who also designed Connaught Circus and the Commander-in-Chief's residence) in cool modern Georgian style to match the nearby bungalows.[61] The word 'Imperial' in the name of the club was removed after independence. With its tennis courts and many other sports facilities, as well as its extensive gardens

Colonial cities: Valletta, Rangoon and new capitals

and organic farm, it remains an exclusive club and a significant institution in the modern capital.

Perhaps the greatest piece of enthnocentrism that the British imposed upon the scheme was the material presence of imperial Christianity. The two grand cathedrals, Anglican and Roman Catholic, are located to the east of the central area, the former in easy reach of the palace. These cathedrals were designed by Henry Medd, trained in the office of Lutyens, then assistant to Baker, and later Architect to the Government of India from 1939 to 1947. The Viceroy Irwin, a devout Anglican, was influential in ensuring that the Cathedral Church of the Redemption was in a prominent position and helped to raise money for it (he also donated the organ). Built in a massive Palladian style, said to be reminiscent of Palladio's Church of the Redentore in Venice, its cool interior retains marks of its imperial past, not least the crowns at each end of the front pew. The grounds are graced by a remarkable Art Deco toilet, an intriguing insertion of modernity into this otherwise atavistic space. Medd's Cathedral of the Sacred Heart was designed to be distinctively Catholic, not least through

56 Anglican Cathedral, New Delhi

the provision of two western towers insisted upon by his clients. These give it the appearance of being a cathedral mysteriously transplanted from Latin America. Nearby is the striking Imperial Hotel, plain and white in its massy Art Deco exterior (though much more colonial in its interior) and surrounded by palm trees, designed by F.B. Blomfield, an associate of Lutyens, and built between 1931 and 1936. It has now been entirely themed according to the Delhi Durbar of 1911, with many prints, portraits and other memorabilia. The visitor wonders what Indian politicians and officials would think of it, but it is yet another piece of evidence of the power of 'heritage'. Most such tourists would be mystified by the rather sour judgement of Jan Morris that New Delhi is 'an anomaly – too late for arrogance, too soon for regrets, too uncertain to get its gradients right. ... The city lacked both the insolence of conquest and the generosity of concessions, and by its deliberate separateness it perpetuated invidious old comparisons.'[62] They might also be surprised that two recent scholars have described the capital as a 'megalomaniac project'.[63]

LUSAKA

The precedents of Canberra and New Delhi were already being discussed when the Colonial Office began to consider pressures for a new capital in Northern Rhodesia. This took place at a time when there were proposals for the amalgamation of Northern and Southern Rhodesia, designed to entrench a tiny white minority in power on both sides of the Zambezi River. This ambition came to fruition with the Central African Federation in 1953 at a time when imperial rulers considered the prospect of African-ruled territories in the area as remote. After the amalgamation of the British South Africa Company territories of North-Eastern and North-Western Rhodesia in 1911, the capital of the colony had been located in Livingstone, close to the Zambezi and the Victoria Falls, in its far south-western corner.[64] The fact that this was always regarded as a temporary expedient was reflected in the fact that government buildings were exceptionally makeshift, with the Governor occupying a wholly unsuitable and uncomfortable building, a former hotel with an iron roof. As European settlers (many of them Afrikaans-speaking) secured further land alienation on the more fertile plateau on the line of rail in the centre of the country, and as the copper mines of the Copperbelt close to the Congo border became more significant, the awkward location of Livingstone became apparent. Copper company representatives and administrators stressed the need for a more conveniently situated capital. In

1930, the trained architect and professor of town planning at University College, London, Stanley Davenport Adshead, was commissioned to produce a report on a potential site and possible plan of a new capital. Given the importance of an adequate water supply, water engineers Sir Alexander Binnie Sons and Deacon were also commissioned to report. In this search, some advocated the mining centre of Broken Hill (Kabwe) on the grounds that using an existing town would reduce expense, but Adshead, having examined the options on the line of rail between Livingstone and the Copperbelt, was impressed with the appeal of a ridge of land on the plateau south of Broken Hill, close to a railway station and a ramshackle collection of small stores which had grown up in association with white farming land. This place was known as Lusaakas, formerly the village of a Lenje headman. It was a thousand feet higher than Livingstone and lay at the centre of the country's butterfly shape near the Kafue River and potentially on a road junction between the so-called Great North Road and others accessing the eastern and western areas of the country. Land there would be very cheap. The modernity of the whole scheme was symbolised by the fact that aerial survey was used to pinpoint the best location, and indeed it was said that one of the advantages of the future Lusaka was that it would provide access to the entire country by air in a matter of hours. The airport thus became central to the entire plan. But the scheme did not have a smooth ride. The worldwide recession ensured that its progress was rocky, halted for financial reasons and then allowed to proceed. It was apparently the assistant secretary of the Northern Rhodesian administration, Eric Dutton, who lobbied hard for the ambitious plan to go ahead and was then instrumental in bringing it to fruition.[65] Once given the green light in 1934, it was decreed that it should be finished in time for the Jubilee of George V in 1935. Construction therefore proceeded in a great rush.

Adshead's original layout was modified by the town-planning engineer of the PWD, P.J. Bowling, but it was the 'imagination and drive' of Dutton that was to be key.[66] All were agreed that a grid plan would be avoided in favour of a segmented layout with a series of focal points and roundabouts. Segments would symbolise multiple aspects of the dominant colonial ideology of segregation and would additionally reflect the didactic and supposedly civilisational objectives of both architecture and layout of the new capital. Kenneth Bradley, the District Commissioner of Mumbwa, about 100 miles to the west of Lusaka, wrote a small book about the new capital which was published in 1935 for private circulation.[67] He was given ten days to write it and copies were presented to 'the distinguished guests who were coming to attend the formal opening'.⁶⁸ Its criteria can therefore be seen as chiming with the views of those 'distinguished guests'. Most importantly, there would be spatial segregation between European and African areas, prompted not only by the fact that this was the colonial norm, but also because Adshead seems to have felt particularly strongly about the supposed lack of African civilisation.⁶⁹ While colonial officials might have avoided the virulence of his racial views, there can be little doubt that the capital's plan reflected the powerful notions of racial and class separation. There was also to be segregation between the commercial and administrative functions, and again a division between shops intended for Europeans and the 'second-class' market for African traders and customers. There was to be no 'untidy mingling of shops and garages with private houses'.⁷⁰ It has been said that Lusaka was designed as the first garden city in Africa – and an enormous number of trees, bushes and other plants were to be deployed – but trees and hedges were to be organised to form screens to emphasise the racial segregation, ensuring that the African compounds would be hidden from passing cars on the major thoroughfares.⁷¹ Within the racialised areas, there would additionally be significant hierarchies: double-storey houses for senior officials, bungalows of varying sizes for others, and flats for single personnel. The grandest avenue, the Ridgeway, would run through this European area. The African areas (the 'Native Side', as Bradley called it, constituting a 'self-contained African town' 'developed on progressive lines') were to be divided into three. One would be for employees of Government House and the administration, which would be closer to the occupants' places of work and be of somewhat superior accommodation; another for servants who would be single, so often known in colonial times, regardless of age, as 'boys'. The third (and most distant) would be for families. In this way, the 'residential area' (meaning the white area) would be 'freed from *piccanins* [children] and other manifestations of domestic untidiness and noise', whereas the presence of Africans who enjoyed more supervisory roles would 'bring a very valuable influence to bear on the more primitive members of the community without themselves suffering any social inconvenience'.⁷² Each African compound (in colonial terminology) would have gathering places, such as the beer hall in the male servants' area, no doubt to alleviate lack of family life. The requirements of security and social surveillance to protect whites ensured that African areas would be separated from European by the business centre and municipal offices, while the Northern Rhodesia regimental barracks would be close to Government House, between the Governor's Village, the African Trades School and the Government Nursery.

Colonial cities: Valletta, Rangoon and new capitals

57 Thatched European bungalow, Lusaka, Northern Rhodesia

Bradley suggested that given the impermanence of traditional African structures, it was essential that the accommodation for Africans should be built of brick, with either superior thatching or tiled roofs. The architect of the buildings of the capital, Jan Hoogterp (who had the necessary credentials of being a pupil of Herbert Baker), visited Nairobi in order to experiment with the manufacture of tiles and was convinced that bricks and tiles could be made anywhere in Africa. This would, apparently, help to improve the standard of structures in African villages, although round huts were chosen, rather than the rectangular ones promoted by missionaries, on the grounds that they were easier to keep clean. That essential perquisite of white settlers and expatriates, a neo-Georgian Gymkhana Club with its adjacent golf course and sporting provisions, was almost as impressive as Government House itself. It was located adjacent to the airport, presumably to provide open land around the runways, but it is tempting to imagine that it was almost as though it would provide an easy escape route if required (though there is no evidence for such a supposition). Government House, the Chief Secretary's residence and the Secretariat offices would all be built in a neo-Georgian style, contrasting strikingly with the 'rondavels' of Africans. This represented the resurgence of imperial neo-Georgian characteristic of the twentieth century. In this, Hoogterp was following his teacher Baker who had designed a neo-Georgian government house for Nairobi completed in 1907.[73] Lusaka was a late manifestation of this revival and it inspired Bradley to allow his rhetoric to run riot in describing Government House, which

> is something more than the residence of a Governor: it is the social centre of a colony, the repository even of all that is most dignified in its life and of such pageantry as can be contrived. It is not only a house, but, as the residence of the King's representative, it is a national treasure, the evidence that a Colony gives to the world of that state of civilisation which it has achieved. The lack of an adequate Government House has for too long deprived Northern Rhodesia of that element of dignified ceremony which its state occasions have rightfully demanded.

He went on that there was a further justification for the scale and design of Government House:

> Northern Rhodesia is a Protectorate in which the Africans outnumber the Europeans by a hundred and twenty to one. To them, this House and its great occasions will be the outward and visible sign at all times of the dignity of the Crown.[74]

That no doubt was the reason for the association of the new capital with the Silver Jubilee in May 1935. The royal connection had already been confirmed when the visiting Prince George (later Duke of Kent) visited the new capital and named one of the avenues after his father.[75] There is something of an irony in the fact that Bradley was not himself able to attend the celebrations for the inauguration of Lusaka. He was to have been flown in from Mumbwa on the day, but no plane arrived. Labour troubles had broken out on the Copperbelt and all planes were required, probably to fly in police and troops.[76] Heavy-handed policing at the Roan Antelope Mine, Nkana, provoked rioting and resulted in the deaths of six strikers.[77]

Such labour unrest was an augury for future political change. Nevertheless, it would be some time before Africans would be able to enjoy the dignity and pageantry of Government House for themselves, although that time would arrive much faster than Bradley's contemporaries imagined. However, his impressive command of imperial rhetoric makes it easy to understand why he was appointed the Northern Rhodesian government's information officer during the Second World War. Yet the planners of Lusaka and the readers of Bradley's book would have been even more astonished by the explosive growth of the population of the city. It was always intended that it would be a relatively small administrative and commercial centre. In 1935 the combined African and European population scarcely reached 10,000. In 1946 it was still under 20,000, but the scale of demographic urbanisation after independence ensured that by 2010, the population of the greater Lusaka urban area had reached 2.4 million. All three new capitals have experienced explosive population growth and all three are indicative of the ways in which empire seemed to remain a going concern in the twentieth century. Canberra represented constitutional change and the emergence of a new Dominion, but supposedly within an imperial framework. New Delhi suggested the lingering hope of the British that the centre could hold and that things might not fall apart or at least be postponed. Lusaka implied that the position of African colonies within the empire still had a long time to run, as had the ideology of imperial racial separation which its layout suggested. Yet all three rapidly emerged as the capitals of wholly independent countries, albeit within a Commonwealth of Equal Nations.

NOTES

1 Asa Briggs, *Victorian Cities* (Harmondsworth, 1968), pp. 277–310.
2 James Belich, *Replenishing the Earth: The Settler Revolution and the Rise of the Anglo-World, 1783–1939* (Oxford, 2009). For architecture, see Philip Goad, *Melbourne Architecture* (Sydney, 2001) and Patricia McHugh, *Toronto Architecture: A City Guide* (Toronto, 1989). See also Allan Levine, *Toronto: Biography of a City* (Madeira Park, BC, 2014). Other significant city histories include John Cookson and Graeme Dunstall (eds), *Southern Capital, Christchurch: Towards a City Biography 1850–2000* (Christchurch, 2000); Vivian Bickford-Smith, *The Emergence of the South African Metropolis: Cities and Identities in the Twentieth Century* (Cambridge, 2016: focusing on Johannesburg, Durban and Cape Town); Nigel Worden, Elizabeth van Heyningen and Vivian Bickford-Smith, *Cape Town: The Making of a City* (Cape Town, 1998) and Vivian Bickford-Smith, Elizabeth van Heyningen and Nigel Worden, *Cape Town in the Twentieth Century: An Illustrated Social History* (Cape Town, 1999).
3 For these architectural developments in Malta, see Malcolm Borg, *British Colonial Architecture: Malta 1800–1900* (Malta, 2001).
4 The main test for the islands came in the Second World War, when it was air power rather than naval defence that became the principal mode of attack, although supplies, famously, still had to come by sea.
5 The Ionian Islands, of which Corfu was the principal one, were returned to Greece in 1864, but only after distinctively British buildings, in neoclassical styles, as well as a cricket ground, were constructed there.
6 It was a pro-cathedral because Malta was part of the diocese of Gibraltar.

7 John M. MacKenzie, 'Presbyterianism and Scottish Identity in Global Context', *Britain and the World*, 10, 1 (March 2017), pp. 88–112, particularly pp. 94–96, based on work by Dr Joseph Sramek.
8 This controversy is discussed in Borg, *British Colonial Architecture*, pp. 83–84. The governor informed the archbishop that the Maltese people did not share his intolerant opinions. The relevant letters can be found in the Maltese National Archives.
9 It also houses the Methodists now, their church having been demolished.
10 There was an Orientalist, Ottoman-style mosque in the Muslim cemetery.
11 Rachel Gordon died in Malta in 1889 on her way home from Ceylon, where her husband Sir Arthur Hamilton-Gordon was governor from 1883 to 1890 after a long career of colonial governorships.
12 Borg, *British Colonial Architecture*, p. 69.
13 The colonial names will be used in this discussion.
14 Michael W. Charney, *A History of Modern Burma* (Cambridge, 2009), p. 18.
15 There is more detail in this section because so little has been written about the Burma/Myanmar example.
16 For example, G.A. Bremner's edited *Architecture and Urbanism in the British Empire* (Oxford, OUP, 2016) contains no reference to Yangon at all, and this is true of most other works on imperial and colonial architecture. Colin Amery, in Robert Fermor-Hesketh, *Architecture of the British Empire* (London, 1986), dismisses its public buildings (p. 133) in four totally inaccurate lines.
17 This may have been partly true, although it has been suggested that there were other reasons, including a more central location, better protected away from the coast, and more capable of dominating some of the non-Burmese ethnicities of the country. Yangon may have been too strong a reminder of the colonial past.
18 See the Yangon Heritage Trust website www.yangonheritagetrust.org/home. I was fortunate enough to interview the manager of the Trust, Thurein Aung, and saw the exhibitions in their offices in Pansodan Street in January 2016. Unfortunately, I had neither the time nor the permission to work in the National Archives.
19 There were of course other towns, some of them with classic colonial architecture. The two hill stations of Maymyo and Kalaw have been considered in Chapter 4.
20 George Orwell's mother was born in Moulmein, and this was the town in which he served as a police officer in the inter-war years.
21 This emphasises the importance of taking a 'four nations' approach to the history of the British Empire. See John M. MacKenzie and T.M. Devine (eds), *Scotland and the British Empire* (Oxford, 2011).
22 Dorothy Laird, *Paddy Henderson: The Story of P. Henderson and Company1834–1961* (Glasgow, 1961), particularly chapter VII. In the early twentieth century, according to an advert in the *Rangoon Times*, Christmas number, 1913, there was a fortnightly service by Henderson from Rangoon to Britain, taking 32 days for the voyage. Other services were supplied by the Bibby Line, the British India Steam Navigation Company, and the Seang Line which served Penang, Singapore, Hong Kong, Swatow and Amoy.

Colonial cities: Valletta, Rangoon and new capitals

23 George Blake, *BI Centenary, 1856–1956* (London, 1956); J. Forbes Munro, *Maritime Enterprise and Empire: Sir William Mackinnon and his Business Network, 1823–1893* (Woodbridge, 2003).
24 Alister McCrae and Alan Prentice, *Irrawaddy Flotilla* (Paisley, 1978); H.J. Chubb and C.L.D. Duckworth, *Irrawaddy Flotilla Company Limited 1865–1950* (London, 1973).
25 Bulloch Brothers were also the agents for the British India Steam Navigation Company, as an advertisement in the *Rangoon Times*, Christmas number, 1912 makes clear. The versatility of this company also ran to launch building, iron and brass founding, iron and steel work, constructional engineering and various classes of insurance.
26 Montgomerie had arrived in Singapore as the medical officer to the colony in 1819, was appointed magistrate, and also became the superintendent of the Experimental Botanic Gardens of the colony. He therefore had extensive experience in the East before he accompanied the troops to Burma.
27 Any examination of collections of postcards and photography of Rangoon will indicate the prominence of the Shwedagon pagoda among the popular images of the city.
28 This map is displayed at the offices of the Yangon Heritage Trust and was on sale in the Strand Hotel. It can be found online.
29 Sarah Rooney and the Association of Myanmar Architects, *30 Heritage Buildings of Yangon: Inside the City that Captured Time* (Chicago, MI and Yangon, 2012).
30 Typically, the identities of its architect and contractor are unknown. It may well have been an 'informal build', but a highly effective one.
31 Rooney and the Association of Myanmar Architects, *30 Heritage Buildings of Yangon*, p. 99.
32 Images of Rangoon in this earlier period are difficult to come by, though there are a few early postcards.
33 See Chapter 1.
34 Giordano Nanni, *The Colonisation of Time: Ritual, Routine and Resistance in the British Empire* (Manchester, 2012).
35 The original General Post Office was badly damaged in the earthquake of 1930.
36 Clark and Greig arrived in Rangoon in 1910 and built the Central Telegraph Office, the Port Authority, the Custom House, Prome Court (residential flats close to the Pegu Club), the State Arts School and the Town Hall. The company pioneered the use of armoured tubular flooring in their buildings.
37 Robinson and Mundy was a firm of engineers, architects and contractors established in Rangoon in 1870 and were responsible for a number of buildings, including the offices of J & F Graham, Finlay, Fleming & Co., the Burmah Oil Co. and the Rowe and Co. department store.
38 Arthur Flavell's company was responsible for, among others, the Irrawaddy Flotilla Company headquarters and the Chartered Bank.
39 The architect of this Roman Catholic School, open to all comers, was Thomas Swales. St Mary's RC Cathedral was originally located on its campus.
40 Andreas Augustin, *The Strand, Yangon* (London, Singapore and Vienna, 2013), pp. 21–29.

41 Ilsa Sharp, *The Eastern and Oriental Hotel: Pearl of Penang* (Penang, E&O, 2008). The Sarkies also owned the Crag Hotel on Penang Hill.

42 Andreas Augustin, *Raffles* (London, Singapore and Vienna, 1986); also chapter 9 of Ashley Jackson, *Buildings of Empire* (Oxford, 2013), pp. 173–193.

43 See Augustin, *The Strand* for the full history, illustrations and literary associations with Rudyard Kipling, Somerset Maugham and others.

44 Charney, *History of Modern Burma*, p. 18.

45 Indian migrants were to be found elsewhere in Burma. For a fictional picture of an Indian family in Burma, see Amitav Ghosh, *The Glass Palace* (London, 2000).

46 The school was nationalised in 1965 and was renamed Basic Education High School No. 6.

47 For elaboration of these arguments see John M. MacKenzie, 'The First World War and the Cultural, Political and Environmental Transformation of the British Empire' in Michael J.K. Walsh and Andrekos Varnava (eds), *The Great War and the British Empire* (London, 2017), pp. 23–38; also John M. MacKenzie, 'European Imperialism: A Zone of Co-operation Rather than Competition' in Volker Barth and Roland Cvetkowski (eds), *Imperial Co-operation and Transfer, 1870–1930* (London, 2015), pp. 35–53.

48 Nicholas Brown, *A History of Canberra* (Cambridge, 2014). For a brief history of the Australian Capital Territory, see the article by Max Neutze in the Australian Encyclopaedia, now Britannica: www.britannica.com/place/Australian-Capital-Territory (accessed 6 July 2018) and for Canberra, www.britannica.com/place/Canberra (accessed 6 July 2018). See also David Gordon (ed.), *Planning Twentieth-Century Capital Cities* (London, 2009).

49 For the history of St John's, see www.stjohnscanberra.org/history (accessed 6 July 2018), an article on the history of the church by Malcolm Allbrook. It was built partly as the result of the philanthropy of a wealthy – and long-lived – Scottish immigrant Robert Campbell. Interestingly, Campbell had been a Presbyterian, but became one of the strongest supporters of the Anglican Church in New South Wales.

50 Charles Turley, *With the Prince Round the Empire* (London, 1926), pp. 46–47.

51 Peter Harrison, 'Griffin, Walter Burley (1876–1937)', Australian Dictionary of Biography, National Centre of Biography, Australian National University, 1983 http://adb.anu.edu.au/biography/griffin-walter-burley-443 (accessed 6 July 2018). This article details the Byzantine and always acerbic relations between Griffin and succeeding Australian administrations and their officials (some of whom would have preferred to keep the planning of the capital in their own hands). Griffin later worked in Melbourne, Sydney and India, where he died.

52 I am grateful to Stephen Foster for a tour of the National Museum in October 2007. For the history of the National Portrait Gallery, see www.portrait.gov.au/content/gallery-history/ (accessed 6 July 2018).

53 Brown, *History of Canberra*, pp. 5–6.

54 David A Johnson, *New Delhi: The Last Imperial City* (Basingstoke, 2015), p. 4.

55 Many Indian politicians, such as Shashi Tharoor, a major critic of the British, see Delhi as a valuable capital (private conversation). See his *Inglorious Empire: What the British Did to India* (London, 2016).
56 Attending this ceremony in 1982, I joined some Indian spectators standing on the low parapet of a fountain. They and I were knocked off by a policeman's *lathi*, or long baton. It was a condign reminder that this treatment was formerly meted out by the British to supposedly errant Indians.
57 Maseeh Rahman, 'Lutyens' Delhi under threat from developers', *Guardian*, 7 October 2003, p. 19. Also available at www.theguardian.com/environment/2003/oct/07/india.conservationandendangeredspecies (accessed 7 July 2008).
58 Quoted in the same *Guardian* article.
59 The major works are Robert Grant Irving, *Indian Summer: Lutyens, Baker and Imperial Delhi* (New Haven, CT, 1981), Thomas R. Metcalf, *Imperial Vision: Indian Architecture and Britain's Raj* (London, 1989) and Johnson's more recent New Delhi. Philip Davies, *Splendours of the Raj: British Architecture in India, 1660–1947* (London, 1985) has indicated (p. 16) some of the diversity of views on the architecture of New Delhi.
60 There is an online article about the differences between Lutyens and Baker: Shashank Shekhar Sinha, 'A Friendship that Faltered on Raisina Hill', https://thewire.in/history/friendship-faltered-raisina-hill (accessed 7 July 2018).
61 According to the club's website, the indoor swimming pool was donated by the vicereine, Lady Willingdon, anxious for somewhere to swim since the viceroy's palace lacked such a facility. She donated 21,000 rupees for the purpose. https://delhigymkhana.org.in/history.aspx (accessed 22 August 2018). It is still known as the Lady Willingdon Swimming Bath and there are also the Willingdon Squash Courts. The club was moved to the site in 1913 and the present building constructed in the early 1930s.
62 Jan Morris, *Stones of Empire: The Buildings of the Raj* (Oxford, 1983), p. 220.
63 Liora Bigon and Yossi Katz (eds), *Garden Cities and Colonial Planning: Transnationality and Urban Ideas in Africa and Palestine* (Manchester, 2014), p. 17.
64 Both the earlier capital of Kalomo and the first site of Livingstone had failed because of high European death rates from blackwater fever. The now overgrown cemetery of the latter, on the banks of the Zambezi, provides testimony of this.
65 Garth Andrew Myers, *Verandahs of Power* (Syracuse, NY, 2003), chapter four, 'Colonial Lusaka'. Dutton had been private secretary to East African governors before taking up his post in Northern Rhodesia. He subsequently worked in Bermuda and Zanzibar, where he was also involved in town planning. See Garth Andrew Myers, 'Intellectual of Empire: Eric Dutton and Hegemony in British Africa', *Annals of the Association of American Geographers*, 58, 1 (1998), pp. 1–27.
66 Kenneth Bradley, *Once a District Officer* (London, 1966), p. 88.
67 Kenneth Bradley, *Lusaka: The New Capital of Northern Rhodesia, Opened Jubilee Week 1935* (London, 1935). Inevitably, this had become a rare item (though it had been in my collection for many years) and it was republished by Routledge in 2013 with an

68 Bradley, *Once a District Officer*, p. 107.
69 Adshead wrote that Africans were 'lazy and stupid' and should be 'treated as slaves'. Above all, 'it would be a mistake to treat them as if they were Europeans', whose expected 'bodily comforts' they had never known. L.H. Gann, *A History of Northern Rhodesia: Early Days to 1953* (London, 1964), p. 259.
70 Bradley, *Lusaka*, p. 28.
71 An appendix to Bradley's book, pp. 65–66, lists 11 indigenous flowering trees, 11 exotic flowering trees, 8 indigenous shade trees, 21 exotic shade trees, 32 flowering and ornamental shrubs, 20 hedges and 9 climbing plants. Apart from the immense passion of Dutton himself, 'a ruthless enthusiast and a demon of energy' (Bradley, *Once a District Officer*, pp. 88–89), two gardeners are mentioned, one British, the other African, George Walton (Bradley, *Lusaka*, p. 59) and Chillika (Myers, *Verandahs*, p. 61). The latter was dignified by only one name, as so common in imperial identification of Africans. For the position of Lusaka within the wider colonial garden city movement, see R.K. Home, 'Town Planning and Garden Cities in the British Colonial Empire, 1910–1940', *Planning Perspectives*, 5, 1 (2007), pp. 223–237.
72 Bradley, *Lusaka*, pp. 45–46. This was not so much gendered as family separation, a reality of labour migration in the colonial era.
73 Metcalf, *Imperial Vision*, pp. 247–248.
74 Bradley, *Lusaka*, p. 44.
75 Queen Mary's Avenue and Prince George's Road added to the royal connection. The prince's visit took place on 3 April 1934, when there was little to see. He laid the foundation stone of the Secretariat building and saw the site of Government House. A.A. Frew, *Prince George's African Tour* (London, 1934), p. 189.
76 Bradley, *Once a District Officer*, p. 107.
77 Andrew Roberts, *A History of Zambia* (London, 1976), p. 203.

CONCLUSION

It is not surprising that in recent years the growing complexities of the study and writing of imperial history have ensured thematic and geographical specialisation. Area studies concentrating on specific geographical regions and continents have rendered it difficult for scholars to break out of their own particular periods and locations. South and South-East Asia, the Far East, the Indian Ocean, Australasia, British North America and the Caribbean have all enjoyed specialist scholarship, developing considerable literatures and complex theoretical positions. Hence, synoptic works on the entire British Empire have become increasingly difficult to write. Studies of material culture have invariably also developed along geographically focused lines. India has always understandably been a special case and this has also been true of the various imperial regions already mentioned. The other approach has been to take one specialist type, such as Gothic religious architecture, and examine it across a broader span. However, a route out of this specialisation into the wider frame adopted by this book is offered by concepts in James Belich's *Replenishing the Earth*.[1] He wrote of consecutive periods as representing 'incremental colonization', 'explosive colonization' and 'recolonization'. These notions were applied to migration and economic boom and bust, as well as to the highly significant growth of cities. But they can be applied differently. It is now possible to see that the globalisation of building types and architectural styles across the world initially constituted incremental colonisation and in the nineteenth century built up into an explosive cultural colonisation. In the twentieth century, we can see aspects of recolonisation occurring in developments in the built environment, not least in the age of 'experts'. Thus, such a conceptual periodisation is helpful in a consideration of the visual and cultural aspects of empire as well for its demographic and economic growth. Indeed, those two categories are of course closely linked.

The British Empire through buildings

Taking a synoptic approach to the built environment of the entire empire, as this book has set out to do, illustrates these processes while also helping to illuminate more conventional political, economic and administrative studies. The reintegration of the 'British World' in terms of material culture is helpful in demonstrating that various key building types reappear across the British Empire, whether in India or the territories of white settlement or the colonies of the so-called 'dependent' empire. Such a focus reveals significant parallels across the empire, parallels which offer insights into the material relationships of imperialism, global cultural change and social formations. It also demonstrates the manner in which the imperial built environment also reflects the dynamics of social change and cultural interactions with indigenous people. When material culture is categorised in terms of chronological phases and functional needs, it becomes apparent that, for example, the militarisation of the landscape usually took place everywhere. This is additionally true of the key buildings that symbolise the exercise of administrative and legal authority, those that marked the increasing power and self-regard of economic enterprises, as well as the churches and other structures that represented the globalisation of religion and ritual, many of them forming the backdrops to the performance of obsessive imperial ceremonial. Moreover, many relatively new building types manifested themselves in worldwide locations in the nineteenth century. These supremely reflected the bourgeois conquest of the globe through imperialism. The middle classes everywhere sought to re-create the institutions which were spreading across Britain (and elsewhere in Europe) in the same period, institutions that represented to contemporary minds 'progress', 'civilisation', 'refinement' and the further dissemination of the intellectual and artistic achievements of the past, a dispersal incorporating a wider class audience, with other races supposedly to follow later. Such institutions included museums, art galleries, libraries, cultural associations of various sorts, print cultures, educational establishments at all levels, gardens, clubs, sporting establishments, public halls and theatres. Originally these buildings were seen as racially exclusive places, providing security from other classes and peoples while also offering zones of observation and surveillance. But they would soon be invaded by a wider constituency in terms of class and race, the institutions progressively and most importantly being adopted and adapted by the colonial 'others'. One of the most significant developments of the later nineteenth and twentieth centuries was that the spread of the bourgeoisie began to incorporate indigenous peoples breaking free from the controls of traditional and then imperial authority, seldom

Conclusion

abandoning their own cultural norms, but creating hybrid forms with Western institutions.

Another category of building spread across the globe at roughly the same time. This was associated with the new technologies of the era. As railway lines penetrated almost everywhere, railway stations became one of the classic building types of the age. The other great global connector was the postal system and the telegraph. By the middle of the century, the buildings representing these developments, posts and telegraph offices (sometimes in separate premises, sometimes together), also spread everywhere, as did the increasingly imposing public expressions of the worldwide banking system. Whereas many of the buildings of the bourgeois public sphere started off by being more or less racially or class specific, the buildings of the new technologies were generally inclusive, since the economic well-being of the systems and companies they represented was entirely dependent on the widest possible customer base. That is not to say that providers and controllers of such buildings were indiscriminate in creating opportunities for access. Very often segregated zones were incorporated into spatial arrangements. This was initially even true of commercial institutions such as markets. There was, however, a sliding scale in such segregation: most pronounced in Africa, less so in India, and barely apparent in the territories of white settlement, if only because First Nations in Canada and Aboriginal people in Australia were generally banished to distant reserves. Nonetheless, these parallels in the development of material cultures across empires were very real and the areas of separation ultimately became class- rather than race-based almost everywhere by the end of the twentieth century.

As these new building types established their near-universal presence, significant developments were also taking place in the architecture of domestic structures, with a mixture of aspects of globalisation (for example in the westernised version of the bungalow) and of distinctive regional adaptations and variants. These affected not only town planning and the growth of suburbs, but additionally the appearance of new settlements often associated with leisure, health, rest and recreation, such as hill stations, resorts, sanatoria and spas. These were also widespread phenomena. Yet again, they often started out as exclusive areas for those who could afford them, unless they were the more broadly based military sanatoria designed to recover the health of troops vital to the security of imperial power and white settler rule. But once again, almost all these locations were invaded by indigenous people, initially as workers and servants and later as consumers.

It has become an obvious truism that the old construction of the imperial/colonial condition as a set of binaries is no longer acceptable. Such binaries were constituted of the modernist and the traditional, the scientific rationality of progress and the precolonial condition of alleged stasis, of liberal sensibilities and the benighted and capricious autocracy of non-parliamentary rulership, of concepts of space and time and their absence, of congested chaotic and insanitary living space and its allegedly organised European equivalent. The built environment of empire seemed in the past to conform to such simplistic oppositional paradigms, so much part of the propaganda of imperial rulers, and it was in these contexts that the binary fallacies seemed to have the longest shelf life. The powerful material presence of colonial Western-style cities and towns, with their characteristic layout and self-consciously impressive public buildings, seemed to represent exactly the supposed modernist ideal when contrasted with traditional communities. In the imperial imagination, such urban spaces, particularly in Asia and Africa, contrasted dramatically with the 'black towns' that seemed to be their antithesis. There was even an attempt to place some aspects of the great traditional cities of previous Asian empires into such a system. European colonialists might penetrate the black towns for drugs, sex, or bazaar purchases, often part of the search for the liberating effects of the bizarre, but they were always excursions into the realm of the 'other', sometimes alluring, but alien and often frightening and dangerous.[2] It might seem that in these respects the settler territories of Canada, Australia and New Zealand were different, but their black-town equivalents, the settlements and reserves of First Nations, Aboriginal and Maori people, were simply located somewhat further away.

The reality is of course that white and black towns (like settler communities and indigenous 'reserves') were wholly interdependent, inseparably linked through processes of development and underdevelopment, through the migration which the white towns called into being, and through the maintenance of systems of cheap and pliable labour. Such linkages may have been less apparent in the territories of settlement, but still the frustration of traditional social and economic patterns in the creation and maintenance of 'reserves' had the same effects. Reserves were also the other side of the coin of land appropriation, white farming and the creation of country towns, as in southern Africa. As colonial cities grew exponentially in the second half of the nineteenth and early twentieth centuries, these effects became increasingly apparent. There has always been the tendency for imperial living space to be divided into racial enclaves,

Conclusion

but such enclavism was further complicated by the separation of social classes among whites as among the indigenous. It is true that enclaves were disrupted by the European need for servants and for workers who were located reasonably close to their employment (as in mines, jute mills, railway works, and so on), but still social demands and what have been called ethno-medical theories ensured that whites attempted to live their lives with a degree of aloofness in separate suburbs, civil lines, cantonments and city zones. Sometimes, whole settlements maintained these patterns, whether in military and civil stations or in the hill communities specifically designed for rest and recreation supposedly separated from the denser populations of indigenous people. However, these hill stations perfectly represented the dilemmas of separation and the impossibility of its achievement. Settlements started from scratch for European use soon filled up with the workers required to offer services and the maintenance of convenient comforts for the white inhabitants. In the territories of settlement such arrangements may have taken mainly class rather than racial forms, but still the ethnic presence of the 'other', however demographically damaged by disease and warfare, could never be wholly eliminated.

When it comes to the architecture of imperial and colonial cities and towns, Mark Crinson has suggested that such buildings produce stock and often extreme reactions. They 'either stand for the rapacity and racial self-delusion of empire or for a world of lost glory and forgotten convictions'.[3] He goes on to mention the presumed absurdity of an English church deposited in very different geographical and climatic circumstances. His objective is to 'demythologise' such architecture in relation to the Middle East and its predominantly Islamic context. The reality, however, is that the colonial built environment can be subjected to even more complex reactions. First, imperial buildings can be found, as this book has argued, in many global settings and different sorts of colonial circumstances. We have to understand the significance of forms that turned up in territories of white settlement, in India, in 'dependent' colonies, in island spaces and also in informal empire. We also need to recognise that the postcolonial reactions to such buildings have been much more diverse than simply rejection. Such buildings have survived and have sometimes been reinterpreted, reused, converted, culturally revalidated and even valued by postcolonial regimes, both in white-ruled territories and in former colonies in the Caribbean, Africa, India and elsewhere. Moreover, in residential housing, as we have seen in earlier chapters, there was clearly a mix of reasons for the adaptation of western styles by indigenous people, if mainly an elite. In West Africa, the Caribbean and Ceylon, imperial styles were adopted for a variety of reasons. They were a badge of the new bourgeoisie, a mark of status; they represented modernism; but they also indicated a degree of mimicry which could sometimes have a satirical edge. Moreover, as empire declined and overlapped with the postcolonial period, indigenous elements became more apparent. To understand these processes fully, we have to identify the significance of reactions to the built environment in specific geographical locations with adaptations to match particular traditional circumstances.

While it is true that European empires liked to create new capitals as material emblems of the modern, some postcolonial states have also set about building new capitals. This impulse has a variety of motivations, including distancing from the former imperial presence, sometimes (at least the propaganda goes) in pursuit of ethnic unity, in a desire to be closer to the geographical middle of territories to enhance contacts with the periphery, in an effort to escape the congestion of the old capital, and to create new institutions. In Africa, Abuja has become the new capital of Nigeria, Dodoma of Tanzania, Lilongwe of Malawi; in Asia Naypitaw for Burma, Sri Jayawardenepura Kotte for Sri Lanka. It has, however, often taken some time for such new capitals to be fully functional or entirely accepted. But even in the pursuit of new capitals, the material culture and buildings of the former colonies have continued to be a very significant presence, with many structures coming to be reinterpreted and reused in new, sometimes unrelated, ways. Many government houses (though not all) have become presidential residences and many of the bourgeois institutions have continued in their old functions, sometimes symbolising indigenous ambitions for middle-class status.

We additionally need to take account of the extraordinary growth in the scale of tourism consonant with social change from the late twentieth century. Tourism has unquestionably promoted the developing notion of 'heritage', as any travel brochure or any observation of the interests and photographic practices of tourists will confirm. That has also fed into the complex of reactions to imperial buildings. The marketing of near-ubiquitous tourist experiences has transformed the privileges of colonialists into those of tourists for the better-off participants from First World countries (including the former Dominions of the British Empire, as well as Japan), and for the rapidly growing tourist constituencies of the newly opulent bourgeois social groups of China, India and elsewhere. There is a sense in which 'heritage' represents a fresh global economic and cultural phenomenon which has incalculable effects upon the consumption of the material remains of past empires, from all periods and on all continents, including those of recent European conquest.

'Heritage' is a form of public history and public history has become a source of fascination for tourists. Many buildings, of course, retain their original purpose and significance, albeit sometimes upgraded for modern usage. But many others have undergone dramatic conversions, not necessarily in structure or design, but in both practical use and purport, signifying wholly different sets of values from those originally intended. This constitutes a novel sort of 'recolonisation', the conversion of what some might consider to be 'dissonant heritage' because representative of a hegemonic ideology of the past. Heritage buildings have acquired a new virtual reality on the World Wide Web, while many have been recolonised by a combination of an indigenous bourgeoisie and the international tourist elite. Some buildings have become heritage because of their perceived aesthetic attributes within a cityscape, thus enhancing their marketing value. Such a collection of buildings would include those in New Delhi and in Yangon. In Chapter 7 we saw the manner in which planned developments in the Lodi estate (known as the Lutyens bungalow zone) in New Delhi could arouse controversy among preservationists. While this may reflect the reaction of residents, a similar tourist imperative has been vital in the preservation and renovation of imperial hotels, which are particularly assiduous in the use of marketing words like 'heritage' and 'colonial', the latter curiously signifying an alleged elegance and leisured lifestyle of the past.[4] This has also been the case in the preservation of aspects of hill stations and resorts in India, Malaysia and elsewhere. A good example of this phenomenon can be found in one of the former treaty ports of the Far East. In Nagasaki in southern Japan, it so happens that the American atomic bomb in 1945 missed the buildings of the international settlement. These are now carefully preserved, not least the home of Robert Blake Glover, the so-called 'Scottish samurai' who was closely involved in the development of Meiji Japan in the late nineteenth century. Other homes and buildings have been moved into what is now known as the 'Glover Gardens'. The number of Japanese visitors to this attraction is considerable, and Japanese people seem to see the complex as emblematic of the modernisation of Japan and therefore, in a sense, of the country's avoidance of direct imperial rule. The old British consulate and the local headquarters of the Hong Kong and Shanghai bank also survive as museum pieces. It has been noticed that in Egypt, there is a desire to preserve the Belle Époque architecture of the 1850s to 1950s period, although it may be that the style is regarded as only incidentally related to imperial rule.[5]

The suggestion that such heritage-making can be related to various linguistic turns, branding, and forms of social legitimisation can well be true of many other such reconstructions as colonial heritage.

There are other intriguing examples where imperial rule was very much a reality. Forts (even ruined ones) throughout the former empire (except those still in use as barracks) have become more significant as heritage hot spots than they were as military redoubts. Heritage can indeed embrace an astonishing range of architectural subjects, from the chattel houses of Barbados to the eighteenth-century naval base at English Harbour, Antigua, from the convict barracks (and many other buildings) of Port Arthur on Tasmania to the still thriving Victorian market buildings of India and the former Dominions. An individual building like Hibbert House in Kingston, Jamaica, intimately connected with the slave trade, has become the headquarters of the National Trust of Jamaica and is extolled for its architectural heritage. Another example can be found in the Burmese hill station of Pyin Oo Lwin (Maymyo), where the governor's former summer retreat has been restored, complete with prints and portraits from the British period and, as the ultimate in imperial chic (or perhaps colonial satire?), visitors are welcomed by mannequins in gubernatorial uniforms in the hallway. It is now a hotel, known as 'Governor's House', also hired out for wedding receptions and other events. The Imperial Hotel in New Delhi has been entirely themed according to the 1911 Delhi Durbar, with prints, portraits and artefacts dating from that period. Surely, many Indian politicians and scholars would not approve of such imperial nostalgia. In Zimbabwe, a country which under Mugabe seemed to have comprehensively thrown off the shackles of white colonial rule, the Victoria Falls Hotel retains the atmosphere, decoration and exhibits that would be recognised by visitors to the Falls many decades ago. Full-size copies of portraits of George V and Queen Mary (among many others from the colonial period) still adorn the walls, and the only concession to nationalism is a Lobengula room with a portrait of the nineteenth-century Ndebele king on the wall, not perhaps particularly appealing to Shona guests. Lobengula regarded many of the Shona chieftaincies as his vassals (and would have seen that part of the Zambezi and the Falls as lying within his kingdom), but in the postcolonial period Robert Mugabe wrought a terrifying revenge against the Ndebele people with his Fifth Brigade. But 'heritage' seems to overwhelm much painful history.

Elsewhere, civic societies and other pressure groups have demanded that buildings from the imperial period, including highly practical ones like railway stations

Conclusion

58 Government House, Maymyo, Burma

59 Victoria Falls Hotel, Southern Rhodesia

The British Empire through buildings

60 Bonsecours Market, Montreal

and banks, should be preserved and maintained. In Montreal, the magnificent Bank of Montreal headquarters in the centre of the city at the Place d'Armes, with its classical portico and dome, has been provided with a museum and has become a central piece of heritage in the city. Older buildings are often given a new lease of life as craft centres or markets. On a small scale, this has saved some of the original rondavels (round thatched huts) in Lusaka, and on a larger one, it has given a new lease of life to the grand Bonsecours in Montreal. The latter, built in 1847 as a market hall, later used as a city hall, an exhibition venue, even temporarily as the parliament in 1849, is now very much a tourist haunt with stalls and boutiques. These examples, illustrating the renegotiation of the resonances of buildings through heritage, can be multiplied across the world.

The functionaries and bourgeoisie of the British Empire were always fascinated by memorialisation. It was thought that the creation of statues and memorials, particularly those to the wars of the twentieth century starting with the Anglo-Boer War, would help to bind the empire together.[6] Here, the reactions of the territories of white settlement that became the Dominions and the colonies in

Asia, Africa and the Caribbean diverged. Among the former, such memorialisation became important contributors to their sense of national identity, to their pride in the emergence of political, constitutional and legal independence. Many of the latter states, after decolonisation, kept some of the memorials that suited them, but destroyed, mutilated or gave away many of the others. In all cases, new statues and memorials reflected the emergent status of independent countries. Naturally, modern countries that have escaped from the trammels of empire emphasise the progression and success of nationalist movements in museums, art galleries and other institutions. Yet often they set this history in the context of the highly visible remains of the empire which was overwhelmed by what they would naturally see as the unstoppable force of their search for freedom. This is partly about historical context, partly about the inevitable nationalist construction of the imperial enemy, but it is also partly about aesthetics and about the recognition of the force and selling power of heritage in a contemporary tourist world. In many places, for example in Yangon, it is because modern architects value the work of their predecessors that buildings which miraculously survived the damage and destruction of warfare are seen as lending a particular tone and character to their city. The book celebrating heritage buildings in Yangon, prepared by the Association of Myanmar Architects, has the subtitle 'Inside the City that Captured Time'. To a certain extent this embracing of heritage (and the attempt to capture aspects of time) is also emblematic of the overturning of racial and imperial exclusivity, transformed into opportunities for everyone (at least everyone who can afford it) to enjoy the originally privileged spaces of empire. It all illustrates the extraordinary capacity of buildings to change their meanings in different eras and generations.

The reconfiguring of buildings was a key aspect of imperialism. In the British imperial period in India, Mughal buildings were adapted as residences for the British (as in the case of the tomb at Lahore). Indigenous forts were taken over as redoubts and barracks for the British military. It is not surprising then that postcolonial nationalists have similarly taken over buildings and developed them. Some buildings have been demolished, certainly, and many statues have been destroyed or removed, but much else has been retained and provided with new meanings. In Asia and Africa there has been a racial shift in this adaptation, while in the colonies of settlement the shift has been in loyalties. Both are united in the manner in which buildings once redolent of a global British imperial presence and ideology have become symbolic of the specific national identity of the modern state. In many places buildings have been adapted to new uses.

The church in Fort William, Calcutta is now a library. Decline of Christian observance has led to the reuse of churches elsewhere too. In Quebec City, the former Anglican St Matthew's Church is also now a library. Elsewhere, churches have been taken over by indigenous worshippers and often converted to new forms of communal and demonstrative worship. In Nicosia, Cyprus, the former lodge of the colonial secretary is now the Cyprus Cultural Foundation. In Quebec City, a former eighteenth-century prison has become the Anglophone Morrin Centre and Library. Town halls, formerly an arena for rival meetings and discourses of different elements in colonial societies (both class- and race-based), have often become emblematic of new nationalist dispensations (albeit contested in different ways). In the former Dominions, town halls have become sites for ceremonial and visible reconciliation between the descendants of white settlers and indigenous. In 2018, Toronto Town Hall became a location for various modes of expression for First Nations people. When it comes to official visits and academic conferences, there is invariably a welcome by indigenous representatives and a symbolic acceptance of alien presence upon their lands, even if this in no way subverts modern power relations.

Aside from tourism, there has often been a more demotic invasion of former imperial buildings. Museums neatly represent this shift. Imperial museums originally stressed the place of the British within the progression of historic cultures (usually depicted as Mediterranean and Middle Eastern), thus celebrating a global British presence. Throughout the empire, native culture was generally displayed through the (for whites) engagingly 'primitive' ethnography of both local and parallel indigenous peoples. But in many former colonial museums, this has been overlaid by the construction of the nationalist period as the latest triumphant and transforming phase of a political continuum. The Victoria Memorial in Kolkata perfectly represents this. Conceived by the Viceroy Curzon as a monument to the reign and person of Queen Victoria and therefore a paean of praise to British rule, it is now a museum of nationalist reaction, an immensely popular attraction for the families of the city. Thus a quintessential imperial building has absorbed nationalism into its fabric. Some of the imperial statuary survives, much supplemented by the statuary of Bengali and Indian heroes, illustrating challenge and reaction to the previous hegemonic dispensation. In New Zealand, Maori meeting halls became an element of display at an early period, together with examples of the glories of Maori carving. In museums such as those in Auckland and Wellington, such Maori material has now come centre stage, not only in reflecting the importance of the original occupants of the land, but also as contributing the vitally distinctive element in the cultural identity of the modern state. This has become equally true of First Nation meeting halls, totems and great sculptural traditions. The Canadian National Museum in Ottawa now gives due prominence to the First Nations while also displaying the cultures of the successive waves of immigrants. Some may see this as a means of justifying settler immigration as but one phase in a long sequence of human movement, but still it acknowledges that the British element was a single constituent and not necessarily even the primary one. In territories of white settlement, indigenous peoples formerly banished out of sight or viewed as strange and primitive cultures contrasting with immigrant modernism have become central to the identity of the modern state, distancing the dominant culture from its European origins by adopting native cultural inputs, in artistic, design, dance, textile and musical forms. Thus within the materiality of the urban setting, indigenous people have become prominently visible, though once again not subverting the realities of power. In Canada, this process has also been important in the reconfiguring and fresh cultural assertion of the métis, mixed-race people. All this constitutes a new form of at least cultural interdependence. Some indigenous may have found this liberating, a source of a new ethnic self-confidence; others may find it just another means for the maintenance of white dominance.

However, in varied ways the built environment of the former territories of empire has been transformed, even if those transformations have sometimes only been superficial. Buildings, far from being mute, are thus capable of communicating in different accents, languages and meanings. James Stuart Duncan, writing of the Kandyan kingdom's capital in central Ceylon, argued that 'the landscape of the city was a political tract written in space and carved in stone. The landscape was part of the practice of power.'[7] This was true of the modern empires, but the fact is that buildings also reflected the extraordinary dynamic of change in use, audience and meaning in the postcolonial world. This can be a passport to their survival but it also unveils significant opportunities for historical analysis. That has been the purpose of this book.

NOTES

1 James Belich, *Replenishing the Earth: The Settler Revolution and the Rise of the Anglo-World, 1783–1939* (Oxford, 2009).
2 Abir Mukherjee's novel *A Rising Man* (London, 2016) sets up precisely this dichotomy between white and black towns in Calcutta. Swati Chattopadhyay, *Representing Calcutta*

(London, 2006) reveals the complexities of representations of the city and the mismatch between British and Bengali projections.
3 Mark Crinson, *Empire Building: Orientalism and Victorian Architecture* (London,1996), p. 1.
4 Even in a less popular tourist destination like Pakistan, Faletti's Hotel, Lahore markets itself on its colonial past (opened 1880), although substantially rebuilt. http://falettishotel.com/ (accessed 19 February 2019).
5 Mercedes Volait, 'The reclaiming of "Belle Époque" Architecture in Egypt (1989–2010): On the Power of Rhetorics in Heritage Making', *Architecture Beyond Europe*, 3 (2013).
6 The fascination with statuary and memorialisation in the British Empire will be examined in another book.
7 James Stuart Duncan, *The City as Text: The Politics of Landscape Interpretation and the Kandyan Kingdom* (Cambridge, 1990), p. 86.

SELECT BIBLIOGRAPHY

ABBREVIATIONS

ABE Architecture Beyond Europe
CUP Cambridge University Press
MUP Manchester University Press
OUP Oxford University Press
PUP Princeton University Press
YUP Yale University Press

PRINTED PRIMARY SOURCES

Baird, J.G.A. (ed.), *Private Letters of the Marquess of Dalhousie* (Edinburgh, Blackwood, 1910)

The Bengal calendar for the year 1789: including a list of the Hon. and United East-India Company's civil and military servants on the Bengal establishment, &c. including also those at Madras, Bombay, Fort Marlborough, China, and St. Helena. [London]: Calcutta printed; London re-printed: for John Stockdale, Piccadilly. MDCCLXXXIX. Entered at Stationers-Hall, [1789]

Coronation Durbar, Delhi 1911, Official Directory (Calcutta, Government Printer, 1911)

Eden, Emily, *Up the Country: Letters Written to her Sister from the Upper Provinces of India* (London, Curzon Press, 1978)

Grant of Rothiemurchus, Elizabeth, *Memoirs of a Highland Lady*, edited with an introduction by Andrew Tod (Edinburgh, Canongate Classics, 1988)

Hervey, Captain Albert, *A Soldier of the Company: Life of an Indian Ensign 1833–43*, edited and introduced by Charles Allen (London, Michael Joseph, 1988)

Hickey, William, *Memoirs of William Hickey*, edited by Alfred Spencer, 4 vols (London, Hurst and Blackett, 1948)

Hodges, William, *Travels in India in the years 1780, 1781, 1782, 1783* (London, the author, 1793)

Select bibliography

Littlewood, Arthur (ed.), *Indian Mutiny and Beyond: The Letters of Robert Shebbeare VC* (Barnsley, Pen and Sword Military, 2007)
Mundy, General Godfrey Charles, *Journal of a Tour in India* (London, John Murray, 1858)
The Rangoon Times, Christmas Numbers, 1912, 1913, 1921, 1922, 1923, 1925
Sheppard, Samuel T., *The Byculla Club, 1833–1916: A History* (Bombay, Bennett Coleman, 1916)
Steer, Valentia, *The Delhi Durbar 1902–3: A Concise Illustrated History* (London, Marshall, 1903)
Wallace, Donald Mackenzie, *The Web of Empire* (London, Macmillan, 1902)
Yule, Henry, and Burnell, A.C., *Hobson-Jobson: The Anglo-Indian Dictionary* (Ware, Wordsworth editions, 1996, first published 1886)

SECONDARY WORKS

Adas, Michael, *Machines as the Measure of Men: Science, Technology and Ideologies of Western Dominance* (Ithaca, NY, Cornell University Press, 1989)
Ahmad, A. Ghafar, *British Colonial Architecture in Malaysia, 1800–1930* (Kuala Lumpur, Museums Association of Malaysia, 1997)
Aldrich, Robert, and McCreery, Cindy (eds), *Royals on Tour: Politics, Pageantry and Colonialism* (Manchester, MUP, 2018)
Anderson, Benedict, *Imagined Communities* (London, Verso, 1983)
Armitage, David, *The Ideological Origins of the British Empire* (Cambridge, CUP, 2000)
Aslet, Clive, *The Age of Empire: Britain's Imperial Architecture from 1880–1930* (London, Aurum Press, 2015)
Augustin, Andreas, *The Strand, Yangon* (London, Singapore and Vienna, The Most Famous Hotels in the World, 2013)
— *Raffles* (London, Singapore and Vienna, The Most Famous Hotels in the World, 1986)
Bach, Brian Paul, *Calcutta's Edifice: The Buildings of the Great City* (New Delhi, Rupa, 2006)
Baillie, Alexander Charles, *Call of Empire: From the Highlands to Hindostan* (Kingston, Ont., McGill-Queen's University Press, 2017)
Barczewski, Stephanie, *Country Houses and the British Empire, 1700–1930* (Manchester, MUP, 2014)
Barr, Pat, and Desmond, Ray, *Simla: A Hill Station in British India* (New York, Scribner, 1978)
Bayly, C.A., *Rulers, Townsmen and Bazaars: North India in the Age of British Expansion, 1770–1870* (Cambridge, CUP, 1983)
Bayly, Christopher, and Harper, Tim, *Forgotten Wars: The End of Britain's Asian Empire* (London, Allen Lane, 2007)

Select bibliography

Beinart, William, and Hughes, Lotte, *Environment and Empire* (Oxford, OUP, 2007)
Belich, James, *The New Zealand Wars and the Victorian Interpretation of Racial Conflict* (London, Penguin, 1986)
— *Replenishing the Earth: The Settler Revolution and the Rise of the Anglo-World, 1783–1939* (Oxford, OUP, 2009)
Bell, Duncan, *Reordering the World* (Princeton, NJ, PUP, 2016)
— *The Idea of Greater Britain: Empire and the Future of World Order, 1860–1900* (Princeton, NJ, PUP, 2007)
Bence-Jones, Mark, *Palaces of the Raj: Magnificence and Misery of the Lord Sahibs* (London, Allen and Unwin, 1973)
Beveridge, Lord (William), *India Called Them* (London, Allen and Unwin, 1947)
Bhageria, Purchottam, with Malhotra, Pavan, *Elite Clubs of India* (New Delhi, Bhageria Foundation, 2005)
Bhasin, Raaja, *Simla: The Summer Capital of British India* (New Delhi, Penguin Books, 1992)
Bhatt, Vikram, *Resorts of the Raj* (Ahmedabad, Mapin Publishing, 1998)
Biagi, Susan, *Louisbourg* (Halifax, Formac, 1997)
Bickford-Smith, Vivian, *The Emergence of the South African Metropolis: Cities and Identities in the Twentieth Century* (Cambridge, CUP, 2016)
Bickford-Smith, Vivian, van Heyningen, Elizabeth, and Worden, Nigel, *Cape Town in the Twentieth Century: An Illustrated Social History* (Cape Town, David Philip, 1999)
Bigon, Liora, and Katz, Yossi (eds), *Garden Cities and Colonial Planning: Transnationality and Urban Ideas in Africa and Palestine* (Manchester, MUP, 2014)
Blair, Louisa, Donovan, Patrick and Fyson, Donal, *Iron Bars and Bookshelves: A History of the Morrin Centre* (Montreal, Baraka Books, 2016)
Borg, Malcolm, *British Colonial Architecture: Malta 1800–1900* (San Ġwann, Malta, Publishers Enterprises Group, 2001)
Bosco, Andrea, *The Round Table Movement and the Fall of the 'Second' British Empire, 1909–1919* (Newcastle upon Tyne, Cambridge Scholars Publishing, 2017)
Bradford, Ernle, *The Great Siege: Malta 1565* (Ware, Wordsworth editions, 1999, first published in 1961)
Bradley, Kenneth, *Lusaka: The New Capital of Northern Rhodesia, Opened Jubilee Week 1935* (London, Jonathan Cape, 1935)
— *Once a District Officer* (London, Macmillan, 1966)
Bremner, G.A., *Imperial Gothic Religious Architecture and High Anglican Culture in the British Empire, c.1840–1870* (New Haven, CT and London, YUP, 2013)
Bremner, G.A. (ed.), *Architecture and Urbanism in the British Empire* (Oxford, OUP, 2016)
Brendon, Piers, *Thomas Cook: 150 Years of Popular Travel* (London, Secker and Warburg, 1991)

Select bibliography

Bridge, Carl, *A Trunk Full of Books: The History of the State Library of South Australia and its Forerunners* (Netley, South Australia, Wakefield Press, 1986)
Briggs, Asa, *Victorian Cities* (Harmondsworth, Penguin, 1968)
Briggs, Tom, and Crisswell, Colin, *Hong Kong: The Vanishing City*, Vol. 1 (South China Morning Post, 1977) and Vol. 2 (South China Morning Post, 1978)
Brown, Nicholas, *A History of Canberra* (Cambridge, CUP, 2014)
Brown, Rod, *Tea and Me, One for Tea: A Country Boy Becomes a Man on an Indian Tea Estate* (Cirencester, Mereo Books, 2015)
Bryant, Julius, and Weber, Susan (eds), *John Lockwood Kipling: Arts and Crafts in the Punjab and London* (New Haven, YUP, 2017)
Butler, Graeme, *The Californian Bungalow in Australia* (Port Melbourne, Lothian Press, 1992)
Cannadine, David, *Ornamentalism: How the British Saw their Empire* (London, Allen Lane, 2001)
Carter, Sarah, *Lost Harvests: Prairie Indian Reserves, Farmers and Government* (Montreal, McGill-Queen's University Press, 1990)
Chang, Jiat-Hwee, *A Genealogy of Tropical Architecture; Colonial Networks, Nature and Techno-Science* (Abingdon, Routledge, 2016)
Charney, Michael W., *A History of Modern Burma* (Cambridge, CUP, 2009)
Chattopadhyay, Swati, *Representing Calcutta: Modernity, Nationalism and the Colonial Uncanny* (London, Routledge, 2005)
Chattopadhyay, Swati, and White, Jeremy (eds), *City Halls and Civic Materialism: Towards a Global History of Urban Public Space* (London, Routledge, 2014)
Cohn, Bernard S., *Colonialism and its Forms of Knowledge: The British in India* (Princeton, NJ, PUP, 1996)
Conner, Patrick, *Oriental Architecture in the West* (London, Thames and Hudson, 1979)
Constantine, Stephen, *Community and Identity: The Making of Modern Gibraltar since 1704* (Manchester, MUP, 2009)
Cookson, John, and Dunstall, Graeme (eds), *Southern Capital, Christchurch: Towards a City Biography 1850–2000* (Christchurch, Canterbury University Press, 2000)
Coombes, Annie, *Reinventing Africa: Museums, Material Culture and Popular Imagination* (New Haven, CT, YUP, 1994)
Courcy, Anne de, *The Fishing Fleet: Husband Hunting in the Raj* (London, Weidenfeld and Nicolson, 2012)
Crawford, George W., *Remember All the Way: The History of the Chalmers-Wesley United Church, Quebec City* (Montreal, Price Patterson, 2005)
Crinson, Mark, *Empire Building: Orientalism and Victorian Architecture* (London, Routledge, 1996)
— *Modern Architecture and the End of Empire* (London, Routledge, 2003)

Select bibliography

Crosbie, Barry, and Hampton, Mark (eds), *The Cultural Construction of the British World* (Manchester, MUP, 2016)
Crowley, John E. *Imperial Landscapes: Britain's Global Visual Culture* (New Haven, CT, YUP, 2011)
Curry-Machado, Jonathan (ed.), *Global Histories, Imperial Commodities, Local Interactions* (Basingstoke, Palgrave Macmillan, 2013)
Dalrymple, William, *The Last Mughal: The Fall of a Dynasty, Delhi 1857* (London, Bloomsbury, 2006)
— *The White Mughals: Love and Betrayal in Eighteenth-Century India* (London, HarperCollins, 2002)
Danschuk, James, *Clearing the Plains: Disease, Politics of Starvation and the Loss of Aboriginal Life* (Regina, University of Regina Press, 2004)
Davidoff, Leonore, and Hall, Catherine, *Family Fortunes: Men and Women of the English Middle Class, 1780–1850* (London, Hutchinson, 1997)
Davies, Philip, *Splendours of the Raj: British Architecture and the Raj 1660–1947* (London, John Murray, 1985)
Davison, Julian, with Tettoni, Luca Invernizzi, *Black and White: The Singapore House 1898–1941* (Singapore, Talisman Publishing, 2006)
Davison, Julian, *Swan & Maclaren: A Story of Singapore Architecture* (Singapore, ORO Editions, 2019)
Denby, Elaine, *Grand Hotels* (London, Reaktion, 2002)
Dobraszczyk, Paul, and Sealy, Peter (eds,), *Function and Fantasy: Iron Architecture in the Long Nineteenth Century* (Abingdon, Routledge, 2016)
Duncan, James Stuart, *The City as Text: The Politics of Landscape Interpretation and the Kandyan Kingdom* (Cambridge, CUP, 1990)
Dunn, Brenda, *A History of Port Royal and Annapolis Royal 1605–1800* (Halifax NS, Nimbus, 2004)
Dutta, Krishna, *Calcutta: A Cultural and Literary History* (Oxford, Signal Books, 2003)
Elquist, Harriet, *Building a New World: A History of the State Library of Victoria, 1853–1913* (Melbourne, State Library of Victoria, 2013)
Fermor-Hesketh, Robert (ed.), *Architecture of the British Empire* (London, Weidenfeld and Nicolson, 1986)
Foster, Stephen, *A Private Empire* (Millers Point, New South Wales, Murdoch Books, 2010)
Fox, Colin, *A Bitter Draught: St. Helena and the Abolition of Slavery* (Elveden, Norfolk, Society of Friends of St Helena, 2017)
Gailey, Andrew, *The Lost Imperialist: Lord Dufferin, Memory and Mythmaking in an Age of Celebrity* (London, John Murray, 2015)
Gann, Lewis H., *A History of Northern Rhodesia: Early Days to 1953* (London, Chatto and Windus, 1964)
Goad, Philip, *Melbourne Architecture* (Sydney, Watermark Press, 1999)

Select bibliography

Goodwin, Godfrey *A History of Ottoman Architecture* (London, Thames and Hudson, 1971)
Gordon, David (ed.), *Planning Twentieth-Century Capital Cities* (London, Routledge, 2009)
Gordon, Joyce, *Nevis: Queen of the Caribees* (Oxford, Macmillan Caribbean, 2005)
Gosse, Philip, *St Helena 1502–1938* (London, Nelson, 1990, first published 1938)
Gough, Barry, *Gunboat Frontier: British Maritime Authority and North-West Coast Indians, 1846–90* (Vancouver, University of British Columbia Press, 1984)
Gravette, Andrew, *Architectural Heritage of the Caribbean: An A-Z of Historic Buildings* (Kingston, Jamaica, Randle Publishers, 2000)
Gunn, Simon, and Bell, Rachel, *Middle Classes: Their Rise and Sprawl* (London, Phoenix, 2011)
Gunn, Simon, *The Public Culture of the Victorian Middle Class* (Manchester, MUP, 2000)
Gupchup, Vijaya, *St Thomas' Cathedral, Bombay: A Witness to History* (Bombay, Eminence Designs, 2005)
Gupta, Samita, *Architecture and the Raj: Western Deccan 1700–1900* (Delhi, B.R. Publishing, 1985)
Hamilton, Douglas, *Scotland, the Caribbean and the Atlantic World, 1750–1820* (Manchester, MUP, 2005)
Harland-Jacobs, Jessica L., *Builders of Empire: Freemasonry and British Imperialism, 1717–1827* (Chapel Hill, University of North Carolina Press, 2007)
Harrison, Mark, *Public Health in British India: Anglo-Indian Preventive Medicine, 1859–1914* (Cambridge, CUP, 1994)
Harvey, Maurice, *Gibraltar: A History* (Staplehurst, Spellmount, 1996)
Head, Raymond, *The Indian Style* (London, Allen and Unwin, 1986)
Headrick, Daniel R., *The Tools of Empire: Technology and European Imperialism in the Nineteenth Century* (Oxford, OUP, 1981)
— *The Invisible Weapon: Telecommunications and International Politics, 1851–1945* (Oxford, OUP, 1991)
Hendrick, Burton J., *The Life of Andrew Carnegie* (London, Heinemann, 1933)
Holmes, Richard, *Sahib: The British Soldier in India* (London, HarperCollins, 2005)
Home, Robert, *Of Planting and Planning: The Making of British Colonial Cities* (Abingdon, Routledge, 2013, first published 1997)
Hoock, Holger, *Empires of the Imagination: Politics, War and the Arts in the British World, 1750–1850* (London, Profile, 2010)
Hosagrahar, Jyoti, *Indigenous Modernities: Negotiating Architecture and Urbanism* (Abingdon, Routledge, 2005)
Howard, Deborah, *Venice and the East: The Impact of the Islamic World on Venetian Architecture 1100–1500* (New Haven, CT, YUP, 2000)
Hughes, Joy (ed.), *Demolished Houses of Sydney* (Historic Houses Trust of New South Wales, 1999)

Select bibliography

Hunt, Tristram, *Ten Cities that Made an Empire* (London, Allen Lane, 2014)
Hyam, Ronald, *Britain's Imperial Century 1815–1914: A Study of Empire and Expansion* (third edition, London, Palgrave Macmillan 2002)
Inglis, Andrea Scott, *Summer in the Hills: The Nineteenth Century Mountain Resort in Australia* (Melbourne, Scholarly Publishing, 2007)
Irving, Robert Grant, *Indian Summer: Lutyens, Baker and Imperial Delhi* (New Haven, CT, YUP, 1981)
Jackson, Ashley, *Buildings of Empire* (Oxford, OUP, 2013)
Johnson, David A., *New Delhi: The Last Imperial City* (Basingstoke, Palgrave Macmillan, 2015).
Kanwar, Pamela, *Imperial Simla: The Political Culture of the Raj* (New Delhi, OUP, 1990)
Kennedy, Dane, *Islands of White: Settler Society and Culture in Kenya and Southern Rhodesia, 1890–1939* (Durham NC, Duke University Press, 1987)
— *Magic Mountains: Hill Stations and the British Raj* (Berkeley, CA, University of California Press, 1996)
Khuhro, Hamida, and Mooraj, Anwer (eds), *Karachi: Megacity of Our Times* (Oxford, OUP, 2010)
Kincaid, Dennis, *British Social Life in India 1608–1937* (London, Routledge 1938)
King, Anthony D., *The Bungalow: The Production of a Global Culture* (London, Routledge and Kegan Paul, 1984)
— *Urbanism, Colonialism and the World-Economy: Cultural and Spatial Foundations of the World Urban System* (London, Routledge, 1990)
— *Colonial Urban Development* (London, Routledge 1976)
— *Aspects of Global Cultures: Architecture, Urbanism, Identity* (London, Routledge, 2004)
— *Writing the Global City: Globalisation, Postcolonialism and the Urban* (London, Routledge, 2016)
Lambert, David, and Lester, Alan (eds), *Colonial Lives Across the British Empire: Imperial Careering in the Long Nineteenth Century* (Cambridge, CUP, 2006)
Lawrence, A.W., *Fortified Trade-Posts: The English in West Africa 1645–1822* (London, Jonathan Cape, 1963)
Lester, Alan, *Imperial Networks: Creating Identities in South Africa and Britain* (London, Routledge, 2001)
Levine, Allan, *Toronto: Biography of a City* (Madeira Park, BC, Douglas and McIntyre, 2014)
Llewellyn-Jones, Rosie (ed.), *Lucknow: City of Illusion* (London, Prestel for the Alkazi Collection of Photography, 2006)
London, Christopher W., *Bombay Gothic* (Mumbai, India Book House, 2002)
Longair, Sarah, *Cracks in the Dome: Fractured Histories of Empire in the Zanzibar Museum, 1897–1964* (London, Ashgate, 2015)
Losty, J.P., *Calcutta, City of Palaces: A Survey of the City in the Days of the East India Company, 1690–1858* (London, British Library, 1990)

Select bibliography

Lutyens, Mary, *The Lyttons in India: Lord Lytton's Viceroyalty* (London, John Murray, 1979)
MacKenzie, John M., *Propaganda and Empire* (Manchester, MUP, 1984)
— *The Empire of Nature: Hunting, Conservation and British Imperialism* (Manchester, MUP, 1988)
— *Orientalism: History, Theory and the Arts* (Manchester, MUP, 1995)
— *Museums and Empire: Natural History, Human Cultures and Colonial Identities* (Manchester, MUP, 2009)
—, with Dalziel, Nigel R., *The Scots in South Africa* (Manchester, MUP, 2007)
MacKenzie, John M. (ed.), *Imperialism and Popular Culture* (Manchester, MUP, 1986)
— *Imperialism and the Natural World* (Manchester, MUP, 1990)
— *Popular Imperialism and the Military, 1850–1950* (Manchester, MUP, 1992)
— *European Empires and the People* (Manchester, MUP, 2011)
MacKenzie, John M., and Devine, T.M. (eds), *Scotland and the British Empire* (Oxford, OUP, 2011)
Magee, Gary B., and Thompson, Andrew S., *Empire and Globalisation: Networks of People, Goods and Capital in the British World, c.1850–1914* (Cambridge, CUP, 2010)
Maudlin, Daniel, and Herman, Bernard L. (eds), *Building the British Atlantic World: Spaces, Places and Material Culture, 1600–1850* (Chapel Hill, University of North Carolina Press, 2016)
McAleer, John, *Picturing India: People, Places and the World of the East India Company* (London, British Library, 2017)
McCarthy, Angela, and Devine, T.M., *Tea and Empire: James Taylor in Victorian Ceylon* (Manchester, MUP, 2017)
McHugh, Patricia, *Toronto Architecture: A City Guide* (Toronto, McClelland and Stewart, 1989)
McQuarrie, John (ed.), *The Hill/La Colline* (Ottawa, Magic Light Publishing, 2015)
Meadows, Douglas, *Modern Eastern Bungalows and How to Build Them* (Calcutta, Thacker, 1931)
Melber, Henning, *The Rise of Africa's Middle Class* (London, Zed Books, 1988)
Metcalf, Thomas R., *An Imperial Vision: Indian Architecture and Britain's Raj* (London, Faber, 1989)
Moore, Brian L., and Johnson, Michelle A., *Neither Led Nor Driven: Contesting British Cultural Imperialism in Jamaica, 1865–1920* (Kingston, Jamaica, University of West Indies Press, 2004)
Moorhouse, Geoffrey, *Calcutta: The City Revealed* (Harmondsworth, Penguin, 1974)
Morris, Jan, *Stones of Empire: The Buildings of the Raj* (photographs and captions by Simon Winchester) (Oxford, OUP, 1983)

Select bibliography

Mount, Ferdinand, *Tears of the Rajahs: Mutiny, Money and Marriage in India 1805–1905* (London, Simon and Schuster, 2015)
Munro, J. Forbes, *Maritime Enterprise and Empire: Sir William Mackinnon and his Business Network, 1823–1893* (Woodbridge, Boydell Press, 2003)
Murray, Craig, *Sikunder Burnes: Master of the Great Game* (Edinburgh, Birlinn, 2016)
Mutch, Alistair, *Tiger Duff: India, Madeira and Empire in Eighteenth-Century Scotland* (Aberdeen, University of Aberdeen Press, 2017)
Myers, Garth Andrew, *Verandahs of Power: Colonialism and Space in Urban Africa* (Syracuse, NY, Syracuse University Press, 2003)
Nanni, Giordano, *The Colonisation of Time: Ritual, Routine and Resistance in the British Empire* (Manchester, MUP, 2012)
Nasution, Khoo Salma, and Berbar, Halim, *Heritage Houses of Penang* (Singapore, Marshall Cavendish, 2009)
Nelson, Louis P., *Architecture and Empire in Jamaica* (New Haven, CT, YUP, 2016)
Nelson, Nina, *Shepheard's Hotel* (Bath, Barrie Books, 1974)
Nilsson, Sten, *European Architecture in India, 1750–1850* (London, Faber, 1968)
Nin, Khoo Su, *Streets of George Town, Penang: An Illustrated Guide to Penang's City Streets and Historic Attractions* (Penang, Areca Books, 2007)
Omissi, David E., *Air Power and Colonial Control: The Royal Air Force, 1919–1939* (Manchester, MUP, 1990)
Panter-Downes, Mollie, *Ooty Preserved: A Victorian Hill Station in India* (London, Century Publishing, 1967)
Parissien, Steven, *Station to Station* (London, Phaidon, 2001)
Patterson, Brad, Brooking, Tom, and McAloon, Jim, *Unpacking the Kists: The Scots in New Zealand* (Dunedin, Otago University Press, 2013)
Pietsch, Tamson, *Empire of Scholars: Universities, Networks and the British Academic World 1850–1939* (Manchester, MUP, 2013)
Porter, Bernard, *The Absent-Minded Imperialists: Empire, Society and Culture in Britain* (Oxford, OUP, 2004)
Preston, Antony, and Major, John, *Send a Gun Boat: A Study of the Gunboat and its Role in British Policy, 1854–1904* (London, Longmans, 1967)
Radford, Denis, *A Guide to the Architecture of Durban and Pietermaritzburg* (Cape Town, David Philip, 2002)
Raible, Chris, *A Colonial Advocate: The Launching of his Newspaper and the Queenston Career of William Lyon Mackenzie* (Creemore, Ont. Curiosity House, 1999)
Ramani, Navin, *Bombay Art Deco Architecture: A Visual Journey 1930–1953* (Delhi, Roli and Janssen, 2007)
Ramnath, Aparajith, *The Birth of an Indian Profession: Engineers, Industry and the State, 1900–1947* (Oxford, OUP, 2017)
Rappaport, Erika, *A Thirst for Empire: How Tea Shaped the Modern World* (Princeton, PUP, 2017)

Select bibliography

Reed, Charles, *Royal Tourists, Colonial Subjects and the Making of a British World* (Manchester, MUP, 2016)
Reksten, Terry, *Craigdarroch: The Story of Dunsmuir Castle* (Victoria, BC, Orca, 1987)
Rich, P.J., *Chains of Empire: English Public Schools, Masonic Children, Historical Causality and Imperial Clubdom* (Washington, DC, Westphalia Press, 2015)
Richards, Jeffrey, and MacKenzie, John M., *The Railway Station: A Social History* (Oxford, OUP, 1986)
Roberts, Andrew, *A History of Zambia* (London, Heinemann, 1976)
Robertson, E. Graeme, and Robertson, Joan, *Cast Iron Decoration: A World Survey* (London, Thames and Hudson, 1977)
Rohatgi, Pauline, Godrej, Pheroza, and Mehrotra, Rohul (eds), *Bombay to Mumbai: Changing Perspectives* (Mumbai, Marg Publications, 1997)
Rooney, Sarah, *30 Heritage Buildings of Yangon* (Association of Myanmar Architects and Serindia Publications, 2013)
Rothschild, Emma, *The Inner Life of Empires: An Eighteenth-Century History* (Princeton, NJ, PUP, 2011)
Sachdev, Vibhuti, and Tillotson, Giles, *Building Jaipur: The Making of an Indian City* (London, Reaktion, 2002)
Scott, Sir Ian, *A British Tale of Indian and Foreign Service: Memoirs*, edited by Denis Judd (London, Radcliffe Press, 1999)
Scriver, Peter, and Prakash, Vikramaditya (eds), *Colonial Modernities: Building, Dwelling and Architecture in British India and Ceylon* (London, Routledge, 2007)
Sharp, Ilsa, *The Eastern and Oriental Hotel: Pearl of Penang* (Penang, E&O, 2008)
— *The Fullerton Heritage: Where the Past Meets the Present* (Singapore, Oro Editions, 2011)
Shorto, Sylvia, *British Houses in Late Mughal Delhi* (London, Boydell and Brewer, 2018)
Sleight, Simon, *Young People and the Shaping of Public Space in Melbourne, 1870–1914* (Farnham, Ashgate, 2013)
Smith, Victor T.C., *Fire and Brimstone: The Story of the Brimstone Hill Fortress, St. Kitts, West Indies, 1690–1853* (St Kitts, Creole Publishing, 1992)
Stern, Robert W., *Changing India: Bourgeois Revolution on the Sub-Continent* (Cambridge, CUP, 1993)
Streets, Heather, *Martial Races: The Military, Race and Masculinity in British Imperial Culturè 1857–1914* (Manchester, MUP, 2004)
Strong, Rowan, *Anglicanism and the British Empire, c.1700–1850* (Oxford, OUP, 2007)
Sunderland, David, *Managing the British Empire: The Crown Agents, 1833–1914* (London, Boydell, 2004)
Sweetman, John, *The Oriental Obsession: Islamic Inspiration in British and American Art and Architecture* (Cambridge, CUP, 1988)

Select bibliography

Talbot, Ian, and Kamran, Tahir, *Colonial Lahore: A History of the City and Beyond* (London, Hurst, 2016)
Tindall, Gillian, *City of Gold: The Biography of Bombay* (Hounslow, Maurice Temple Smith, 1982)
Varnava, Andrekos, *British Imperialism in Cyprus, 1878–1915: The Inconsequential Possession* (Manchester, MUP, 2009)
Waldron, Anthony, *Exploring the Capital: An Architectural Guide to the Ottawa-Gatineau Region* (Vancouver, Figure1 Publishing, 2017)
Whidden, James, *Egypt: British Colony, Imperial Capital* (Manchester, MUP, 2017)
Wilkie, Benjamin, *The Scots in Australia, 1788–1938* (Woodbridge, Boydell, 2017)
Woollacott, Angela, *Settler Society in the Australian Colonies: Self-Government and Imperial Culture* (Oxford, OUP, 2015)
Worden, Nigel, van Heyningen, Elizabeth, and Bickford-Smith, Vivian, *Cape Town: The Making of a City* (Cape Town, David Philip, 1998)

ARTICLES, CHAPTERS AND THESES

Allan, J. Alex, 'The Melbourne Public Library', *Australian Builder* (March 1951), pp. 138–141
Ballantyne, Andrew, and Law, Andrew, 'The Genealogy of the Singaporean Black and White House', *Singapore Journal of Tropical Geography*, 22 (2011), pp. 301–313
Bhasin, Raaja, 'Viceregal Lodge and the Indian Institute of Advanced Study', pamphlet, Shimla, IIAS, Rashtrapati Nivas, 2009
Bremner, G.A., '"Some Imperial Institute": Architecture, Symbolism, and the Ideal of Empire in Late Victorian Britain, 1887–93', *Journal of the Society of Architectural Historians*, 62, 1 (2003), pp. 50–73
— '"Imperial Monumental Halls and Tower": Westminster Abbey and the Commemoration of Empire, 1854–1904', *Architectural History*, 47 (2004), pp. 251–282
— 'The Architecture of the Universities' Mission to Central Africa: Developing a Vernacular Tradition in the Anglican Mission Field', *Journal of the Society of Architectural Historians*, 68, 4 (2009), pp. 514–539
— 'The Corporatisation of Global Anglicanism: Architecture, Organisation and Faith-based Patronage in the Nineteenth-century British Colonial World', *ABE*, 2, 2012
Chattopadhyay, Swati, 'Politics, Planning and Subjection: Anticolonial Nationalism and Public Space in Colonial Calcutta' in Chattopadhyay, Swati, and White, Jeremy (eds), *City Halls*, pp. 199–216
— 'The Other Face of Primitive Accumulation; the Garden House in British Colonial Bengal' in Scriver, Peter, and Prakash, Vikramaditya (eds), *Colonial Modernities*, pp. 169–197

Select bibliography

Chopra, Preeti, 'South and South-East Asia' in Bremner, G.A. (ed.), *Architecture and Urbanism in the British Empire*, pp. 278–317
— 'The Bombay Town Hall: Engaging the Function and Quality of Public Space, 1811–1918' in Chattopadhyay, Swati, and White, Jeremy (eds), *City Halls*, pp. 158–176
Cowell, Christopher, 'The Kaccha-Pakka Divide: Material, Space and Architecture in the Military Cantonments of British India (1765–1889)', *ABE*, 9–10 (2016)
Deschamps, Simon, 'From Britain to India: Freemasonry as a Connective Force of Empire', *Revue Electronique d'études sur le monde Anglophone,* put online 15 June 2017 (accessed 5 June 2018)
Drinkall, Sophie, 'The Jamaican Plantation House: Scottish Influences', *Journal of the Architectural Heritage of Scotland*, II, 1 (1992), pp. 56–68
Dutta, Arindam, '"Strangers within the Gate": Public Works and Industrial Art Reform' in Scriver, Peter, and Prakash, Vikramaditya (eds), *Colonial Modernities*, pp. 103–105
Fraser, W. Hamish, and Mavor, Irene, 'The Social Problems of the City' in Fraser and Mavor (eds), *Glasgow*, Vol. II: 1830–1912 (Manchester, MUP, 1996), pp. 352–393
Gregory, Jenny, 'Town Halls in Australia: Sites of Conflict and Consensus' in Chattopadhyay, Swati, and White, Jeremy (eds), *City Halls*, pp. 115–135
Harvie, Christopher, '"The Sons of Martha": Technology, Transport and Rudyard Kipling', *Victorian Studies*, 20, 3 (spring 1977), pp. 269–282
Hassam, Andrew, 'Portable Iron Structures and Uncertain Colonial Spaces at the Sydenham Crystal Palace' in Felix Driver and David Gilbert (eds), *Imperial Cities* (Manchester, 1999), pp. 174–175.
Hinson, Andrew, 'A Hub of Community: The Presbyterian Church of Toronto and its Role among the City's Scots' in Tanja Bueltmann, Andrew Hinson, and Graeme Morton (eds), *Ties of Bluid, Kin and Countrie: Scottish Associational Culture in the Diaspora* (Markham, Ont. Stewart Publishing, 2009), pp. 119–133
Home, Robert, and King, Anthony D., 'Urbanism and Master Planning: Configuring the Colonial City' in Bremner, G.A. (ed.), *Architecture and Urbanism in the British Empire*, pp. 51–85
Home, R.K., 'Town Planning and Garden Cities in the British Colonial Empire, 1910–1940', *Planning Perspectives*, 5, 1 (1990), pp. 223–237
Hosagrahar, Jyoti, 'Negotiated Modernities; Symbolic Terrains of Housing in Delhi' in Scriver, Peter, and Prakash, Vikramaditya (eds), *Colonial Modernities*, pp. 219–240
Hughes, Matthew, 'The Practice and Theory of British Counterinsurgency: The History of the Atrocities at the Palestinian Villages of al-Bassa and Hallul, 1938–39', *Small Wars and Insurgencies*, 3–4 (2009), pp. 528–550
Inglis, Andrea Scott, 'Claiming the Higher Ground: The Nineteenth-Century Hill Station in Australia as a Manifestation of Empire' (Ph.D. thesis, University of Melbourne, 2004)

Select bibliography

Izamida, Hideo, 'A Study on British Architects in East and South-East Asia, 1830–1940', *Journal of Asian Architectural and Building Engineering* (January 2003), pp. 131–136
— 'Scottish Architects in the Far East, 1840–1870', *Journal of the Architectural Heritage of Scotland*, II, 1 (1992), pp. 99–103
Kalman, Harold, and Nelson, Louis P., 'British North America and the West Indies' in Bremner, G.A. (ed.), *Architecture and Urbanism in the British Empire*, pp. 239–277
Kelkar, Madhu, 'The Sanitary Crusader, Arthur Crawford and the Politics of Sanitation in Bombay', *South Asian Journal of Multi-Disciplinary Studies*, 2, 2 (2016), pp. 1–15
Khuhro, Hamida, 'The Making of a Port' in Khuhro, Hamida, and Mooraj, Anwer (eds), *Karachi*, pp. 34–35
MacKenzie, John M., 'Empires in World History: Characteristics, Concepts, and Consequences', introduction to the Wiley-Blackwell *Encyclopedia of Empire* (Malden MA and Oxford, Wiley-Blackwell, 2016), pp. lxxxiii–cx
— '"The Second City of the Empire": Glasgow – Imperial Municipality' in Felix Driver and David Gilbert (eds), *Imperial Cities* (Manchester, MUP, 1999), pp. 215–237
— 'Missionaries, Science and the Environment in Nineteenth-Century Africa' in Andrew Porter (ed.), *The Imperial Horizons of British Protestant Missions, 1880–1914* (Grand Rapids, MI and Cambridge, Eerdmans, 2003), pp. 106–130
— 'Irish, Scottish, Welsh and English Worlds? The Historiography of the Four-Nations Approach to the History of the British Empire' in Catherine Hall and Keith McClelland (eds), *Race, Nation and Empire: Making Histories, 1750 to the Present* (Manchester, MUP, 2010), pp. 133–153
— 'The British Empire: Ramshackle or Rampaging?', *Journal of Imperial and Commonwealth History*, 43, 1 (March 2015), pp. 99–124
— 'Presbyterianism and Scottish Identity in Global Context', *Britain and the World, Historical Journal of the British Scholar Society*, X, 1 (March 2017), pp. 88–112
— 'Scottish Orientalists, Administrators and Missions: A Distinctive Scots Approach to Asia?' in T. M. Devine and Angela McCarthy (eds), *The Scottish Experience in Asia, c.1700 to the Present: Settlers and Sojourners* (London, Palgrave Macmillan, 2017), pp. 51–73
Merrington, Peter, 'The State and the "Invention of Heritage" in Edwardian South Africa' in Andrea Bosco and Alex May (eds), *The Round Table, the Empire/Commonwealth and British Foreign Policy* (London, Lothian Foundation Press, 1997), pp. 127–133
Micots, Courtnay, 'Status and Mimicry, African Colonial Period Architecture in Coastal Ghana', *Journal of the Society of Architectural Historians*, 74, 1 (March 2015), pp. 41–62

Select bibliography

Mushtaq, Muhammed Umair, 'Public Health in British India: A Brief Account of Medical Services and Disease Prevention in Colonial India', *Indian Journal of Community Medicine*, 34, 1 (2009), pp. 6–14
Myers, Garth Andrew, 'Moving Beyond Colonialism: Town Halls in Sub-Saharan Africa's Postcolonial Capitals' in Chattopadhyay, Swati, and White, Jeremy (eds), *City Halls*, pp. 237–254
— 'Intellectual of Empire: Eric Dutton and Hegemony in British Africa', *Annals of the Association of American Geographers*, 58, 1 (1998), pp. 1–27
Pieris, Anoma, 'The Trouser Under the Cloth' in Scriver, Peter, and Prakash, Vikramaditya (eds), *Colonial Modernities*, pp. 199–218
Prakash, Vikramaditya, 'Between Copying and Creation: The Jeypore Portfolio of Architectural Details' in Scriver, Peter, and Prakash, Vikramaditya (eds), *Colonial Modernities*, pp. 115–125
Scriver, Peter, 'Stones and Texts: The Architectural Historiography of Colonial India and its Colonial-Modern Contexts' in Scriver, Peter, and Prakash, Vikramaditya (eds), *Colonial Modernities*, pp. 27–50
— 'The Public Works Department of British India' in Scriver, Peter, and Prakash, Vikramaditya (eds), *Colonial Modernities*, pp. 69–92
Shorto, Sylvia, 'A Tomb of One's Own: The Governor's House, Lahore' in Scriver, Peter, and Prakash, Vikramaditya (eds), *Colonial Modernities*, pp. 151–168
Singhal, Bindu, 'Glimpses of Indo-Saracenic Architecture', *Architecture and Design*, 17, 5 (Sept./Oct. 2000), pp. 98–101
Tindall, Gillian, 'Existential Cities' in Fermor-Hesketh, Robert (ed.), *Architecture of the British Empire*, pp. 74–103
Volait, Mercedes, 'The Reclaiming of 'Belle Époque Architecture in Egypt (1989–2010): On the Power of Rhetorics in Heritage Making', *ABE*, 3, 2013
Walker, Paul, 'Institutional Audiences and Architectural Style: The Napier Museum' in Scriver, Peter, and Prakash, Vikramaditya (eds), *Colonial Modernities*, pp. 127–147
Welter, Volker M., 'Arcades for Lucknow: Patrick Geddes, Charles Rennie Mackintosh and Reconstruction of the City', *Architectural History*, 42 (1999), pp. 316–332
Whidden, James, 'The Levantine British: Defying Race Categories in Colonial Alexandria', *Britain and the World*, 12, 1 (March 2019), pp. 51–66
Wilton-Ely, John, 'The Rise of the Profession of Architect in England' in Spiro Kostof (ed.), *The Architect: Chapters in the History of the Profession* (Berkeley, University of California Press, 1977), pp. 180–208
Withey, Matthew, 'The Glasgow City Improvement Trust: An Analysis of its Genesis, Impact and Legacy and an Inventory of its Buildings, 1866–1910' (Ph.D thesis, University of St Andrews, 2003)

Index

Abyssinia 39
Adelaide 74, 98, 105, 117, 128, 134, 144, 182, 200, 217, 241
Adelaide, Queen 229
Agra 36
airfields 243, 245
Alberta 41, 77, 97
Alexandria, Egypt 108, 202
Allahabad 88, 200
America/American (USA) 7, 17, 34, 59, 64–5, 89, 97, 99, 109, 110, 125, 130, 136, 146, 215, 242, 265
America, North 7, 28, 31, 40, 56, 100, 165, 166–7, 196, 214, 259
Anderson, Benedict 5
Anglo-Boer War (1899–1902) 40, 64, 96, 181, 203, 268
Antigua 53, 266
apartment blocks 188–9
architects 5, 14, 17, 32–5, 44, 69, 86–7, 105, 108, 146–7, 179, 188, 199–201, 212–15, 217, 228–30, 231, 234, 238, 269
  Adam, William and Robert 32
  Adams, John 146
  Adshead, Stanley Davenport 249–50
  Anderson, Arthur 153
  Baker, Sir Herbert 100, 181, 202–3, 241, 245–7, 251
  Barry, E.M. 231
  Bayne, Richard Roskell 143

  Begg, John 88, 114, 236
  Bidwell, R.A.J. 239
  Blomfield, F.B. 248
  Bloodsworth, James 74
  Blore, Edward 74
  Bodley, George Frederick 200
  Boileau, Major J.T. 113
  Bonavia, Giuseppe 230
  Brassington, J.W. 102
  Broughton, Bishop William 196, 201
  Bude, Capt. Henry de 203
  Burges, William 146, 200, 205
  Butterfield, William 200
  Caldwell, J.L. 199
  Campbell, John 98
  Chisholm, Robert Fellowes 93, 131, 133, 201
  Conybeare, Henry 146, 205
  Cowper, Col. Thomas 92
  Crookshank, Sydney 71, 88
  Darwood, John 238
  Ellis, R.E. 144
  Emerson, William 88, 143, 146, 200
  Forbes, Major William Nairn 91, 199
  Foster, Thomas Oliphant 237
  Fuller, Col. J.A. 102
  Fuller, John 146
  Garstin, John 91
  Gibbs, James 87, 196
  Goodwyn, Capt. Henry 209
  Granville, Walter 102, 205

Index

Gray, Sophia (Sophy) 197
Griffin, Walter B. and Marion M. 242–3
Hall, Capt. William 198
Henderson, E.J.W. 76
Hoogterp, Jan 251
Hoyne-Fox, Henry 72, 201, 235
Irwin, Henry 71, 88, 114
Jacob, Samuel Swinton 86, 88, 132
Janzen, Hendrick 201
Kay, William Porden 75
Khan, Bahadur 147
Kingston, George Strickland 74
Köhler, W.H. 129
Lawson, Robert 212, 215
Lutyens, Edwin 245–8, 265
McCallum, Henry 133
Maclaren, James 154
Mant, Major Charles 88
Medd, Henry 247
Molecey, George 146
Murdoch, John Smith 101
Murzban, Cowasjee 147
Paris, Walter 146
Pearson, John L. 100, 135, 200, 230
Ram, Ganga 131
Reed, Joseph 128
Robe, Major William 198
Ross, David 212, 215
Russell, Robert T. 246
Scamp, William 229
Scott, David Clement 214
Scott, George Gilbert and J.O. 146–7, 199–200
Shute, John 32
Sinclair, John Houston 135, 202
Smith, Major Robert 203
Smith, Capt. Robert N. 203
Spence, Basil 99
Stark & McNeill 179
Stevens, C.F. 157
Stevens, F.W. 71, 146
Storm, W.G. 210
Strachan, James 144
Street, G.E. 205
Swan & Maclaren 179

Thatcher, Frederick 200
Troup, Alexander 152
Turnbull, Thomas 212
Vernon, Walter Liberty 128
Vixseboxse, J.E. 135
Whitmore, Col. George 228–9
Wierda, Sytze 103
Wild, James 202
Wilkins, Gen. Henry 93, 146
Wittet, George 88, 131
Wren, Christopher 32, 196
Wyatt, Capt. Charles 69
  see also engineers/engineering
architecture 1–18, 23–35, 41, 44, 65–78, 85–9, 105, 112, 130, 132–5, 143, 145–9, 152, 156, 164–5, 173, 178–9, 181, 187–9, 227–8, 231, 234, 238, 245, 249, 259, 263, 265–6
  amateur 17, 33, 105–6, 135, 196–7, 214
  catalogues 104, 176
  climate and 4, 9, 14, 16, 17, 25, 29, 41, 61, 66, 71, 86, 87, 92, 104–5, 109, 114, 117, 138, 164, 167–9, 177, 182, 188, 197–8, 207
  Creole 171–2
  destruction 12, 23–45, 53, 76, 203, 231, 243, 269
  domestic 3, 5, 9, 11, 13, 16, 28–30, 42, 56, 61, 64, 71, 76, 89, 109, 117, 156, 164–84, 186, 188, 214, 246, 251, 261, 269
  'heritage' architecture *see* heritage
  historicist 27, 76, 85–6, 88, 198
  hybrid 1, 6–7, 14, 25, 26, 29–30, 85–8, 97, 103, 131, 173, 178–80, 198, 201–2, 205, 214, 227, 229, 236–8, 245
  imperial style 24, 27, 65, 89, 177, 189, 264
  indigenous 2, 13–14, 28–30, 35–6, 40, 56, 59, 65–6, 85, 87, 105–7, 133, 164–71, 178, 182, 251, 268
  pattern books 33, 86, 91, 132, 177, 209
  prefabricated 71, 74, 104–5, 176, 198
  religious 89, 195–219, 259
  see also gardens; garden city

Index

Argentina 8, 145
Armitage, David 203
Armstrong, Bishop John 201
Art Deco 17, 27, 89, 103, 156–7, 179–80, 188, 247–8
Art Nouveau 27, 89, 179
Arts and Crafts 38, 77, 88, 117, 154, 178
 see also crafts
Asiatic Society of Bengal 127, 130, 139, 216
Asiatic Society of Bombay 92, 127
Aslet, Clive 10, 12
Auckland, NZ 76–7, 98, 134–5, 138, 184, 211, 270
Auckland, Gov.-Gen. Lord 60, 113
Australia/Australian 5, 7, 8, 15, 16, 28, 33, 34, 40, 67–8, 74–6, 84–5, 94–8, 105, 110, 117, 127, 129–30, 134, 137–8, 144, 150–2, *156*, 165, 174, 177, 182–3, 196, 198–9, 211, 213–15, 217, 218, 227, 241–4, 259, 261–2
Awadh 36, *38*, 65

Bangalore 88, 203
banks 28, 41, 109, 114, 138, 152–3, 235, 237–8, 261, 265, 268
Barbados 53, 73, 166, 170, 266
Baroque 27, 30, 87, 89, 95–9, 103, 131, 137–8, 152, 198, 199, 229, 230, 243
barracks 9, 36, 51, 56–8, 63–5, 77, 107, 117, 250, 266, 269
 see also cantonments
Barry, Sir Redmond 128
Beato, Felice *37*, *38*
Belich, James 227, 259
Belle Époque 265
Bengal 70, 92, 127, 139, 172, 173, 175, 203, 205, 216, 233, 244, 270
Benin City 39–40
Bentinck, Gov.-Gen. Lord William 61, 113
Beveridge, Henry, and William, Lord 184–5
black-and-white house 179–80
'black towns' 166, 185, 262
Blantyre, Malawi 214
Bombay (Mumbai) 38, 41, 56, 62, 63, 70–1, 88, 91–3, 102, 111, 114, 115, 127, 131, 139, *141*, 143, 146–8, 151, 153, 155, 157, 184, 185, 186, 188, 199, 205, 208, 209, 236
bourgeoisie 9, 16, 31, 39, 83, 86, 89–90, 94, 109, 115, 124–57, 164, 183, 185, 215, 260–1, 264–5, 268
 see also class, social
Bowling, P.J. 249
Bradley, Kenneth 249–52
Bremner, G.A. 11, 200
Brisbane *see* Queensland
British Columbia 41, *59*, 77, 97, 154, *155*, *174*
British Museum 128, 133
British South Africa Company 40, 248
Buckingham and Chandos, Duke of 71, 112
bungalow 11, 29, 63–5, 77, 111, 114, 117, 152, 164, 172–83, 243, 245, 246, 250, *251*, 261, 265
Burma (Myanmar) 39, 44, 72–3, 115, *116*, 201, 231–40, 264, *267*

Cairo 42–3, 108, 154–5
Calcutta (Kolkata) 11, *12*, 33, 38, 56, 69–70, 88, 91, *102*, 127, 130–1, 139, *140*, 143, 146, *149*, 151, 155, 157, 173, 185–7, 199, *200*, 208–9, 215–17, 239, 244–5, 270
Canada/Canadian 5, 7, 9, 15, 33, 34, 59, 64–5, 68, 77, 84–5, 89, 97–100, 103, 127, 129–30, 133, 136–7, 150, 152, *153*, 167, 174–5, 182, 197–9, 210, 217, 241, 262, 271
 First Nations 15, 40–1, 56–7, 97, *165*, 213, 261, 262, 270–1
Canberra *see* urban planning
Candacraig 115, *116*
cantonments 39, 51, 60, 63–4, 88, 111, 113, 175, 187, 234, 263
 see also barracks
Cape Dutch *see* Dutch style
Cape province, South Africa 2, 40, 57, 64, 85, 100, 116, 129, 135, 172, 200, 201, 210, *211*, 213

289

Index

Cape Town 96, *101*, 103, 129, 135, 138, 152, 154, 180–2, 197, 210, 217
Caribbean 4, 7–8, 44, 52–3, 56, 68, 73, 105, 106, 124, 125, 130, 154, 166–73, 196, 205, 207, 217, 259, 263, 269
Carnegie, Andrew 130
Casa Loma 175
cathedrals 25, 29, 36, 42–3, 59, 107, 135, 198–207, 212, 214, 229–30, 238, 247–8
  see also churches
Cawnpore (Kanpur) 205, *206*, 216
Ceylon (Sri Lanka) 85, 101, 105, 110, 114–15, 133, 141, 172, 173, 264, 271
Chang, Jiat-Hwee 11, 187
Charlottetown, Prince Edward Island 77, 97
'chattel houses' 166, 266
Chattopadhyay, Swati 11–12
Chennai *see* Madras
China/Chinese 8, 14, 41, 106, 109, 114, 178–9, 205, 219, 238, 240, 248, 264–5
Christchurch, NZ 199, 212
church architecture *see* architecture, religious
Church of England *see* churches, Anglican
churches 15, 25, 29, 36, 41, 42, 43, 56, 60, 64, 87, 89, 100, 104, 106, 107, 108, 111, 115, 129, 195–219, 232, 260, 263
  Anglican 42, 43, 112, 113–14, 135, 211–12, 195–205, 207–8, 212, 214–15, 229–30, 242, 247, 270
  Baptist 195, 205
  commemorative 100, 205–7, 230
  Congregationalist 195, 212, 215
  evangelicals 108, 195–6, 204, 208
  Methodist (Wesleyan) 195, 203, 205, 212, 215, 230
  Roman Catholic 36, 43, 89, 195, 201, 203–4, 210–11, 214–15, 227, 229–30, 247
  Scottish 195–6, 197, 204, 207–13, 230
  see also cathedrals; missions

Church of Scotland *see* churches, Scottish
Churchill, Winston 40
cinemas 3, 9, 25, 28, 156–7
city halls *see* town halls
city improvement *see* urban planning
civilisation 14, 24, 27, 44, 65–6, 83, 126, 132, 136, 178, 249–50, 252, 260
class, social 3–5, 16, 26, 28, 31–5, 84, 124–6, 134–5, 139, 142, 150–2, 154, 157, 166, 182–9, 204, 214–17, 250, 260–4, 270
  see also bourgeoisie
classical style 13, 27, 33, 65, 69–71, 74–7, 87, 89, 91, 95, 96, 98–103, 109, 126–8, 130–1, 134–5, 139, 146, 148, 152, 154, 178–9, 196, 198, 199, 203, 207–9, 215–17, 227–30, 235–8, 268
clubs 9, 25, 28, 108, 112, 114–16, 126, 136–42, 154, 156, 180, 189, 218, 234, *235*, 240, 246–7, 251, 260
colleges 25, 32–3, 88, 127, 129, 131, 209, 213, 243
Colombo 133, 141, 155, 173
Colonial Office, London 33, 186, 248
Combermere, Gen. Lord 60
Connaught, Duke and Duchess of 62, 142
contractors 34, 106, 234, 238, 246
courts *see* law courts
crafts 32, 34–5, 85, 86, 88, 105–8, 131–2, 179–80, 201, 219, 229, 245, 268
  see also Arts and Crafts
Craigdarroch 174
Crinson, Mark 108, 263
culture, imperial 3–4, 6, 12, 24, 85, 196, 241
culture, material 11, 12, 24, 259–61, 264
Currie, Sir Donald 154
Curzon, Viceroy Lord 62, 244, 270
customs houses/buildings 56, 90, 98, 109, 145
Cyprus 116, 270

Daceyville 183
Dalhousie, Gov.-Gen. Lord 33, 61, 70, 127, 216
Dalrymple, William 36

Index

Davies, Philip 10
Delhi 35–7, 39, 61–2, 64, 173, 186–7, 203, 204, 244
  see also urban planning, New Delhi
Dufferin, Gov.-Gen./Viceroy Lord 65, 77, 201
Duncan, James Stuart 271
Dunedin 15, 152, 174, 182, 212
Dunsmuir, Robert 174
Durban 95, 138, 148
durbars 39, 60–2, 71, 92, 104, 244, 248, 266
Dutch 52, 57, 85, 101, 103, 109, 129, 172, 201
Dutch style 85, 135, 142, 172, 180–1
Dutton, Eric 249

East India Company (EIC) 8, 30, 32, 55–6, 65, 69, 71, 73, 90, 139, 146, 199, 207–9, 216, 244
Eden, Emily 60, 113
education 5, 9, 25–6, 31, 34, 88–9, 115, 124–6, 132, 134, 147–8, 209, 213, 260
Edwardian 89, 96, 100, 137–8, 180, 243
Egypt 9, 17, 33, 42, 107–8, 155, 231, 265
engineers/engineering 5, 14, 23–5, 32–4, 69, 86, 91, 92, 105, 113–14, 125, 132, 144, 145, 146, 147, 178, 179, 186, 198, 199, 203, 205, 209, 228–30, 233, 235, 249
  military 33, 69, 91, 92, 105, 113, 203, 209, 233
  see also architects; Public Works Department (PWD)
England/English 14, 17, 32, 55–6, 61, 62, 66, 87, 100, 101, 102–3, 104, 111–15, 147, 148, 157, 179, 181, 182, 195, 197–8, 203, 207, 230, 263
environment, natural 2, 3–5, 9, 23, 53, 138, 184
Episcopal Church of Scotland *see* churches, Scottish
estate houses *see* plantation houses

Fairview, St Kitts 170–1
Fergusson, Sir James 10, 36
Fermor-Hesketh, Robert 10
First World War 97, 98, 100, 109, 115, 183, 240, 242–3
Flemish style 95, 102, 143, 152
forts 26–7, 29, 38–40, 42, 51–9, 64–5, 67, 72, 77–8, 83, 107, 150, 227–31, 266, 269
  Bombay (Fort George) 56, 71, 139, 146
  Calcutta (Fort William) 56, 215, 270
  Delhi (Red Fort) 61, 64
  Louisbourg, Cape Breton 57
  North-West Frontier, India 40, 54–6, 78
  St Kitts (Brimstone Hill) 53, 54
'four nations' 2, 14, 108, 203, 219
Fraser, Lt Alexander 233–4
Fredericton, New Brunswick 77, 97, 201
Free Church of Scotland *see* churches, Scottish
Freemasons 100, 114, 125, 137, 157, 215–19
Freetown 116, 218, 219
French style 43, 85, 98, 100, 103, 128, 147
Frere, Sir Bartle 93, 146
Friendly Societies 218–19

garden city 183, 246–7, 250
gardens 25, 28, 29, 36–8, 68, 69, 100, 103, 111–12, 129, 135, 138, 140, 147, 169, 170, 173, 175, 180, 214, 217, 228–30, 238, 246, 250, 260
  botanic 74–5, 112, 115, 117, 125
  'Glover' 109, 265
  see also parks
Geddes, Patrick 37
Georgian architecture 30, 73, 76–7, 97, 98, 103, 127, 136, 138, 139, 169, 174, 182, 245, 246, 251–2
Gibraltar 8, 58
Glasgow 2–3, 71, 179, 186, 212, 233–4
globalisation, cultural 9, 11, 16, 24–7, 31, 54, 78, 94, 130–1, 134, 136, 145, 148, 157, 175, 177, 195–6, 216, 218, 240, 259–61, 263–4, 269–70
Gothic 11, 27, 71, 74, 75, 76, 87, 88, 93, 98–100, 102–3, 112, 114, 127, 129, 144, 146–7, 175, 198–201, 205, 209–15, 227, 229–30, 238, 242, 259

Index

Government Houses 9, 27, *37*, 52, 56, 61, 65–78, 100, 113–15, 134–5, 142, 154, 217, 245, 252, 264, 269
Grahamstown 84, 135, 182, 200, 201, *211*
Grant, Elizabeth 63
Greece/Greek 66, 197
Greek Revival 92, 98, 210, 229, 231
Gregory, Jenny 94–5
Gregory, Sir William 133
Grenada 53, 207
Grey, Sir George 129
Groote Schuur 180–1

Halifax, Nova Scotia 41, 64, 77, 96, 137, 145
Havell, E.B. 245
health 4, 15–16, 25, 26, 39, 67, 71, 83–4, 110–12, 115–17, 125, 143, 164–5, 183, 185–7, 234, 261
heritage 44, 53, 64, 95, 138, 153–4, 155, 157, 169–70, 231, 237, 245, 248, 264–9
Hervey, Capt. Albert 63
Hickey, William 69
hill stations 16, 67, 71, 105, 109–18, 127, 140, 151, 261, 263, 265, 266
  Africa 116
  Australia 117
  Burma 115, *116*, 266, *267*
  Darjeeling 111, 112, 114, 140
  Jamaica 116–17
  Mahabaleshwar 63, 111
  Malaya 114–15
  Naini Tal 71, 112
  Nuwara Eliya 114, 141
  Ootacamund 71, 110–11, 127, 140
  Poona (Pune) 63, 74, 141
  Simla (Shimla) 61, 71, 110–14, 127
Hobart *see* Tasmania
Hong Kong 8, 42, 72, 103, 110, 155, 184
Hosegrahar, Jyoti 187
hotels 9, 34, 62, 71, 90, 107–8, 111, 114–15, 117, 138, 149, 154–6, 239, 248, 265, 266, *267*
Hudson's Bay Company 30, 59

hunting 2, 31, 40, 61, 84, 111, 165
Hyderabad 63, 66, 112

Imperial Institute, London 11, 13
Indian Revolt/Uprising (1857) 33, 35–9, 62, 64, 66, 92, 148, 176, 203, 244
indigenous (society) 4–8, 15, 17, 24–6, 28–9, 34–5, 38–9, 40–2, 52–3, 55–6, 59, 63, 65–9, 83–6, 104, 106, 111, 117–18, 126, 146, 148–50, 157, 164–6, 178, 189, 195, 201, 203, 205, 212–14, 232, 234, 238, 241, 260–71
Indo-Saracenic 10, 30, 87–9, 93, 102, 131–2, 135, 144, 201, 236, 245
informal empire 6, 8, 17, 26, 39, 104, 107–9, 145, 195, 202, 219, 263
international style 156, 180, 188
Ireland/Irish 7, 14, 17, 32, 51, 66, 171, 195, 210, 215, 240
iron 86, 104–5, 113, 129, 144, 151, 174, 178–9, 182, 198, 248
  cast-iron 71, 104–5
  corrugated 104, 113, 176
Irrawaddy Flotilla Co. 154, 232, 238
Irving, Robert Grant 10
Irwin, Viceroy Lord 247
Islamic 9, 29, 42–3, 87, 107–8, 202, 207, 214, 239, 244, 263
Istanbul 107–8, 205
Italianate architecture 27, 75, 76, 133, 138

Jackson, Ashley 11
Jacobean 76, 77, 112, 170
Jacobethan 71
Jaipur 86, 131–3
Jamaica 11, 53, 103, 116, 164, 169–70, 207, 266
  Hibbert House 169
Japan/Japanese 8, 39, 72, 109, 115, 153, 180, 203, 231, 232, 239, 264, 265
Jerusalem 57, 108–9, 207
Johannesburg 96, 103, 180–1, 203

Karachi 93, 102, *103*, 144, 146
Kennedy, Dane 110

Index

Kenya 14, 41, 57, 96, 116, 140, 202
Khartoum 43
King, Anthony D. 11, 175, 185
Kipling, John Lockwood 147
Kipling, Rudyard 112–13, 145, 216
Kitchener, Lord Herbert 62, 216
Kolkata *see* Calcutta
Kuala Lumpur 89, 115, 141
Kumasi, Ghana 39

La Trobe, Charles 74, 128
labour force 8, 27, 34–5, 40, 60, 84–6,
   105–8, 150, 165, 167, 172, 201, 213,
   238, 252, 262
Lagos 67, 186
Lahore 38–9, 131, 150, 155, 269
Lang, Revd John Dunmore 210–11
Larnach, William 174
law courts 9, 27, 28, 56, 88, 90, 92, 101–3,
   135, 147, 236–8, 243
legislatures *see* parliament (buildings)
leisure and recreation 3, 9, 57, 63, 68, 105,
   109–11, 115, 117, 126–7, 136, 151,
   177, 234, 261, 263, 265
   see also sport
Levant 17, 107, 108
libraries 3, 15, 25, 70, 92, 98–9, 100, 104,
   111, 114, 125–31, 134–5, 147,
   215–16, 243, 260, 270
Light, Sir Francis 71, 114
Lilongwe 12
Livingstone, Zambia 142, 248–9
Livingstone, David 106, 205
log cabins 166–7
Longair, Sarah 135
Lucknow 35–9
Lusaka *see* urban planning
Lytton, Viceroy Lord 61–2, 112

Mackenzie, William Lyon 136
Mackinnon, Sir William 232
Macquarie, Mjr. Gen. Lachlan 74, 98, 216
Madras (Chennai) 56, 70–1, *72*, 88, 93, 102,
   104, 112, 131, 133, 140, 141, 144,
   146, 155, 157, 201, 203, 208–9

maidans 38, 56, 102, 131, 141, 147, 199, 209
Malabar 71, 133
Malaya 33, 41, 89, 105, 110, 114, 172, 178–9
Malta 8, 41, 57–8, 126, 227–31
Mandalay 39, 115, 232
mandated territories 8–9, 107, 207
Manitoba 41, 77
Maori *see* New Zealand
markets 96, 142–4, 201, 250, 261, 266, 268
Masons *see* Freemasons
Mauritius 117, 130, 172
Maymyo (Pyin Oo Lwin) 115, *116*, 266, *267*
mechanics' institutes 126–7, 134–5
medicine *see* health
medieval 24, 51, 54, 85, 87, 101, 103, 196,
   198, 199, 201
Medley, Bishop John 201
Melbourne 74–5, 94–5, 98, 101, 104–5, 117,
   128, 134, 137, 144, 151, 182–4, 200,
   211, 227, 241, 243
memorials 93, 134, 205, *206*, 230, 243, 246,
   268–70
Metcalf, Thomas 10
middle class *see* bourgeoisie
Middle East 8, 17, 43, 107–9, 195, 214, 238,
   239, 263, 270
military 2, 4, 6, 9, 14, 16, 25–7, 30, 32, 33,
   51–65, 71, 78, 83–6, 95, 104, 105,
   110, 113–17, 125, 137, 139, 148, 150,
   152, 166, 175, 180, 215–16, 233–4,
   243, 245, 261, 263, 266, 269
   residences 60, 62, 71, 77, 246
   see also barracks; engineers/
   engineering
mint 90, 91, 98
Minto, Viceroy Lord 139, 244
missions 2, 5, 11, 15, 25, 29, 30, 34, 43, 106,
   108–9, 195–6, 201, 203–5, 212–15,
   219, 251
   Lovedale *2*, 213
   Scottish 108–9, 204, 209, 213–14
   see also cathedrals; churches
modernism 14, 17, 27, 76, 99, 101, 102,
   104, 156, 180, 187, 189, 214, 243,
   262, 264, 271

Mombasa 57, 135, 155, 202
Montgomerie, Dr William 233–4
Montreal 97, 102, 127, 129, 137, 153, 209, 217, 268
Morrin College/Centre 127, 270
Morris, Jan 10, 248
Moulmein 232
Mughal 31, 35–8, 56, 60, 61, 65, 87, 110, 173, 244, 246, 269
Mumbai *see* Bombay
Mundy, Gen. G.C. 60
museums 2, 12, 15–16, 25, 39, 40, 43, 73, 88, 91, 92, 98, 125, 126–36, 145, 242, 243, 260, 268, 269, 270–1
Muslim *see* Islam
'Mutiny' *see* Indian Revolt/Uprising
Myers, Garth Andrew 12

Nairobi 12, 116, 142, 155, 251–2
Nelson, Louis P. 11–12
neoclassical *see* classical style
Nevis 104
new capitals *see* urban planning
New Delhi *see* urban planning
New South Wales 33, 41, 74, 97, 117, 128, 151, 153, 173, 174, 183, 210–11, 216, 242
New Zealand 5, 7, 8, 15, 33, 34, 40, 59, 165, 262, 270
Newfoundland 40, 97, 197, 199
Nigeria 116, 264
Nilsson, Sten 10
Norman 24–5, 26–7, 143, 198, 210, 214
Northern Rhodesia (Zambia) 3, 77, 96, 142, 176, 227, 248–52
 see also urban planning, Lusaka
Nova Scotia 57, 64, 77, 96, 137, 144, 196

Ontario 41, 97, 126, 127, 130, 133–4, 136, 199, 241
Orient Club, Colombo 141
Orientalism 2, 24
Orientalist architecture 29, 142, 173, 214, 217

Ottawa 77, 99, 101, 103, 129, 210, 241, 271
Ottoman 57, 69, 107, 207

Palestine 41, 108–9
Palladian 198, 230, 246–7
Palladio, Andrea 32, 247
parks 4, 9, 25, 37, 70, 98, 105, 114, 125, 134
 see also gardens; garden city
parliament (buildings) 68, 95, 96–101, 103, 129–30, 134, 217, 231, 243, 246, 268
Pellatt, Sir Henry 175
Penang (Prince of Wales Island) 58, 71–2, 93, 94, 114, 155, 167, 178–9, 203, 231, 239
Perth *see* Western Australia
piazza 126, 168–72
Pietermaritzburg 94, 95, 210
plantation 8, 11, 26–7, 31, 53, 73, 105–6, 110, 114, 117, 140, 166–73, 207
 houses 33, 73, 105, 170–1, 168–73
Pocock, J.G.A. 203
Pondicherry (Puducherry) 35
post and telegraphs 26, 90, 106, 108, 111, 114, 144, 146–9, 151–2, 213, 236–7, 261
Prakash, Vikramaditya 11
Prince of Wales 37, 58, 131, 142, 242
propaganda 2, 205, 262, 264
Protestant *see* churches
Presbyterian *see* churches, Scottish
Pretoria 100, 103, 203, 241, 245
Public Works Department (PWD) 3, 32–4, 86–7, 113, 132, 147, 176, 180, 249

Quebec 35, 64–5, 77, 85, 97, 102, 126–7, 196, 198, 209, 215, 217, 241, 270
Queensland 74, 76, 98, 117, 200, 217

race 3–5, 12, 15, 23, 24, 26, 28, 32–5, 68, 84, 86, 90, 92, 95, 109, 111, 113, 126, 138–42, 150, 165–6, 168, 185–6, 205, 216, 234, 240, 250, 260–3, 269
Raffles, Stamford 58, 72

Index

railway stations 2, 28, 88, 89, 142, 145, *147*, 148–52, 157, 232, *233*, 249, 261
   Victoria Terminus, Bombay 143, 147, 151
railways 32, 34, 40–1, 61, 85, 112, 114–15, 143, 144–6, 152, 154–5, 176, 184, 188, 205, 214, 234, 245, 260, 263
   Canadian Pacific (CPR) 154
Rangoon (Yangon) 39, 44, 72, 142, 154–5, 186, 201, *202*, 231–40, 265, 269
Renaissance 27, 32, 56, 72, 95, 98, 103, 112, 128, 137, 152, 237
residences *see* architecture, domestic
Residencies *see* Government Houses
Rhodes, Cecil 180
Richards, Edwin Percy 186–7
Romanesque 93, 97, 128, 203, 210, 230, 235–6
Rome/Roman 24–5, 26, 36, 66, 195, 228
Romney Manor, St Kitts 170
Royal Engineer Establishment, Chatham 32
Royal Engineers 86, 117, 198
Royal Indian Engineering College, Cooper's Hill 32
Royal Institute of British Architects 32
Royal Military Academy, Woolwich 32
Royal Navy 30, 41, 180
Ruskin, John 13
Russell, William Howard 36

Said, Edward 24
St Helena 8, *53*, 73
St John's, New Brunswick 41
St Kitts 53, *54*, 169–70, *171*
St Martin-in-the-Fields 87, 198, 208, 210, 212
St Nicholas Abbey 170
Salisbury (Harare) 52, 67, 202
Saracen Iron Works 71, 179
Sarkies brothers 239
Saskatchewan 41, 97
schools 15, 104, 106, 107, 110, 117, 125, 132, 147, 152, 201, 210, 212, 213, 238, 239, 240, 245, 250

Scotland 14, 51, 66, 71, 101, 105, 136, 171, 204
Scott, Ian 63
Scottish baronial 71, 117, 174
Scottish/Scots 14, 101, 104, 108–9, 112, 114, 115, 124, 130, 131, 152, 167, 171, 179, 195, 197, 199, 204, 206, 207–12, 215, 217, 230, 232–3, 234, 236, 265
Scriver, Peter 6, 11
sculpture 25, 26, 100, 106, 133, 147, 171, 188, 201, 271
Second Empire style 97–8
Second World War 3, 39, 41, 72, 76, 187, 231, 232, 242
Selwyn, Bishop G.A. 59
Seven Years' War 35, 57
shipping 32, 41, 144–5, 148, 153–4, 180, 207, 231, 232, 237, 239
'shop houses' 167
Sierra Leone 116, 201, 218, *219*
Simla (Shimla) *see* hill stations
Singapore 8, 58, 72, 93, 110, 133, 155, 164, 167, 178–80, 182, 186, 217, *218*, 231, 233, 239
Singh, Ranjit 38, 61
Sir Alexander Binnie Sons and Deacon 249
Skinner's (St James's) Church, Delhi 203, 204
slaves/slavery 8, 11, 52–3, 85, 106, 166, 167–72, 201, 205–7, 266
Somerset, Lord Charles 129
South Africa 2, 7, 15, 33, 34, 64, 68, 84, 94, 96, 100–1, 103, 105, 116, 129–30, 152, 154, 165, 180–2, 196, 210, *211*, *213*, 217, 236, 248
South Australia 74, 98, 117, 128, 129, 217, 241
Southern Rhodesia (Zimbabwe) 14, 52, 67, 116, 172, 182, 202–3, 248, 266, *267*
sport 9, 12, 25, 28, 63, 84, 108, 110, 125, 137, 139, 142, 151, 157, 196, 240, 246, 251, 260
   see also leisure and recreation
Sri Lanka *see* Ceylon

Index

Stamp, Gavin 10
statuary 25, 66, 91, 92, 97, 103, 126, 129–30, 147, 268–70
Stewart, James Horne 174
stores (retail) 63, 104, 179, 236, 239, 249
'Straits Eclectic' style 178–9
Straits Settlements 71, 85, 179
suburbs *see* urban planning; urbanisation/urbanism
sugar 11, 53, 85, 105, 138, 167–8, 172
Sydney 42, 74–5, 94, 97–8, 134, 137, 151–4, 182–4, 196, 201, 210–11, 241

Tasmania 74–5, 98, 138, 266
technology 16, 26, 28, 31, 40, 55–6, 58, 86, 89, 144–52, 156, 157, 161, 184, 245, 261
telegraphs *see* post and telegraphs
tents 14, 27, 59–65, 67, 77–8, 104, 166, 198, 242
terraced housing 182–4
theatres 3, 9, 12, 25, 28, 93, 104, 108, 114, 128, 131, 142, 156, 230, 260
Thomason College of Civil Engineering, Roorkee 33
Tindall, Gillian 10
Toronto 18, 97, 126–7, 133, 136, 137, 151–2, 154, 175, 182, 184, 210, 227, 270
Tortola 73, 103
tourism/tourist 44, 53, 57, 64, 96, 106, 107, 108, 112, 115, 144, 152, 170, 245, 248, 264–5, 268–70
town halls 11, 90–6, 111, 114, 127, 131, 148, 238, 268, 270
town planning *see* urban planning
trams 184, 188
transport 26, 32, 86, 94, 111, 114, 148, 151, 182, 184–9
Tudor 77, 113, 142, 180

universities 25, 77, 88, 124, 125, 127, 128, 129, 130, 134, 136, 147, 205, 209, 213, 243, 249

urban planning 2–3, 6–7, 16, 25, 32, 85, 94, 144, 164–89, 203, 232, 233, 241–2, 245, 249–50, 261
    new capitals 17, 39, 227, 240–51, 264
        Canberra 75–6, 101, 178, 227, 240–4, 246, 248, 253
        Lusaka 12, 77, 142, 178, 241, 243, 248–53, 268
        New Delhi 10, 30, 39, 70, 77, 100, 178, 187, 241, 244–8, 253, 265, 266
urbanisation/urbanism 9, 11, 31, 83, 90, 164, 166, 177, 181–9, 227–53, 259–63

Valletta 57, 126, 227–31
Venice 13, 87, 93, 102, 147, 247
Victoria, Australia 31, 59, 74, 85, 94–5, 98, 117, 127–8, 151, *156*, 173
Victoria, British Columbia 59, 77, 97, 154, *155*, 174
Victoria, Queen 74, 92, 93, 126, 130, 138, 157, 238, 270
Victorian 83, 99, 146, 174, 212, 230, 234, 266

Wales/Welsh 14, 51, 195
Wellesley, Gov.-Gen. Marquess 69–70, 72
Wellington, NZ 77, 98, 101, 151, 200, 212, 216, 218, 270
West Africa 41, 52, 110, 124, 154, 168, 263
West Indies *see* Caribbean
Western Australia 67, 76, 98, 129
Winnipeg 77, 97, 217
women 29, 34, 110, 137–9, 141, 172, 208, 214, 216–7
    see also architects, Sophia Gray; architects, Marion M. Griffin; Eden, Emily; Grant, Elizabeth
Yangon *see* Rangoon

Zambia *see* Northern Rhodesia
Zanzibar 12, 135–6, 205, *206*
Zimbabwe *see* Southern Rhodesia

EU authorised representative for GPSR:
Easy Access System Europe, Mustamäe tee 50,
10621 Tallinn, Estonia
gpsr.requests@easproject.com

www.ingramcontent.com/pod-product-compliance
Lightning Source LLC
Chambersburg PA
CBHW042118300426
44117CB00021B/2982